GC959.3

THAILAND'S POLITICAL HISTORY
From the Fall of Ayutthaya in 1767 to Recent Times

CHINE
BIRMANIE
HAUT LAOS
TONKING
EMPIRE D'ANNAM
CHIENG-MAÏ
ROYME DE SIAM
CAMBODGE
COCHINCHINE FRANÇAISE
GOLFE DE TONG-KING
GOLFE DE SIAM
LUANG-PRABANG
HA-NOY
HUE
BANGKOK
JUTHIA
SAIGON
OUDONG
Lao-Kay
Lai-Chu
Tuyen Quang
Thai Nguyen
Lang Son
Bac Ninh
Hung Hoa
Son-Tay
Hai Dzuong
Hung Yen
Nam Dinh
Ning Binh
Thanh-Hoa
Ha-Tinh
Kouang-Binh
Kouang-nam
Kouang-ngai
Binh-phu
Nha-trang
Binh thuan
Bien-hoa
My-tho
Vinh-long
Ha-tien
Chaudoc
Kampot
Compong-Som
Pnompenh
Compong Soai
Pursat
Battambang
Chantaboun
Siemreap
Stung-treng
Khong
Bassac
Oubon
Souren
Korat
Plateau Désert
Kemarat
Lakon
Nong-han
Saniaboury
Ponpissay
Khassy
Pitchilouk
Nakansavan
Zimme
Labong
Karens
Ligor
Songkhla
Tenasserim
Me Kong
C. Cambodge
Bches du Mé Khong

THAILAND'S POLITICAL HISTORY

From the Fall of Ayutthaya in 1767 to Recent Times

B. J. Terwiel

River Books

First published and distributed in Thailand in 2005 by
River Books Co., Ltd.
396 Maharaj Road, Tatien,
Bangkok 10200
Tel: (66) 2 225 4963, 225 0139, 6221900
Fax: (66) 2 225 3861
Email: riverps@ksc.th.com
www.riverbooksbk.com

A River Books Production.

Publisher: Narisa Chakrabongse
Editor: Paisarn Piammattawat
Design: Charoenkwan Klinphut

ISBN 974 9863 08 9

Frontispiece: An etching map of Siam, 1893, Paris.
(Courtesy The Old Maps & Prints, River City)

Printed and bound in Thailand by Sirivatana Interprint Co., Ltd.

Contents

Preface

The forerunner of this book was published in 1983 and carried the title *A History of Modern Thailand*. It had been intended as the first volume in a new Australian Series of Histories of Southeast Asia started by Queensland University Press. Eight further volumes had been announced when suddenly QUP abandoned its 'Asian experiment' before it had a chance to prove itself. As a result the book was deprived of its projected companion volumes, and the one remaining volume was hardly noticed beyond Australia and Singapore. As a result I regularly received complaints that the book remained very hard to obtain but was unable to remedy the situation.

Meanwhile much time has elapsed. During the process of revising *A History of Modern Thailand* some newly discovered sources had to be incorporated, sometimes leading to changes in the argument. Then the time frame was enlarged to take the Post World War II situation into account. In addition numerous stylistic changes were made to improve readability. A further concluding chapter completed the revision. The end-product was so far removed from the original book that it warranted being given a new title.

The chief aim of this book is to provide a readable historical account based on contemporary sources. In order to draw the reader into the situation I have avoided, as much as possible, to rely upon interpretations by fellow-historians. In particular I have consciously avoided to react upon standardized nationalistic myths about what happened in Siam, preferring to make my own judgment after immersing in the available documents of the time. This book may thus be regarded as a fresh, admittedly personal look at old source material.

Acknowledgements

Much of the preparation of the forerunner of this book took place in Hamburg, at what was then called the Abteilung Thailand, Burma und Indochina of the Seminar fur Sprache und Kultur Chinas, Universität Hamburg, where I spent some six months under the auspices of a Von Humboldt-Foundation Research Fellowship. I am also grateful for assistance received in gaining access to collections at the National Libraries of Bangkok and Copenhagen, the Library of the Instituut voor Institut voor Taal- Land- en Volkenkunde at Leiden, the Library of the School of Oriental and African Studies in London, and especially the National Library of Australia and the Menzies Library in Canberra. I thank the editors of Oxford University Press (East Asia Branch) for granting permission to use extracts of Simon de La Loubère's Kingdom of Siam.

A Note on Transliteration

There always have been problems with the rendering of Thai words into the Latin script. The latter is a relatively limited code, well suited to transmit European languages, but rather problematic for accurately transmitting Thai. In the first place, the Thais make use of five tones, and often it is the tone that is the decisive marker with which to distinguish between one word and another. Secondly the Thai language has a rich array of vocals, among them sets of slurred combinations that do not occur in many European languages. Thirdly, the language is replete with words that have been borrowed from Pali and Sanskrit and which are spelled in an archaic manner that does not resemble its pronunciation.

In this work I decided to use a much simplified system of transliteration that ignores the Pali or Sanskrit spelling and indicates an approximate equivalence with spoken Thai without indicating the tone. The chief reason for choosing this system is to provide an idea of how Thai concepts sound to those who are unfamiliar with the Thai language. Excepted from this system are in the first place some words that have internationally become known with a variant spelling, such as the monetary unit 'baht', the name 'Chulalongkorn', the office of 'Phrakhlang', and the 'Chaophraya River'. Thai family names are presented in the simplified system, apart from those instances where Thais themselves have chosen to transcribe these family names in a different form.

As for the word Siam, that at present has a rather archaic sound, it was until 1939 the universally accepted word for the country, it proudly adorned stamps and the Thais did not perceive of the appellation as pejorative. In the pre-1939 section of the book the term is therefore not avoided.

List of illustrations, maps and tables

new breed of minister, to the right. Bottom left shows a candidate for the first election, stating: 'If you elect me, I shall help you and the public shouting: 'Hurrah'. The final cartoon shows Phibun (with Field Marshall's staff) and his wife La'iad in their home at Chidlom Road, surrounded by people asking for favors. (Collection of Paisarn Piammattawat) (Page 278)

Maps

Tables

Plate 1. An engraving of a mandarin family, hand-colored, 1762, Paris.
(Courtesy The Old Maps & Prints, River City)

1

BACKDROP:
SOCIETY DURING THE LATE-AYUTTHAYA
PERIOD (*CIRCA* 1680-1750)

Land and People

T he geological structure of Mainland Southeast Asia is
dominated by mountain ridges that run chiefly in a North-
South direction. They determine the general direction of the
larger rivers, flowing southwards and also the position of the
large alluvial lowland that forms the heartland of Siam. In the
northern part of the region that concerns us here the rivers Ping,
Wang, Yom and Nan at first run almost parallel, joining in the
lowlands to form the mighty Chaophraya River. In the middle of
the Chaophraya lowlands, at the point where yet another large
waterway, the Pasak River, joins the Chaophraya the old Thai
capital city of Ayutthaya was situated.

In this lowland a network of rivers and canals were the
chief human thoroughfares and only in the direct vicinity of
these waterways villages and towns could be found. Waterways
also connected the Chaophraya lowlands with regions southwards. The Thais communicated by water via the Gulf of
Thailand along the coast to Phetburi, Kuiburi, Chumphon –
where the Isthmus of Kra could easily be crossed towards the
southernmost part of Tenasserim – and along the Gulf further
south towards Nakhon Si Thammarat, Songkhla, Pattani and
regions where Malay was spoken. When reaching the Gulf the
Thais could also follow the coast in a south-eastern direction, to
Bang Plasoi (now called Chonburi) and Chanthaburi, before reaching Khmer-speaking regions.

Towards the east and west Ayutthaya was also connected
overland to a series of trade routes. Towards the east one path
went via Prachinburi and Kabinburi towards the Cambodian
realm, another to Nakhon Ratchasima and the richly populated
Mun and Chi Rivers. Westwards some difficult terrain had to be
crossed overland to reach Tavoy and Mergui, the chief ports of
the Tenasserim region which at some times fell under
Ayutthayan control, later to become dominated by Burma.

In the late seventeenth century the country that is studied
here did not possess borders in the modern sense of the word.
While the Chaophraya lowlands and many regions directly adjacent were governed directly from Ayutthaya, further away there
were regions where a measure of control was exercised in an
indirect way. The relationship between the city and many far

away towns was thought of in terms of a mighty center surrounded by tributary states. The exact conditions between Ayutthaya and each of its outer centers differed from case to case. Outer regions, such as Nakhon Si Thammarat in the south, Chiang Mai in the north or Nakhon Ratchasima in the northeast formally acknowledged Ayutthaya's supremacy by regularly sending a sign of subservience as well as valuable produce at the same time functioning in many ways as independent principalities. In times of war they would have to contribute troops to the central army at short notice. In return they knew that because of their alliance with the greater power they would be protected from military attack.

There are some early estimates of the size of the Siamese population that depended on Ayutthaya, the most interesting one undoubtedly that recorded in the latter part of the seventeenth century by Simon de La Loubère. After remarking that the capital city is thinly inhabited[1] and the country as a whole even less so, we are told that the reason for the lack of people lies in a high level of taxation and other impositions. Finally La Loubère cites indigenous sources:

> *The Siameses do therefore keep an exact account of the men, Women, and Children; and in this vast extent of Land, according to their own Concession, as they reckon'd up the last time but Nineteen Hundred Thousand Souls. From which I question not that some retrenchment is to be made for Vanity and Lyes, ..., but on the other hand thereunto must be added the Fugitives, which do seek a Sanctuary in the Woods against the Government.*[2]

Less than two million people were thus registered, whereby it is not clear whether this included the population of one or more tributary states.

The Social and Administrative System in Theory

In the following pages it is described how during the late-Ayutthaya period (the late seventeenth and first half of the eighteenth centuries) these Siamese were administered. Its hierarchy and its rules and regulations are stated without reference to specific instances. The system of administration is described as if each member of the administration actually fulfilled his duties, and as if the king were really guided in every respect by the *Phra Thammasat*,[3] the code of laws believed to have been passed on through the ages.

By far the most important office in the country was that of the king. The Thais had clearly formulated ideas on what virtues the ideal king should possess. He should be generous, moral, self-sacrificing, honest, mild, ascetic, balanced, congenial,

[1] In many history books rather exaggerated figures as to the population of the capital circulate. Thus Fouser blithely tells us that seventeenth century Ayutthaya might have had a million inhabitants (Beth Fouser, *The Lord of the Golden Tower, King Prasat Thong and the Building of Wat Chai Watthanaram*, Bangkok: White Lotus, 1966, p. xiii). Gervaise seems more down to earth when he reports that the city could supply about sixty thousand adult men, and the villages directly adjacent another sixty thousand. Nicolas Gervaise, *Histoire naturelle et politique du royaume de Siam*, Paris: Claude Barbin, 1688, p. 47.

[2] S. de La Loubère, *The Kingdom of Siam*, p. 11. In the Thai annals there is a reference that has been interpreted by Frankfurter to mean that the first general registration of all towns and cities took place in the beginning of the sixteenth century (O. Frankfurter, Events in Ayuddhya from Chulasakaraj 686-966'. *The Siam Society Fiftieth Anniversary Commemorative Publication. Selected Articles from the Siam Society Journal*. Vol.1, 1904-29. Bangkok: The Siam Society, 1954, p. 52). This view was based on the reading of the 'Luang Prasert' version of the annals. In various other versions the reference seems to be rather that a compilation of all royal ceremonies was made. See Richard D. Cushman (transl.), *The Royal Chronicles of Ayutthaya*, Bangkok: The Siam Society, 2000, p. 19.

[3] From the Sanskrit *dharmasastra*, or Pali *dhammasat*, book of laws.

patient and law-abiding. The person most worthy of this office was usually decided upon after the position had become vacant. The eldest male child from the union of the previous king with his queen would stand a good chance of being chosen by a grand council.[4] If such a person was not available, or if he was not considered suitable, often the previous king's brother, one who had gained experience through occupying a senior office, such as that of *maha uparat*,[5] would be elevated to the position of monarch.[6] Once the decision on the succession had been made, it was formalized as soon as possible with an anointing ceremony. If circumstances prevented a full-scale anointing at short notice, it was possible to carry out a provisional installation, which might be followed later by the full ceremony. As the Thai name for the ritual – *Phra Ratchaphithi Boromaphisek*, or 'royal ceremony of the great anointment' – indicates, the sprinkling and pouring of lustral water was the central act.[7] The idea that water is a suitable medium, which can be pervaded and saturated with sacred power, was widespread in Siam.[8] The water to be used for the creation of a new king was collected from various places around the kingdom, preferably from spots that were considered sacred in their own right. Siam's chief religious specialists would further increase the water's spiritual power by chanting appropriate words over it. The formal installation of a new king included, besides the anointment, handing over of the regalia, consisting of an array of objects such as: the state umbrella; a betel-chewing set; a pair of slippers; a fan and fly-whisk. Among the insignia of his new rank, the king would receive a golden plate on which a long string of royal epithets and honorable names was engraved.[9] The new king would solemnly declare that he would rule for the well-being of the populace and protect and defend all those now coming under his command. Among his first duties were a procession around the capital city, thus symbolically receiving the territory, and the acceptance of pledges of loyalty from all members of his family and senior state officials.

After a king had been thus formally confirmed in office, he became very much a being apart. Nobody was allowed to approach his person: guards were always at hand to prevent this. His wives, aided by many other women, usually young females of good family who were presented to serve him, would supervise the preparation of the king's food. Women tidied his sleeping quarters and waited on him at table. On the relatively rare occasions that the king moved outside his palace, his progress would bring ordinary life to a halt. If his boat was encountered on the river, all other craft would move out of the way and the approaching royal boat would only meet with ships that were no longer propelled, their rowers having thrown themselves face down.

If the royal boat passed that of a state official, the official was obliged to come out of the central high seat with its protec-

---

[4] H. G. Quaritch Wales, *Siamese State Ceremonies: Their History and Function*, p. 67, and *Supplementary Notes on Siamese State Ceremonies*, p. 11; S. de La Loubère, *The Kingdom of Siam*, p. 101.

[5] From the Sanskrit or Pali *maha uparaja*, 'Great Viceroy' or deputy-king.

[6] This frequently occurred during the Ayutthaya period, leading some commentators, such as Schouten, to take the brother's succession as the rule rather than the exception. See F. Caron and J. Schouten, *A True Description of the Mighty Kingdoms of Japan and Siam*, p. 100.

[7] It is somewhat misleading to call the ceremony a 'coronation', for, although a crown formed part of the regalia to be carried about in procession and presented, the actual placement of that crown on the king's head as symbol of his changed status, which has been a feature of the Siamese ritual only during the Bangkok period, is probably a result of European influence. There is no reason to suspect that the crown occupied a pre-eminent position in the ceremony during Ayutthaya times.

[8] La Loubère, *The Kingdom of Siam*, p. 81, and B. J. Terwiel, *Monks and Magic: An Analysis of Religious Ceremonies in Central Thailand*, pp. 251-2.

[9] For details, see Wales, *Siamese State Ceremonies*, pp. 102-6.

[10] La Loubère, *The Kingdom of Siam*, p. 42.

[11] N. Gervaise, *The Natural and Political History of the Kingdom of Siam*, p. 121. For further details see J. Kemp, *Aspects of Siamese Kingship in the Seventeenth Century*, pp. 1-19.

[12] Officially the palace was called Phra Ratchawangbowonsathan-mongkhon. See *kromphra* Damrong Ratchanuphap, *Tamnan Wangna*, PP, vol. 11, p. 1.

[13] La Loubère, *The Kingdom of Siam*, p. 95 and p. 100. La Loubère states that the *uparat* carried the honorary prefix of *chaophraya*, which caused Wales to surmise that it was not the *uparat*, but the *chaophraya uparat*, a person of lower rank, mentioned in the Law of Civil Hierarchy, who was described by La Loubère. There can be little doubt but that Wales is wrong in this identification. The person seen by La Loubère is indeed the 'deputy king', while the entry in the Law of Civil Hierarchy refers to the chief of that prince's department. Further supporting literature on this issue can be found in F. H. Giles, 'Analysis of Van Vliet's Historical Account of Siam', *Journal of the Siam Society* (hereafter *JSS*) 30, pt 3 (1938), pp. 353ff. I am grateful to Dr. M. Vickery in this respect for his comments on the Law of Civil Hierarchy.

[14] Wales, *Ancient Siamese Government and Administration*, p. 236. The *baht* was a lump of silver weighing some 15 grams.

[15] *Chaofa* seems to be an old Tai title (i.e., one that has been used not only among the Siamese but also among other Tai-speaking groups, such as the Shans, where the term is often spelled *Hsawpha*). It appears for the first time in Siamese history in the late sixteenth century as an honorary prefix to the titles of King Naresuan. In late-Ayutthayan times the title was bestowed only on princes and princesses as a mark of royal elevation to the highest rank. For further details on the use of the title, see M. Vickery's review of R. B. Jones's *Thai Titles and Ranks*, *JSS* 62, pt. 1 (1974), pp. 158-73.

[16] Wales, *Ancient Siamese Government*, p. 236.

[17] Caron and Schouten, *A True Description*, p. 98.

tive hood and prostrate himself on the small platform just in front of it. No one in the boat would stir until the king was well away.[10] If the king proceeded by land, all people close enough to notice his conveyance were obliged to prostrate themselves fully and nobody would venture to catch a glimpse of the monarch, either because of genuine respect for that august body passing near by or out of fear of being caught in the act and punished by one of the guards. Such occasions gained immensely in dramatic impact by the fact that absolute silence was maintained when the king moved among the populace.[11]

One of the princes of the highest rank, frequently a younger brother or a son of the king, would be chosen to fill the office of *maha uparat*. The *uparat* occupied, at least during late-Ayutthaya times, a palace situated at some distance from that of the king. In accordance with the Siamese notion of east being the most auspicious direction, undoubtedly because that is the direction in which the sun rises, the palace of the *uparat* was considered to lie 'in front' (i.e., to the east) of the king's palace, and therefore in common parlance it was referred to as the *Wang Na*, or Front Palace.[12] The prince who was *uparat* was the second highest dignitary in the country, as measured by the attributes of rank and honor that were attached to his office. The holder of this office was the only dignitary who was automatically excused from having to prostrate himself before the king during royal audiences and council meetings.[13] Although the *uparat's* wealth was not such that he could rival the king's display of power, some of the glamour of the king's office was reflected in the *Wang Na*, where a miniature court was kept.

The various members of the royal family each received an allowance from the king. In late-Ayutthaya times, the *uparat* had 40,000 *baht* a year;[14] a prince of *chaofa* rank[15] would receive 8,000 *baht* and children and grandchildren of the king not of *chaofa* rank would receive amounts varying between 1,600 and 4,000 *baht* each. The queen, if such a person was appointed, received 24,000 *baht*. The other most important women attached to the king would each be able to maintain their own quarters in the women's compound. They received amounts varying from 400 to 4,000 *baht* each, from a total of 16,000 *baht* spent annually on that section of the royal household.[16]

Not much is known about the women's compound in late-Ayutthaya times. It is certain that young women of rank were often presented by their families to serve the king.[17] It is also clear that it was possible for the queen to conduct business and acquire goods.[18] The women's compound was run and organized by women, and had an elaborate organization in which a complex hierarchical system could be discerned. This was where the king's wives and concubines lived and also where the princesses were brought up and might obtain a good education.

Daughters of noble families who had been presented to the court were trained as dancers and musicians. The king could choose whom he liked from among the accomplished women. If a concubine gave birth to a child, her status as mother of a royal child, *chaochommanda*, was raised above that of other concubines. Mature and experienced ladies would become teachers or supervisors of other daily activities. It was a place where princesses, often prevented from marrying by their exalted rank, could make a career. The ladies of rank would each have a retinue of women, often drawn from the wealthy families of Ayutthaya, who would gladly assign a daughter to serve a great lady in return for an education and for the prestige and honor of being associated with the royal court.

Some princes, mature and trusted advisers to the king, would receive the nominal headship of an administrative government department. Most departments were called *krom*, and the princes who had become nominal heads would attach the word *krom* as a prefix to their titles and names. The use of the word *krom* as a sign of princely rank probably goes back to the second half of the seventeenth century, to the reign of King Narai (r. 1656-1688).

There were many subdivisions among the princes of *krom* rank, the lowest being called *kromamu'n*, a higher rank being a *kromakhun*, and a yet higher one *kromaluang*. In theory it was possible for the king to bestow even higher *krom* ranks, such as *kromaphra* or even *krom somdetphra*, but this rarely occurred. The order of the different princely *krom* ranks, ranging from *kromamu'n* to *krom somdetphra*, duplicates a range of civilian ranks whereby a *mu'n* would be lower than a *khun*, a *khun* below a *luang* and a *luang* below a *phra*.[19]

An important part of the palace organization was that of the *mahatlek*, or the corps of royal pages. As far as can be determined, all young men in the *mahatlek* were drawn from outside the royal family. It was a great honor to be accepted in the corps of pages, for these young men were the personal assistants to the king. Although their rank was not as high as that of many other members of the nobility, they were highly respected. In the latter part of the seventeenth century it seems that the inner core of the *mahatlek* consisted of four groups of ten young men, each group commanded by a young officer holding the rank of *chamu'n*. Members of this core probably had direct access to the king. The Law of Civil Hierarchy reveals that these sections of the *mahatlek* were themselves hierarchically structured; within each section there were five different ranks. From de La Loubère's account of Siam published in 1693, it is possible to identify the honorary names of the four *chamu'n* in 1687. His 'Meuing Vai, Meuing Sarapet, Meuing Semeungtchai and Meuingsii' are in fact the *chamu'n* Waiyaworanat, Saraphetphakdi, Samoechairat, and Sisaorak.[20]

[18] La Loubère, *The Kingdom of Siam*, p. 101.

[19] It is possible that the custom of attaching these particular terms of civilian ranking to distinguish between princely titles reflects the earlier situation when *krom* titular headships were first bestowed upon princes. At that time a fairly small department may have had as its head *(chao krom)* a person of *mu'n* rank, a middle-size department may have had a *khun* and a major department may have been ruled by a *luang*. In subsequent times these direct links probably were lost as the number of civilian titles grew and increasingly higher titles were given to the *chao kroms*. The series of princely ranks thus may throw light upon an early stage of the Siamese administrative system.

[20] Compare La Loubère, *The Kingdom of Siam*, p. 100, with the Tamnaengnaphonlaru'an, in the *Kotmai Tra Sam Duang* (hereafter *KTSD*) 1: 223. It is interesting to note that the four officers in question are divided into two 'at the head of the elephant', and 'two at the tail of the elephant'. This most probably indicates their position with regard to the royal elephant.

The pages entered royal service at the age of fifteen or sixteen. Some in an inner group prepared the king's betel quid; while others were responsible for his personal weapons. Other pages read his documents, helped keep his accounts, or carried messages to provincial officials. The importance of being in the corps of pages lay not only in being near the august presence and being intermediaries between the king and various other people; it also meant having a chance of obtaining acquaintances within the palace and gradually learning the practice of statecraft. After a young page had served some four or five years, the king would have had ample opportunity to assess his character, intelligence and degree of devotion to duty. Upon reaching the age of twenty, it was customary for a page to leave the king's service in order to spend at least one Lenten season as a fully-fledged Buddhist monk. Upon successful completion of his season in a monastery, the young man was considered ready to accept responsibilities and could present himself to the king to be considered for an appointment. If he had made a good impression, he could expect to be elevated to one of the middle ranks of the civilian administrative system and appointed to his first duties in office. For example, the king could place him in one of the provincial courts as a representative of the central administration.

An interesting feature of the inner *mahatlek* at that time was that on certain official occasions when the presence of all forty-four pages was required, they had to arrange themselves in two groups, twenty-two on the king's right-hand side and twenty-two on the left.[21] Each page would know on his appointment whether he belonged to the right-hand side *mahatlek* or to the left-hand side *mahatlek*. Similarly, members of the king's bodyguard would be either right- or left-hand-side guards. It seems that this gave rise to the custom of tattooing certain soldiers either on the right arm or on the left.[22] The chief state officials also knew beforehand whether they had to range themselves at the king's right hand or at his left. Provincial towns were called right-hand towns or left-hand towns, possibly an indication of whether the provincial governor would have to stand to the right or to the left during audiences.[23] Similarly some government departments would themselves be split up into a right and a left side, in imitation of the royal court.[24]

Once a royal page had successfully completed his period of serving the king, he would most likely be appointed first to the administrative rank of *okluang* (also known as *luang*, because by the late seventeenth century the prefix *ok* was becoming obsolete), thus already outranking administrators who were *(ok)khun* and *(ok)mu'n*. In late-Ayutthayan civil administration, most of the executive officers fell under one of six categories. These six were, from lowest to highest: *(ok)mu'n*, *(ok)khun*, *(ok)luang*, *(ok)phra*, *(ok)ya*, and

[21] La Loubère, *The Kingdom of Siam*, p. 99.

[22] J. O'Kane, transl., *The Ship of Sulaiman*, p. 96. Soldiers with tattooed arms were also found in the provinces (see La Loubère, *The Kingdom of Siam*, p. 83). For a wider view of the history of Siamese administrative tattooing, see B. J. Terwiel, 'Tattooing in Thailand's History', *Journal of the Royal Asiatic Society*, 1979, pt 2, pp. 156-166.

[23] Wales, *Ancient Siamese Government*, p. 114.

[24] It is possible that the ritual feature of the division of the king's audience into a right-hand a left-hand side was adopted some time during the first millennium AD by the Tai peoples when Chinese influence was strong; see B. J. Terwiel, *The Tai of Assam, and Ancient Tai Ritual*, vol. 1, *Life-cycle Ceremonies*, pp. 10-1.

(ok)phaya. While there were a vast number of officials with the rank of *khun* and *mu'n*, there were just over a hundred officials mentioned in the laws with the title *luang*, eighty-eight had the title *phra*, twenty-four were *ya*, and seventeen individuals were named as *phaya*.[25] On solemn ceremonial occasions, when officials appeared in official dress, they wore high, white, cone-shaped hats. It was possible to see at a glance what rank a person occupied, because the protocol prescribed different types of decorative bands round the base of the cone. An officer of *mu'n* rank had a silver-colored band and a *khun* a narrow golden one without decoration. A *luang* was entitled to a golden band two inches wide, a *phra*, gold with leaf decorations and the two highest ranks had golden bands profusely decorated with rosettes and embroidery.

Among those of *ya* and *phaya* rank could be found the heads of the most important government departments as well as the six chief ministers. These were:

1. The *chaophraya Chakri*, chief of the division known as *Mahatthai*, which could be translated as Department of Civil Affairs. Near the end of the Ayutthaya period this minister became responsible for control over the provincial towns to the north of the capital. He was president of the king's council and may be regarded as the highest-ranking noble in the country. Like the king and the *Uparat* (as well as some other senior ministers) he was allowed to place his personal seal on official documents issued under his command. His seal carried the image of a *Ratchasi*, the stylized Siamese lion.[26]

2. The *chaophraya Maha Senabodi*, head of the *Kalahom*, titular commander-in-chief of the armed forces. During the late-Ayutthaya period he supervised control of the southern provinces. Both the *Mahatthai* and the *Kalahom* devoted much of their attention to organizing and supervising the provincial *corvée*. The *Maha Senabodi*'s seal carried the image of the *Khotchasi*, a mythical animal representing a lion with an elephant's trunk.

3. The *(ok)phaya Tharamathibodi*,[27] head of the *Mon-thienban* Department. This department was popularly known as *krom Wang* (Palace). There is some evidence for the notion that this office once outranked all other ministries,[28] but in late-Ayutthaya times this was certainly no longer the case. The *krom Wang* ministry looked after the upkeep and maintenance of the palace and its inmates. It supervised certain troops attached to the palace and organized the labor of slaves and freemen who worked for the royal monasteries.

4. The *phaya Yomarat*, head of the *phra Nakhonban* Department, also known as *krom Mu'ang* (City). Most

[25] These numbers have been extrapolated from *An Index of Officials in Traditional Thai Governments*, by Yoneo Ishii, Osamu Akagi, and Shigeharu Tanabe, Vol. 1, pt. 1.

[26] *Ministry Seals of Thailand*, a wall-chart prepared by the Agency for International Development, United States Operations Mission to Thailand, 1966.

[27] Wales prefers to read the name as *Thammathibodi*, or Minister of Justice, ignoring the Thai spelling with a long a in the first syllable (*Ancient Siamese Government*, p. 92). It is most likely, however, that the Siamese title is derived from a Pali or Sanskrit word meaning 'palace'. I suspect that the Sanskrit *dhaman*, meaning 'dwelling-place', 'house', 'abode', was the root of the word.

[28] M. Vickery in his review of Ishii et al., 'An Index', in *JSS* 63, pt. 2 (1975), pp. 428-30.

officials who looked after the peace, order, and safety of the city of Ayutthaya worked in this *krom*. Their tasks included fire prevention measures, police duties, and the maintenance of a criminal court and a prison.

5. The *(ok) ya Phonlathep*, chief of the *Kaset* Department. In popular parlance this was known as *krom Na* (Department of Lands). The most important tasks performed by this *krom* were the collection of the government's share of the rice crop, the upkeep of a registry of lands and the settlement of boundary disputes.

6. The *(ok) phaya Sithammarat*, chief of the *Kot*, or Treasure-box. This department was also known as *krom Phrakhlang*, or the Treasury. It was charged with the collection of all taxes on imported and exported goods. As Ayutthaya became a major trading city, the office of the *Phrakhlang* gained more expertise in dealing with people from many countries. The Treasury also became the storehouse of knowledge about foreign countries, and most of the king's dealings with the world outside Siam took place by way of the palace of the *Phrakhlang* in a section called *krom Tha* (Harbour Section). Sometime during the late-Ayutthaya period, the chief of the *Kalahom* seriously displeased the king, and thereupon the responsibility for manpower control in the southern provinces was transferred from the *Kalahom* to the *Phrakhlang*. As a result, the *Phrakhlang's* ministry changed character, and many new *kroms* were added to handle the extra work.[29]

During much of the Ayutthaya period, these six dignitaries formed what can be styled the Siamese 'inner cabinet', for these chiefs of the six ministries channeled various sources of revenue and controlled most of Siam's manpower. Each year, hundreds of ranking officers would receive a sum of money from the king called *biawat*.[30] In late-Ayutthaya times, a chief minister would receive 4,000 *baht*, while a relatively lowly court official would be given as little as 80 *baht*. The king's expenses on *biawat* have been reported as high as 120,000 *baht*.[31] The yearly *biawat* cannot be regarded as equivalent to an official's salary. Salaries derived usually from fees paid for specific services by the populace. It must be seen rather as a sign of the king's *largesse*, a token of the honor of having been of assistance to the king.

Ayutthaya took control of the whole of the Chaophraya Delta, expanded its influence in all directions including the important sultanates in the southern peninsular region. By virtue of the many natural resource in the vast region that was dominated by Ayutthaya a steadily expanding number of

---

[29] This arrangement apparently was not wholly satisfactory, and one of the first measures of King Rama I was the return of many, but not all, of the southern provinces to the jurisdiction of the *Kalahom*.

[30] Literally 'scribbling money'. The word *bia* is an extremely old Tai word, originally meaning 'cowry shell', going back to the time when the cowry was the chief form of currency. The shell was still legal tender in Ayutthaya times, to a value of 6,400 shells per *baht*.

[31] Wales, *Ancient Siamese Government*, p. 236.

Chinese gained access to the court and helped organize a regular trade, the Thais supplying rice, sugar, natural dyes, wood and animal products and the Chinese bringing manufactured goods. Stimulated by a growing trade, the country's administrative system underwent reform and change. New departments were created as the need arose, and occasionally when the king wanted to please or punish some of his ministers, departments were merged, or holders of one office were appointed to act as chiefs of a completely different department. For example, in 1687 it seems that the head of the Ecclesiastical Department, an officer carrying the title of *(ok)ya* and the name of *Phra Sadet*, held the commission of *Phrakhlang*.[32]

This outline of the system of ranks and titles clearly shows that the Siamese possessed a quite intricate formal hierarchy. The office to which a person was appointed carried a rank, such as *mu'n*, *phra*, or *phaya*, and also a formal name, such as *Chakri*, or *Yomarat*. For the sake of brevity the names mentioned thus far are not the complete names bestowed upon the holders of an office. For example, strictly speaking, the *Chakri* was known as *chaophraya Chakri Si'ongkharak Samuhanayok Akhamaha Senathibodi Aphaiphiri Bara Kromphahu*, a string of words extolling the minister's role as royal bodyguard, his rank as chief general, and his fearlessness and bravery. Thus in late-Ayutthaya times it was an established custom to link many positions in the administration with a particular rank and name, so that in the course of time as people moved up in the administrative hierarchy, they would change both rank and name. Officials became known by the ritual name attached to the office they held. To their intimate family and friends, the individuals would naturally retain their given names, those obtained from their parents, although such names may have been rarely used.[33]

One of the most interesting state ceremonials, with which the king obtained a measure of control over his corps of officials, was the ritual of pronouncing the oath of loyalty.[34] This oath to the king was sworn regularly, the most solemn occasion taking place on the third day of the waxing of the moon of the fifth lunar month, in March or April, most likely in connection with the elaborate New Year ceremony. In the morning, Buddhist monks prepared a bowl of water, and all officers drank a cupful while declaring that terrible things might befall them if they were unfaithful to the king. Careful watch was kept to see whether each official drank effortlessly, or if he had any difficulty in swallowing. Nobody was exempt from this ceremony. If an official absented himself he could be punished with death, for such behavior was reckoned tantamount to treason. Nobody was allowed to wear golden rings during such a ceremony, apparently in the belief that some magically charged rings might make the wearer invulnerable against the effects of swearing a false oath. Some soldiers, presumably the

---

[32] La Loubère, *The Kingdom of Siam*, p. 80.

[33] In the intimate circle, the Siamese usually avoid using a person's real name and even his or her nickname. The strategy of most people is instead to substitute certain kinship terms. For example, contemporaries find out who is slightly older or higher in status and that person obtains the honorary name of *phi*, or 'older relative', while those slightly less in status become *nong*, 'younger relative'.

[34] *Ibid.*, p. 81.

king's bodyguard, had to take the oath every month, a measure undoubtedly inspired by fear for the king's safety.[35]

Large parts of the Chaophraya lowlands were under the direct control of the capital, Ayutthaya. At some distance from Ayutthaya, secondary seats of power were maintained, ruled by an Ayutthaya-appointed governor *(chaomu'ang)*, who would have a council of advisers representing many of the chief departments of the capital. Such secondary seats of power were towns like Kamphaeng Phet, Sawankhalok, Phitsanulok, Nakhon Thai, Phetchabun, and Nakhon Ratchasima towards the north and north-east of Ayutthaya; and places such as Nakhon Si Thammarat, Patthalung, and Pattani in the south. In principle, the governors of such secondary seats of power ruled over all the subsidiary towns immediately surrounding them. Each of these provincial seats of power had its own relationship with Ayutthaya; some retained more control over their own affairs than others. Further away, Ayutthaya liked to be surrounded on all sides by petty states that acknowledged Ayutthaya's leadership in international affairs but who would usually not tolerate the indignity of having representatives of the Ayutthayan government attached to their courts. These petty kingdoms regularly sent a token of allegiance, together with some valuable gifts.

At times when Ayutthaya was powerful and mighty, it might have counted Tenasserim, Chiang Mai, Luang Prabang, Champasak, Cambodia and some of the states at the southern end of the Malay Peninsula as areas more or less aligned with it, but at no time did Ayutthaya have the administrative apparatus to assume direct control over these outer regions, probably with the exception of Tenasserim and its subordinate towns.[36]

Besides these ways in which administrative personnel could be distinguished by ranks, names and amount of *biawat*, other differences between one rank and another were ceremonially stressed. High officials would have a state boat, with rowers fore and aft and a seat in the middle. Over the seat a woven bamboo hood *(kup)* was erected, and not only did the color in which it was varnished indicate whether the official belonged to a right-hand side department or to a left-hand one (red for the former, black for the latter), but also the hood would carry a decorated band near the edges which showed his rank.[37] As a state official, a man would have the right to travel under a single-tier umbrella, the multi-tiered ones being reserved for the king himself. Special insignia of rank issued by the king were silver equipment with which to prepare betel leaf and areca nut.[38]

Apart from all these ways of distinguishing between one official and another, which were concomitant with the maintenance of an elaborate court and administration, the Siamese were also in the habit of reckoning a person's worth by noticing where someone was placed on the *saktina* scale. Unlike the

[35] Wales, *Siamese State Ceremonies*, chap. 14, and *Supplementary Notes*, pp. 23-7.

[36] La Loubère, *The Kingdom of Siam*, p. 82.

[37] The *kup* is better known as the Siamese type of howdah used on the back of an elephant. For the boating *kup*, see La Loubère, *The Kingdom of Siam*, p. 41.

[38] Throughout Southeast Asia the preparation of a betel quid has acquired ritual significance, and in many countries it is possible to assess a person's rank by the quality of his betel-box.

insignia of rank and status, the *saktina* system encompassed all Siamese, at least in theory. Everyone from the lowliest beggar and the slave to the chief princes had a place according to *saktina*. The only Siamese who fell outside the system because of his rank and power was the king himself. Originally, the *saktina* system must have evolved from a custom of allotting plots of land to able people. It is likely that the king gave a certain number of complete villages to his chief advisers, including land and inhabitants, and the peasants thus donated would have had the duty of performing services for their over-lords.[39] Some time during the Ayutthaya period this practice of allotting land to the different categories of citizens developed into the *saktina* system. By late-Ayutthaya times it was already fully developed, and most Siamese must have known what their position on the *saktina* scale was. By this time, the system's link with an allotment of land had already been lost, the only remaining trace of this origin being the fact that the units of the *saktina* scale were still counted in areas of *rai*, each *rai* corresponding approximately to one-quarter of an acre, and that the word *na*, 'arable land', was often used in the proclama-tions allotting a specific number to a particular type of person.[40] Another feature that undoubtedly goes back to the origin of the system is the exclusion of the king. After all, in the-ory he is the only one who controls all land, so if a number were allotted to him it would have to be one comprising all the arable fields in the kingdom, which at that time was immeasurable.

In the fully-fledged *saktina* system, the *uparat* is given by far the highest number of *rai*, namely 100,000, by virtue of being a close relative of the monarch and holding the office of head of the Front Palace. A *chaofa* prince would readily be allotted either 15,000 or 20,000 *rai*, but if such a prince were to be elevated to *krom* rank, the *saktina* position would be increased to an impressive 40,000 or 50,000. Offspring of the king and various middle and lower-ranking mothers would be allotted 6,000 or 7,000 and if they were promoted to *krom* status, their amount would be raised to 11,000. This class of royalty, at that time known as *phra chao lanthoe*, seems to have been the last category in which one was eligible to become a *krom* prince. Members of a further category, *momchao*, offspring of the ranking princes, would obtain 1,500 on the *sak-tina* scale, but these were not mentioned as candidates for *krom* rank.

It is notable that princes reaching *krom* rank range on the scale from 11,000 to 50,000, which means that their places in the *saktina* scale are all higher than those of the most honored administrators outside the royal family. The absolute top a com-moner could reach was a rank of 10,000, well above many members of the royal family, who ranged usually between 500, and 1,000 *rai*.

[39] A different version of such a system could be observed in the Shan states in the days when the Shan *Sawbhas* still wielded immense power. The *Sawbha* would allot villages to his wife and chief concubines, and these villages would provide servants and goods to the appropriate section of the palace. In return, the villages would be exempt from various other forms of taxation.

[40] See the 'Aiyakan Na Tamnaeng Na Phonlaru'an' and the 'Saktina Thahan Huamu'ang' in the *KTSD* vol. 1. I have also consulted the edition by *kromaluang* Ratchaburi Direkru't.

At the top of the *saktina* scale for commoners, at 10,000 *rai*, were found the six most important ministers, the heads of the *Mahatthai* and *Kalahom*, as well as the heads of the *Wang*, *Mu'ang*, *Na*, and *Phrakhlang*, and also the governors of some important provincial towns. A few others also rated as high, not necessarily because they wielded immense political power, but because they had the highest standing in ceremonial matters, for example, the *Phra Sadet*, principal of the Ecclesiastical Department, and two *Maha Ratchakhru*, the dignitaries heading the Department of State Ceremonial.

The *saktina* scale may be likened to an ascending system of titles, with distinct 'slots' into which a person was fitted. Directly under the 10,000 came the category of 5,000, directly below that were places at 3,000, then followed positions allotted values of 2,400, 2,000, and 1,600. From 1,600 to 600 the places dropped by measures of 200, and then in smaller and smaller intervals from 600 to 500, 400, 350, 300, 250, 200, 150, 100, 80, 50, 30, 25, 20, 15, 10, and 5. Altogether there were twenty-seven steps on the civilians' ladder.[41]

There is no direct link between attaining a rank in the system of *mu'n*, *khun*, *luang*, *phra*, *ya*, and *phaya* and an exact place on the *saktina* scale. Though in general the *phaya* may be found among the top stages of the *saktina* ladder, there were two civil servants with *phaya* rank who stood only at *saktina* 400, a *saktina* rank well below many an official of only *khun* or even *mu'n* rank. There is only a vague correspondence between the two systems in so far as the higher *saktina* numbers would be allotted to persons in more responsible positions; often these persons would also be given ranks attached to these positions. Of the two scales, the *saktina* one seems to be the most accurate in indicating how much responsibility a person carried. Moreover, the *saktina* system covered people who did not qualify for elevation to a rank.

A person who reached the *saktina* rank of 400 could consider himself a member of the administrative elite; he would have to present himself to the king in a ritual called *thawai tua* (literally offering, presenting oneself), and from then on was considered to belong to the *khunnang*, the nobility. Perhaps no more than two thousand persons had *saktina* of 400 or higher, out of an estimated population of two million.[42] Belonging to the *khunnang* entitled an official to receive the king's annual gift of money, *biawat*. At the same time, this privilege influenced his legal position regarding inheritance, for the king claimed a share of the *khunnang's* personal wealth upon his death.[43] The *khunnang* and their offspring were exempt from *corvée* without having to apply (and pay) for exemption. *Khunnang* were allowed to be represented in courts of law by another person. All those of *saktina* 400 and above were, in principle, eligible to attend royal audiences.[44]

[41] The positions of 250 and 350 appear to have been seldom or never used. They did exist, at least as legal categories, as can be seen from the *Kotmai Lilit*, which was gleaned from *kromaluang* Ratchaburi Direkru't, *Kotmai Lem 1*, pp. 728-9 and 732-3.

[42] Chai-anan Samutwanit, *Saktina kap Phatanakan khong Sangkhom Thai*, as cited by A. Turton, 'Thai Institution of Slavery', in *Asian and African Systems of Slavery*, ed. J. L. Watson, p. 253.

[43] J. Low, 'On the Laws of Mu'ung Thai or Siam', *Journal of the Indian Archipelago and Eastern Asia* 1 (1847), p. 351.

[44] Akin Rabibhadana, *The Organization of Thai Society in the Early Bangkok period, 1782-1873*, p. 103.

It is not known for certain why the Siamese developed and maintained such an elaborate formal system in which all Siamese were given places on a numerical scale. A possible reason for the perseverance of the system in Siamese society lies in the fact that the *saktina* system already in early Ayutthaya times became intricately interwoven with the legal system. According to the administration of the law, it made quite a difference to a person whether he or she belonged to a low or a high point in the scale. A high official found guilty of a particular crime might have to pay a higher fine than a commoner. For example, after being convicted of adultery, a man of 10,000 on the *saktina* scale could be fined 2,000 *baht* of silver, a person of *saktina* 5,000 could pay up to 1,200 *baht*, while a lowly beggar of a rank of *saktina* 5 could be fined a maximum of 160 *baht*. The same principle was also true for the laws on compensation. Judges had a table dividing the population into *saktina* categories ranging from 5 to 10,000, each category subdivided into five lists, setting out the amounts due to an injured party when: only his dignity was injured; he was hurt physically by another person's hand; by a wooden instrument; by a blunt or sharp metal instrument. The latter four types of injury were further subdivided into ten, ranging from simple bodily damage such as bruises, through broken limbs and blindness to death resulting from the injury. For each of the twenty-seven stages on the *saktina* list, forty-two different injuries were legally recognized and the amount of compensation for each was prescribed by law. The compensation to a slave for having a limb broken unlawfully ranged between 50,000 and 70,000 cowry shells, depending on the nature of the injury; if he were blinded the sum was set at 105,000 shells. The compensation for similar injuries to an official at 10,000 *saktina* was, for a broken limb, a sum between 6,280,000 and 8,792,000 cowry shells, and 12,756,000 for being blinded.[45]

The *saktina* system is of particular interest to the historian because in theory it encompasses the whole Siamese population. By examining all those who, for example, were worth 50 or less on that scale, one may obtain a few glimpses of the lives of ordinary people.[46]

A rating of 50 *rai* on the *saktina* scale was given to scribes *(samian)* and legal counselors *(thanai)* attached to officers of *mu'n*, *khun*, *luang*, and *phra* rank, provided that these officers had not yet reached the *saktina* of 1,000. Artisans attached to a great variety of departments often had 50 *rai*, as did soldiers in charge of a small group of ordinary soldiers. For example, a *naimuat* (literally, master of a group) or a *sarawat* (assistant supervisor) would be worth 50. Also given a rating of 50 *rai* were messengers, or first-class soldiers who could fire a cannon *(changpu'n)*, and those who could manufacture a cannon, such as the people who kept the fire going, made the cast and smelt-

---

[45] Extrapolated from the *Kotmai Lilit*, cf. the *kromasak* section of *kromaluang* Ratchaburi Direkru't, *Kotmai Lem 1*. We must imagine that indeed vast amounts of shells were in circulation, in a thirteenth-century inscription we are told of 'heaps of cowry shells' and as late as the beginning of the nineteenth century the poet Sunthon Phu describes the women in the provincial market of Chonburi as carrying a large purse with cowries.

[46] The following paragraphs are based upon a survey of the Law of Civil Hierarchy and the Law of Military Hierarchy, *kromaluang* Ratchaburi Direkru't, *Kotmai Lem 1*, pp. 165-260.

ed the metal. The lowest of the court Brahmans, those responsible for the maintenance of a shrine, fell in this category, as well as those guarding a herd of elephants. In a subsidiary department of the *Mahatthai*, the position of clown was rated at the level of 50 *rai*, as were a group of palace women described as a dwarf, a half-size person, a transvestite and an albino (probably forming an entertainment group).

A rating of 30 *rai* was allotted to the man in charge of a platoon of ten regular soldiers, but in some more specialized *kroms*, every ordinary soldier might be given this status. This was the case with the buglers and gong-carriers who formed part of all marching armies. In the *Phrakhlang* department, 30 *rai* was allotted to some skilled workmen who did not reach the dignity of full artisan status.

A *saktina* level of 25 was given to a foreman, probably one supervising unskilled work. It was also the level allotted to some food distributors, cleaners, and watchmen.

A level of 20 was given to an ordinary man of the social class of *phrai*, or freeman, who was head of a household. It was also the level of some unskilled laborers in the palace, such as water-carriers, and palanquin bearers attached to the female section of the palace.

A rating of 15 *rai* was allotted to commoners in general *(phrai rap)*, both men and women. It also was the number attached to women servants in departments other than the palace.

The base level for commoners was 10 *rai*. None of the fixed positions in government departments descended to this level.

The lowest in the scale, 5 *rai*, was given to beggars, mendicants, slaves and the descendants of slaves.

The list of officials and their *saktina* positions reveals that, although women are not found among the holders of the highest offices, when they are appointed to a position they are given a *saktina* rating commensurate with their responsibilities. Some important women at the palace rated 1,000. Among the helpers and servants, it is clear that a woman and a man doing the same work obtain the same position on the scale. This may be seen as an indication of an aspect of Siamese culture, probably related to the *corvée* system, which gave Siamese women considerable responsibilities at home while the men were forced to labor for the government.[47]

Examining the *saktina* system in some detail has shown clearly that a large number of Siamese were classed in various categories of *phrai*, or commoners [– the term being applied to all between *saktina* rank 10-350 inclusive –] such as *phrai* who supervise, *phrai* with family and base-level *phrai* have been encountered. Below the *phrai* were the mendicants and slaves. Legally speaking, the whole population can therefore be divid-

---

[47] It has often been remarked by travelers that the position of women in Siamese society is relatively high. Women are often in control of a large share of the family finances. This feature may thus possibly be traced back to Ayutthayan times. Only with regard to religious and ceremonial life are Siamese women severely disadvantaged. Some of the reasons for their exclusion from this aspect of culture are explored in B. J. Terwiel, *Monks and Magic*.

ed into four broad classes: royalty *(chao)*, nobility *(khunnang)*, commoners *(phrai)*, and slaves *(that)*, beggars for convenience being thrown in with the latter category.

While the *saktina* system provides us with an insight into the hierarchical subdivisions within the whole population, one ought not forget that this is but one fairly legalistic system, revealing only part of the social reality. Just as in order to understand more fully a noble's position, his title, department, name, insignia, and *saktina* number must all be taken into account, so the lower ranks need to be distinguished further before a person's position can be adequately assigned.

One method of looking at the ordinary people at the lower end of the scale is by noting their position with regard to *corvée*. In principle, all *phrai* had to serve the king six months each year. All commoners were therefore registered in bands *(mu)* and departments *(krom)*, and in addition it was noted whether a person belonged to the right-hand part of the popula-tion, the 'guards' *(thahan)*, or to the left-hand part, the 'civil-ians' *(phonlaru'an)*. This information was recorded for all men and women. The children were assigned partly to the section of their mother and partly to that of their father, according to an intricate set of tables.[48] Each *mu* and *krom* had its administrative personnel, the *chaomu* and *chaokrom* being responsible for those registered under their names. There was a special gov-ernment department, the *krom Satsadi* or *Suratsawadi*, which maintained the lists on which all men, women, and children were noted. With the help of these lists, it was possible to assess the strength of *corvée* groups in all districts. From time to time the government held a census *(samanokhrua)* during which fresh lists were made up to serve as a new basis for the *corvée*.

Corvée was supervised by government administrators appointed for this task. The *phrai* assigned to work under such an administrator called their supervisor the *nai*, or 'master'. Some of the *phrai* served the king throughout the year; they were the king's personal retainers who had specific functions at the court, such as helping look after the elephants, doing guard duty or porterage. The king was responsible for their keep. Most *phrai*, however, did not fall into this category. They served the king at their own expense for six alternate months a year, one month on *corvée*, one month off. During the months when they worked for the king, they were assigned work by their *nai*. Often their tasks were carrying earth for public works, making bricks, helping provide building material by cutting and sawing wood, or providing the king with minerals by working in the mines. There were many *phrai* who were left to their devices for the remaining six months. If a commoner was pros-perous and wished to avoid *corvée* service, in late-Ayutthaya times he could buy himself an exemption. In 1688 it reputedly cost fifteen *baht* for a year's exemption.[49]

---

[48] *KTSD* vol. 2: 13-9.

[49] Gervaise, *The Natural and Political History*, p. 60.

Apart from the commoners who were free to dispose of their own time during the months that they did not have to serve *corvée*, a large number of men were attached to particular nobles or princes. Each man of rank was allowed to maintain his own band. The more important the person was, the larger the number of men who worked for him, rowed his boat and protected his property. These men would still be subject to the king's *corvée* and would have to divide their time between *corvée* for the king and tasks for the prince or noble. The ranking prince or noble would be responsible for their maintenance. Understandably, men of rank would often use their influence to protect 'their' *phrai* from the onerous *corvée*, and thus being assigned for duties to a private individual became a way of escape from performing duties for the king.

Another very popular method of changing one's status was to sell one's freedom and thereby attach oneself to a master. According to the Siamese legal system, it was possible to borrow large amounts of money using oneself and one's dependants as collateral. So long as the borrowed sum was outstanding, the person who had furnished the sum had a right to the labor of the borrower. In other words, people worked instead of paying interest. Debt bondage was not identical with slavery, because the bonded person retained his civil rights. He could buy himself free for the original sum of money, or change master by persuading another man to furnish the amount owed. A person who had made such a contract may be called a fiduciary slave, a person held 'in trust'. People who had become fiduciary slaves had, in theory, to serve four months each year in government *corvée*, four months for their master in order to 'pay interest', and were given four months in which to look after themselves.[50] If a master wished to keep a fiduciary slave during the months that they had to serve *corvée*, he had to pay the government a sum of money smaller than that necessary to obtain *corvée* exemption for an ordinary *phrai*.[51] The number of fiduciary slaves was large.[52]

Whilst fiduciary slaves retained their basic civil rights, there were several categories of people who were completely owned by their masters and thus counted as their personal property. These were people who had borrowed upon their person more than the legal limits set for fiduciary slaves, war-captives, the offspring of slaves and people who had been given to a monastery in perpetuity. The state could not demand *corvée* from these 'absolute' slaves.

It is therefore clear that many men were liable to be called up every alternate month to do government service. Their families and farms were often left in charge of their wives, who were not subject to *corvée*. Adult married women were often, therefore, used to taking full responsibility and much of the burden of keeping the farm going fell upon the women's shoul-

---

[50] R. Lingat, *L'esclavage privé dans le vieux droit siamois*, pp. 84-5; and Wales, *Ancient Siamese Government*, pp. 200-1.

[51] Wira Wimoniti, *Historical Patterns of Tax Administration in Thailand*, p. 39.

[52] O'Kane, *The Ship of Sulaiman*, p. 122 and p. 131.

ders. Of necessity, the division between 'typical' men's work and 'typical' women's work became rather blurred in Siam. When a man was available, he would do the most strenuous labor, such as plowing the field, but a strong woman would not hesitate to tackle such tasks in the absence of men.

The System in Practice

The administrative system above has been described in detail, because it provides the framework within which the state functioned in the Ayutthaya period. However, that system as laid down provided norms which were often difficult to follow, so individuals tended to bend the rules to suit their private needs and ambitions. In order to obtain a more realistic historical perspective, it is therefore necessary to balance the depiction of the given system with a few remarks on its practical limitations.[53] The office of the king appears to have been potentially extremely powerful. The king officially assumed the headship of the judiciary; he was by right the commander-in-chief, and in theory he appointed and dismissed all officers of state. Once a king had been anointed, only very subtle forces prevented him from acting arbitrarily. One may have hoped that the king's accession promise to behave in accordance with the ancient time-honored laws would be taken seriously. His senior advisers may have indicated by silence or veiled allusions that they disagreed with one of the king's pronouncements. An unpopular king may have found it difficult to obtain reliable information upon which to act.

The power of an anointed Siamese king was so great that the whole system was weakened when an incompetent individual came to the throne. Only a quite exceptional individual could fulfil the monarch's duties in the manner intended by the law. For this very reason the succession often caused problems. Although the eldest son of the king and his queen had precedence, in reality, more often than not it was another relative of the king who succeeded him. Sometimes there were rival claimants and the assumption of power resulted in much bloodshed. The very divine powers and status of the reigning king often prevented a peaceful succession. The king was so elevated and ritually superior that even just to discuss his succession openly could be regarded as treason. Thus officially, as long as the king was in charge, only the king himself arranged for his succession, and when the king neglected to do so, dangerous rivalry could occur. Thus, paradoxically, it was the very power and exaltation of the office that caused a weakness in the system. 'Despite the absolutism and divinity of kingship, the court history of Siam in the seventeenth century is replete with intrigue, coups and vicious succession disputes.'[54]

[53] This was the focus of a recent study by Neil A. Englehart, *Culture and Power in Traditional Siamese Government*, Ithaca: Cornell University Press, 2001.

[54] Kemp, *Aspects of Siamese Kingship*, p. 41.

The remarkable exaltation of the king's person not only often hampered a smooth succession but in addition it prevented a clear and open flow of information.

> *He often times punishes ill Advice, or recompences good. I say good or bad according to his sense, for he alone is the Judge thereof. Thus his Ministers did much more apply themselves to divine his sentiments, than to declare him theirs, and they misunderstand him, by reason he also endeavours to conceal his Opinion from them.*[55]

In order to keep track of what was happening, the king therefore had to send out trusted men to find out the truth. The *krom Mahatlek* was probably the most important source of informers. This indirect and devious manner of obtaining information was not conducive to effective government. If a king ordered a major task to be done without specifying the details, his advisers would often have to improvise. Consequently if the job was poorly performed, the responsible officers would break the bad news by stages, trying to avoid ascribing the blame to him who first suggested the action, while also making a valiant effort to shield themselves. The difficulties arising from the ineffectual system of passing on information led to a proliferation of methods for finding out the truth. Often the invisible powers would be invoked to assist the king in assessing information, or he would resort to trial by ordeal.[56] The king had to take strong measures in order to keep reasonable control over the court. As described, all his officers had to swear allegiance regularly and give proof of their good intentions by swallowing sanctified water. If there was any doubt in the king's mind regarding the loyalty of any of his subjects, he could have them flogged, deprived of rank and title, or punished in whatever way he thought fit.

The state offices were all in the hands of the king and all appointments were subject to his approval. The system did not provide for hereditary offices. Yet the government servants formed a class apart, for only they had access to an education which would lead to an administrative career. Often a son followed in his father's footsteps and rose high in the nobility. Usually this system was moderated by a lengthy period of apprenticeship at the court, during which a promising youth would be attached to the *Mahatlek*. The king's control over the *Mahatlek* gave him a powerful weapon in his efforts to create an effective administration. He could obtain information through the corps of pages, from whom he would select officers to represent his interests in the various *kroms* in the capital as well as in the provinces. Through his control over the *Mahatlek* the king also gained a measure of power over older, experienced civil servants who had managed to place a younger relative among the pages.

---

[55] La Loubère, *The Kingdom of Siam*, p. 103.

[56] Many types of ordeals are mentioned by G. E. Gerini in 'Trial by Ordeal in Siam and the Siamese Law of Ordeals', *Asiatic Quarterly Review*, April 1895, pp. 415-24, and July 1895, pp. 156-75.

A legal weapon in the hands of the king was the fact that by tradition he had the right to hold a person's whole family responsible for the misdeeds of one of its members. A father would be held accountable for the behavior of his son, and *vice versa*. This principle was extended to chains of command, a senior officer being responsible for the faults of a junior.[57] It also applied regionally, because in some cases where a culprit could not be found, the neighbors were punished.[58] Siam shared this principle of law with traditional China.

While it was possible therefore, for a senior official to place his sons on the first step of the ladder leading up to a career in the administration, he had to relinquish parental control in doing so. It was the king's favor that catapulted a young man into powerful positions, and the king's ire could annihilate all ambitions at a stroke. The court was therefore a fairly dangerous place. From de La Loubère we can glean that it was a hotbed of intrigue:

> *The Ministry there is tempestuous: not only thro the natural Inconstancy, which may appear in the Prince's [i.e., the king's] Mind; but because that the ways are open for all persons to carry complaints to the Prince against his Ministers. And though the Ministers and all the other Officers, do employ all their artifices to render these ways of complaints ineffectual, whereby one may attack them all, yet all complaints are dangerous, and sometimes it is the slightest which hurts, and which subverts the best established favour.[59]*

There are accounts of the most senior ministers of state being flogged or otherwise punished at the king's command. De La Loubère adds that 'these examples, which very frequently happen, do edify the people'.[60] Indeed, the king's relation to his courtiers may be seen from the ordinary people's point of view as much less threatening. Commoners did not have the honor of being admitted to the presence of the king; at the same time they did not run the risk of incurring his displeasure. Occasionally there may have been a feeling of mischievous joy at the news that a particular officer had been punished, because for the common people officers of state were often equated with forms of oppression.

Officers of the Department of Land (*krom Na*) collected one quarter of a *baht* for each *rai* of rice land. There was a tax on boats and on distilleries of alcohol, as well as on the retail of alcoholic drinks. Half a *baht* annually was paid for possessing a durian tree, one *baht* for a betel tree, and for each areca-nut tree a number of nuts had to be delivered to customs officers.[61] Whenever a state official acted for the people, whether it was to give a voucher for the payment of land tax or that on fruit trees, he exacted a fee for administrative costs. From this fee the

---

[57] La Loubère, *The Kingdom of Siam*, pp. 105-6.

[58] Gervaise, *The Natural and Political History*, p. 60.

[59] La Loubère, *The Kingdom of Siam*, p. 106.

[60] *Ibid.*

[61] The amounts of taxation are those valid in the 1680s and subject to change (La Loubère, *The Kingdom of Siam*, pp. 93-4).

officer paid his scribes and legal staff as well as personal expenses. It was because of the existence of a large number of fees that the administration thrived. It is likely that in the lower echelons of the civil service, efforts were made to increase the value and number of fees. To counteract this, from time to time the king announced an official list of administrative fees.

The immense power of the king may have been seen by the commoners as a check upon the greed of the king's agents. If a case of oppression found its way to the king's ear, punishment of the offender was almost assured. An apt illustration of the system and its restraints may be drawn from the method of organizing *corvée*:

> *In every quarter there is a mandarin who supervises the public works: he is called a* nai. *For this post they generally choose a severe man who punishes defaulters rigorously. Often he is corrupted and bribed with gifts which they give him voluntarily or which he extorts from them, but he is always punished as an extortioner if the king becomes aware of his malpractices.*[62]

One of the king's weapons against an unchecked oppression of the commoners by his officers was the fact that one *krom* could be appointed to supervise the work of another *krom*. The *krom Mahatthai* supervised the 'civilian' *corvée*, but there was a separate *krom* that registered men, women and children on lists which formed the basis upon which the *Mahatthai* officers could do their work. The *Mahatthai* officers directed the *nai* and their bands of workers. In principle, the various departments were to keep each other in check. In practice, however, the state officers tended to assist one another. A clear example is given from the provincial administration:

> Oc-Pra Sassedi[63] *makes and keeps the Rolls of the People. 'Tis an Office very subject to Corruption, by reason that every particular person endeavours to get himself omitted out of the Rolls for money. The* Nai *do likewise seek to favour those of their* Band, *who make presents to them, and to oppress those with labour who have nothing to give them. The* Maha Tai, *and the* Sassedi, *would prevent this disorder, if they were not the first corrupted.*[64]

The difference between the system in theory and the actual practice is especially apparent in the administration of *corvée*. As explained, large numbers of people escaped the six months' service by changing their legal status and becoming fiduciary slaves; also it was common practice to avoid registration. This malpractice must have been particularly widespread in the late seventeenth century, because it led to the proclamation of new laws regarding the upkeep of the manpower lists.[65] Even during times when the central government had a firm grip

---

[62] Gervaise, *The Natural and Political History*, p. 60.

[63] An officer of *Okphra* rank of the *krom Satsadi*.

[64] La Loubère, *The Kingdom of Siam*, p.84.

[65] 'Phra Aiyakan Ban Phanaek', *KTSD* vol. 2: 1-26.

on the populace, a number of people avoided registration by moving about or by claiming to be somebody else.

An interesting aspect of *corvée* in the late seventeenth century is that people could be set to work in mines and forests to provide the king's warehouses with supplies. In fact, especially in the outer provinces where little public work was being conducted, the maintenance of a supply of forest products and minerals became the chief task of many commoners. In these outer regions many people made their living by extracting forest products or minerals, and the king would not force them to abandon this work for six month's *corvée*. Instead he allowed them to pay tax by delivering some of their produce to his agents. These people had gained a special place on the rolls and were known by names such as 'salt-levy commoners' *(phrai luang suai klu'a)* or 'tin-levy commoners' *(phrai luang suai dibuk)*.

Plate 2. An engraving of a canal scene in Ayutthaya, hand-colored, Paris.
(Courtesy The Old Maps & Prints, River City)

Canal d'Ajuthia. — Dessin de Thérond d'après une photographie.

Plate 3. Drawing of Wat Mongkhon Bophit in Ayutthaya by W. Korn, after A. Berg,
Berlin, 1864.
(Courtesy The Old Maps & Prints, River City)

2

TUMULT AND REFORM

(1767-1782)

B etween 1759 and 1767 the Siamese lost many battles, much manpower, wealth and resources. However, out of the devastation arose a military genius who built up an efficient, hard-hitting army, with thousands of men marching and fighting, accustomed to bloodshed. This man, usually known by the name of Taksin, occupied the centre of the Siamese stage from 1769 until 1782. Before we deal with this person, the dramatic circumstances that propelled him to the fore will be described.

The Fall of Ayutthaya as recorded in the Royal Chronicles

The Thai Annals deal extensively with the defeat of the Thai capital of 1767. However, one needs to bear in mind that the oldest descriptions of this event in the chronicles were recorded more than a century later, by which time the state of Siam had largely recovered from these traumatic events. All of these accounts commence with the Burmese invasion of 1760 of the Mon territory of Tenasserim that was traditionally subject to the Siamese. The older accounts then report that the Burmese King Alaungphaya, hearing about unrest and succession troubles in Ayutthaya, used the opportunity to invade Siam from the south.[1]

The provinces of Kuiburi, Pranburi, Phetburi and Ratburi fell to the Burmese without resistance. This gave the invaders such a momentum that they rapidly entered the heartland and began a siege of the capital. During the siege, when the royal palace of Ayutthaya was already being damaged by gunfire, the Burmese king was severely hurt by an exploding gun. Not long after he died and the siege was lifted.

The resulting succession struggle sparked a rebellion against the Burmese occupying army by the Chinese in Tenasserim, who sent tokens of allegiance to Ayutthaya. The Burmese, now united under King Hsinbyushin, invaded again in 1765. Siamese attempts to stop the invasion in the southwest failed repeatedly and a second invasion from the north also proved unstoppable. The Burmese met strong resistance at the wooden stockade at Bang Rachan, but when the Siamese defenders asked to be given large guns to be able to attack the Burmese, the defenders in Ayutthaya decided against such a measure, fearing that these guns would fall into the hands of the enemy. Subsequently the stockade was overrun and Ayutthaya found itself under siege once more.

[1] The Royal Autograph version that was composed in the middle of the nineteenth century suppresses this information. Also in the depiction of subsequent events this version does not agree with the oldest accounts. It is not the right place here to analyse the ideological agenda of those who recast the Thai annnals around 1855. In the summary of events in this chapter it was decided to rely upon the older versions.

Of the many skirmishes mentioned in the Siamese annals, all agree that three Siamese army commanders and their troops were sent out of the besieged city to intercept Burmese supply lines. One of them, the Governor of Phetburi, attacked, but the other two, named in the Annals as the Governor of Tak and *luang* Saraseni, hid and watched without coming to his rescue. After the death of the Governor of Phetburi the remaining two did not return to the capital but established a fortified outpost.[2]

The Burmese gradually tightened their grip on Ayutthaya. The Siamese then sent the *phraya Kalahom* to negotiate, whereupon the Burmese reminded him that some sixty years before Siam had been a tributary state which rebelled. The siege continued for more than two years; even the most intrepid forays were unable to break its hold. Finally the Burmese breached the walls and captured the city on Tuesday, the ninth day of waxing moon in the fifth month, year of the boar, which corresponds to April 7, 1767.[3]

The Fall of Ayutthaya: the Background

Virtually all history books that deal with the fall of Ayutthaya in 1767 present the events leading up to this debacle in the same manner. They point out that when the reign of King Boromakot (1733-58) ended, a dispute arose about the succession.[4] Up till 1755 it had been generally accepted that Prince Thammathibet would inherit the throne, especially since this prince had demonstrated his intelligence and great gifts as a poet.[5] However, in 1755 Thammathibet was accused of having amorous relations with young women who had been presented to the king. On being found guilty he was executed in accordance with the law. This execution raised the question of the succession to the throne. There were two other sons of *chaofa* status, namely Ekathat and his younger brother Uthumphon. Apparently neither of these candidates was outstanding, and Boromakot hesitated to indicate his preference until just before his death. Among the king's many sons who were not of *chaofa* rank was an ambitious and able person who had been given the distinction of a *krom* rank: *kromamu'n* Thepphiphit, who later was to play a major role in Siamese politics.

On his deathbed King Boromakot selected Uthumphon to be king, hence in 1758 he was proclaimed monarch and officially anointed. A major crisis ensued confrontation which normally would have led to one party annihilating the other, a surprising compromise was reached between the brothers. Uthumphon voluntarily stepped down and he disappeared from public life by becoming a Buddhist monk, whilst Ekathat was made king.

The two appointments, almost immediately one after the other, had serious consequences for the court and the adminis-

[2] Cushman, *The Royal Chronicles of Ayutthaya*, pp. 512-3.

[3] *Ibid.*, p. 520.

[4] W. A. R. Wood, *A History of Siam, from the Earliest Times to the Year A.D. 1781*, pp. 243-50; R. B. Smith, *Siam or the History of the Thais, from 1569 A.D. to 1824 A.D.*, pp. 90-9; M. L. Manich Jumsai, *Popular History of Thailand*, pp. 250-301; Abha Bhamorabutr, *A Short History of Thailand*, pp. 60-8; Rong Syamananda, *A History of Thailand*, pp. 89-92; G. Coedes, *The Making of Southeast Asia*, pp. 161-2.

[5] For details on Thammathibet, see *Chaofa Thammathibet, Phra Prawat lae Phra Niphon Bot Roykrong.*

tration. Uthumphon had been accepted by a group of able administrators who had heeded Boromakot's advice. Ekathat, on the other hand, had successfully challenged the succession. As a result, many senior officers who had declared themselves for Uthumphon found themselves summarily dismissed, while a group of Ekathat's personal friends, who had backed him against his younger brother, were rewarded by being appointed heads of ministries.

The deposed officers were dismayed at the turn of events and banded together to try and re-establish Uthumphon as king. Prince Thepphiphit was conspicuous among the conspirators. When Uthumphon was told about the attempt to overthrow Ekathat's rule, he decided to forestall this. He personally revealed the identity of the group of dissatisfied men, on condition that they were not to be executed. *Kromamu'n* Thepphiphit was therefore exiled and the others imprisoned.

It was a bad time for the Siamese to be divided, because King Alaungphaya of Burma was at the height of his power and the Burmese were extending their realm by reestablishing a ring of vassal states all around Burma proper. This included the effective suzerainty over the Shan States, Chiang Mai and other northern-Tai *mu'angs*, leading to efforts by the Burmese to be recognized as masters of the northernmost Lao principalities. The Burmese also tried to regain full control over Tavoy, Mergui and Tenasserim, a region that had come to be regarded as part of the Ayutthayan sphere of influence.

In 1759 Burmese troops took the southern Mon principalities, and when the Siamese retreated, the Burmese, using their advantage, moved on deep into Siamese territory, travelling from the south upwards through Phetburi, Ratburi, and Suphanburi. The Burmese king took advantage of the apparent weakness of the Siamese defense and sent for reinforcements while he pressed on towards Ayutthaya. During the first months of 1760, Ayutthaya itself was threatened. King Ekathat found himself desperately in need of experienced men, some of whom belonged to Uthumphon's faction. He was forced to ask Uthumphon to leave the *Sangha*[6] and take charge of the capital's defense. The able administrators who had been arrested for plotting against Ekathat were released from prison. Just before the rainy season was expected, the besieging Burmese were suddenly struck with a major setback as described, King Alaungphaya was seriously injured, precipitating a Burmese retreat,[7] dying on the way home. He was succeeded by his son, the crown-prince Naungdawgyi, who clearly lacked his father's power and ambition.

For the time being Siam appeared to have been saved, whilst the two factions at court resumed their struggle for influence. In 1762 Uthumphon once more retired to a Buddhist monastery, leaving his brother as the sole monarch. In the

[6] The *Sangha* is another word for the Buddhist order of monks and novices.

[7] The Siamese and Burmese chronicles do not wholly agree as to what befell Alaungphaya. The older Siamese chronicles, in accordance with the accounts by the Burmese, simply mention that Alaungphaya became ill. Only the relatively recent Royal Autograph Edition of 1855 relates that Alaungphaya died after having been severely wounded by an exploding gun. For the Siamese versions, see Cushman, *The Royal Chronicles of Ayutthaya*, p. 483. The Burmese version as related in the Hmannan Yazawindawgyi can be found in *luang* Phraison Salarak (transl.), 'Intercourse between Burma and Siam as Recorded in Hmannan Yazawindawgyi', *Journal of the Siam Society*, Vol. 11, Pt.3, p. 11. Where the Royal Autograph Edition differs from the older versions almost invariably it seems to present the Siamese in a heroic light and therefore this source should be regarded with suspicion.

following year Naungdawgyi of Burma was succeeded by his brother Hsinbyushin, a much more effective and strong leader. In 1765 Hsinbyushin led an army into Siam proper, following the southern route explored by his father, and ordered the troops poised along Siam's northern towns to move southwards. King Ekathat sent a massive army down south, but when his troops approached the Burmese, the latter attacked so boldly that the Siamese force had to retreat in confusion. Many elephants and provisions fell into enemy hands. The Burmese were able to extend their effective control over most of western Siam, taking stronghold after stronghold and living off the local resources. Often the towns fell after little or no resistance, but occasionally the Siamese resisted the invaders and gave battle before finally submitting.[8]

Once more the Siamese mustered a huge army to meet the Burmese, but again this force was compelled to retreat. By the beginning of 1766 the enemy had reached the outskirts of the capital. A long siege began, and eventually, in April 1767, the capital fell. The victors took all they could carry in weapons and other valuables and also transported a large number of prisoners to Burmese territory, leaving only a relatively small force behind to keep the peace. King Ekathat met with his death during the fall of the city, and Uthumphon died not long after.

Factors Related to the Fall of Ayutthaya

The picture that emerges from most historical sources is one where the chief blame for the fall and destruction of Ayutthaya is placed upon King Ekathat. The story of how he weakened and undermined the strength of the court through personal ambition, thereby losing all to an outside enemy, has the makings of a classical literary tragedy. While having two kings and their factions must be considered a factor of importance in the fall of Ayutthaya, it is doubtful whether that aspect alone suffices to account for the long series of misfortunes that befell Siam between 1759 and 1767. Another major factor was that the Siamese military was no match for the Burmese. During the reign of Boromakot there had been peace and security. At that time the relations with the Burmese court were quite friendly. No major battles were fought by Siamese armies in any of the outer regions. When King Alaungphaya pushed the Siamese out of Tenasserim in 1759, the Siamese had not been at war for a generation or more. They relied on the latent force of their populace. If one of the *mu'angs* under Ayutthayan control should become disloyal, the king could readily summon a massive army to march upon the vassal town and subdue it.

For the maintenance of order in Ayutthaya itself, the king had professional soldiers who performed guard duties, but the

---

[8] The stubborn resistance at the stockade of Bang Rachan, in the province of Singburi, has been mentioned above. Especially the relatively unreliable Royal Autograph Edition of the Thai Annals have greatly stressed the heroic deeds of the Thai defenders. As a concomitant of nationalistic history textbooks the heroes of Bang Rachan are much remembered in Thailand, the stockade having been reconstructed and a huge monument having been erected. For details, see Khana Kammakan Fu'nfu Burana Khai Bang Rachan, *Wirachon Khai Bang Rachan* (published at the royal opening of the Bang Rachan monument). Recently it was made into a major Thai film.

number of troops involved was not very great. During peacetime much of the central army was engaged in caring for a large number of elephants, which would form an essential part of the country's army in case of war. The traditional system of warfare between Siam and Burma seldom involved a direct large-scale confrontation. However, if a Siamese army were to engage a major enemy in battle, the traditional strategy of the Siamese was to amass a sufficiently large number of men to satisfy the enemy of the seriousness of the Siamese intentions. A huge number of people could be involved, who at short notice could be moved by land or water towards the opposing party. They would not attack, but barricade themselves behind bamboo fences, and might first send out a front guard to test the situation. Both parties would continuously spy upon each other regarding the strength and condition of their troops.

Although the use of a type of gunpowder was long known and cannons had been cast in Southeast Asia since the first half of the sixteenth century, they were not used in a European manner. La Loubère succinctly tells us the reason: 'Kill not is the order, which the King of Siam gives his Troops, when he sends them into the Field: which cannot signified that they should not kill absolutely, but that they shoot not directly upon the Enemy.'[9] The Persian assessment of Siamese warfare attests to the same:

> They have no intention of killing one another or inflicting any great slaughter because if a general gained a victory with a real conquest, he would be shedding his own blood, so to speak. The fixed custom is that when two factions have lined up before one another, a group from each side comes forward, beating kettledrums and playing flutes and the infantry and the horsemen on both sides begin dancing and shouting and raising all the noise they can. Every so often one army advances and the other retreats and in that way one that has some luck manages to catch the other off guard. They rush up and surround their rivals and when the victorious group like a pair of compasses draws a line around the other army the vanquished being a dot in the centre, admit defeat and place their will in the circle of obedience.[10]

A successful general managed to give the opposition the impression that he was fully confident of his success. He selected the bravest troops to fight skirmishes, ready to press forward if they perceived an advantage. The cannon blasts, the power of the decorated war elephants, the roar of war drums and the stirring sight of colourful troops pressing forward with pennants in the air were used at the right moment to intimidate the opposition. These armies moved slowly. It was impossible to go quickly with heavily laden elephants and other beasts of

[9] La Loubère, *The Kingdom of Siam*, p. 90.

[10] O'Kane, *The Ship of Sulaiman*, p. 90. An eyewitness account of warfare in the early seventeenth century is given by C. van Nyenrode, published in F. H. Giles, 'A Critical Analysis of Van Vliet's Historical Account of Siam in the 17th Century', p. 181.

burden. The slow, coordinated rolling forward was itself part of the effort to cause the enemy to give in or withdraw and avoid battle.

In 1759 the Burmese armies had been engaged in various battles. They were the attackers, driving away the Siamese from Tavoy, Mergui and Tenasserim. They met with very little, if any, resistance. It might be argued that the incursion into the heart of Siam was provoked by the Siamese lack of resistance. Apparently the Ayutthayan court was unable to muster rapidly the forces needed to stop Alaungphaya. Siamese morale must then have suffered considerably, but it was to receive much heavier blows during the 1765 and 1766 invasion. This time the Siamese were somewhat better prepared and they raised a truly impressive army, reputedly some sixty thousand men, apparently much larger than that of the invaders. At the first encounter, however, the Burmese appeared undaunted by the large numbers opposing them, directly attacking en masse the main Siamese force. The first battle, not far from Suphanburi, in which the great Siamese army was routed, may be regarded as the decisive one. The Burmese demonstrated to the Siamese that the new phase evolved over the last century in mainland Southeast Asian warfare was there to stay. This referred to the direct, fast, and efficient attack where troops were pushed to the limit and men killed indiscriminately in order to gain a victory. At that time the Siamese leaders had neither the effective command nor the measure of control over the troops to withstand such all-out attacks. Therefore, they once again had to take refuge in the capital.

In 1351, when the Siamese had moved from old Ayutthaya (south-east of present site) across the Chaophraya River[11], it was an almost impregnable city. It was surrounded by broad waterways and in the course of the centuries it had been provided with strong fortifications. In the 1760s it was bristling with weapons and lacked neither provisions nor valiant men. Yet in 1767 this city was subdued. The inner divisions at the court certainly played a role, but arguably this was only one factor contributing to the debacle. The fact that large numbers of capable men managed to slip out of the city in order to reach safer regions must also have weakened Ayutthaya. The court's rejection of Prince Thepphiphit's offers to come to Ayutthaya's assistance was a sign that there was no unified defense. A great fire occurring during the later stage of the siege probably further undermined morale.

One factor that may well have played a decisive role was Ayutthaya's expansion beyond its protective ring. Major monasteries had been established at various places surrounding the city. These contained brick buildings, often with equally solid brick walls.[12] It is not known when or if the Siamese first realized that these monasteries could become fortresses from

---

[11] Taking the references to ancient Ayodhya and Ayudhya (Ayutthaya) in Kasetsiri. *The Rise of Ayudhya: A History of Siam in the Fourteenth and Fifteenth Centuries*, Kuala Lumpur: Oxford University Press, 1976 to refer to one and the same city, it follows that in 1351 the Siamese did not establish a brand-new capital. The annals seem to imply that in that year they founded a new dynasty and on that occasion moved a short distance to a strategically better position.

[12] One of these was the famous Wat Chai Watthanaram, built in 1630. See Fouser, *The Lord of the Golden Tower*, 1996. For more details on monastery building outside the city walls, see F. H. Turpin, *Histoire civile et naturelle du royaume de Siam*, pp. 293-319.

where the Burmese could bombard the city. At any rate they did
not manage the threat, because the enemy troops took monastery
after monastery until only the walled city was in Siamese hands.
From these vantage points the Burmese kept an iron grip on the
capital and were able to erect tall towers from the tops of which
they could shoot over Ayutthaya's walls into the heart of the city.

The Rise of Taksin

The man who later was called Taksin, or *phraya*[13] Tak, was born
in 1734. His father was a Chinese immigrant who, like many
other immigrants from that country, was a Teochiu speaker. He
must have been remarkably resourceful, for it has been recorded that he successfully bid for the gambling monopoly in
Ayutthaya, which meant that he was allowed to run gambling
dens in the capital district, for which he paid the government a
prearranged tax. This automatically gained him a place in the
official Siamese bureaucracy. He became known formally as
khun Phat Nai'akon and married a Siamese woman. His son,
the future Taksin, grew up fully bilingual.

There is a strange legend attached to this son's early childhood.[14] Apparently, when he was only three days old he was
found with a snake coiled around his body. His father took this
as an omen that the child had to be killed, but his mother
resisted this interpretation with the utmost vehemence. The parents' quarrel became known at the residence of the *chaophraya*
Chakri, the chief of the *Mahatthai* Ministry, who happened to
live just across the road from *khun* Phat. The Minister decided
to settle the issue by adopting the boy. The *chaophraya* Chakri
noticed that from that moment onward his financial dealings
were more successful, which is why he called the boy Sin
(wealth). The boy was diligent and clever, receiving the best
education available in the land, first at a monastery school (Wat
Kosawat) and later at the palace, where he served several years
in the *Mahatlek*, the corps of royal pages.

The extraordinary appearance of a snake that did not bite
the baby and the fortunate intervention of the country's chief
minister are typical of miraculous legends that become attached
to the personal history of famous men. It is not the intention
here to present them as factual. Yet it is quite possible that *khun*
Phat and his wife arranged for their promising son to be adopted into a Siamese household that was far more elevated in rank
and status than their own. It has been customary in Siam for
parents to present a bright child to a family in better circumstances. This practice is called *liang*. The child makes himself
useful in the rich person's household, and in return he benefits
from the resources of his foster-parents. If he is very intelligent,
his foster-parents will not deny him a first-rate education.

[13] In Ayutthaya times this title is more
often than not known as *phaya*, and
this has been its rendering in chapter
1. However, gradually the spelling
phraya came to be fashionable, and
eventually it supplanted that of
phaya. For simplicity's sake henceforth
in this book both *phaya* and
chaophaya are given in their later
spellings of *phraya* and *chaophraya*.

[14] Various versions of this legend can be
found, in G. E. Gerini, 'Shan and Siam',
Imperial and Asiatic Quarterly Review,
1898, pp. 158-9; K. P. Landon, *The
Chinese in Thailand*, pp. 6-7; J.
Stransky, *Die Wiedervereinigung
Thailands unter Taksin, 1767-1782*,
pp. 50-1; M. J. Smith, 'Taksin the
Savior of Siam', *Sawaddi*, March-
April 1968, pp. 18-9; and Pradit
Kraiwong, *Taksin Maharat*.

Following the footsteps of most privileged young men, Sin became a Buddhist monk during his twentieth year. He chose to live at Wat Kosawat, where he had received his first formal schooling. What is remarkable, however, is that young Sin did not leave the order after having completed the prescribed period of one Lenten season. Instead he remained a full three years, studying and learning. Only men who are attracted to a disciplined and studious life tend to prolong their traditional retreat in the *Sangha*.

After three years in the order, Sin returned to the court, where he obtained a position as one of King Boromakot's assistants in matters dealing with the *Mahatthai* Ministry. After King Boromakot had died in 1758 and the first wrangle over the succession had been settled in favor of Prince Ekathat, Sin was sent on an inspection tour to some northern provincial *mu'angs*. Soon afterwards he was appointed *luang* Yokrabat in the small provincial town of Tak. This *mu'ang* was not a very important one, being one of the many fourth-ranking provincial towns where the *luang* Yokrabat would automatically have a *saktina* of 500. In 1760 Sin rose to the position of deputy-governor[15] with a *saktina* of 600, and when the governor of Tak died he was appointed to the post of governor, or *chao mu'ang*, with a *saktina* of 3,000 and the rank of *phraya*. From this period date his popular names of *phraya* Tak, and Taksin. As governor of the town, he was automatically its chief military commander, and when the Burmese invaded Siam again in 1764 he played a prominent role in a battle near Phetburi. Western Siam was gradually invaded by the Burmese, and Taksin spent the years between 1764 and 1766 as one of the senior officers in the Ayutthayan army.[16]

Taksin gained a reputation as an able leader and a brave soldier, albeit rather impulsive. This latter aspect of his character brought him into serious trouble when he was engaged in Ayutthaya's defense. It was the rule that no cannon could be fired before permission had been obtained from the palace. Taksin, on duty at a monastery on the eastern side of Ayutthaya and seeing a tempting target, did not follow the prescribed cumbersome procedure and ordered a large cannon to be fired. As a result of this breach of discipline, Taksin was brought before a court and severely reprimanded for his headstrong behavior. According to Prince Damrong,[17] this reprimand caused Taksin to think about fleeing from the capital. His real motivation may have been disgust with those who did not allow him to press a military advantage and who rigorously stuck to the rules, or a growing awareness that Ayutthaya was incapable of withstanding the prolonged Burmese onslaught. What seems certain is that in November 1766 he used the opportunity of taking part in a raid outside Ayutthaya's walls to withdraw his troops from the direct command of his superiors and occupy a

[15] Gerini, *Shan and Siam*, p. 159.

[16] It is often reported that he was appointed governor of Kamphaeng Phet, a *mu'ang* of the second rank, and thus a major promotion. However, in the troubled times just before the fall of Ayutthaya, this promotion was probably never put into effect. The remark by King Mongkut that *phraya* Tak bribed the *chaophraya* Chakri in order to obtain this promotion must be viewed as an unsupported opinion. It is unlikely that Taksin would have been so keen to gain the governorship of a town which was then in Burmese hands. See 'Brief Sketches of Siamese History', *Siamese Repository*, 1869, p. 258.

[17] *Kromphra* Damrong Ratchanuphap, *Phongsawadan Ru'ang Thai Rop Phama*, PP, Pt 6, Vol. 6, p. 129.

strategic stronghold not far from the city. Taksin remained there several months until in January 1767 a big fire broke out in the capital. He chose that moment to retire from the battle-field altogether and with about a thousand men broke through the Burmese siege. There are some indications that many of Taksin's followers were Chinese.[18] The direction in which Taksin and his troops fled may have been influenced by their ethnic background. They could have fled north or eastwards, but went in a south-easterly direction towards the regions where Chinese settlers were numerous. Taksin and his follow-ers were now outcasts, pursued by Burmese, and also liable to be attacked by Siamese. His escape was successful; he reached *mu'ang* Chonburi and moved further on towards Rayong.

Reputedly at this stage Taksin held a meeting, declaring that as Ayutthaya's power had dissipated he would create an independent army in the eastern part of Siam. By acclamation he was elected the absolute leader (*chao*) and when local village headmen came to offer their services, *chao* Tak appoint-ed them to such ranks as *mu'n*, *khun*, *luang*, and *phra*, thus assuming the legal right to do so. The leaders of the town of Rayong presented food, but at the same time secretly invited troops from Chanthaburi to come and attack *chao* Tak. This plot failed and *chao* Tak was able to establish his power over the whole region of Rayong and Chonburi. To the east, the ruler of Chanthaburi prepared himself for a confrontation with this new forceful half-Chinese general. After several attempts to solve the issue by diplomacy, in June 1767 a full-scale battle erupted. *Chao* Tak conquered the town of Chanthaburi, gaining control of all of southeastern Siam, which included a long stretch of the coast and several small harbors, as well as a number of ships.[19]

The Country's Subjugation

It was now two months after Ayutthaya had fallen and central Siam was under Burmese control. Had the Burmese maintained a strong military presence, they might have continued their occupation of Siam for a long time. However, the main armies were pulled back to Burma, leaving only a few thousand men under the command of a Mon general. This man had distin-guished himself in Burmese eyes by taking the stockade at Bang Rachan, where Siamese defenders had long defied Burmese attempts to dislodge them. The Siamese, deprived of the immense power, wealth, and status of Ayutthaya, had fallen back upon their provincial administrative system to regain a measure of order. The governors of towns (*chao mu'ang*) and their staff could no longer expect directives from the king's central bureaucracy; for the time being many were responsible to no one but themselves. However, there were *mu'angs* of

---

[18] *Ibid.*, p. 131.

[19] Stranski, *Die Wiedervereinigung Thailands*, p. 55.

various types: some were relatively large centres, traditionally supervising a number of subordinate *mu'angs*, and others occupied strategic positions. Soon, however, it was possible to recognize a series of regional leaders in the area that was not directly ruled by the Burmese and Burmese-appointed governors. If Taksin had not boldly escaped from Ayutthaya, the leader of southeastern Siam would undoubtedly have been *phraya* Chanthaburi. Directly east of Ayutthaya, the rulers of Phimai and Nakhon Ratchasima, respectively *kromamu'n* Thepphiphit (safely returned from exile) and *luang* Pheng, vied for control of the Khorat Plateau. To the north of Ayutthaya was the important provincial town of Phitsanulok, to which many Ayutthayan officials had fled. The governor of Phitsanulok soon declared his independence, and the Burmese, not having sufficient troops to deal with this problem, allowed this to happen. Even further northwards, the town of Sawangkhaburi also became an independently governed center under the inspired leadership of the chief Buddhist monk, *phra* Fang, renowned for his supernatural powers, who took over the rule of this region, helped by many other monks. He marched south and besieged Phitsanulok, but returned to Sawangkhaburi after six months when it showed no sign of yielding. In the south, the acting governor of Nakhon Si Thammarat declared himself absolute ruler and governed in his own right.[20]

The Burmese had appointed governors in the regions they had conquered between 1764 and 1767, but they could no longer spare the manpower to rule even that area effectively. It was not long before the boldest of the self-appointed independent rulers, *chao* Tak, decided to attack Burmese-held territory. In October 1767, six months after the fall of Ayutthaya, he went westwards with an army of some five thousand men and more than a hundred boats. He took the stronghold at Thonburi and ordered the execution of the Burmese-appointed governor. The Burmese headquarters just outside Ayutthaya were alerted, and troops were sent south to quell the disorders and re-establish Burmese control. *Chao* Tak did not wait for reprisals, but marched out to meet the enemy. He won the first skirmishes, put the Burmese-led troops to flight and pushed his advantage by attacking the main Burmese camp, which he overran.[21] In one bold and decisive campaign he thus succeeded in taking the lower part of the Chaophraya valley, the traditional heartland of Siam, and as commander of this part of the country, *chao* Tak now became a chief contender for the throne of the Siamese kingdom as a whole.

Chao Tak's exultation at having delivered the old capital from the Burmese must have been tempered by his realization of the magnitude of the tasks confronting him. Sooner or later the Burmese could be expected to send a massive army to re-subjugate Siam, the capital of which lay in ruins and which

---

[20] For details, see Damrong Ratchanuphap, *Phongsawadan Ru'ang Thai Rop Phama*, pp. 143-53; Stranski, *Die Wiedervereinigung Thailands*, pp. 43-8; and Chaloem Yuwiengchai, 'Prawatisat Nakhon Si Thammarat samai Krung Thonburi', in Rai-ngan Kan Samana Prawatisat Nakhon Si Thammarat, Nakhon Si Thammarat Withayalai Khru, *Prawatisat Nakhon Si Thammarat*, pp. 218-9. Several other contenders for power sought refuge in Cambodia and Cochin-China. See Chingho A. Chen, 'Mac Thien Tu and phraya Taksin: A Survey on Their Political Stand, Conflicts and Background', *Proceedings, Seventh IAHA Conference 22-26 August 1977, Bangkok*, pp. 1545-8.

[21] According to Wood (*A History of Siam*, p. 252), the Siamese contingent under Burmese command began to desert and ran over to Taksin.

would have to be rebuilt. Moreover, though Taksin had proven to be the country's most daring general, this did not automatically give him the right to rule. There were many men in the country who, less than a year before, used to be superior to him in rank and position. He had no royal blood in his veins and would have to deal with immense opposition if he were to declare himself Siam's absolute ruler. Indeed, it is likely that at first he ruled simply as a military man, issuing effective orders to restore law and order, proclaiming it to be illegal to oppress farmers and the poor. From the earliest days when he had had distanced himself from the besieged capital, he had set himself up as a leader of the common folk, a protector of the people, who ordered his soldiers to be just, assist those in need and foster the Buddhist religion.[22]

There has been much speculation as to why *chao* Tak did not make Ayutthaya his base. According to legend, he had a dream in which the former kings drove him away from the old capital and he therefore had to search for new headquarters.[23] It is impossible to ascertain whether indeed such a dream upset the leader. Many other possible motives for the abandonment of Ayutthaya have been suggested. For example, the fields in the Ayutthaya region had been left untended, making it difficult to supply the city. It would have needed an enormous effort to rebuild Ayutthaya's fortifications. Not only would this have been costly; it would have had to be completed with great speed to provide effective shelter for the city's defenders.[24] Whatever the exact reasons, it remains a fact that *chao* Tak decided to make his headquarters in the fortress at Thonburi, a stronghold that had traditionally guarded the approach to Ayutthaya from the sea. At Thonburi, on the west bank of the Chaophraya River, the existing fortifications provided him with a much more manageable township, closer to the other towns already under his command and easier to reach from the sea.[25]

Before he left the devastated city of Ayutthaya, *chao* Tak took some measures that are indicative of his stature as a leader. He organized the ceremonial cremation of King Ekathat's corpse and treated with consideration the few members of the royal family and palace staff who were still living in the city. At the same time, there could be no doubt who was lord and master, for he took as his personal consorts four ladies from the palace, one of them the daughter of *kromamu'n* Thepphiphit. Less than two years later Thepphiphit's daughter and one of the other high-ranking women were found guilty of consorting with other men. Taksin's punishment was merciless: the culprits were publicly raped before their arms and heads were hacked off.[26]

The Burmese soon attempted to resume their hold over central Siam. In 1768 some two thousand soldiers from Tavoy were sent to reinforce those still stationed at Ratburi, southwest of Thonburi. *Chao* Tak's quick reaction to the news of the

[22] Stranski, *Die Wiedervereinigung Thailands*, p. 61.

[23] This has given rise to some romantic poetry; see, for example, Montri Umavijani, *A Poetic Journey Through Thai History*, pp. 10-5.

[24] Some of the arguments surrounding *chao* Tak's decision not to revive Ayutthaya can be found in L. Sternstein, 'From Ayutthaya to Bangkok', *Hemisphere* 17, no. 11 (November 1973), pp. 14-21.

[25] Whichever argument the reader may prefer, one should avoided looking at this decision with the benefit of hindsight. *Chao* Tak did not know he would succeed in becoming the ruler of Siam; it was by no means certain that he would be able to withstand the Burmese, nor could it be taken for granted that he would be able to hold a throne against a throng of men with better claims to the throne. King Boromakot had 123 children, many of whom were still alive. Moreover, the choice was not simply between Ayutthaya and Thonburi; according to the *Phra Ratcha Phongsawadan Krung Thonburi*, Taksin did at first not rule out the possibility of making Chanthaburi his permanent headquarters.

[26] Stranski, *Die Wiedervereinigung Thailands*, pp. 73-4.

Burmese reinforcements is in line with his intrepid character. He went by sea with a large number of troops to the mouth of the river Mae Klong, thus trapping the Burmese fleet that had been stationed there since early in the Burmese invasion. At the same time a land force under the command of his trusted comrade Bunma[27] attacked the Burmese from a different direction. This bold maneuver succeeded in putting the enemy to flight, and *chao* Tak thus extended the territory over which he held sway and captured much-needed ships and weapons.

Some time early in 1768, reputedly encouraged by his chief advisers, who reported to him that everyone – officials, tradesmen, soldiers, and farmers – wanted him to be proclaimed king, *chao* Tak agreed to this, though there is no firm evidence of his formal anointment.[28] It was clear from the outset, however, that King Taksin would not be a traditional king, surrounded by protocol and removed from ordinary people. He was a man who often insisted on knowing even the smallest details, and he would not allow court procedure to isolate him. At the beginning of his reign, he was, after all, a king without a proper palace; indeed, he then possessed as yet only a small part of his kingdom.

Taksin realized that most of the outer regions that traditionally had been subject to Ayutthaya, did not recognize him as the new overlord, and that soon this would result in armed confrontation. As usual, he preferred to take the initiative and in 1768 he marched against Phitsanulok. The ensuing battle turned out unfavorably for Taksin, who was wounded in the leg and had to retreat. The ruler of Phitsanulok, who considered that he had decisively defeated his chief opponent, now in his turn proclaimed himself to be Siam's king.

Before he could consolidate his position the ruler of Phitsanulok became seriously ill and died, leaving his son in charge. The latter, probably fearing that claiming a throne was rather hazardous, did not follow his father's lead and contented himself just with the title of *chao*. Meanwhile, *phra* Fang of Sawangkhaburi again marched south, began his second siege of Phitsanulok and after three months took and ransacked the town. The monk-ruler now held the northern part of what used to be Siam.

Taksin had not been seriously wounded at Phitsanulok and before long decided to march to the northeast, where some of the Burmese-led troops had joined *kromamu'n* Thepphiphit. Fierce battles were fought on two fronts and Taksin's troops were victorious. Thepphiphit escaped further eastwards, but eventually was captured, brought before Taksin and soon afterwards executed. Late in 1768 yet another military venture was begun: the subjugation of the southern regions. Taksin sent two armies southwards, this time remaining in Thonburi. However, when these armies were defeated by the ruler of Nakhon Si

[27] At this stage in his career, Bunma carried the title *phra* Maha Montri. This man was the younger brother of the man who would take the throne after Taksin had abdicated, and he became Siam's *uparat*, playing a key role in the country's affairs.

[28] Turpin (*Histoire civile*, p. 336) states: 'Il fut appelé au commandement par la voix unanime des grands & du peuple. Il ne prit d'abord que le titre modeste de défenseur de la nation; & couvrant ses desseins ambitieux du voile de la moderation, il ne voulut paraître que citoyen, pour être véritablement Roi.'

Thammarat, Taksin went to their assistance with a fleet of warships and managed to subjugate the region. He stayed in the south until March 1769, as usual enforcing strict rules upon the soldiers, forbidding them to kill the farmers' cattle or to rob the populace. He kept them busy building more warships. He also provided funds for the repair of monasteries, and large amounts of rice were donated to Buddhist monks and novices. In a typical gesture he ordered a sum of money to be given to every mendicant when it was *wanphra*.[29] In the descriptions of Taksin's rule, such episodes of 'merit-making' are often encountered, usually immediately after order has been forcefully restored. It is quite likely that the two types of activities are linked. Up till the present day there are still many Siamese who feel that an act of merit is called for immediately after the performance of an act that carries demerit. Although Buddhist doctrine does not allow for it, many Siamese feel that the effects of the meritorious activity will offset the ill effects of the evil deed.[30]

F. H. Turpin's *Histoire civile et naturelle du royaume de Siam*, which was published at the beginning of Taksin's reign and mentions events up to 1769, confirms the new king's position, his reputation as a stern warrior and his distribution of ranks and titles among those who aided them. Two further aspects relevant for an assessment of King Taksin are mentioned by Turpin. The first concerns his measures to alleviate famine and second is his 'well-known' hatred of Buddhist monks.[31]

It is not certain whether the food shortages of 1768 and 1769 can be fully attributed to the effects of the war. Turpin also mentions drought, a perpetual hazard to the farmers in central Siam. In addition, there were plagues of rats and insects, attacking rice and vegetable crops. He reports the outbreak of a severe contagious disease, one that affected people's cerebral function with loss of memory, impaired speech and intermittent periods of madness and lucidity.[32] The severity of the outbreak is attested by the statement that 'every morning the river was filled with corpses.'[33] Whatever the cause of the food shortages, it is certain that when Taksin returned from the south his leadership was direly needed. Not only were many people starving, but also bands of robbers were making life uncertain.

Using treasury funds, Taksin imported large amounts of rice, which he distributed free of cost. In this respect, he took the same measures as did previous kings in similar circumstances. In addition, he ordered all government employees, regardless of rank or status, to work on fields that lay fallow. This latter decree was probably unprecedented and reflects the pragmatic and impulsive character of the general-king. Also it may have been inspired by Taksin's personal dislike of pomp and ceremony.

The second aspect touched upon by Turpin, Taksin's 'aversion' to Buddhist monks, is more difficult to assess. Turpin is unambiguous in his report, which may be translated as follows:

[29] *Wanphra* is the Buddhist regular 'sacred' day held four times each lunar month.

[30] Thus the Thai executioner declared in an interview that he was not worried about the fact that he killed people, because after each execution he bought food for the monks. See the *Far Eastern Economic Review*, 23 July 1976, pp. 24-5.

[31] Turpin, *Histoire civile*, pp. 334-40.

[32] *Ibid.*, p. 338.

[33] A. Pallegoix, *Description du royaume Thai ou Siam*, vol. 2, p. 259.

He had learned by experience that the priests, in the abuse of their power over the unlettered masses, were wont to foment sedition and stir popular feeling. He took a violent dislike to them, which he did not try to conceal, and considered that the respect they enjoyed was a slight on his authority. He therefore wished for the extermination of these idolatrous priests who, poor by profession, enjoyed the fruits of the labour of the artisans and farmers, without doing anything in return.[34]

Turpin continues with an example of how Taksin treated the 'idolatrous' priests:

A Sancrat[35] *of great renown was accused of incontinence. Phia-Thae*[36] *made him appear before his tribunal and condemned him to a trial by fire. The soles of his feet were burned by the glowing charcoal, and that was the proof that he was guilty. He would have been condemned to decapitation had not powerful interceders obtained his pardon, under the specious pretext that his death would cause a scandal, and that when their servants were done away with, the gods would be less respected.*[37]

These two quotations need to be examined separately. The first one, in which Taksin is accused of wishing to kill all Buddhist monks because he felt the respect given them was a slight on his own authority, does not fit in with the facts known about him from other sources. Firstly, Taksin had of his own free will once stayed a considerable time in the Buddhist order. Secondly, in Rayong, in Thonburi, and again later in Nakhon Si Thammarat he had exhorted people to respect the Buddhist religion and had personally dispensed rice to the monks and novices. Taksin appears to have been not only a competent general but also a devout practicing Buddhist. If there is any truth in Turpin's account, the dislike reputedly felt by Taksin might have been directed towards priests who did abuse their position, who broke the rules and who by their bad behavior undermined the venerable *Sangha*. Taksin's preoccupation with the good name of the order of monks is also testified in Siamese sources.[38] It is possible that Turpin's informants had in mind the priest-general *phra* Fang and his monks who had control over the northern part of Siam. These were Taksin's political enemies, and in addition, their involvement in warfare would have made them renegade Buddhist priests in the eyes of a devout Buddhist.[39] Turpin's remark about idolatrous priests enjoying the fruits of the labor of others without doing anything in return must be accounted for by the fact that Turpin's informants were French missionaries who held Buddhism in contempt. The statement reflects not so much Taksin's views as the prejudices of the authors of the documents upon which Turpin based his account.

---

[34] Turpin, *Histoire civile*, p. 337. B. O. Cartwright's English translation of Turpin, which was published in 1908 in Bangkok at the American Presbyterian Mission Press under the title *History of the Kingdom of Siam*, is not wholly accurate, and these passages have therefore been rendered into English with the original at hand.

[35] *Sangkharat*, or leader of the Buddhist church in the country.

[36] Turpin, working from missionaries' reports, consistently spells Taksin's name in this manner, probably a misreading from a manuscript where the name might have been spelt Phaia-Thac.

[37] Turpin, *Histoire civile*, pp. 337-8.

[38] *Phra Ratcha Pongsawadan Phra Ratchalekha*, vol. 2, pt 1, pp. 4-6.

[39] According to the ancient rules of the *Patimokkha*, a priest is not allowed to involve himself with military affairs. He is not even allowed to look and enjoy the sight of a military parade. See Ñanamoli Thera, transl., *The Patimokkha, 227 Fundamental Rules of a Bhikkhu*, pp. 58-9. If a Buddhist priest engages in war and intentionally kills a human being, he is automatically expelled from the order and forfeits all respect.

Turpin's example of the high-ranking priest being tortured, found guilty, but let free under some spurious pretext also must be read with caution. According to Siamese sources, there was indeed an inquiry into the behavior of the patriarch, who, it was rumored, had planned to enrich himself at the expense of various wealthy citizens. Taksin ordered the patriarch to appear before a tribunal, and when the venerable monk refused, he forced him to undergo a trial by fire. The ordeal turned out unfavorably for the patriarch and accordingly he was sentenced to leave the order of monks.[40] This apparently was the story upon which Turpin's informant built his account. A chief priest thus did have the soles of his feet burnt, but this may not be seen as an example of Taksin's blind jealousy. The trial by fire was a well-accepted method of finding out whether or not a person was guilty. A broad ditch was filled with burning pieces of wood and after some time the accused man was forced to walk through the hot charcoal and ashes. The gods and benevolent powers were invited beforehand to protect the innocent. Since people always walked barefoot and often had strong, hardened foot-soles, it was not uncommon for a man to come through the ordeal unscathed.[41]

The year 1770 was again full of martial activity. In March of that year Taksin boldly went up north, skirting *phra* Fang's domain, towards the Burmese-dominated city of Chiang Mai. He succeeded in reaching this heavily fortified town with an army of fifteen thousand, but was unable to find a weak spot in its defenses. Realizing that the task was too much for his present resources, he ordered a retreat. The Burmese attacked the withdrawing army and succeeded in causing a stampede. Taksin reputedly drew his sword, forcing his troops to make a stand and give battle. Finally he reached the town of Phichai, where his boats made a rapid return to Thonburi possible. There, ships loaded with rice had just arrived, and large amounts were distributed throughout the population. Taksin can hardly have had time to recuperate from his unsuccessful excursion to Chiang Mai when he set out again for the north, but this time to eliminate a less formidable foe, the 'renegade-monk' *phra* Fang in Sawangkhaburi. It is possible that this second exploit of 1770 was prompted by intelligence gathered on the first, namely that *phra* Fang's hold over the region was not very firm. This time he did not leave much to chance: between May and July three armies were sent up, the chief one numbering some twelve thousand soldiers led by Taksin himself, flanked on each side by forces of five thousand men. The armies traveled mainly by boat, the most efficient means of transportation. The defenders of Sawangkhaburi were not able to withstand the first attacks and Taksin incorporated the northern region into his kingdom. He stayed some months in order to supervise and direct the region's submission. As usual, he ordered his troops to desist

[40] Stranski, *Die Wiedervereinigung Thailands*, p. 78.

[41] For details, see G. E. Gerini, 'Trial by Ordeal in Siam and the Siamese Law of Ordeals', and La Loubère, *The Kingdom of Siam*, p. 86.

from plundering and he invited the farmers to reoccupy their farms. Taksin's attitude to religion and his talents for organization are demonstrated in his manner of dealing with the problem of the purification of the northern Buddhist Order.[42] *Phra* Fang had fled, but his four chief advisers were caught, disrobed and transported to jail in Thonburi. All the monks in the region were assembled. Those who had killed, stolen, or consorted with women, thus having broken one or more of the four rules of the *Sangha* which entail expulsion, had no right to wear monks' robes and were told to change over immediately into civilian clothes. They would be employed in positions in the new state administration. Those who pleaded not guilty would have to prove their innocence by diving under water for the prescribed time.[43]

> *The King pronounced a solemn invocation and adjuration...*
> *After this adjuration the King sat down on a chair by the*
> *river-bank to watch the proceedings. Many of the priests*
> *succeeded in the Ordeal, but others who were not equal to*
> *the occasion were ignominiously divested of their robes*
> *and then executed. Their remains were thrown into a heap*
> *and burnt.*[44]

The monks who safely came through the ordeal received new robes and positions in the hierarchy of the *Sangha*. Taksin then summoned a group of fifty learned monks from Thonburi to supervise the continued purity of the doctrine, paid homage at the important Buddhist sanctuaries of the north and donated funds to some of the monasteries.

Taksin's handling of the case of the aberrant monks must have seemed proper and just to the traditional ecclesiastical authorities. It demonstrates that he venerated the *Sangha*, having ensured that all unworthy individuals had been removed. Further proof of Taksin's friendly attitude towards Buddhist monks is the fact that at some moment in his reign, he decided to include monks who held the exalted position of member of the *ratcha khana* (the highest advisory body in the Siamese Buddhist order) and those who possessed a *parien* diploma in ecclesiastical studies, among the officials who received a regular sum of money from the king's purse. The fact that he included some monks in the select group so honored confirms Taksin's sincere admiration for scholarly monks, and it denies Turpin's picture of a man who wished the extermination of all priests.

By the end of 1770 the early years of Taksin's rule were completed. In a frenzy of activity he had managed to do battle with each of the contenders for the throne and brought most of the region that used to be governed by the kings of Ayutthaya under his control. He had traveled with his armies in all the outer regions and had personally supervised the setting up of a unified administration.

---

[42] The following account is based upon Gerini, 'Trial by Ordeal', pp. 123-4; Stranski, *Die Wiedervereinigung Thailands*, pp. 90-1; and C. J. Reynolds, 'The Buddhist Monkhood in Nineteenth Century Thailand', pp. 30-1.

[43] The Siamese sources state that the prescribed time was three *klan*, or three 'exertions'. Since we do not know how long one 'exertion' lasted, it is impossible to determine the severity of the trial.

[44] Gerini, 'Trial by Ordeal', pp. 423-4.

The beginning of Taksin's rule seems to have been characterized by sternness and steadfastness, well suited to the turbulent years after the devastation of Ayutthaya. He provided a rallying point when Siam was hopelessly divided and he repulsed the foreign occupying troops. Although information on these early years is scanty and incomplete, nevertheless it shows Taksin to have been a pragmatic and quite popular ruler. His popularity was partly based upon his military successes, which provided a measure of pride and self-esteem for the humbled nation; partly upon the efficacy of his measures to restore security, rules and regulations, and partly upon his forthrightness and unwillingness to bend the laws for personal gain or that of his chief advisers. Taksin was a man of the people. This is confirmed by hints in the literature that he was reluctant to assume the position of king, preferring the more modest title of 'preserver of the kingdom'. It can be seen in his concern for the common soldiers, including raising their wages considerably above what had been customary.[45] His care for the ordinary folk is shown in his decree preventing people from falling into debt through immoderate gambling.[46]

Consolidation

By 1771 Taksin could regard himself as master of a large kingdom. This was when he took the next step in the formation of a viable state: the creation of a capital. Up to 1771 Thonburi had remained little more than a fortress surrounded by a rapidly growing population of traders, soldiers and administrators. If Taksin had harbored thoughts of returning to Ayutthaya, a possibility that has been mooted in the literature,[47] in 1771 he must have abandoned such plans and come to a firm decision to make Thonburi the new capital. In that year he organized a massive *corvée*, collecting manpower from Thonburi as well as from the provinces, comprising both those who traditionally belonged to the 'military' *(thahan)* as well as the 'civilians' *(phonlaru'an)*. They were employed in digging out waterways and heaping up earthen walls around Thonburi. On two sides of the town canals were constructed, both to help develop these regions as rice-growing areas and as a defense measure, because in case of emergency these regions could be flooded quickly to hinder enemy movement.[48]

In 1771 the king decided on a military expedition to Cambodia, which had become a Siamese vassal state during Ayutthayan times but asserted its independence since the Burmese invaded Siam.[49] Just after the end of the rainy season of 1771, two large armies moved eastwards. One of these armies, numbering some ten thousand men, was under the command of the elder brother of Taksin's old friend Bunma,

[45] Pallegoix, *Description du royaume Thai*, vol. 2, p. 97 and p. 262.

[46] Before this decree came into effect, many people had been thrown into jail and were forced to part with their belongings and often with their freedom and that of their wives and children because they attempted to recoup gambling losses by betting more than they possessed. Taksin therefore issued a decree absolutely forbidding the lending of money to the players. Gamblers henceforth could only play with what they brought along. Since it was now forbidden for them to exceed staking that amount, it was no longer possible for the managers of such establishments to enforce extra payment. This has been extrapolated from the preamble of 'Phraratchakamnot Mai', no. 26, *KTSD* 5, pp. 290-1.

[47] Sternstein, *From Ayutthaya to Bangkok*, pp. 19-20.

[48] Stranski, *Die Wiedervereinigung Thailands*, p. 74.

[49] A detailed description of the events leading to this invasion can be found in Chen, 'Mac Thien Tu and phraya Taksin', pp. 1544-50.

mentioned earlier.[50] King Taksin, commanding the second army of about the same size, traveled by boat. At first the Siamese troops met with little resistance, taking the Cambodian harbor town of Bantheay Meas (Thai: Phutthaimat) which at that time was a Chinese enclave, called Ha Tien.[51] However, early in 1772 an army from Annam temporarily managed to expel the occupying Siamese troops. Taking advantage of the problems the Siamese had in Cambodia during 1772 and 1773 the Burmese attempted to invade Siam proper from their base in Chiang Mai, and Taksin had to battle repeatedly to retain the northern town of Phichai, north of Phitsanulok.

It will never be known whether at this stage Taksin could have held out against a full-scale Burmese attack. By a stroke of fortune, the Burmese were deflected from settling their score with Taksin by the outbreak of a rebellion in the predominantly Mon areas of Burma. Taksin, always quick to seize an opportunity, attacked the Burmese stronghold at Chiang Mai. Late in 1774 he moved his armies northward. When by January 1775 Taksin himself arrived before the walls of Chiang Mai, his armies had encircled the town and were ready to attack. The town fell relatively easily and the Siamese captured a considerable number of cannons and guns. King Taksin, as was his wont after a successful campaign, paid homage in the chief temples and donated valuable presents to some monasteries. On the return to Thonburi he had to divert his army to the town of Tak, where he had once been governor, to defeat a Burmese-led attack.

The year 1774 is also noteworthy for Taksin's decree on the tattooing of the populace. Every person of *phrai* status was to have his wrist tattooed, receiving a mark indicating who was his master *(nai)*, and another mark indicating in which *mu'ang* he resided. Persons who willfully had themselves falsely tattooed, as well as those illegally in possession of tattooing implements, would be liable to suffer the death sentence.[52] Although during Ayutthaya times the practice of tattooing certain soldiers with a distinguishing mark on the arm had already been known – originally probably as a safety measure for identifying the king's or governor's bodyguard[53] – the decree to tattoo each and every *phrai* probably constituted an innovation. The measure undoubtedly would have assisted the quick identification of ordinary subjects and must have greatly facilitated the allocation of *corvée* duties. There can be little doubt that this decree was obeyed; Taksin did not suffer people to ignore an official decree.

When Taksin eventually arrived back in Thonburi in February 1775, he heard that a large-scale Burmese invasion was reported at the southwestern part of the central plain. This was the long-expected confrontation. Orders were given to his not-yet-demobilized army to proceed southwards immediately,

---

[50] It is quite likely that the future Rama I was, at this time, not yet promoted to the *phraya* Chakri position, and that the official Thai sources often depict his career wrongly. This has been noted by Stranski in *Die Wiedervereinigung Thailands*, p. 129.

[51] Ha Tien was a Chinese town founded in 1700 which remained an autonomous port for almost eighty years.

[52] 'Phraratchakamnot Kao', no. 34, *KTSD* 5, p. 95.

[53] See La Loubère's remarks on the 'painted arms' soldiers in *The Kingdom of Siam*, p. 83 and pp. 96-7.

as he called up reserve troops from the northeast. In the circumstances, he forbade his troops to rest or even visit their families. When he learnt that one of his senior officers had disobeyed the order, Taksin personally beheaded him. He instructed the army to hold back the Burmese at Ratburi and arrived there himself in mid-February. When, during deliberations with the highest officers, one officer disagreed with Taksin about what tactics to follow and uttered incautious remarks, that man was also beheaded and his body exposed as a frightful example of what a breach of discipline would entail. The troops from Nakhon Ratchasima arrived rather belatedly, because some of the soldiers had insisted upon visiting their families and had even brought along women and children. Taksin had these families executed. It seems that on the verge of the long-awaited full-scale clash with the Burmese, Taksin would not allow even the slightest disobedience. At this crucial moment, he pushed himself and his soldiers with all his willpower to the utmost of their capacity. The ensuing battles between the Siamese and Burmese were convincingly won by the Siamese, and in April they returned victoriously to Thonburi.

Furthering anything that might strengthen his position, Taksin sent a personal appeal to the Chinese emperor requesting cannons and sulfur with the annual fleet to China. He mentioned in his request that these would be helpful in his battles with Burma, their common enemy. Apparently the Chinese were not amused by the idea of such an insignificant ally, for the answer was a carefully worded snub.[54]

In March 1776 the Burmese invaded northern Siam and captured the major town of Phitsanulok, gaining control of large tracts of the region. Fortunately for the Siamese, the Burmese King Hsinbyushin died, and after one unsuccessful effort to regain Burmese control of Chiang Mai, the new king called off the whole expedition. Siamese troops were sent in different directions to harass the retreating enemy. When one section of Taksin's army failed to make contact with the Burmese, Taksin called eleven senior officers before a military tribunal, found them guilty and had them all executed. This illustrates Taksin's passion for discipline and the ruthlessness with which this passion was pursued. This was the man who at this time was being defied by the Catholic missionaries at Thonburi.

Taksin and the Missionaries

The conflict between King Taksin and the Christian community of Thonburi arose in September 1775.[55] In accordance with established practice, Taksin had arranged for the court to hold a regular ceremony of swearing the oath of allegiance, during which all senior government servants would swallow some

[54] For details, see G. W. Skinner, *Chinese Society in Thailand: An Analytical History*, pp. 22-3. The Ch'ing court was apparently strongly influenced against Taksin by information received from Cochin-China. See Chen, 'Mac Thien Tu and phraya Taksin', p. 1549. This was not the first time that Taksin had contact with outside powers regarding military supplies. Already in 1770 the Dutch had sent cannons from Batavia. See W. Blankwaardt, 'Notes upon the Relations between Holland and Siam', *JSS* 20, pt 3 (1927), p. 257.

[55] Since Taksin's behavior towards the Catholic missionaries is often brought forward as proof of the king's 'madness', the events are here given in some detail.

water that had been blessed by a group of Buddhist monks. The Catholic bishop, Mgr. Lebon, deciding that this ritual was against Christian principles, had taken aside the three members of his flock who held government positions and administered the oath himself in the name of the evangelical saints. The bishop then blithely proceeded to make out certificates stating that these three men had formally sworn the king's allegiance. Apparently he had not fully informed himself of the Siamese law in this matter, which stated that all the king's servants, of whatever race or creed, had to undergo the ceremony and that refusal to do so would be regarded as treason, punishable by the death penalty.

The three officials, armed with their certificates, were promptly imprisoned. Three days later the bishop and his two missionaries were brought before Taksin. When the king heard that the bishop would not recommend his charges to say the appropriate oath and drink the water, he was furious and had all six culprits stripped and tied between pillars. The three officials received fifty lashes of the rattan, but the three priests were freed without a lashing, apparently in the hope that the example would make them realize that the authorities were in earnest. Later that night the six appeared before a tribunal. The three officials were solemnly commanded to make their formal oath and the priests were invited to submit a formal apology to the king. The six adamantly refused. The following day all six appeared again before Taksin, and he displayed even more anger than before. This time the bishop and his missionaries received one hundred lashes and were sent to prison manacled with irons around their necks and limbs. The three officials were also sent to prison under the same circumstances. After two months of confinement, the three officials indicated their willingness to comply with the rules, and they were marched off to a Buddhist monastery, where they drank the water of allegiance.

The three officials having repented, the case should have been closed. However, the priests persisted in their original attitude. The situation was further complicated by a rumor that a cloth, stained with the bishop's blood, was being smuggled to Europe in order to gain general support for the unfortunate priests. As a result, all communication between the prisoners and local Christians was forbidden until the matter had been investigated. At the same time the Burmese threat on two fronts in the north developed into a serious situation. In January 1776 Taksin himself went there without having resolved the awkward confrontation with the missionaries. The bishop and his two helpers remained in jail, constantly hindered in their movements by the shackles and irons.

There they remained until August 1776. In July of that year, after intercessions by various Catholics and an English officer resident in Siam, most of their irons had been removed.

In August they were again led before a tribunal, where they were presented with a document to sign. The document in question was a general statement in which the signatories promised not to act against the person of the king. However, it included a special clause allowing people to drink the water of allegiance and the priests refused to sign, at the same time informing the court that they promised to refrain from actions against the king. A day later the last chains were removed and it appeared that they were to be freed. However, this was a false hope; soon they were back into prison, shackles and all. At the beginning of September 1776, after signing a general statement only, they were finally released.

The confrontation between Taksin and the missionaries can be viewed in various ways, Pallegoix in his *Description du royaume Thai* gladly provides the details, because they show how these brave men were willing to die for their faith.[56] The case also provides an instance where the regulations and prescriptions of the Catholics clashed with those of traditional Siam. Looking at it from Taksin's point of view, the missionaries simply incited people to act against the law. The ceremony of the oath of allegiance was an important frequently held ritual, administered not only in the capital but also in outer regions. It was a valuable security measure. Taksin could have ordered the priests' execution, but, because they were foreign nationals as well as religious leaders, he did all he could to try and convince them to retract. Having failed to do so, a truce developed between the king and the Christians.

Taksin and Buddhist Meditation

For some time the country remained poised for the next Burmese invasion, but when this did not materialize Taksin began to realize that under Hsinbyushin's successor, Singu, Burma was not likely to send a large army. For the first time since the fall of Ayutthaya, the king could give his mind to things other than warfare.

His involvement with the study of Buddhist meditation probably dates from this time. Taksin ordered a search for the most authoritative texts on the subject, and in 1777 the most senior monks of the country presented him with relevant Pali texts. He obtained similar books from foreigners.[57] He must have already had some training in Buddhist meditation and methods of concentration when as a young adult he spent three years in the *Sangha*. Now, at a much later stage of his life, he arranged for monks with a great reputation as teachers on this subject to advise him regularly on his exercises.

The king's widening interests at this time are also demonstrated by the fact that he sponsored the edition of a

[56] Pallegoix, *Description du royaume Thai*, vol. 2, pp. 263-70.

[57] Reynolds, 'The Buddhist Monkhood', p. 32.

famous Siamese text on cosmology, reputedly written in the mid-fourteenth century.[58] Taksin planned a magnificent launching ceremony, to which he invited people from all nations. Unfortunately, Bishop Lebon knew the work to be full of superstitions, totally unsuitable for Christians and forbade members of his congregation to attend. Taksin was annoyed when he saw the absence of that small but noticeable community and angrily proposed to have all the missionaries executed. Reputedly the *phraya* Chakri managed to appease him, and the following day Taksin shrugged off the affair, saying: 'I am leading this nation in the right and proper direction, and if the Christians do not want to follow my lead, worse luck for them, it is their own business [or words to that effect].'[59]

Late in 1778 Taksin ordered an invasion of what was traditionally Laotian territory. The reasons for this campaign are not altogether clear. Taksin had communicated with Laotian rulers and had established what seemed to be cordial relations with some of them. Apparently he had some reason to believe that their friendly statements were but lip-service, and probably felt that a demonstration of Siamese might be appropriate. A minor provocation sufficed as an excuse for sending the two brothers Thong Duang (the future Rama I) and Bunma, who had become his trusted top generals, with some thirty thousand men to the Laotian territories.[60] The invasion of Laos was a success, at least from the Siamese point of view, and in April 1779 the men returned home, bringing with them large numbers of Laotians, many of whom were settled in the district of Saraburi.

While his armies were on the warpath, Taksin remained in the capital. He became more and more interested in meditation. Already in 1778 a Danish visitor, J. G. Koenig, had remarked on the king's passionate and all-consuming interest:

He believes that according to their religious creed he will one day be a god. To be able to draw breath so that one does not perceive any movement in the pit of the stomach is considered a sign of his commencing divinity. Moreover there are some other sure signs thereof, consisting in his being able to sit perfectly rigid for hours like the idol Rill, with meditative features and fixed eyes, and lastly he believes that by reading he is going to have white blood, as the gods are said to have that too. With these capacities he believes he will finally succeed in flying.

He relates all this nonsense to all who appear before him, and asks them whether they do not think them possible, and whether they do not believe that one day he will be able to fly, whereupon he is assured by all his courtiers, doctors and Talapoins[61] that he surely is right.[62]

---

[58] This edition became well known; it has been published many times under the title *Traiphumi Phraruang*, and it has been translated into French by G. Coedes and C. Archaimbault as *Les trois mondes (Traibhumi Brah Ryan)*. Regarding the date of compilation of this work, the critical remarks of Vickery ought to be taken into account. See M. Vickery, 'A Note on the Date of the Traibhumikatha', *JSS* 62, pt. 2 (1974), pp. 275-84.

[59] Pallegoix, *Description du royaume Thai*, vol. 2, p. 271.

[60] Further details can be found in D. K. Wyatt, 'Siam and Laos, 1767-1827', *Journal of Southeast Asian History* 4, no. 2 (September 1963), pp. 13-32.

[61] The word *Talapoin* is used in the older literature in European languages to indicate a Buddhist monk. It has often been stated that this word is derived from the Siamese word *talapat* or *talipat*, a fan made out of the tan leaf, which monks and wise people often carry. However, Gerini has pointed out that the origin is more likely to be found with the Mon words for 'Our Lord' or 'Lord of Piety' (see G. E. Gerini, 'Historical Retrospect of Junkceylon Island', *JSS* 2, pt. 2 (1905), pp. 175-6 and especially p. 259).

[62] J. G. Koenig, 'Journal of a Voyage from India to Siam and Malacca in 1779', *Journal of the Straits Branch of the Royal Asiatic Society*, no. 26 (January 1894), pp. 164-5.

Dr. Koenig, a European scientist and a pupil of Linnaeus, did not hesitate to label the king's ambition to fly as 'nonsense'. However, the Buddhist scholars and advisers could not dismiss it so easily. Famous Buddhist saints reputedly had achieved such powers. Taksin asked top-level advisers to check on the possibilities. The head of the Siamese *Sangha* personally went with him through a list of the thirty-two marks of a great man (*mahapurusha*) and found it was possible to identify twelve on the king's body.[63] This probably encouraged Taksin into believing that he was a person destined for greater things than ordinary people.

Two monks, *phra* Wannarat and *phra* Rattanamuni, especially stimulated and encouraged Taksin. They judged Taksin's accomplishments as proof of having reached the status of *sodaban*, the first stage towards enlightenment. According to Siamese textbooks the *sodaban*, literally 'one who has entered the stream [of insight]', was a saintly person who had reached such a state of perfection that he could not have more than seven further births among men and angels before reaching the blissful stage of *nipphan* (nirvana). Taksin, ambitious and enthusiastic, seems to have accepted the two monks' opinion that he was a *sodaban*. This belief was soon to lead him into direct conflict with the Buddhist order.

Meanwhile, the king's behavior in respect to the Christians displayed little of what they would have called saintliness. Late in July 1779, the time had arrived for soldiers to be paid. When the Christian contingent, which formed part of his personal bodyguard, arrived to receive their money, the king suddenly exclaimed that the Christians would have to do without. He accused them of not appearing at the royal ceremonies and even of refusing to play music on the official festive days. He added that he was considering expelling all Christians from the country. A few days later a state procession was held and a group of Christians, alarmed at the news of a possible expulsion, acted against their bishop's advice and attended this non-Christian ritual. Bishop Lebon thereupon threatened to expel from the church all those who had attended. Of the eleven culprits, ten confessed and demanded pardon; one refused.[64]

The head of the Treasury, *phraya Phrakhlang*, a Muslim by faith, had apparently urged Taksin to carry out his threats against the Christians. Some time later, during a royal audience, Taksin addressed the *Phrakhlang* and warned him, using words to this effect: 'The other day you caught me in a moment of anger against the Christians and you even tried to increase my rage. They are united and firm in their religion, but you are like a two-faced animal. You may rest assured that if I had acted hastily and excessively against them, you would have paid for it, you would have been the real victim.'[65] As an after-

[63] Reynolds, 'The Buddhist Monkhood', pp. 32-3.

[64] Pallegoix, *Description du royaume Thai*, vol. 2, p. 272.

[65] *Ibid.*, p. 273.

math of this public reproof, Taksin decided to allow the Christian soldiers to receive their remuneration after all.

The above incidents may serve to convey the eccentric manner in which the king held his daily audience, or the fear even his chief advisers might sometimes have felt. At the same time it shows that Taksin had, probably somewhat begrudgingly, developed an admiration for the principled staunch defenders of the Catholic faith. Perhaps the most important conclusion to be drawn is that in 1779 Taksin admitted he had a short temper and could act hastily.[66]

At the beginning of 1780, Bishop Lebon and his two helpers were again brought before a court, found guilty of having broken a law, imprisoned and finally deported. Apparently the priests had been asked to comment upon the king's attempts to reach superhuman powers through meditation and especially upon the possibility of the king being able to fly. The Catholic leaders had told him frankly that flying was incompatible with the physical form of the human body. Naturally this advice would have been unwelcome. However, the priests also found it necessary to tell the king that polygamy was unlawful in their eyes. According to information collected more than forty years after these events, the bishop and his clergy each received a hundred cuts of the bamboo and were banished from the kingdom.[67]

There exists yet another account of Taksin's preoccupation with the acquisition of supernatural powers which probably belongs to this period. Reputedly he demanded from the courtiers who had assembled at a regular audience to know who could go up to heaven. There was an awkward silence, which finally was broken by a reply from the governor of Patthalung, who boldly declared that this was something beyond human experience, at least as long as the human was still alive. The story goes that Taksin answered: 'That is right! These are boldly spoken words which are right!' This is given as one of the possible reasons why the governor of Patthalung gained himself the nickname of *Khanglek* or 'he who speaks courageously.'[68] If this episode really did take place, it would demonstrate that the Thonburi courtiers had become very reluctant to enter into a debate with the king, uncertain what his reaction would be. It also may be taken as an indication that Taksin appreciated a simple, brave, and direct answer.

The Final Years

Early in 1780, King Taksin heard that a Siamese boat had been intercepted off Ha Tien. The crew had been massacred and the cargo taken. Taksin immediately requested an inquiry, but the Vietnamese rulers were tardy in their reply. Aggravating matters

---

[66] See also Koenig, 'Journal', p. 165. Sir John Bowring mentions that if a king in anger calls for his sword, the sword-bearer cannot give it, on penalty of death. He is not to be the instrument of the king's anger, but at any risk must refuse to place the means of gratifying the king's passions within his reach. See Bowring, *The Kingdom and People of Siam*, vol. 1, p. 435.

[67] J. Crawfurd, *Journal of an Embassy to the Courts of Siam and Cochin China*, p. 182.

[68] Luang Siworawat, *Phongsawadan Mu'ang Patthalung*, PP vol. 12, pt 15, p. 35.

further, a secret communication from the Tay-son brothers – who had recently conquered most of the region now called Vietnam – to Ha Tien, proposing a joint surprise attack upon Thonburi, was discovered just at the time when a large Vietnamese fleet was maneuvering off the Cambodian coast. The more important Vietnamese residents in Thonburi were interrogated, and during November 1780 more than fifty of them were executed. Other Vietnamese were deported to the frontier areas.[69]

This was also the time that Taksin had to quell a secessionist uprising which was led by an Ayutthayan Buddhist monk named *phra* Maha Da.[70] The scanty information on the Maha Da movement indicates that it had millenarian overtones. *Phra* Maha Da went among the people sprinkling holy water, and he appointed assistants to whom he gave traditional titles up to the rank of *phraya*, a prerogative reserved for independent rulers. Taksin was able to suppress the movement and had Maha Da arrested, brought to Thonburi and executed.[71]

During 1781 and 1782 the irascible king became involved in two conflicts with sections of his people which must have seriously damaged his prestige. The first conflict was with a large number of Buddhist monks. It may be seen as the outcome of Taksin's strenuous efforts to master various types of meditation practices. He questioned the *Sangha* on whether a layman who had reached the state of *sodaban* would be higher, ritually speaking, than an ordinary Buddhist monk who had none of the accomplishments of a *sodaban*. If the answer were that a genuine lay *sodaban* was more worthy than an ordinary unaccomplished monk, and if it were accepted that the king was such a *sodaban*, ordinary monks would have to pay homage to the king.

The supreme patriarch and some of the country's highest monks pondered over this question and advised the king in no uncertain words: 'Although a layman can be a *sodaban*, he is still in a defective, inferior guise. A monk, even though he may come from the common classes, is in a complete, superior guise because he wears the yellow robe. Monks who observe the four percepts of purity should not pay homage to a layman who is a *sodaban*.'[72] This statement is fully in accordance with ecclesiastical jurisprudence in Siam, and Buddhist monks have never been obliged to prostrate themselves, bow down, or even raise their hands in a polite 'thank-you' gesture before a layman even if he were king.

Taksin, however, apparently feeling that the rare combination king-*sodaban* was such a special case that the simple, often ignorant Buddhist monk ought to show respect, took this answer as a personal affront. He was so certain of his higher status that he decided to force the issue, calling monks before him and testing whether or not they would pay homage and prostrate before their King. The patriarch found himself in a

[69] Chen, 'Mac Thien Tu and Phraya Taksin', pp. 1562-3.

[70] The title *maha* was used in connection with the name of a Buddhist monk to indicate a high degree of learning.

[71] Stranski, *Die Wiedervereinigung Thailands*, p. 138.

[72] Translated by Reynolds in 'The Buddhist Monkhood', p. 33.

very similar situation to Bishop Lebon six years earlier; this was a matter of principle. To his credit, it has been recorded that he and many other monks would not bow down. Taksin punished all of them. The supreme patriarch was demoted, as were many other high-ranking Buddhist monks, some even being given fifty or a hundred lashes. More than five hundred monks were sentenced to cart dung, a defiling and rather abhorrent task. Naturally, there were many monks who, when confronted with the fierce and angry monarch-*cum-sodaban*, did bow down, if not out of reverence, then out of fear.

This conflict between Taksin and a large section of the *Sangha* has often been misreported and misunderstood. Taksin did not try to be worshipped as a god, he never claimed to be a Buddha, he had not accepted the idea that he was a Bodhisattva: he simply objected to the idea that a recently ordained, simple young Buddhist monk should be higher in status and ritual rank than a king who had proved to his own satisfaction that he had advanced far along the path towards enlightenment. Taksin was unwise to take the advice of his most knowledgeable informants as a personal insult and rush into a confrontation. He lost considerable good will by literally forcing monks to bow to his will. Although nobody would have dared to tell him so face-to-face, virtually all principled, traditionally minded Siamese would have sided with the monks who had ruled against the king's wish. This confrontation must have been a major factor in the uprising that followed not long after.

The second serious problem that arose between Taksin and a section of the populace developed from his hasty attempts to suppress illegal trade and corruption. Apparently there had been a flourishing illegal trade in rice, salt, rhinoceros horn, ivory and valuable wood. People who engaged in this trade avoided paying tax and customs duty, hence made many thousands of *baht* profit. These illegal practices were first brought to light by a denunciation. When he heard about the corrupt practices, Taksin apparently wanted to find out speedily who had been involved. He encouraged people to inform him on these matters and acted rapidly on every report, taking the sworn evidence of an informer as sufficient proof of a person's guilt; he had people flogged if they denied the accusations. Some of the informers were rewarded with government positions.[73]

The harsh methods of punishing those who had made illegal profits, and a general dissatisfaction with his method of dealing with many of the most revered Buddhist monks, appear to have been the chief factors leading to the undoing of King Taksin. There were troubles in Ayutthaya again where a group of rebels had killed the governor. In March 1782 the king sent a contingent of troops under *phraya* San to restore order. However, the rebels marched towards Thonburi, with a close relative of *phraya* San reputedly among them. If *phraya* San did not join the rebels, at

[73] Stranski, *Die Wiedervereinigung Thailands*, p. 139.

least he did not prevent them from entering the capital. Taksin's palace was beleaguered one night, but his Christian bodyguard managed to hold his opponents back. Aware of his vulnerable position, Taksin negotiated his abdication, using the newly appointed supreme patriarch and his two meditation teachers *phra* Wannarat and *phra* Rattanamuni as go-betweens. Taksin succeeded in obtaining permission to withdraw from the scene, and during the evening of the day of his abdication he became a Buddhist monk and took up residence at Wat Chaeng.

The main army was in Cambodia at that time, together with many prominent and powerful figures such as the head of the *Mahatthai* Ministry, Thong Duang, who now carried the title *chaophraya* Mahakasatsu'k, his brother Bunma, now known as *chaophraya* Surasi, and Taksin's son *kromakhun* Intharaphitak. In the capital, *phraya* San's troops at first looted the Treasury, but soon some form of government was established. *Phraya* San, the senior administrators such as *chaophraya* Mahasena and *phraya* Ramanwong, and the most senior relative of Taksin's available, *kromakhun* Anuraksongkhram, all joined to restore order and form a government. Although Siamese sources do not state this explicitly, it appears that *kromakhun* Anuraksongkhram was accepted as the new head of state.

This interpretation is somewhat unorthodox. It is based on two facts. Firstly *kromakhun* Anuraksongkhram, who had been arrested and imprisoned by *phraya* San, suddenly emerged as a free man and leader of Thonburi's defense. Secondly, Taksin's successor is invested in Chinese records with Taksin's family name, a name that would have been appropriate to *kromakhun* Anuraksongkhram. The yearly Chinese trade fleet may have been sent early because of the troubled situation with a letter stating that Taksin had abdicated in favor of his younger relative. The Chinese court appears to have had no official account of the events of early April the change of power took place.[74]

Meanwhile, *chaophraya* Mahakasatsu'k had heard about Taksin's abdication and acted promptly to put himself forward as Taksin's successor. He asked his brother Bunma to keep *kromakhun* Intharaphitak isolated, and sent an urgent message to his nephew *phraya* Suriya Aphai, governor of Nakhon Ratchasima, asking him to march post-haste to Thonburi and seize control. *Phraya* Suriya Aphai raised more than a thousand Siamese and Laotian troops and marched on Thonburi less than a fortnight after Taksin's abdication. *Kromakhun* Anurak-songkhram marched up to give battle, lost the fight and was taken prisoner. *Phraya* Suriya Aphai took possession of Thonburi, and when *chaophraya* Mahakasatsu'k arrived with a large force he found the capital waiting for him and nobody challenged his claim to be Siam's new king.

[74] Skinner raises the problem of Rama I's Chinese name and gives several possible explanations for this. However, he does not consider the possibility that indeed Taksin's relative may have sent the tribute mission of 1782. See Skinner, *Chinese Society in Thailand*, p. 24.

The man who had risen to become Taksin's most trusted general was a strict disciplinarian and a veteran of many campaigns. Ironically, this general now became the instrument of Taksin's destruction. As soon as the new leader had taken control of Thonburi, he ordered a ruthless purge. Among those who died were more than forty members of *kromakhun* Anuraksongkhram's clique, including the prince himself, also *phraya* San and his supporters, and many people who had been personally attached to Taksin. Taksin's son Intharaphitak and six followers were brought to Thonburi as prisoners and killed.

Taksin himself, now in the 'superior guise' of the yellow robe, was taken from his monastery and put to a court martial, where he had to listen to charges pertaining to the later years of his rule. He was accused of having ill-treated the former supreme patriarch and of having sentenced people without giving them an opportunity to defend themselves before a tribunal. Taksin was found guilty, and the new ruler ordered him to be beheaded in the fortress Wichaiprasit.[75] The execution took place on 7 April 1782. When he died, Taksin was forty-seven years old.[76]

A Controversial Man

Most of the historical works that mention King Taksin state that during the later years of his reign he lost his ability to rule. It has been suggested that Taksin suffered from delusions of grandeur, or that he developed 'a kind of Caesar complex'.[77] The information that has been collected above indicates, however, that Taksin's unorthodox behavior was consistent throughout his reign. It has been shown that his treatment of law-breaking Catholic missionaries, offending Buddhist monks, and illegal traders during the later years of his rule was quite similar to his treatment of deserters, officers who did not promptly follow orders, those who contradicted him, and those who hampered him in achieving full control over the country during the earlier years.

Taksin may have been physically smaller than many,[78] but he consistently set himself high goals. Even before Ayutthaya fell, it was clear that he could not abide a setback to his career, being unable to accept the fact that he was court-martialed for disobeying an order. From that moment onwards, throughout his fifteen years of rule, Taksin drove himself mercilessly and the high standards he set himself were applied to those he selected as his aides.

The idea that during the later years of his rule Taksin began to suffer from a mental disease is rejected in the account presented here. Possibly such an idea was put forward as one of the legitimizing measures by those who succeeded him. Taksin was a remarkable person, quick off the mark and volatile. At the

[75] Stranski, *Die Wiedervereinigung Thailands*, p. 158.

[76] In southern Thailand, particularly in Nakhon Si Thammarat, it is often said that Taksin was saved and sent in exile to the south. People point to the remnants of a building at Lan Saka, which is called 'Taksin's palace', where reputedly the abdicated monarch lived for many years enjoying a peaceful old age. (I thank Dr. A. Diller of the Australian National University for calling my attention to the existence of this palace and its reputation). However, it is most unlikely that Taksin was indeed allowed to live. If Rama I had been willing to let that happen, he would undoubtedly have preferred to keep Taksin under close observation. Probably the legend is to be interpreted as a reflection of the important role Taksin played in the south, not only during the time he resided there, in late 1768 and early 1769, but also when he reinstated the old ruler of Nakhon Si Thammarat and elevated him to a special honorary rank of *chao prathetsarat*, a title that was disallowed by Rama I. Morever, when Taksin was executed, one of his consorts, the daughter of this governor, was sent back to Nakhon Si Thammarat, where she gave birth to a male child. This son of Taksin became governor of the city. See J. Low, 'On the Government of Siam', *Asiatic Researches* 20, pt 2 (1836), p. 268.

[77] K. Wenk, *The Restoration of Thailand Under Rama I, 1782-1809*, p. 7.

[78] Koenig, 'Journal', p. 164.

same time he remained absolutely sincere, determined and uncompromising. These characteristics helped him become Siam's supreme military leader, one of the most remarkable generals of his time. These same characteristics hampered him when the campaigns were over and when, during the last five years of his reign, he could lay down his sword and take up the scepter. The qualities that were virtues in a general who had to win battles became liabilities to a sedentary ruler. As an army commander he could give short shrift to officers who lacked courage or to men he disliked for being sycophants or hypocrites, but not so as a peacetime king. While Taksin was a highly successful general, he cannot be regarded as an altogether successful king.

Taksin was undoubtedly aware of what the behavior of a monarch ought to have been: a king should be just, he ought to protect the population, lift the nation's moral standards, and lead when leadership is called for. Taksin fulfilled these kingly duties in many instances, such as when he ordered his soldiers to respect farmers' property, when he cleansed the Buddhist order in Sawangkhaburi, and when he proudly sponsored the copying of an ancient document on cosmology. However, when the period of rapid and hurried establishment of order, of improvisation and extemporization, was over and the king remained in Thonburi for lengthy periods of time, a good measure of caution and statecraft was needed. An absolute king surrounded by a court during a period of relative peace must be able to act slowly; he must be able to win friends in whom he can confide and who are willing to act for him. Taksin probably realized that during the last years of his rule he had disappointed many people, and that he should have refrained from trying to change people's convictions by sheer force, or combat corruption by a frenzy of punishments. He must have sometimes felt that his personality did not suit Siam's highest office. During the last years of his reign apparently he was unhappy and irascible. He abdicated readily as if he were glad to be rid of that office and welcomed the opportunity to withdraw from the secular world. If his successor had taken the risk of letting Taksin live, Siam would have been one unusual, but very serious Buddhist monk the richer.

Plate 4. A drawing of King Rama I to commemorate the sesquicentennial of the Chakri Dynasty in 1932.

3

INNOVATION IN THE GUISE OF ORTHODOXY

(1782-1809)

Background

T hong Duang who was later to become the founder of the Chakri dynasty was born on 20 March 1737[1] as the fourth child of a ranking Thai government official and his Chinese wife. The boy's given name was Thong Duang. As was appropriate for the son of an established officer in the government administration, Thong Duang was sent to the court at Ayutthaya, and at the age of eight he became page to Prince Uthumphon. In 1757 he served the customary Lenten season as a Buddhist monk and afterwards returned to the court, where he resumed his position as one of Uthumphon's men. He must have been directly affected when King Boromakot died and a succession struggle developed between Uthumphon and Ekathat. Not long before the large-scale Burmese invasion of 1764 began, Thong Duang had been appointed *luang* Yokrabat to the governor of the provincial town of Ratburi. There he married, and when the Burmese took Ratburi he went to live with his wife's family not far from the coastal town of Samut Songkhram. During the siege of Ayutthaya, Thong Duang seems to have been cut off from his family. After the fall of Ayutthaya, when communications improved, it was clear that his family was divided between two camps: his younger brother Bunma had joined Taksin in south-eastern Siam, but his father and the other members of his family were living in Phitsanulok, where the governor asserted his independence. Thong Duang's father became Phitsanulok's *chaophraya* Chakri, and it is likely that, as the governor's chief adviser, he played a role in the battle against Taksin.

Bunma had become one of Taksin's favorites, and it was he who persuaded his elder brother to join their army. During the fifteen years of Taksin's reign, the two brothers steadily rose to become Taksin's most trusted military commanders. Apparently they never came into conflict with the short-tempered king. Between 1767 and 1782 Thong Duang took part in eleven military campaigns. During the first battle he had been given the title of *phra* Ratcharin. Two years later he held the important position of *phraya* Yomarat, and by 1770 had already gained the rank of *phraya* Chakri. During the later years of Taksin's reign, the *phraya* Chakri was entrusted with the command of several campaigns in Laos and Cambodia. In late 1781 he marched east-

---

[1] Prince Dhani Nivat, 'The Age of King Rama I of the Chakri Dynasty', *JSS* 46, pt 1(1958). p. 51.

wards once again to assert Siamese domination over Cambodia. In the previous chapter has been described how at the beginning of 1782 Taksin was suddenly forced to abdicate and how *phraya* Chakri (who by then had been elevated even further and possessed the personal title of *chaophraya* Mahakasatsu'k) managed to claim command of the country.

There can be no doubt that the man who was accepted as the new king was usurping the throne. It has been argued that *kromakhun* Anuraksongkhram, Taksin's nephew, had already been chosen to be the successor. The battle between *phraya* Suriya Aphai and *kromakhun* Anuraksongkhram may, therefore, be seen as the decisive move in a *coup d'état*. *Chaophraya* Mahakasatsu'k may have been contemplating such a move for some time and Taksin's sudden abdication may only have hastened events. Several pieces of information support this interpretation of events, such as the hurried message sent by *luang* Sorawichit, and the sending of *phraya* Suriya Aphai with orders to establish control over Thonburi. The latter incident is often presented as a routine measure to quell disorders in the capital, but the civil disturbances seem to have ceased before *phraya* Suriya Aphai could possibly have arrived there, and his forces had to fight a reasonably organized, if small, army from Thonburi. Moreover, the large number of executions that took place during the first days after the chief general entered Thonburi appear excessive for a 'quelling of disorder' and more in line with the aftermath of a *coup d'état*.

Probably the details will never be known, because the *coup* was successful and thereupon an elaborate process of legitimization was set into motion. Whether or not the new king had previously contemplated this move, it is certain that he had been in disagreement for some time with several of Taksin's decisions, because he did not wait long before reversing them. Also, it may be safely assumed that the king, who later became known as Rama I and also as Phra Phuthayotfa Chulalok,[2] had not been in agreement with Taksin's idiosyncrasies and his personal style of ruling. From the very first day after he was accepted as Siam's new ruler, on 6 April 1782, Rama I took measures which seem to be related specifically to a wish to distance himself from Taksin's unusual style of government and to stress the dignity of the highest office, which had suffered during Taksin's years.

A New Capital

Fifteen days after taking full command, the king-elect attended a ceremony to establish a 'city pillar' on the land just opposite Thonburi, across the River Chaophraya.[3] This can be seen as a firm commitment to move the country's capital to the other side

[2] The name Phra' Phuthayotfa Chulalok is the name of the king's statue in the royal pantheon, and this name has been used posthumously to refer to the king. The designation Rama I, which is widely used in later Western sources, was invented by King Wachirawut, 1910-25. During Rama I's lifetime, he was simply known as 'the king', and referred to by one of his many titles.

[3] For details on the Siamese 'City pillar', see B. J. Terwiel. 'The Origin and Meaning of the Thai 'City Pillar', *JSS* 66, pt 2 (1978), pp. 159-71.

of the river. The speed with which such a major policy decision was reached indicates that for some time the Thonburi site had been considered unsatisfactory. As Thonburi had grown in size and importance, Taksin's palace, hemmed in by two monasteries, had become much too small. Moreover, the Thonburi bank of the river was the concave side, subject to constant erosion. In addition, the eastern bank, even though it was low and swampy, would be easier to defend against a massive Burmese attack, because the wide loop of the Chaophraya River would provide a natural defense. The strategic argument may have weighed heaviest in this case, because news must have filtered through that a month before Rama I took command a new ruler had emerged in Burma. An additional thought might have been that an immediate move would demonstrate that there was a clean break with all that Taksin stood for. The fact that Rama I did not wait until a proper palace was built, rather rapidly moving to a building provided with a temporary stockade, supports this interpretation of the move to the east bank.

The construction of Rama I's palace, which involved driving a large number of piles into the marshy ground, must have proceeded at a feverish pace, because it had to be completed before July, when the new ruler's ceremonial elevation to the throne would take place.[4] In July the new residence of the *Uparat*, the *Wang Na*, was also officially opened. It was decided to build a city of considerable size and to create a grid of canals similar to that of the old capital of Ayutthaya. As well, the layout of Rama I's palace followed that of the Ayutthayan royal palace.

The decision to create a replica of Ayutthaya cannot be seen simply as falling into line with an old pattern, or Ayutthaya being the best paradigm that could be remembered. Instead, the recreation of a city along Ayutthayan lines was, like many of Rama I's decisions, replete with symbolic meaning. By ordering his craftsmen and surveyors to build a new Ayutthaya, he underlined his intention to rule in the manner of an Ayutthayan king. At the same time he affirmed that Siam was again a country in its own right, with a splendid capital to demonstrate this. During the years of frantic construction that followed, many shiploads of bricks were taken from Ayutthaya and Thonburi, where derelict buildings were completely demolished to furnish the basic materials from which new palaces, fortifications and monasteries were created. Invariably the removal of Ayutthayan bricks has been seen as an economic means of supplying the architects and craftsmen with building material. However, it could be argued that cheap manufacture of bricks from the many local deposits of river clay would have been equally possible, and that Rama I could have left the old capital in its half-ruined state. Again, the decision to take bricks from Ayutthaya may have had ritual value: by using parts of the

---

[4] Most historical sources place the assumption of the throne in June, but the *Thiphakorawong chronicle* leaves little doubt about the real date. Possibly the first person to transpose the Siamese date into the Western Calendar overlooked the fact that 1782 was a year with two eighth lunar months, and that the coronation took place in the repeated lunar month.

old buildings of the legendary capital, some of its glamour and greatness was transferred to the new city site, which obtained a new long name, beginning with the syllables Krungthep. The old name of the village Ban Kok survived in the international appellation Bangkok.[5]

The ceremonial ascent of the throne took place according to the old traditions, with senior monks chanting for three days over the container of water which would be used to transform the general into a king. At an auspicious moment, the new ruler crossed from Thonburi to Bangkok in a formal procession and then carried solemnly by palanquin to his new palace, anointed and presented with a suitable array of royal names.

A New Bureaucracy

After his formal elevation to kingship, the founder of a new dynasty can be expected to announce the elevation of his relatives and the presentation of their new titles and names. Rama I raised as many as nineteen relatives to the highest princely rank of *chaofa*.[6] In these appointments the new king especially honored his two elder sisters. He not only made them and all their offspring *chaofa* but also gave them the personal rank of *kromphra*; and an official of the rank of *phraya* was assigned to be the head of the elder one's personal staff.

Bunma, the king's younger brother, who had served Taksin since the early days and proved himself a brilliant tactician and army leader, was elevated to the office of *Maha Uparat*, Ruler of the Front Palace. Six of the other *chaofa* princes obtained *kromaluang* rank (including the king's eldest son), and two reached *kromakhun* status. The king's generosity towards his own family is clear from the fact that the more common princely honor of *kromamu'n* rank was not given to the immediate relatives but only to the husband of the king's half-sister. The princely appointments in general seem to differ from traditional norms in that so many obtained the rare title of *kromaluang*. It is quite possible that Rama I deliberately did this because Taksin had not given such high titles to members of his own family. It can be seen as yet another sign of reaction against the previous rule.

The nominations of the civilian state ministers included few surprises. The *kroms Mahatthai, Kalahom, Mu'ang*, and *Na* were all headed by close companions of Rama I whom he had learnt to trust during military campaigns. The remaining two senior executive posts, that of the headship of the *krom Wang* and the *krom Phrakhlang*, were filled by men who had already served with distinction under Taksin. The names and ranks of more than fifty other senior appointments were announced.

---

[5] Ban Kok means 'Village of the Wild Plum Trees'.

[6] One of Rama I's daughters had been accepted in Taksin's court and had given birth to a son. This daughter had died before Rama I's accession, but the grandchild, Taksin's son, was recognized as *chaofa* Supantuwong (see Chula Chakrabongse, *Lords of Life*, p. 82).

Those who had played an active role in the *coup d'état* that had put Rama I in power were amply rewarded. *Phraya* Suriya Aphai, the king's nephew, obtained both the rank and title of *chaofa* and *kromaluang*, and the honorable name of Anurakthewet. He was also awarded the right to be seen under a three-tiered umbrella with an inlaid mother-of-pearl handle and received two special ceremonial boats. A certain *nai* Saeng, who had helped by sending a secret note,[7] rose to become *phraya* Thipphakosa. *Nai* Bunnak, who had first planned the suppression of disorders in Thonburi, became governor of Ayutthaya with a rank of *chaophraya*. *Luang* Chana and *luang* Sura, who had assisted *nai* Bunnak, became officials with *phraya* rank. *Luang* Sorawichit, who had first brought the news of the disturbances in Thonburi, also was raised to be *phraya*.

Thus, for the second time in fifteen years, Siam's bureaucracy was changed dramatically. The promotion of large numbers of executive officers from the lower ranks, whose members would in normal times not have been able to penetrate the higher levels of administration, accounts to a certain extent for the spirit of innovation which characterizes the reign of Rama I. Although the country was no longer ruled by a king who seemed to relish unorthodoxy, even under Rama I's apparent policy of narrowly applying the rules as of old, there was ample scope for fundamental reform. A sign of the king's willingness to adopt judicious reform measures was the reorganization of the provincial administration. The *krom Kalahom*, which during late Ayutthayan times had been deprived of the administration of the southern provinces, was given the jurisdiction over twenty *mu'angs*, the *krom* Tha, or Harbour Department (traditionally a part of the *krom Phrakhlang*) was assigned the responsibility for nine central and eastern *mu'angs;* the remaining northern provinces[8] were given to the *krom Mahatthai*.

Also in 1782, the new king regulated some affairs of the *Sangha*. He reinstated to the highest ecclesiastical council three monks who had been stripped of their rank because they had refused to prostrate themselves before Taksin. These three monks were given special honors because they had proved steadfast, and they were given ultimate authority on matters regarding the interpretation of Buddhist scriptures. The two monks who had led Taksin to believe in his special status of *sodaban* were ordered to leave the *Sangha* altogether, for they were given to disingenuous flattery and their influence had caused grave dissension among the Buddhist monks. Rama I demoted monks who had been elevated by Taksin, reversing Taksin's rule that certain monks receive money stipends, and he changed some of the monks' titles he considered unorthodox. One government official accused of having stolen while he was a Buddhist monk, and forcibly defrocked under Taksin's rule – presumably a victim of his drive to fight corruption – had his

---

[7] Thadeus and Chadin Flood, ed.. *The Dynastic Chronicles Bangkok Era, the First Reign, Chaophraya* Thiphakorawong edition, vol. 1 (hereafter *DC First R*), p. 10. This could be taken as another indication supporting the hypothesis that the *coup* was not altogether improvised.

[8] Including one central province, that of Chachoengsao.

case re-examined, was officially declared free of guilt and invited to rejoin the *Sangha*.

The *Uparat* apparently had been wronged once by one of the two monks who had influenced Taksin, and he therefore demanded that the man be tortured and executed. However, the king decided that his life should be spared and then appointed him to a post in the *krom Mahatthai*. It would seem that the king went out of his way to demonstrate his power *vis-à-vis* his brother. Besides, at the beginning of the reign there were already signs of hostility between the king and his younger brother, which later in the reign would result in serious confrontations. In 1783 there was an unsuccessful attempt upon the *Uparat's* life, in which a personal friend of the king was implicated, possibly further cooling relations between the two brothers.[9] In the subsequent investigations, it transpired that two monks claiming supernatural powers had been among the instigators. They were reputed to be able to make themselves invisible and had thus gained access to the Front Palace. Probably the sight of Buddhist monks was so familiar that the conspirators had used this guise to gain easy access. Not long afterwards, the king issued a proclamation requiring every monk to obtain a certificate of identification bearing his name, his monastery of residence, the name of his preceptor, and the seal of the highest ecclesiastical official in his place of residence.[10]

Administrative Measures

Just as in 1771, when people from the capital and the provinces came and built Thonburi's fortifications, so in 1783 and 1784 large numbers of workers descended upon Bangkok to dismantle the constructions at Thonburi and create a new city. An order to tattoo all members of the *phrai* class throughout the provinces may be seen as connected with this massive work. The amount of labor thus raised was still insufficient, and ten thousand Cambodians were brought in to dig a wide canal, almost three and a half kilometers in length, which would serve as a moat for the region where the Chaophraya River did not provide protection. These Cambodians also dug another canal right through the city, which would, it was hoped by the king, become the place where people would enjoy going boating and hold spontaneous singing contests during the wet season, just as had been the custom in Ayutthaya. When the Cambodians had finished digging the canals, thousands of Laotians were pressed into helping with the construction of walls and parapets all around the city. In 1783, the definitive buildings of the royal palace and of the *Uparat* were begun, together with many of the chief officials' residences. The new city was built speedily, so that the kingdom would have a safe and unassailable center

[9] Of the senior conspirator, *phraya Aphaironnarit*, it is said in a different context that he had served the present king in many military campaigns, that he had fought gallantly, and that he was an honest man. *DC First R*, p. 10.

[10] C. J. Reynolds, 'The Buddhist Monkhood in Nineteenth Century Thailand', pp. 42-43.

from which the country could be ruled, even if foreign armies invaded. The organization of such large numbers of workers for such a protracted period must be regarded as a feat of historic dimensions. It illustrates the effectiveness of Rama I's administration and the measure of control it exerted over the population. The strict military discipline which had been enforced during Taksin's reign and in which Rama I also firmly believed made it possible to bring together tens of thousands of people and to assign and supervise the completion of a great variety of tasks.

By 1784, Bangkok began to look like a capital city. An audience hall, a temple, a library, and various other buildings had been erected within the palace compound. The king developed a fixed routine in his palace. At daybreak he would present food to a group of Buddhist monks. Then he often took time to deal with the court finances before mounting the throne and ordering the royal bodyguard to let in members of his family and the *Mahatlek* pages. After they had had a chance to discuss matters, the audience was opened to include non-royal senior members of the administration. In the middle of the day and during the afternoon, the king relaxed. After an early evening meal he listened to a sermon in the audience hall, before giving his attention to the evening audience.[11] A steady stream of information from various government departments and the provinces thus found its way to the king and his senior advisers. Out of the discussions would arise further business, instructions might have to be written and sent to provincial officials. Matters of general importance often arose from the daily business, and from time to time the king would order the Department of Registration *(krom Satsadi)* to disseminate a royal edict.

These edicts serve as an indication of the range of matters brought to the king's notice. At the same time they show what type of information may have stirred the king into action and what image he wished to present to the wider public. Thus from 1782, the year of his succession, dates an edict prohibiting all civil servants from indulging in gambling. Any administrator caught at it could lose all his prerogatives, and both the gambler and the person responsible for organizing the game would receive thirty cudgel strokes.[12] Sometimes the preamble to an edict, which indicates what caused the king to proclaim a new ruling, is quite revealing, not only of the king's intentions but also of the state of the country. Thus it was declared in March 1784:

Nowadays there are but few amongst the populace who are truthful and who make a living in a law-abiding manner. There are many people who are dishonest, who fear neither past, present nor future, who only think about accumulating wealth and spend it on their own families and wives. They intrigue with rogues in order to set up [slave-selling] rackets. They take children, wives, siblings, grandchildren

[11] *DC First R*, pp. 305-7.

[12] K. Wenk, *The Restoration of Thailand under Rama I, 1782-1809*, p. 32.

and servants and, having sold them at one place, they take them to be sold at one or two other places ... . Such shameless and fearless rogues are more numerous now than in the past, and they need to be punished.[13]

The king declared such rackets illegal and decreed that if a legal suit against a breach of the rule were proved,[14] all guilty would be flogged three times and for three days be publicly exposed. The slave was to be restored to the master to whom he originally belonged. The seller and guarantor would be forced to repay those they had cheated and also to perform hard labor for the government, attending elephants if they were males, and helping grind rice at the government storage units if they were female.

Sometimes matters were brought before the king that caused him to remind litigants of the proper procedures for solving disputes. The question of interpretation of the Buddhist texts, for example, which had led to a quarrel among senior monks, caused the king to proclaim: 'Henceforth it is forbidden ... to bring a case concerning monks quarreling over the Vinaya ... before the king, asking for his generous consideration. This darkens things for Siamese monks. Let [cases] be presented to the Supreme Patriarch, the *Phra Rachakhana*, and the abbots.'[15]

Not all administrative matters mentioned for 1784 were dominated by procedural considerations. Six years earlier, in 1778, when Rama I was Taksin's chief army commander and had invaded Laos, he had brought back to Thonburi the miraculous Buddha image known as Phra Phuthapatimakon Kaewmorakot, or the Emerald Buddha.[16] When a beautiful temple had been constructed in the new royal palace, the king ordered the ceremonial transport of the Emerald Buddha to this new abode. This temple also became the place where members of the *Mahatlek* would assemble twice a year in order to drink the water of allegiance.

By 1784 Rama I's administration was proving effective, and it was in this year that the king made the somewhat surprising decision to exhume Taksin's remains and to provide the previous ruler with a proper cremation. Both the king and his *Uparat* attended the final rites. It is not clear what motivated them in doing so. Possibly this was a sign of respect for Rama I's former chief, but it could also be seen merely as the outcome of growing confidence. Those who are inclined to ascribe less laudatory motives to the monarch might even suggest that it could have been intended to prevent the development of a cult at the monastery of Bangyiru'atai, where Taksin had been buried.

An equally surprising measure was the king's announcement that he intended to hold a formal second anointment. While it was not altogether unknown for a king who had been

---

[13] 'Phraratchakamnot Mai', no. 39, *KTSD* 5, pp. 350-52.

[14] The careful statement that guilt had to be proved might have been inspired by a wish to show the difference from Taksin, who had not shown much regard for legal niceties.

[15] Reynolds, *The Buddhist Monkhood*, pp. 45-46.

[16] For the history of the Emerald Buddha, see C. Notton, transl. *The Chronicle of the Emerald Buddha*.

installed somewhat hurriedly to hold a proper ceremony some
time later, this could hardly apply to Rama I, whose anointment
had been prepared for several months and had lasted several
days. Moreover, considerable time had passed and the king had
no reason to feel seriously challenged.

It appears that the king identified his rule with the creation
of a new capital and that he wished to underline the intimate
relationship between his ascent to power and the creation of a
new city by deciding to undergo a second formal anointment as
part of the elaborate celebration of the completion of the
transfer from Thonburi to Bangkok. With much pomp and
ceremony, the king was bathed, dressed, anointed and presented with regalia and the kingdom.[17] Not long afterwards, the new
capital city was formally opened. Poor people received free
meals at many points around the city, and along the new city
wall 'wish trees' were set up for three days from where daily
eighty *baht* worth of coins were scattered around. The people
were entertained with spectacular theatrical performances and
other forms of amusement. A focus of the celebration was the
Temple of the Emerald Buddha. The *Dynastic Chronicles* place
the official opening of the capital, together with the second
anointment of the king, in the year 1147 Chula Era, the year of
the snake, the seventh year of the decade, which corresponds
with 1785-86 in the international calendar, and historians have
hitherto accepted this date. However, these events are reported
as having taken place before the large-scale Burmese invasion,
and a senior government adviser who was demoted early in
1785 is reported to have played a role during the anointment.[18]
Therefore it has been decided here to correct the year and place
these events some time during 1784.

Having been reaffirmed in his position of king, and
celebrated the official opening of the new capital, Rama I was
in a position to give his full attention to the crisis that developed
in late 1784.

The Great Invasions

At that time some disastrous flooding had occurred and much
of the year's rice crop had been destroyed. The price of rice rose
to eighty *baht* for a cartload, and many people suffered because
of the scarcity of food. In accordance with time-honored
custom, the king ordered large amounts of rice from the royal
granaries to be distributed to the people. At that time, King
Bodawpaya of Burma was completing his annexation of Arakan
and, encouraged by the wave of military successes which had
gained him overlordship over Burma, he decided to launch a
massive attack upon Siam. The Burmese opened up five
different fronts simultaneously: one army was sent down to the

---

[17] For details, see *DC First R*, pp. 74-84.

[18] This was *chaophraya* Thanmathikon, the head of the *krom Wang*, who was punished for neglect of duty during the Burmese invasion.

far southern provinces; one moved southwards and then up toward Phetburi and Ratburi; the main army took the Three Pagoda Pass and headed straight for the capital; another army crossed the mountain ridges further north and entered Siam near the town of Tak, and a large number of troops were also deployed in the Chiang Mai region.

Upon the news of a general invasion, the Siamese troops were divided into three forces: a southern flank led by the heads of the *krom Mu'ang* and the *krom Wang*, the main army under the *Uparat's* command, aided by a supporting army under the chief of the *krom Mahatthai*, and a northern flank led by two of the king's nephews, assisted by the heads of the *krom Kalahom* and the *krom Phrakhlang*.

Bodawpaya's army and that of Siam's *Uparat* made contact just north of the town of Kanchanaburi. The first skirmishes between the advance units showed the Burmese in good fighting spirit and the Siamese were at first worsted. Morale was low. When the *Uparat* sent small forces into the jungle areas to harass the Burmese supply line, he learnt that his commanders did not carry out orders. Almost a decade of respite from Burmese invasions had resulted in a much slacker discipline, so the *Uparat* arrested those commanders who were at fault and had them beheaded. From then on the Burmese supply routes were effectively attacked, and soon the Burmese camp suffered from lack of food.

Rama I anxiously awaited news from the front, and when no good news was forthcoming, he decided to rally the whole reserve army and went with his fleet up-river to Kanchanaburi. With great pomp and ceremony, trumpet-blasts, drum-beating and victory flags unfurled, he entered his brother's encampment. The *Uparat* was, however, extremely annoyed at receiving unsolicited aid. By that time the Burmese were starving, and the *Uparat* felt he could soon risk a decisive battle. He urged the king to return to the capital and to be ready to render assistance where it was really needed. The king agreed to this and left the same evening.

Meanwhile, smallpox broke out among the beleaguered Burmese, and in due course the *Uparat* attacked and captured the Burmese camp. Bodawpaya decided to pull back his army and was harassed all the way to Burmese territory. The victorious Siamese troops were immediately diverted southwards, and the troops of the northern flank under the chiefs of the *Kalahom* and *Phrakhlang* departments suddenly ran into a major Burmese camp near Ratburi, an encampment that had escaped the notice of the southern Siamese army under the ministers of *Mu'ang* and *Wang*. The ensuing battle was a close contest, but finally the Siamese gained the upper hand and pursued the fleeing Burmese to the border.

When the *Uparat* arrived by boat in Ratburi and heard that his troops had given battle while the original southern army had failed to make contact, he sent a message to Bangkok asking permission to execute the ministers of *Mu'ang* and *Wang*. These two were close friends of Rama I, and the request was refused; the king told his brother that he could punish them but that their lives had to be spared. The guilty generals were then stripped of titles and ranks, and their heads were partly shaved before they were marched around the camp. Subordinate officers of that army were all flogged.

The *Uparat* then returned to Bangkok to confer with his brother. It was decided that the king would march northwards, where troops were badly needed: the *Uparat* took a fleet to the southernmost provinces, where the Burmese seemed to have wrought havoc. Most of the northern region had readily fallen to the Burmese troops. The area was only sparsely populated, and Chiang Mai City still lay in ruins as a result of the fighting in 1776. Only the city of Lampang, under the inspired leadership of *phraya* Kawila, offered resistance and was under siege. The Siamese troops under the command of Rama I's nephews had stalled and prevaricated. It was the imminent arrival of the king, who threatened to behead all the commanders who had failed to fight, that spurred them on. One Burmese encampment was taken, and upon reaching a second fortified position it was found that the enemy had begun a general retreat northwards. The Siamese then broke the siege of Lampang. Though Burmese troops still remained further north at the town of Chiang Saen, it was decided to recall the troops to Bangkok. Possibly the precarious food situation had a bearing upon this decision. Officers who had fought bravely were rewarded. The two army generals who had been punished by the *Uparat* and stripped of their ranks and titles were accepted back in government service, the former *chaophraya* Thanmathikon receiving the rank of *phraya* Sithammathirat and the former Yomarat becoming *phraya* Mahathirat.

Meanwhile the *Uparat* had sailed to Chumphon and begun marching overland in the direction of the southernmost Burmese army. When contact was made with the Burmese vanguard, the Siamese immediately engaged in a full-scale battle and were able to rout them, causing the withdrawal of all remaining enemy troops. The *Uparat* restored peace and order, punished some government officials, and rewarded others. Having settled these affairs, the *Uparat* decided of his own accord to extend Siamese influence. Rather than return to Bangkok, he sent messages to various independent sultans in the Malay Peninsula asking them to accept Siamese overlordship. The sultans of Pattani, Kedah, Kelantan and Trengganu resisted, but after Pattani was effortlessly taken the other states accepted Siam's superior status. When the king was informed of his brother's exploits, he expressed his pleasure but also ordered him to return. The *Uparat* returned victoriously, taking weapons and prisoners as well as much rice from the south, because the food scarcity was not yet over. The king accepted the newly conquered provinces and incorporated them into the Bangkok administration, raising the fourth-class Siamese provincial town of Songkhla to a third-class one and relegating the Malay states to Songkhla rule.

After the war, the king reconsidered the *corvée* duties and issued a proclamation by which commoners belonging to the category of *phrai luang*, who had been obliged to work in the king's service six months each year, were now required to work only four months in a year.[19] This relinquishing of the State's claim upon a large proportion of the population's time may be related to the rice shortage of the previous season. The king's advisers may have felt that the heavy demand upon people's time had aggravated a situation which developed into a serious lack of food. In addition, however, it is likely that the king was aware of the fact that people tried to attach themselves to powerful individuals and become *phrai som* in order to escape the onerous state duties;[20] therefore the lessening of the *corvée* burden was also an attempt to gain better control over the general populace.

At the beginning of 1786 a massive Burmese army crossed the mountains again, this time making certain that ample stocks of food were available along the route. The Siamese king and the *Uparat* moved up with troops to meet the invaders, leaving *phraya* Phonlathep, head of the *krom Na*, in command of Bangkok. The advance units of the Burmese and Siamese met and fought fiercely but inconclusively for three days, after which the Siamese suddenly poured in heavy reinforcements and broke through the Burmese lines. When the Burmese supreme commander found out that his vanguard had been beaten, he hastily withdrew, leaving many weapons behind.

It was this battle which finally convinced the Burmese of Siam's status as a truly independent country, a status temporarily lost through the fall of Ayutthaya. Siam pressed its temporary advantage to regain control in the Tavoy area, as well as pushing its influence further north to encompass the whole Chiang Mai area, which had long been under Burmese overlordship. Although the Burmese continued to be regarded as a traditional enemy who was only waiting for a moment of Siamese weakness to take advantage and invade the country, from 1786 onward the skirmishes between the two countries were largely the result of Siamese initiatives.

The position of Siam as an international power was affirmed in 1786 when the Chinese emperor officially acknowledged Rama I as the new king of Siam. Interestingly, the imperial edict, quoted by G.W. Skinner in his *Chinese Society in Thailand*, referred to Taksin as Rama I's father: 'We see that the present head of their state has succeeded to his father's

---

[19] See 'Phraratchakamnot Mai', no. 12. *KTSD* 5, p. 239.

[20] This is quite clear in 'Phraratchakamnot Mai', no. 7, dated 1789. The king also tried to increase the number of *phrai luang* by offering a reward to people who caught unmarked commoners and brought them to be tattooed. A person convicted of maliciously plotting to subvert the law on this point could be sentenced to death (see 'Phraratchakamnot Mai', no. 17, dated 1787).

estates and aspirations. He has sent envoys to pay tribute and his sincerity is commendable.'[21] Skinner surmises that the mention of Taksin is either the result of some translator substituting the term 'son' for 'son-in-law', or that Rama I deliberately sent a misleading allusion to a 'proper succession'. However, if *kromakhun* Anuraksongkhram had been chosen to succeed Taksin, as has been suggested above, it must have been during his short period of power that a tribute mission was sent, together with a letter indicating that the new king was a close relative of Taksin. The Chinese imperial court may have assumed the ruler who sent a mission in 1784 to be the same as the one of 1782. The remark that Rama I may have inherited his 'father's' aspirations may have been sarcastically intended, for Rama I had boldly requested a thousand copper shields for his troops, apparently disregarding the fact that the export of copper was expressly banned by Chinese law.[22]

In November 1786 a Portuguese boat arrived at Bangkok with a message for the king, seemingly following on contacts which had been made at the beginning of his reign. Some extracts of Rama I's reply to the queen of Portugal[23] reveal his preoccupation with the Burmese:

> *Recently in a great battle I defeated six Burmese armies which had penetrated into my country and thereby gained a great deal of booty, weapons, horses and elephants ... . With regard to Your offer of help, I have difficulties in the transportation of the troops and ammunition which I need. I am deeply gratefully for Your Majesty's offer ... and would feel very much obliged to receive 3,000 muskets which, in accordance with my wishes, the governor of Goa could send to me during this year. I will make payment upon receiving Your Majesty's instructions about this.*

> *I am delighted with Your request to establish a factory in my country for the convenience of Your Majesty's Christian subjects. Your representative may search for a suitable location for it, and also for a church; moreover, priests may be sent.*[24]

Rama I was quite amicably disposed towards Christians, at least sufficiently so to support the idea of establishing a church. This concession can be seen more as an indication of his awareness of the European eagerness to build churches than of his religious tolerance. He considered the Buddhist faith the best for his subjects, and when some years after the letter had been sent, one of his officials wanted to join the Catholic church, Rama I forced him to become a Buddhist monk and imprisoned his family.[25]

In the Chiang Mai region, some of the northern Tai leaders revolted against the Burmese in 1787 and captured the

---

[21] G. W. Skinner, *Chinese Society in Thailand*, p. 24.

[22] *Ibid.*

[23] Queen Mary, who reigned from 1777 to 1816.

[24] Wenk, *The Restoration*, p. 120.

[25] A. Pallegoix, *Description du royaume Thai ou Siam*, vol. 2, pp. 278-79.

Burmese governor of Chiang Saen. Knowing that they needed powerful allies in order to survive such an open challenge, they handed the prisoner over to *phraya* Kawila, the governor of Lampang, famed for his stubborn resistance against the massive Burmese army a few years before. *Phraya* Kawila in his turn sent the prisoner to Bangkok. There the Burmese governor revealed his country's intent of re-establishing Chiang Mai as a fortified city. Upon hearing that the Burmese were invading again, the *Uparat* quickly marched north,[26] where the presence of Siamese troops was sufficient to establish Kawila as the vassal ruler of the region with the task of rebuilding Chiang Mai. This was probably the time when the Siamese *Uparat* married Kawila's younger sister, the beginning of an alliance between the two generals that was to last until the *Uparat's* death in 1803.

During the time that the *Uparat* was in the north, Rama I decided to lead an army to Tavoy and invade Mon territory, which had long been under Burmese rule. He managed to reach the city, which had largely been abandoned by the defending troops, but fearing a ruse he decided to return without giving battle.

A Strong Siam

A feeling of relative peace and security prevailed in the years between 1787 and 1793. The building of Bangkok continued, and fortifications were steadily improved. This was the time of the curious incident mentioned in the *Dynastic Chronicles* arising from the visit of a French ship to the capital city. The captain's younger brother was apparently a pugilist of some renown, and he sent a challenge to the Siamese by way of the *krom Phrakhlang*. The *Uparat* took it upon himself to find a first-rate boxer. Prize money was set at fifty *chang*, or four thousand *baht*. The Siamese champion was prepared according to tradition and, in order to increase the man's chances, magical herbs were added to the oil with which he was rubbed.[27] In the fight, the Frenchman apparently tried to close in on the Siamese boxer, but the latter, in accordance with Siamese rules, kept out of his reach, occasionally darting forward to deliver a blow and jumping back whenever the Frenchman moved forwards. The Europeans were not familiar with this light-footed technique, and impatiently the captain leapt into the ring and seized the Siamese in order to force him to 'give battle'.[28] The *Uparat*, outraged by this breach of the rules, jumped into the ring and with a well-placed kick brought the captain down. General pandemonium broke out; the two brothers were beaten up and had to be carried back to their ship. Probably realizing that the French brothers had been rather severely punished for their provocation, the king sent some medical practitioners to their ship to

[26] Wenk, following the Phongsawadan Yonok, mentions a Burmese invasion in some particulars not unlike that which has been described as part of the massive attacks of 1784-85 (see *The Restoration*, pp. 66-68).

[27] The rubbing of oil is standard practice in Thai boxing; see H. Stockmann, *Muay-Thai: The Art of 'Siamese Un-armed Combat*, p. 32.

[28] I disagree with Wenk's rendering of this story, in which he describes the slipperiness of the oil being the cause of the European's irritation. The account in *DC First R* does not warrant that interpretation.

offer treatment. Once the brothers had sufficiently recovered, they left Bangkok.

The king's decision to organize the revision of the Siamese version of the Buddhist *Tripitaka* may also be seen as a sign of the state of Siam being secure. Considerable funds had already been channeled into the copying of the sacred texts on strips of palm leaves. Men were employed to transliterate Laotian and Mon versions into the characters traditionally reserved for sacred writing in Siam,[29] and these rewritten texts were kept in the library building of the main palace. However, when it was brought to the king's notice that the old texts contained many mistakes, he decided to organize a council of learned men to sift through all extant versions and write an authoritative set. In this Rama I was guided by examples of former great kings who had sponsored Buddhist councils. Two hundred and fifty men of learning worked for five months at the revision of the texts. When the work was completed in 1789, a great festival was organized to commemorate the new *Tripitaka*. However, during the fireworks the roof of the royal library caught fire and the new edition had to be carried out in order to escape the flames. The king decided that this was a sign that the existing library had not been suitable and ordered a more imposing edifice to be built.

The second Siamese attempt to establish control over the Mon regions was triggered off in 1792 by the decision of the Burmese authorities to replace their governor at Tavoy. This governor rose in rebellion and asked the Siamese to assist him, offering Rama I the overlordship of the whole Mon country, stretching from Mergui and Tenasserim up to Martaban and Rangoon. After due consideration, Rama I decided to send troops under the chief of the *krom Mu'ang*, *phraya* Yomarat, and later the *Uparat* moved with another contingent to the border region in order to be able to render assistance if necessary. The Siamese troops were not warmly received, however, and the *phraya* Yomarat advised the destruction of the Tavoy fortifications, the taking of much of the population as slaves and a withdrawal. The *Uparat* agreed to this and ordered his soldiers to begin executing this plan. However, Rama I overruled his brother and ordered the uprooted people to be repatriated. Rama I personally took command and ordered troops from Cambodia and Laos to be moved up. He sent his brother southwards to cross the Isthmus of Kra and to send up a fleet so as to increase the Siamese mobility.

Burmese troops arrived before the Siamese had consolidated their position, however. The first skirmishes outside Tavoy early in 1793 turned out unfavorably for the Mon and Siamese, and when many Mon troops crossed over to the Burmese side, Rama I decided to beat a hasty retreat. During this retreat, the Siamese armies suffered heavy losses, which for the time being put an end to their ambitious plans.

---

[29] During the Ayutthaya period, there was a strong Cambodian influence, and formal documents were often written in Cambodian characters, to which Siamese tone-markers could be added. The Cambodian script was again adopted as the most formal manner of writing in the time of Rama I, and the *Tripitaka* was rendered completely in Cambodian characters.

Legal Measures

The king again devoted his attention to internal matters of state. From 1794 dates the law regarding the management of gambling houses. This law[30] not only provides an example of the type of decisions Rama I made, and the detailed manner with which the legal provisions are set out, but also gives some insight into the social system and the values prevailing at that time.

In the preamble it is told how Taksin had forbidden gamblers to borrow any money. Rama I had at first let this innovative measure stand, for it was perceived that it was in the common interest of the people, preventing them from falling into debt. However, as a result fewer people were attracted to gambling houses, the holders of the royal patents were bidding less for the right of keeping these institutions, and the State revenue therefore diminished. Moreover, some licensed patent-holders, who had illegally furnished players with stakes, could not recoup from gamblers hiding behind Taksin's law.

In order to solve these problems, in 1784 the king decided to abolish Taksin's regulation and to allow gamblers to borrow again. However, in order to ensure that players would gamble within their means, license-holders were given orders to lend up to a certain amount only, depending on the wealth of an individual. A list of examples was attached. If a gambler of *phrai*, or commoner, status had a family of two or three persons, possessed one or two pairs of buffaloes, four or five cartloads of rice, and twenty or thirty *rai* of rice-fields, up to two *chang*, or 160 *baht*, could be lent. If the commoner had no family and could not demonstrate that he had any possessions, he would be allowed to borrow 20 *baht*. In the case of women gamblers, the license-holder was advised to scrutinize them carefully before allowing them to borrow. If a woman had rings on both hands, was well dressed and accompanied by three or four slaves who carried valuable betel-chewing equipment, one *chang* or 80 *baht* would be the maximum allowed. In general, the king allowed women to borrow half the amount permitted to men. Thus an unaccompanied single woman, not a slave (for slaves were strictly prohibited from gambling) and with no apparent wealth, could be lent a maximum of 10 *baht*.

The years 1794 and 1795 saw several other royal proclamations which provide some insight into the social fabric of the time. For example, it was brought to the king's attention that the law books gave no guidance on the problem of whether someone who had borrowed money upon the security of his person and had neglected to pay for more than ten years would have to pay the whole interest due to the money lender. The king ruled in the affirmative.[31] Another problem concerned the laws of inheritance. In a former proclamation, apparently in an attempt to prevent much litigation, it had been ruled that after fifteen

---

[30] 'Phraratchakamnot Mai', no. 26, *KTSD* 5, pp. 284-92.

[31] 'Phraratchakamnot Mai', no. 28, *KTSD* 5, pp. 295-97.

days' duration, no suits could be entered.[32] The king amended this to read that cases dealing with criminal charges and impeachment could be entered at any time and that the fifteen days' limit ought only to be applied in cases of quarrels, insults and fights connected with an inheritance.[33] In another instance the king proclaimed that he had had numerous cases of people who borrowed money upon their own person although they were still bound to a previous money lender. Henceforth the judges who supervised the drawing up of such contracts ought to examine carefully the financial history of the persons involved.[34]

The Two Brothers

Although Rama I appears to have been a capable administrator who managed his team of government civil servants skillfully, he did not succeed in maintaining a cordial relationship with his brother the *Uparat*. The *Uparat* was strong, brave, quick of action, and a capable military leader. In contrast, the king was much more cautious, intent upon knowing exactly where his path led before he would step. During the excursions to Mon territory, the king's overruling of his senior officers' advice cost the Siamese dearly. The *Uparat*, on the other hand, could look back upon an unblemished military record. As a result of his successful campaigns, Siam had expanded its influence both southwards and northwards. In this situation, feelings of rivalry between Rama I's palace and that of the *Uparat* could flourish. In 1796, during the preparations for a boat race where the king's crew would vie with that of his brother, the latter secretly had a team of rowers trained, in the hope that the king's crew would be tricked in believing they would easily win. When the ruse became known, the king cancelled the boat race. For two months the *Uparat* did not appear at the daily royal audience and when he finally did so, he asked for an increase of his annual allowance of one thousand *chang*, or eighty-thousand *baht*.[35] The king answered that the provisions for *biawat* were already a heavy burden, and suggested that his brother trade in order to supplement his income. This caused a break in the relations between the king and the heir-apparent. The Front Palace armed itself, and preparations for a battle were made. It was only through the intercession of the two elder sisters that bloodshed was prevented and peaceful relations restored.

The *Uparat* may have shone as an inspiring military commander, but during the 1780s and 1790s Rama I left his own mark upon the court as a patron of the arts, particularly in the revival of a literary tradition. The chief creative artist on the literary scene was not the king but one of his advisers, the same *luang* Sorawichit who had warned the king about Taksin's

[32] The simplicity and directness of the former proclamation has the flavour of Taksin's ruling, but there is no indication in the law which guides us in the establishment of the age of the former rule.

[33] 'Phraratchakamnot Mai', no. 28, *KTSD* 5, pp. 297-99.

[34] 'Phraratchakamnot Mai', no. 30, *KTSD* 5, pp. 303-5.

[35] This is double the amount the *Uparat* received in late Ayutthayan times.

abdication and who had been promoted to *phraya* Phiphatkosa. Some time later he became *chaophraya Phrakhlang*. The literary revival took the form of re-creating the 'great classics' which had featured in earlier days. Examples of these works are *Unarut*, based on a story from the *Mahabharata*, and *Dalang* and *Inao*, which were derived from the Javanese Pantji cycle. *Chaophraya Phrakhlang* translated a history of the Mon struggle against the Burmese, an apt topic considering the campaigns between 1791 and 1793, and also *Sam Kok*, a Chinese historical novel. Another Chinese historical novel, *Sai Han*, is attributed to the king's nephew, *chaofa* Anurakthewet, who had by then been promoted to kromphra rank. Yet another courtier, *phraya* Thammapurohit, translated the Sinhalese chronicle *Mahavangsa*. Probably the best-known work of foreign derivation in Siamese literature is the *Ramakien*. The wide range of sources translated should be seen as an inheritance of the broad interests of the Ayutthayan court rather than as a reflection of Bangkok's international contacts. Rama I intended not only to build a new Ayutthaya, inspired in architecture and layout by the old city, but also to stimulate a similar cultural scene. At the same time, the literary works were not mere faithful imitations; there was scope for personal poetic styles that are recognizably late eighteenth century.[36]

Some of the literature written at that time was typically Siamese, such as a poem in the *nirat* style, attributed to Rama I himself and dated 1786, just after the massive Burmese invasion had been repelled. Another typical Siamese genre was the royal chronicle, of which an Ayutthayan version was brought up to date by one of the court officials. This work was completed in 1796.

Meanwhile, the Burmese tried several times to bring Chiang Mai under their control, but each time Bangkok's *Uparat* came to the rescue. *Phraya* Kawila, safe under Siamese protection, even began conquering traditional Shan towns and moving the population towards regions more firmly under his control. These incursions provoked the Burmese ruler Bodawpaya into a large-scale attack upon Chiang Mai in 1802. Again the *Uparat* moved up north with both his personal troops and some from the king's force. The fact that the king's own troops did not fight as bravely as those under the *Uparat's* own command may have rekindled the dormant feelings of rivalry between the two brothers. During the campaign of 1802 the *Uparat* became ill, but it has been recorded that already before his illness[37] he had been considering a palace revolution, encouraging his sons Lamduan and Inthapat secretly to prepare themselves for taking over the government. It is quite possible that he had also taken Kawila into his confidence.[38]

The *Uparat* did not recover from his disease. His condition deteriorated gradually. Realizing his powers were waning

---

[36] Much of the information in this paragraph is based upon Prince Dhani Nivat's article 'The Reconstruction of Rama I of the Chakri Dynasty', *JSS* 43, pt 1 (1955), pp. 21-48.

[37] *DC First R*, p. 266.

[38] This is a conjecture, based mainly upon the cordial relations existing between the two men and Kawila's sudden wish to break off relations with Siam when he heard of the *Uparat's* death and the execution of members of his family.

and his early demise would weaken the chances of his party taking power, seemed to drive him to despair. At one moment he threatened to take his own life and Lamduan had to wrest a sword from his father's hands. The *Uparat* lamented that he had personally won the treasures which surrounded him and on his death these would revert to the descendants of his brother, rather than to his own offspring. This incited them to seize power. The *Uparat's* chief adviser, a certain Thong-In, joined the conspirators. The preparation for the *coup d'état* included the testing of some magical means by which the plotters reputedly could become invulnerable. Unfortunately for the *Uparat's* party, the test failed, several members died, and these had to be secretly buried in Lamduang's compound. Rumors reached the king's palace around the time when the *Uparat* died, and Rama I sent some agents to infiltrate the ranks of those who were intriguing. Before long the whole plot was known to the king, the group was arrested and the guilty were executed.

With the death of the king's brother at the age of sixty, the last period of Rama I's long reign begins. Two features of this period deserve special attention, namely the codification of Siamese law and the proliferation of state ritual.

The Legal Code

With respect to legal matters, Rama I had always shown a keen interest in the meticulous drawing up of decrees. He appears to have taken his judiciary function quite seriously. His legal advisers based themselves upon Ayutthayan laws, which were quite inadequately documented, and this often led to difficulties. The first effort to bring a variety of legal sources together and establish a 'pure' set of rules concerned the laws of appeal. These were studied by a court official, *luang* Thammasat, who in 1801 produced a summary in verse, the so-called *Kotmai Lilit*.[39] In 1804, however, when the king's legal advisers brought a certain inconsistency in other texts to his notice, Rama I ordered a complete overhaul of all Siamese laws. A committee of eleven went through all the court documents on legal matters, arranged them in sections, and discussed various versions. Rama I himself checked and revised the purged set of laws and ordered copies to be made. The new body of laws received the seals of the *krom Mahatthai, krom Kalahom* and *krom Phrakhlang*, and have therefore became known as the *Kotmai Tra Sam Duang*, or Laws of the Three Seals.[40] It is quite possible that the old documents upon which the Laws of the Three Seals were based were then deliberately discarded so as to underline the authority of the new body of laws.[41]

[39] I have used the version as published by *kromaluang* Ratchaburidirekru't, *Kotmai Lem 1*, pp. 681-705. It is interesting to note the conversion of *bia*, or cowry shells, into silver. During Ayutthayan times, 6,400 *bia* had been equivalent to one *baht*. However, after the fall of Ayutthaya the shells had been rare and their value increased relative to the *baht*. Foreign merchants were quick to exploit this situation and brought in many shells, so many that the value dropped even below that of Ayutthayan times. In the *Kotmai Lilit*, it appears to have been as low as 8,000 *bia* to one *baht*.

[40] There have been various editions; for this study, two versions have been consulted: the Khurusapha edition of 1963 and the version in *Kotmai Lem 1*, mentioned in note 39.

[41] Dhani Nivat 'The Reconstruction of Rama I', p. 28.

State Ritual

The second feature of Rama I's later years is the great stress laid on ceremonial. Every royal celebration was the occasion for a massive display of pomp and ceremony. Between 1802 and 1809 there were no less than twenty-seven royal tonsure ceremonies. In addition, this is the period during which a large number of the king's trusted relatives and advisers died, including *kromaluang* Thepharirak and the king's half-brother *kromaluang* Chakchetsada. These deaths in the royal family led to elaborate cremation rituals. When one of the king's daughters miraculously escaped from drowning, she was raised in rank and title and for three days the court held a festival in her honor. In 1806, three years after the death of the previous *Uparat*,[42] the king's eldest son, who was then thirty-two years old, was formally anointed and became the new chief of the Front Palace. The celebrations lasted many days. Rama I once organized a great elephant procession, in which the senior members of court marched along carrying imitation weaponry.[43] Members of the court were encouraged to have ceremonial boats constructed, and they were allowed to use their imagination regarding the boat's ornamentation, taking care not to outshine the king's barge. Buddhist ceremonies were good occasions for a display of the courtly splendor, and both the elaborate *Kathin* ceremony and the great Mahachat preachings were held during the first reign.[44]

The proliferation of court ritual continued unabatedly throughout the first reign. This feature cannot be seen simply as Rama I's reaction against King Taksin's lack of formality, because during the later years of Rama I's life there was no longer any reason to fear a comparison between his rule and that of his predecessor. Neither is this preoccupation with ceremonial just a matter of legitimation of a new rule; the only direct threat to the throne now came from within the ruling family.

Three further considerations seem necessary to appreciate this proliferation of ritual. In the first place it must be realized that Rama I had created a 'new Ayutthaya', resplendent with palaces and temples. By organizing a multitude of court ceremonies, the king may have been motivated by the wish to make the new city come to life. Secondly, the king was a devout Buddhist of mature age, and for that reason it is likely that he was interested in playing a key role in a variety of rituals which would increase his personal store of good *karma*, the merit of which would ensure him a fortunate rebirth. When, for example, in 1809 the king invited two thousand monks to come and chant for three days at the Temple of the Emerald Buddha, half of these monks were fed from money provided by the king, and the responsibility of the other half was divided among the rest of the

---

[42] I follow Wenk, *The Restoration*, p. 15, in accepting this year as the one of the appointment of a new *Uparat*.

[43] *DC First R*, p. 302.

[44] For details, see G. E. Gerini, *A Retrospective View and Account of the Origin of the Thet Maha Ch'at Ceremony*.

court. The resources poured into the building, upkeep, and improvement of the temples brought immense merit to the king. Most Siamese would have heartily agreed with the king's spending on the *Sangha*, because the merit channeled from state funds would increase the chances of a happy, prosperous Siam, whose enemies would remain powerless. The third consideration regarding the manifold state rituals concerns Rama I's personality. Although there are only few accounts that allow a judgement on this matter to be made, those there are agree that throughout his rule Rama I never relaxed protocol. For example, when he was more than seventy years old, as the vassal-king of Cambodia went to take his leave and entered the audience hall without the customary formal announcement, the Siamese king took offence, and 'King Phra Uthairacha was greatly humiliated in front of the officials'.[45]

King Rama I died in 1809, just over twenty-seven years after he had seized the throne. It had been a remarkable period in which the Siamese had successfully withstood a large-scale invasion. The country's prestige had risen considerably, and its sphere of influence had greatly expanded. The great project of building a new capital city had progressed throughout the reign, and this had given a stimulus to artists and craftsmen. New initiatives found scope, and as the city took shape it began to diverge from the capital as Rama I had known it during his youth. The new times and novel circumstances made for considerable reform. The *corvée* duties had been lessened, and the legal position of various social classes had been greatly simplified. There was also greater internal security. For most people, life in Siam under Rama I was fundamentally different from life as it must have been in Ayutthaya.

---

[45] *DC First R*, p. 307.

Portraits de la reine de Siam et de sa fille
LE SINISTRE
Dessin de Henri Meyer, d'après une photographie de notre correspondant. — Voir l'article, page 275.

Plate 5. An engraving from Le Journal Illustré, *1880, Paris using an earlier picture of a Siamese queen and her daughter. The inset depicts the Chaophraya River and Wat Chang (now called Wat Arun).*
(Courtesy The Old Maps & Prints, River City)

4

TRADE AND POETRY
(1809-1824)

After Rama I's death, the senior court officials and princes decided to recognize Prince Itsarasunthon, the eldest son of the deceased king who during the last two years had occupied the position of *Uparat* as the person to be anointed king. This decision was not unanimously supported, however, and a few days later a plot against the succession was discovered. The other candidate, the son of Taksin and Rama I's daughter, had proved himself to be a very able prince.[1] He had plotted with the minister of the *krom Na*, *chaophraya* Phonlathep, and others to take power. This had been revealed in an anonymous letter and all the conspirators were executed, more than forty persons in all, including the prince's male offspring.[2] The prince's wealth, palace, servants and rice were given to the eldest son of the new king-elect.

The day after the execution, the shortened version of royal anointment began, and when the complex ceremonies had been performed, the customary swearing-in of members of the court and government officers took place. There was no immediate announcement of a list of royal appointments comparable to that after Rama I took office. Most experienced officials retained their positions which is indicative of the fact that the same family remained in power. The Front Palace was given to the new king's only full brother, *kromaluang* Senanurak,[3] who now became *Uparat*. The few senior administrative appointments represented minor changes, mainly a shifting around of men who already held positions of great responsibility. Thus the head of the *krom Phrakhlang* became head of the *krom Mahatthai*, a post that had been vacant, and a personal attendant of the previous king of *phraya* rank took the position as head of the *krom Phrakhlang*. The chief of the *krom Mu'ang* was moved to become *chaophraya* and head of the *Kalahom*, and the *phraya* who had discovered the planned *coup d'état* was rewarded with the *krom Mu'ang*.[4]

The first decree of the new king was an order to grant an amnesty to certain types of prisoners and to clear the courts of pending litigation matters. The court costs for both defendants and accusing parties were borne by the Crown.

Another early decision was the ordering of a complete census of manpower, which involved checking the numbers of people for whom each *nai* was responsible, the tattooing of appropriate symbols on the wrists of subjects who had not yet been tattooed or who had changed status, and the making of a

---

[1] At Rama I's rise to power, the boy was raised to be *chaofa* Suphantawong, and later to *chaofa* Aphaithibet. Subsequently Rama I changed this name to Thammathibet. On the occasion of the anointment of Prince Itsarasunthon (the future Rama II) to *Uparat*, Prince Thammathibet was among the few to receive further honors, and he was appointed to *kromakhun* rank and changed his name to Kasatranuchit.

[2] See *chaophraya* Thiphakorawong, *Phraratchaphongsawadan Krungratanakosin, Ratchakan thi Song* (hereafter *PKRt Song*), pp. 2-3. The attempted *coup* is confirmed in the records of the court astrologers, in *Chotmaihethon, chabap Phraya Munlathonrak*, p. 29.

[3] For details on Prince Senanurak's career, see *momratchawong* Saengsom Kasemsi and Wimon Phongphiphan, (comps.), *Prawatisat Thai Samai Ratanakosin Ratchakan thi Nu'ng thu'ng Ratchakan thi Song*, pp. 20-1.

[4] Further details, also regarding the senior appointments during the reign itself can be found in *PKRt Song* pp. 6-9.

new written record. In the decree, the king decided on the following measures:[5]

1. The settling of all disputes regarding people's registered status, during the general registration drive.

2. The general announcement to reach all the run-away *phrai*, prisoners-of-war, and debt-slaves who were in hiding, to return to their old patrons. If they gave *themselves* up they would not be punished. If the *phrai luang* and redeemable slaves felt unable to return to their old patrons, on this one occasion they could choose themselves a new patron. However, once they had chosen, they could not use this right again. Moreover, this right was only given to *phrai* in Bangkok and its immediate surroundings; provincial people had to remain in their provinces.[6]

3. The forceful arrest and imprisonment of those run-away people who did not give themselves up voluntarily.

4. The tattooing of all people according to their patrons, and the punishment of all those who connived to circumvent the registration.

5. The lowering of the period of *corvée* for *phrai luang* in the provinces to one month of service in every four months, releasing them to work for themselves the other three months.

The offer to run-away and unregistered people to select their own patron was without precedent. It indicates the existence of a serious problem regarding the registration of *phrai*. So many people had been able to escape the rules and regulations that a massive drive was warranted, and in order to prevent the overfilling of prisons and the courts from having to deal with too many cases, the king offered this novel incentive. It is not known, however, how successful the 1810 decree was in establishing a better record of the population.[7]

The king did not grant the right to choose a new patron to provincial *phrai*, because he wanted to prevent further population movement from the provinces to the city. For the same reason, the *corvée* burden in the provinces was lowered. The shortage of people in the provinces was most striking in the northern regions, which had been severely affected by the wars with Burma. Though the custom of taking a census of the work force may be regarded as customary at the beginning of a reign, the specific instructions refer to the circumstances of that time; they indicate problems of administration pertaining to the whole country.

Following the census of the work force in 1810, during the next year the king ordered a survey of the arable land. The instructions to the provincial governors have been preserved, and these provide further interesting information regarding the

---

[5] The full text of the edict was printed in *Prawatkitchakanthahan Samai Krungratanakosin*, pp. 16-20. A rough translation can be found in H. G. Q. Wales, *Ancient Siamese Government and Administration*, pp. 131-4.

[6] The provincial men are called *lek huamu'ang*, rather than *phrai* of one category or another. This has led Gesick to assume that there existed a fundamental difference between *phrai luang* and *lek huamu'ang* (see L. M. Gesick, 'Kingship and Political Integration in Traditional Siam, 1767-1824', pp. 174-75). I rather doubt this interpretation and suspect that the words *lek huamu'ang* are used in order to indicate that the king was making certain laws only for the benefit of people in the provinces. Rama II was concerned to stimulate the repopulation of the countryside.

[7] While the effect of the decree cannot be measured, it seems unwarranted to assume that it was ineffectual, as does Englehart, *Culture and Power*, p. 35.

administration of Siam at the beginning of the second reign. In the document,[8] the governors were told that the main aim of this impending land survey was to decide which land was pledged to the Buddhist Order and which belonged to the people. All lands were to be measured and changes in land use or ownership had to be reported to the *Yokrabat* and the *Sena*,[9] and applications had to be made at the *krom Na* for certificates of ownership.

Already during Ayutthaya times there have been surveys of the agricultural regions in order to facilitate the enforcement of the tax on certain trees and the collection of a proportion of the rice crop for transportation to the king's warehouses.[10] Undoubtedly it was the *krom Na*, the Department of Lands, under the guidance of the *phraya* Phonlathep, which supervised the collection of rice tax, the opening up of new lands, and the mediation in boundary disputes. Taksin and Rama I perpetuated the system, because the court consumed large amounts of rice, and the *krom Na* maintained its departmental activities. Yet the document of 1811 is the earliest that reveals the details of one such survey. Since no documentation regarding the land and tree surveys before this date have been found, it is impossible to determine with certainty in which aspects the proclamation of Rama II differs from previous ones.

The region surveyed in 1811 covered the whole central plains area and some of its immediate surroundings. The size of the area covered was surprisingly large. It reflected, at least from the *krom Na's* point of view, the region that could be administered directly from Bangkok. Towards the south, this direct administration included Phetburi; further south were regions that were administered through the *Kalahom*. Towards the east, the territories of Chanthaburi and Trat were not included: these came under the jurisdiction of the *krom Tha* (part of the *krom Phrakhlang*).[11] If the *krom Na's* responsibilities reflect central control, the eastern territories directly controlled by the capital were very much the same as they were fifty years earlier. It is to the north that the greatest changes seem to have taken place. During the 1810 survey the whole area of Sukhothai and Sawangkhaburi was included, as far north as the borders of the states of Phrae and Lampang. During late-Ayutthayan times, the *mu'angs* of Kamphaeng Phet, Phitsanulok, Phichai, and Phetchabun were governed through appointed governors and a few representatives of the central power, and it is unlikely that they would have been included in a direct survey from the capital.

The inclusion of the northern region reflects Siam's expansion to the north. Since the reign of Rama I, the area covered by the *mu'angs* of Phrae, Nan, Lampang, Lamphun, Chiang Mai, and Chiang Rai had become the kingdom's northern protective belt. A second reason for the inclusion of such a large northern area in the survey could be the fact that

[8] 'Rangthongtra thu'ng Huamu'ang ru'ang Khaluangrangwatna oktra-chongthidin', in *Chotmaihet Ratcha-kan thi Song*, C.S. 1173, pp. 37-42.

[9] The *Sena* is an officer of the *krom Na*, responsible for the collection of tax on rice lands (Wales, *Ancient Siamese Government*, p. 89).

[10] La Loubère mentions one-quarter of a *baht* per *rai* land tax as well as tax on various fruit trees (*The Kingdom of Siam*, p. 93).

[11] *DC First R*, p. 13.

the region had been severely depopulated and was thus relatively easy to cover.

King Rama II appointed eight committees to supervise the land survey, two of them headed by a man of *phraya* rank, with the remaining six groups under less exalted officials. Each of the committees contained representatives from the departments of *Mahatthai*, *Kalahom*, *Na*, and *Mahatlek* and an officer of the *Wang Na*. This would seem a standard procedure followed to minimize risks of collusion and bribery. After all, each committee was empowered to issue title deeds, so that its officials were likely to be approached by parties wishing to influence their decisions.

After the list of the committee members' names, a series of specific instructions follow. These are quite varied, ranging from matters concerning methods of measuring to describing the rate of taxation. Since the document has hitherto received little publicity, and is quite revealing regarding domestic situations in Siam at the beginning of the nineteenth century, the range of clauses are here translated and annotated in summary.

> a. When a title deed is issued, the document must contain the name of the owner, his place of domicile, and a description of the type and size of the fields. The leader of the measuring party and the representative of the *krom Na* must press their seals on the document in each other's presence, and each page must be marked on the back.

Comment: Officials of more than one department had to be involved in order to increase the chance of creating an accurate and truthful picture of land holding. After all, such documents form the basis of one of the chief sources of revenue.

> b. If landowners wish to possess only a small area of land and they feel that the officers of the committee have issued too much in their name, they have three days in which they can rectify this.

Comment: This clause is indicative of a situation of a good supply of arable land and a relative scarcity of people to work it. It confirms the picture obtained from the general census instructions regarding the provinces.

> c. Before measuring takes place, the customary ceremonies ought to occur, including an offering to the spirits of the field and the measuring rope ritual. The prices for ritual objects and administration costs are determined: one *baht* for pulling the ritual rope, three-quarters of a *baht* for white cloth, one quarter for an umbrella, half a *baht* for a water container, one-eighth for a mat, one-eighth for blessing the water, and

one-and-a-half *baht* as the cost for obtaining the fully
sealed title deed for land [up to] one hundred *rai*. The
oath-taking ceremony by the group of officials involved
in the measuring must be done every Buddhist prayer
day, four times each lunar month in the precinct of a
monastery. Persons who become tired while pulling and
wish to hand over their place at the rope to somebody
else ought to finish their oath before handing over.

Comment: The king's instructions regarding religious ceremonies were basically intended to increase the chance of
obtaining honest and trustworthy records. The various
ceremonies appear to be of a kind related to judiciary rituals,
such as the ordeals by fire and water and the regular oath of
allegiance to the king. Thus far no a more detailed description
of this rope-pulling ritual has been found.

    d. The type of tax called *khawchatsu'* ought not to be
       levied upon upland farms which are mentioned in title
       deeds.

Comment: The tax *khawchatsu'* was, as will be shown in the
following paragraphs, usually two buckets (40 litres) of rice per
rai, and was not levied in all places.

    e. If there are people with valid title deeds on certain lands
       and other people take that land [against the owner's
       wishes], let the committee and the *Sena* drive the
       squatters away.
    f. In the regions of Bangkok, Ayutthaya, Angthong,
       Suphanburi, Nakhon Chaisi, Samkhok, Nonthaburi, and
       Sakhonburi, the tax is forty litres of rice per *rai* as tax
       khawkha, and another forty litres as tax *khawchatsu'*,
       to be brought to the Bangkok granaries. In the region
       of Chainat, Uthai Thani, *mu'ang* San, *mu'ang* Sing,
       mu'ang In, *mu'ang* Phrom, Manoram and Lopburi, the
       tax is forty litres per *rai*, tax *khawkha*, also to be taken
       to the Bangkok granaries. In the regions of Prachinburi,
       Nakhon Nayok, Chachoengsao, and Chonburi, the tax
       is forty litres *khawkha* and forty litres *khawchatsu'*, to
       be put in the granary of Prachinburi. At Saraburi,
       Phetburi, and Samut Prakan, the same taxation is
       imposed and the grain is to be put in the municipal
       granaries. At Nakhon Sawan there had been a shortage
       of rice in the granary, so during the year 1810/11, the
       tax *khawkha* is set at forty litres per *rai*. Ratburi,
       Kanchanaburi and Kamphaeng Phet farmers are
       charged forty litres *khawkha* per *rai* for the town
       granaries. In Phetchabun, Tharong, Buacham, Chai-
       badan, Khamphran, Sukhothai, Phichai, Sawankhalok,
       Phichit, and Phitsanulok, the tax is one-fourth of a *baht*

per *rai*, and the amounts, together with details of land holdings, have to be forwarded to Bangkok.

Comment: This could be the earliest detailed record of land taxation in Siamese history. Though there must have been similar types of instructions before Rama II's time, these have not been preserved. It shows the areas that delivered rice directly to Bangkok – Nakhon Sawan this particular year being exempted – and where subsidiary government storage centers were kept. We may safely surmise that this was in the form of paddy or unhusked rice, in order to minimize the risk of mould. These subsidiary centers were kept as a defense measure so that armies could draw upon them. There was one such secondary storage place in the east, at Prachinburi, one near Bangkok, at Samut Prakan, and five in the west. This reflects the fact that the main external threat to the country was still felt to be Burma. The actual taxation amounts varied; close to the capital they were highest, and further away they were lower. This was in accordance with the *king's* policy to make the outer regions attractive for farmers. The northern belt, which was particularly affected by the wars and depopulation, was taxed not in rice but in silver. Since the king was following a policy of attracting farmers to the region, the taxation of these northern provinces must have been equal to that of other outer provinces, such as Kamphaeng Phet and Ratburi, or even less. Therefore we may draw the conclusion that in 1811 a coin of one-fourth of one *baht* would buy not more than forty litres of unhusked rice, or possibly a little less. This is confirmed in the calculations made eleven years later, when the value of that amount of rice is almost equal to one-fourth of a *baht*.[12]

> g. If the measuring rope is lying on the field during measuring, and someone accidentally steps over it, let that person perform a *tham khwan* ceremony with balls of puffed rice and sugar, flowers, and candle for the measuring rope. The government officer is strictly forbidden to ask for restitution in money.

Comment: Siamese are taught from a very early age not to step over worthy objects, and the measuring rope must be considered important. When such a rope is accidentally stepped over, its *khwan*, or 'invisible vital element', may escape; hence the appropriateness of holding a *tham khwan* ceremony.[13] The *king's* instruction seems to be a reaction upon hearing that such practices may have been provoked in the past and his wish to put a stop to this manner of raising money from the general populace.

> h. The fields of Laotian, Cambodian, Burmese, Manipurian,[14] and Mon war slaves who have been assigned lands of government officials, mainly in the

---

[12] J. Crawfurd, *Journal of an Embassy to the Courts of Siam and Cochin China*, p. 385.

[13] The *tham khwan* ceremony belongs to the ancient Tai tradition. For references and further details, see B. J. Terwiel, 'The Tais and Their Belief in Khwans', *South East Asian Review* 3, no. 1 (1978), pp. 1-16.

[14] Probably Burmese war slaves, captured during the wars with Burma.

districts of Bangkok, Nonburi, Samkhok, Ayutthaya, and Saraburi, and who have been assigned buffaloes and oxen need to be measured and title deeds must be issued. Even when people rent or borrow fields, both *khawkha* and *khawchatsu'* tax need to be paid.

Comment: This ordinance appears intended to close a possible tax loophole. The fact that a piece of land was worked upon by a war slave or by someone who borrowed the land did not constitute a case for exemption from the two types of tax. Incidentally, the distribution of war captives seems to be limited to the heartlands of the kingdom, probably the result of a deliberate policy which would make it difficult for such slaves to escape and flee back to their country of origin.

i. If there are disputes regarding such [borrowed] fields, the leader of the government measuring party should decide according to the laws, but he is not allowed to accept payment for this adjudication.
j. If people have large stretches of land upon their title deeds, but it is found that these are not cultivated, they must be given to the *krom Na* official and the capital city be notified.
k. If one works upon the fields on an official ceremonial day, the *krom Na* official should hand the fields over to others.
l. Hoarding land and letting it lie fallow is absolutely forbidden.

Comment: At first sight, the latter three regulations may throw some doubt upon the question whether there was private ownership of lands in Siam. Nominally the whole kingdom belonged to the king. However, there can be little doubt about the general acceptance of the principle of private ownership. Land could be owned, sold, donated, and inherited. Only on the death of an official who had a *saktina* of more than 400 would the king receive one-fourth of the estate. People of lower status passed all their possessions on to their relatives. The three stipulations mentioned here were intended to encourage land to be worked upon and to discourage any circumstance that would lead to arable land lying fallow.

In the document's concluding paragraph officials are told to submit their census data to the capital, and warned that conniving to provide false information was reprehensible and would be punished under the law.

Both the decree on the population census and the one on the land survey reveal at least partially the complex system of administration that existed in the early nineteenth century. In addition, they show the direction of the new king's thought. He apparently had been convinced of the need to make regulations that would encourage the re-population of some provinces and the resumption of lands. At the same time, he saw that the ordinary people had to be protected against rapacious civil servants.

A series of royal appointments elevating the new king's close relatives to higher ranks was announced only in early 1814, after Rama II had been in office a considerable time.[15] We cannot be sure what the king's motivation was in waiting so long before creating a number of new princes of *kromamu'n* rank, but it is quite likely that the discovery and subsequent execution of a contender for the throne within the family may have delayed such appointments. Rama I's queen, now the mother of a king, was given the title of *kromsomdet* Amarintharamat. Seven of the king's half-brothers, four of his sons, and two nephews were all given *kromamu'n* ranks and new names, but other relatives were also among those promoted. Altogether twenty-two persons were elevated to *krom* rank. Hitherto Rama II had apparently given little attention to honoring his own family. A notable exception was the ceremonial bathing ritual of the eldest son of his most senior wife, held in 1812 with proper pomp and ceremony.[16] This son had been born before Rama II's accession to the throne, in 1804, and had received the name *chaofa* Mongkut. The ritual bath can be seen as a token of the king's acceptance of the young prince as a promising youngster of the highest rank. In 1816 this was further underlined by the very elaborate manner in which the cutting of Mongkut's topknot took place.[17]

In 1813 the king ordered a large party of Laotians to come and construct a sluice at the lower end of the Bangkaew Canal, because the water had been running off too fast and the canal had fallen dry, an intolerable situation in a country where rivers and canals formed the chief communication channels.[18] The next year the king ordered a new fortification to be built along the stretch of river between the capital and the sea.[19]

The years 1815, 1816, and 1817 were probably long remembered in Siam as the years during which some shocking incidents occurred in the court. First *phra* Inthra Aphai, one of Taksin's sons, was discovered to have been engaged in a love affair in which three of the king's women were compromised. According to the law, all four were executed. Then the *Uparat*, the king's full brother, became ill and died, aged thirty-seven. Not long afterwards the *Sangha* was shaken by a scandal. The Buddhist monk who had been chosen to become patriarch of the Siamese Buddhist Order was accused of homosexual activities. A committee of three princes of *kromamu'n* rank investigated the matter, found the man guilty, and sent him to gaol. Unfortunately this did not conclude the matter, for *kromamu'n* Sisuren, one of the king's half-brothers and a friend of the imprisoned man, wrote anonymously a poem on the case in which the king himself was slandered. Another committee of

[15] *Chotmaihethon*, pp. 31-2.

[16] *PKRt Song*, pp. 43-8.

[17] *Ibid.*, pp. 82-5.

[18] *Ibid.*, pp. 51-2.

[19] *Ibid.*, pp. 61-2. See also Shigeharu Tanabe, 'Historical Geography of the Canal System in the Chao Phraya River Delta', *JSS* 65, pt 2 (1977), p. 42.

inquiry investigated the poem, and on grounds of style it was decided that prince Sisuren must have been the author. During interrogation the prince died. However, the case was further investigated by the king's eldest son, *kromamu'n* Chetsadabodin,[20] and eleven courtiers who had been involved in the production and distribution of the poem were condemned to death.[21]

The year 1817 also saw the beginning of a new state festival, namely the commemoration of the Buddha's birthday, enlightenment and passing into *nirvana*, coinciding with the full moon of the Siamese sixth lunar month. This festival was presided over by the new patriarch.[22] The *Dynastic Chronicles, Second Reign*, also report a case of self-immolation for religious reasons. A certain *nai* Nok, having done many good deeds during his life, wished to proceed to the state of *nirvana*, and thus, after having prepared himself, he set fire to himself under the sacred fig-tree in front of the old temple of Wat Chaeng. Many people came to pay respect to the corpse.[23]

The first half of Rama II's reign was relatively quiet. Though the king had to be on guard against Burmese hostilities; all was not quiet in the Laotian principalities; there were signs of Vietnamese expansion into areas that had come under Siamese control during the first reign; in the far south the Siamese overlordship of Kedah was being undermined; yet none of these troubles developed into the type of provocation that caused the king to order that firm measures be taken.

During the early part of Rama II's reign, Siam's relationships with the outside world also caused little concern. China was still regarded as the greatest power on earth, and the trade with China dominated foreign relations. As often as possible the king would send a tribute mission to the Chinese court, and consequently obtained lucrative trade concessions. He also sent an ecclesiastical mission to Sri Lanka, in the hope of fostering closer relations which would benefit Theravada Buddhism. The mission returned and reported favorably on their adventures.[24] Siam attracted the attention of traders of various nations. A few American ships came, one bringing a letter from the American president. These were received very much in the same manner as a Siamese tribute mission was received in China: they were allowed to trade and departed laden with sugar. The Portuguese, also well acquainted with Siamese customs, came with a letter from their king, and eventually a Portuguese consul was permitted to settle in Bangkok, receiving the customary title at the Siamese court of *luang* Aphaiphanit.

The French had relatively little trade interests. Their presence was mainly limited to some Catholic missions. The largest Catholic community was situated in the Southeastern port of Chanthaburi, where a congregation of some 500 persons, almost all of Vietnamese extraction could be found.[25]

---

[20] In the following six years Prince Chetsadabodin gradually was trusted with much of the daily government of the country, leading up to his elevation to the throne in 1824.

[21] *PKRt Song*, pp. 80-2, and *Chotmaihethon*, p. 35.

[22] This festival has been regularly held ever since that time. It is called Wisakhabucha. Further details can be found in *Kromphra* Damrong Ratchanuphap, *Phraratchaphongsawadan Krungratanakosin Ratchakan thi Song*, vol.2, pp. 4-10.

[23] *PKRt Song*, pp. 87-88. For further details, see R. Lingat, 'Les suicides religieux au Siam', *Felicitation Volumes of Southeast-Asian Studies Presented to His Highness Prince Dhaninivat Kromamun Bidyalabh Bridhyakorn*, vol. 1, pp. 71-5.

[24] *PKRt Song*, pp. 94-7.

[25] For details see B. J. Terwiel, 'Towards a History of Chanthaburi, 1700-1860: The French Sources', *International Conference on Thai Studies*, August 22-24, 1984, Bangkok, Vol. 8, pp. 1-19.

The Later Years

In 1818 the king was inspired by a report from members of the tributary mission returning from China that the emperor had created a large pleasure ground with rare plants and animals. This gave rise to the Siamese version of such grounds, and before long many *corvée* workers were engaged in the creation of the courtly garden, complete with artificial lakes, islands and pavilions. This new project constituted a break with Rama I's plans for the new capital. Rama II definitely had abandoned the idea of being guided and restrained by emulating the old capital. The pleasure gardens became the place where the king's passion for poetry and dance could be given free rein. Much of the literary heritage, so carefully reconstituted along traditional lines during the reign of Rama I, was rewritten in a new and modern style. The king gathered a large circle of artistic people, chosen from his own relatives, the nobility and the commoners. Among the latter, the poet Sunthon Phu was outstanding. In 1818 this gifted man was just in his early thirties. His abilities were greatly appreciated by the king, who honored him with the rank of *khun* and later with that of *phra*.[26]

The later years of the second reign also did not bring any serious external threats to the kingdom, which allowed the king to proceed with his development of Siam's defense and with the further building of Bangkok. An example of the first interest is the development of the town of Samut Prakan, at the mouth of the river Chaophraya, where a 'city pillar' was set up.[27] The great *prang* at Wat Chaeng, which was begun during the second reign, is a good example of the second type of pursuit.[28] However, these years were replete with minor problems of statecraft, and from time to time disturbing situations developed.

In 1819 there was a big prison revolt. Burmese prisoners of war killed their warders and took to the streets, where they were overpowered.[29] A much greater crisis occurred when a particularly virulent strain of cholera reached Siam. An epidemic had begun in India in 1817 and had arrived at Sri Lanka during the following year. From there it spread in various directions by way of trading vessels. In 1819 it reached Penang; by April 1820 it had reached Bangkok. The death toll in Bangkok was great. The monasteries could not keep up with the cremations; many corpses were thrown in the river. During the emergency the king issued a decree to his people explaining how the sickness had come from abroad and how ordinary medicine had no effect. Therefore a special royal ceremony for the expulsion of evil was held: sacred stanzas were chanted, all around the city large guns were fired, and a procession was held with the nation's most sacred objects. The king temporarily relieved all people of their duties and exhorted all to make merit, chant

[26] Sunthon Phu's works are still being reprinted and read. They often provide glimpses of social life and rules of behaviour which must have been valid during Rama II's time. Some of his works have been thoroughly studied, notably his *Suphasit Son Ying*, translated and annotated by K. Wenk ('Ein Lehrgedicht für junge Frauen – Suphasit son ying – des Sunthon Phu', *Oriens Extremus* 12, pt 1 (1965), pp. 65-106), and Wenk's book *Phali Lehrt die Jüngeren-Phali son nong*. For Sunthon Phu's biography, see C. Notton, transl., La vie du poète *Sounthone-Bhou*.

[27] *PKRt Song*, pp. 154-55.

[28] Further details can be found in Prungsi Wanliphodom, 'Phraprang Wat Arunratchawaram', in *Chaloem Phrakiet Phrabatsomdet Phraphuthaloetla*, pp. 41-51.

[29] *Chotmaihethon*, p. 36.

sacred mantras, and practice munificence. Even those on palace duty were requested to remain home and look after their families. All through the province of Bangkok, the king advised people to let the animals roam around freely in the markets, and prisoners (with the exception of Burmese war prisoners) were freed. The populace was asked not to kill any living being, thus avoiding harmful acts. Soon the epidemic abated. At that time there was a rumor that the disease was the result of the recent building activities in the palace. In order to build a mound in the palace pleasure grounds, large rocks had been taken from the sea, and it was thought that this could have caused the guardian spirits to be angry and that these could have sent the cholera as a punishment.[30]

Not long afterwards news arrived that in Vietnam a similar epidemic was raging. To ward off this danger the king ordered the court's most famous magical specialists to memorize the strongest and most difficult spells. Day and night there were chanting sessions, and yet another warding-off ceremony was held during which bells were beaten and guns were fired.[31]

This was also the time when news reached the capital that the Burmese were again planning to invade Siam. A large army was raised and moved towards the central-western side of the kingdom. *Kromamu'n* Chetsadabodin, the king's eldest son, was given charge of the main force. During 1821, when it became clear that the Burmese were not invading after all, the armies were pulled back. Many conscripts were rescheduled to continue the work on making a large mound in the palace, and instead of fighting the Burmese they cut trees, made rafts, and fetched large rocks for the king's pleasure garden. The troops that had been sent as a precaution to the southwestern region of Phetchaburi under the command of *kromamu'n* Sakdiphonlasep had been accused of having oppressed the populace. The *Phrakhlang*, *chaophraya* Senathibet, sent strict orders that the army could not requisition boats and food from the people without offering compensation:

> *If a farmer has only one wagon-load of rice, you ought to buy only half that amount. If the price of six pots of sugar is one-and-a-quarter baht, offer one baht for seven pots as a government price. Good relations between the army and the populace are in the interest of the country and must be fostered.*[32]

The mild, coaxing letter is indicative of the style of government under Rama II.

Meanwhile, the resident counselor of Singapore, aware that friendly relations had been established between the government of Siam on the one hand and those of Portugal and the United States on the other, had taken it upon himself to send a British trader, John Morgan, with a letter for the Siamese

[30] *PKRt Song*, pp. 115-6; *Chotmaihethon*, p. 37; and Crawfurd, *Journal*, p. 455. The latter reports that the *Phrakhlang* estimated that one-fifth of the populace had died from the cholera epidemic. Although Crawfurd takes this to mean one-fifth of the whole population of the country, it may be surmised that the losses in Bangkok were relatively higher than in provincial towns. For more details see B. J. Terwiel, 'Asiatic Cholera in Siam: Its First Occurrence and the 1820 Epidemic', in N.G. Owen (ed.) *Death and Disease in Southeast Asia*, Singapore: Oxford University Press, 1987, pp. 142-161.

[31] *PKRt Song*, pp. 128-29.

[32] *PKRt Song*, pp. 136-37.

king, informing him of the British presence in Singapore and the hope that commercial links between the countries would be strengthened. A gift of a double-barreled gun and two mirrors accompanied the letter. Morgan arrived in May 1821 and was duly interviewed by the *Phrakhlang* and subsequently by *kromamu'n* Chetsadabodin. They questioned him mainly on the relations between Britain and Burma, since this was foremost in Siamese thought at that moment. Morgan presented his gifts and letter to Rama II and received permission to trade. He met, however, with many obstacles in the disposal of his cargo. The difficulties Morgan encountered must be interpreted as a snub, probably delivered on the highest orders. The reason for this somewhat ungracious Siamese behavior is not difficult to ascertain: Morgan had brought a quantity of opium, a product that had been expressly declared contraband by the king, and thus the semi-official contact between the Siamese and the British was marred.[33]

A year later, probably unaware of the unfortunate impression Morgan had made upon the Siamese, the British sent an official envoy, John Crawfurd, to Bangkok. Crawfurd arrived at an awkward moment, because the Siamese king had recently sent a trading vessel to Bengal, which returned during Crawfurd's stay having incurred a great trade loss.[34] Moreover, official envoys were expected to be the bearers of a missive from the hands of the highest authority. When Crawfurd could produce no letter from King George IV, but only a document signed by the king's representative in India, his prestige must have suffered considerably.

At that time, when a European vessel arrived in Bangkok, the king's officers not only would charge duty on the merchandise, and a harbor tax dependent upon the ship's tonnage, but also would insist upon having the first choice of buying, paying less than the market price. Only after the court's agents were satisfied that they had bought all that was of interest to them did they allow the trader to have free access to the public.[35] While the Europeans were thus unable to exploit an open market, and therefore it was difficult for them to be certain of large profits, there were possibilities for those who adapted to the Siamese system. Up to August 1821, the cargoes of twelve American ships had been sold, and sugar had been taken on the return journeys.[36]

Crawfurd attempted to obtain for British traders free trade with the merchants of Siam, but the *Phrakhlang* struck that clause from the final draft of the treaty.[37] Although Crawfurd was unable to improve the trading possibilities for British merchants, he accumulated knowledge about Siam's commercial position in the international trade network of eastern Asia. He noted that trade with China dominated the whole pattern. Probably this had been the case from the end of the seventeenth

[33] O. Frankfurter, 'The Unofficial Mission of John Morgan, Merchant, to Siam in 1821', *JSS* 11 (1914-15), pp. 1-8.

[34] Crawfurd, *Journal*, p. 141.

[35] *Ibid.*, pp. 144-5; G. Finlayson, *The Mission to Siam and Hue the Capital of Cochin China, in the years 1821-2*, pp. 168-77.

[36] Frankfurter, 'Unofficial Mission of John Morgan', p. 6.

[37] Crawfurd, *Journal*, p.172.

century onwards, when King Phraphetracha decided to cut most links with European powers. After the fall of Ayutthaya, Taksin had hastened to dispatch trade missions to China. In a general statement about the reign of Rama I, the pre-eminent position of China in matters regarding trade is clear:

> *The greatest revenues in that era came from the Chinese junk trade. There were Chinese junks built like the Chinese style* tuakang *(tiller steerage) ships, with a* rahu *demon head at the bow. Some of these demon heads were painted green, some red. The junks measured each from five to seven* wa[38] *across the beam. There were a large number of them. Some belonged to the Crown, some to members of the royal family, some to government officials, and some to merchants.*

> *These ships were either built in Bangkok or in provincial areas outside the capital. They were loaded with merchandise to be sold in China every year. Some ships sold only their cargoes of merchandise, some ships sold both their cargoes of merchandise and the ships themselves as well. The profits of this junk trade were tremendous.*[39]

What was true for the first reign also applied to the time of Rama II. When Crawfurd arrived in Bangkok in early 1822 the annual fleet from China had already arrived. This fleet comprised approximately 140 boats. Products carried from China to Bangkok included massive amounts of crockery, such as cups, dishes and bowls,[40] tea, brassware, copperware, silk, sugar candy, playing cards, dice, paper, and dried vegetables. Apart from these goods, the vessels would often carry large numbers of people. Crawfurd mentions in his *Journal of an Embassy to the Courts of Siam and Cochin China* how one junk had been known to bring twelve hundred passengers to Bangkok, and he was told that the annual immigration of Chinese to Bangkok was at least seven thousand.[41]

For the return journey, the fleet would carry rice, black pepper, sugar, cotton, tin, cardamom, hides, feathers, ivory, various woods for furniture making, sapan wood, mangrove bark,[42] stic-lac,[43] edible swallows' nests, and sea cucumbers *(bêche-de-mer)*. The goods exported to China were much more valuable than those brought from China to Bangkok, and the Chinese had to make up the difference in money. Boat-building also continued steadily, and every year between six or eight junks of the largest size were manufactured in Bangkok.[44]

Apart from the annual Chinese fleet, there was an extensive coastal trade with ports controlled by Cambodia, with the region later known as Cochin-China, especially with the harbor of Saigon, and with places far to the south, including Pattani, Kelantan, Trengganu, Pahang, Singapore, Malacca, Penang,

---

[38] The *wa* is equal to two metres.

[39] *DC First R*, vol. 1, pp. 304-5.

[40] When some crockery was damaged in transit, it could be used to decorate monastery edifices simply by chipping off pieces and using them in mosaics. Most of the decorations of the gigantic *prang* at Wat Chaeng (now Wat Arun) were thus obtained.

[41] Crawfurd, *Journal*, p. 412; however, his figures often appear rather inflated, as is discussed below.

[42] Both sapan wood and mangrove bark were used in the Chinese tanning and dye industry.

[43] Excretion from the lac beetle, used as sealing wax.

[44] Elsewhere Crawfurd states that from eight to ten were manufactured (*Crawfurd Papers*, p. 117).

Batavia, Semarang, Cheribon, Palembang, and Pontianak. This trade around the Gulf of Siam and further south into the Indonesian archipelago was conducted with vessels smaller than those used in the trade to China. From the Siamese point of view, most of the coastal trade and that into the archipelago was a corollary of the trade with China: some of the goods obtained from the annual fleet were exported to these smaller ports, and goods China wanted were brought back to Bangkok. Through this secondary trade network Siam also became linked up with other markets and obtained goods from India and Europe. A large number of the coastal trade junks belonged to the king.[45] Crawfurd reports that the Siamese trade with many parts of the Malayan archipelago had greatly increased, Siam exporting mainly rice, sugar, salt and oil, and importing products for the Chinese market as well as European goods. Singapore was rapidly gaining importance for this trade,[46] not only because of its strategic position, but also because just then the relations between the Siamese and the Dutch were not very cordial.[47]

Regarding the general appreciation of the king's rule, Crawfurd states that the country had prospered under his administration and that the monarch was generally regarded as one of the mildest sovereigns who had ruled Siam for at least a century and a half.[48] The person of the king is described as short, of ordinary features, and somewhat corpulent.[49] With respect to the court, Crawfurd had the impression that there were two factions, one led by the prince Chetsadabodin and the head of the *krom Phrakhlang*, *phraya* Suriyawongkosa, the other by 'the prince Caw-fa' and his maternal uncles.[50] Crawfurd was not familiar with the Siamese system of princely titles and did not realize that *chaofa* was a title, not a name. This title had been bestowed upon many of Rama I's younger relatives, as well as on Rama II's sons Mongkut and Chuthamani. From the context, and from the allusion to the *chaofa's* uncles, it may be deduced that prince Mongkut is meant as a central figure of one of the two 'parties'. As to the nature of these 'factions', it may be assumed that this refers to the question of who was most worthy in the king's eyes to occupy the vacant position of *Uparat*. Prince Chetsadabodin was already in his mid-thirties and had served his father well on many occasions. According to the *Dynastic Chronicles*, Chetsadabodin had been assigned the task of receiving people's petitions, and often late at night the king would consult with this son regarding the day's legal affairs.[51] On the other hand, in 1822 Prince Mongkut was in his eighteenth year, young and untried, but senior to his elder half-brother in rank because Mongkut was the eldest son of the queen, a status which had been underlined by the splendor of the ceremonies that had marked his leaving childhood.

---

[45] Crawfurd, *Journal*, p. 413.

[46] *Ibid.*, p. 414, Frankfurter, 'Unofficial Mission of John Morgan', p. 8.

[47] There had been remonstrations against the Siamese because of alleged kidnapping of Javanese subjects. (Frankfurter, 'Unofficial Mission of John Morgan', p. 7). That there was reason for the Javanese protests is borne out by Crawfurd's account of kidnapped slaves from Semarang (*Journal*, p. 148).

[48] Crawfurd, *Journal*, pp. 136-7.

[49] *Ibid.*, p. 94.

[50] *Ibid.*, p. 105.

[51] *PKRt Song*, p. 203.

Crawfurd provides also a summary account of the *corvée* system. He states that all adult males were compelled to serve the state four months a year. This confirms the general idea mentioned above, that Rama II did not lower the *corvée* period for the general populace to three months a year, as is often mentioned in history books: only certain groups in the provinces had been given an alleviation of the *corvée* burden. Exemption from *corvée* was granted to members of the *Sangha*, to the Chinese, to slaves, to government civil servants, to men who had three sons already serving, to those who could provide another person to serve instead, and to those who had been able to purchase a certificate of exemption from the government. In certain parts of the country, a commutation of *corvée* was given to people because they provided the capital with certain goods, such as sapan wood, saltpetre, ivory or animal hides.[52] This information complements that of Siamese sources. Instead of *corvée* the Chinese paid a head tax of two *baht* and one-and-a-half *fu'ang*[53] per annum, of which two *baht* went to the government and the remainder was the tax collector's fee. This head tax was much lower than the amount needed for a Siamese to buy himself an exemption from *corvée*. In 1822 there appear to have been some 31,500 people paying this head tax in the capital district. Crawfurd estimated that there were another seventy thousand Chinese adult males spread over the rest of the country. Unlike the *phrai*, the Chinese were not tattooed but had to wear on the wrist a badge, bearing the seal of the taxation officer.

Crawfurd's mention of slaves among the people who were exempt from *corvée* also agrees with the picture that can be obtained from Siamese sources. Already during Rama I's reign it had been recorded that a registered slave did not have to perform *corvée*,[54] his master being charged with a slave's head tax.[55] Crawfurd mentions that all ordinary *phrai* could pay the government a sum of six to eight *baht* for an exemption of one month's work. This sum must have been absolutely out of reach for most common people. Only wealthy *phrai* would have been able to make use of this right. The alternative of sending a substitute for oneself must have been a much more practicable solution for a fairly prosperous *phrai*.

The category of people who supplied goods instead of serving *corvée* was known in Siamese laws as *phrai luang suai*. By freely amassing specific products, they were an indispensable link in the trade with China. The *Dynastic Chronicles of the Second Reign* mention the quest for *suai* products from a quite different perspective. In his general assessment of the whole reign, *chaophraya* Thiphakorawong mentions government servants negotiating the supply of *suai* products with bands of runaway *phrai* and slaves.[56] This indicates the king's dependence upon *suai* products as well as the propensity for compro-

---

[52] Crawfurd, *Journal*, pp. 374-5.

[53] A *fu'ang* is one-eighth of a *baht*.

[54] 'Phraratchakamnot Mai', no. 17, *KTSD* 5, p. 257.

[55] A figure mentioned by Wales (*Ancient Siamese Government*, pp. 200-1) is that of an annual sum of five *baht*. It is not certain, however, that this sum would have remained unchanged over a long period, nor is it certain that this sum was charged for all classes of slaves.

[56] *PKRt Song*, p. 205.

Table 1. Estimated Siamese revenue in 1822, two Crawfurd accounts (in *baht*)

	Crawfurd Papers	Crawfurd's *Journal*
Land tax	258,000	2,295,338
Spirit tax	264,000	460,000
Gambling monopoly	260,000	460,000
Shop tax	165,000	121,880
Fishing tax	64,000	64,000
Chinese poll tax	200,000	201,250
Monopoly edible nests	100,000	100,000
Monopoly tin	60,000	54,000
Monopoly pepper	320,000	400,000
Other monopolies	335,000	109,000
Custom duties	200,000	264,000
Corvée	7,344,000	20,000,000
Fruit trees	-	520,000
Sugar	-	105,000
Turtle eggs		5,000
Total revenue	9,650,000	25,159,468

mise which pervades the whole period. Rather than meet the problem of run-away slaves with force, the king's agents traded with them for mutual benefit.[57] With regard to the land tax, Crawfurd mentions a fixed tax on all lands producing grain, according to their extent, without regard to their quality, and a tax on orchards, according to the number and type of trees. All lands cultivated with rice were taxed 2 1/2 *thang* per twenty Siamese fathoms square, or *rai*. This is half a *thang* higher than that announced at the beginning of the reign. Crawfurd sheds no light upon the distinction between *khawkha* and *khawchat-su*'. Since the former was the most widespread, and as Crawfurd did not travel inland, it may be surmised that his information relates to *khawkha* tax and that this had been raised by half a *thang* between 1811 and 1822.

Apart from these items of general information, Crawfurd provides a lengthy statement about Siam's revenue. Many of the estimates regarding the various taxes provide a measure with which to gauge trade, the number of people involved and the relative importance of certain occupations. The state's income from the

---

[57] *Crawfurd Papers*, p. 133, describes how the king naturally pays a sum considerably less than those goods would be worth in Bangkok.

Table 2. Two accounts of spirit tax for fourteen towns in Siam (in *baht*)

Town or region*	Amount in Weight	Finlayson Value	Crawfurd Value
Bangkok	18 *piculs*	72,000	144,000
Ayutthaya	6 *piculs*	24,000	48,000
Sukhothai	1 *picul*	4,000	8,000
Prachinburi	1 *picul*	4,000	8,000
Rayong	1 *picul*	4,000	8,000
Kamphaeng Phet	1 *picul*	4,000	8,000
Chainat	20 catties	1,600	1,600
Nakhon Ratchasima	2 *piculs*	8,000	16,000
Vientiane	3 *piculs*	12,000	24,000
Kanchanaburi	20 catties	1,600	1,600
Chumphon	30 catties	2,400	2,400
Pathiu	20 catties	1,600	1,600
Chaiya	8 catties	640	640
Patthalung	30 catties	2,400	2,400

* The spelling of names in Finlayson and Crawfurd is inconsistent, and in some cases the identification in this list is tentative. Pathiu was a town just north of Chumphon, and Chaiya is not far south of that town.

monopoly of pepper, together with the rate of taxation, for example, could lead to an estimate of plantation size. However, the tax figures published in Crawfurd's Journal are extremely suspect.

It appears that Crawfurd, in order to aggrandize his mission's importance and to stimulate British interest in the kingdom, deliberately changed many of the figures he had collected, boosting the Siamese revenue, at least on paper. A clear indication of this process can be obtained from a comparison of the figures in *The Crawfurd Papers* and those published in the *Journal* (see table 1).

Crawfurd's original estimate of Siam's revenue of less than ten million *baht* is boosted by more than fifteen million *baht* in his official report. The discrepancies in the two accounts can occasionally be explained by the fact that Crawfurd uses a different method of calculating totals, as in the case of the land tax and the value of *corvée*. In other instances, however, it is impossible to divine the methods used to reach the figures.

One of Crawfurd's companions, George Finlayson, provides a list of the spirit tax in fourteen towns and Crawfurd also provides such a list in his *Journal*.[58] Again, the two lists show great discrepancies (see table 2).

There can be little doubt that Finlayson and Crawfurd based their report upon the same list of figures, for in all cases where Crawfurd differs from Finlayson, he has given exactly double the amount. Moreover, only in the cases where Finlayson mentions *piculs* does Crawfurd differ; where catties are mentioned he gives the same figure. Therefore it appears that both men drew up their lists from figures that mentioned *piculs* and catties, and that Crawfurd took a *picul* of spirit to be worth twice as much as did Finlayson. Finlayson's total comes to less than 150,000 *baht*, while Crawfurd's figures add up to almost 275,000 *baht*. From table 1 it can be seen that neither figure bears resemblance to Crawfurd's two final estimates of the spirit tax.

As to the question of whether Crawfurd or Finlayson is right with regard to the value of a *picul*, there can be little doubt that Finlayson calculated from the accurate unit of measurement. A *picul* (Thai: *hap*) was equal to fifty catties (Thai: *chang*), and this was already so established in Ayutthayan times.[59] Crawfurd, however, took the *picul* to be twice as heavy, apparently assuming the Siamese *chang* to be equivalent to the 'standard catty', of which there were one hundred to the *picul*. The *chang* was worth eighty *baht*, whereas the 'standard catty' was worth only half that.[60] Finlayson's list in table 2 can be taken as the more accurate one. The list of towns seems to cover a very large area, with each town at some distance from the other. It is tempting to surmise that the Siamese had, for the purposes of tax on alcohol, divided the country up in fourteen districts and that the list represents thus a complete picture. However, until further evidence is found, this must remain but speculation.

[58] Finlayson, *Mission to Siam*, p. 248; Crawfurd, *Journal*, p. 379.

[59] La Loubère, *The Kingdom of Siam*, p. 164. The standard Thai-Thai dictionary also gives one hap the value of fifty *chang* (*Photchananukrom Chabap Ratchabanthitsathan*, p. 963.)

[60] A succinct statement of the ancient Siamese system of weights can be found in G. B. McFarland's *Thai-English Dictionary*, p. 59, where the difference between a *chang* and a 'standard catty' is shown. The 'standard catty' was probably introduced into the Siamese system as a result of the intensive trade with China, for the measure was used in China.

The Court

The news that worried the administrators throughout 1822 and 1823 was the growing confrontation between Burma and Great Britain. The Siamese were by no means certain how to interpret these events, and many feared that the Burmese would emerge the stronger of the two parties. It was decided to keep troops alert near the border.

Internally, the court was amused by a strange incident between the two chief ministers. One evening, after these two had attended the cremation rites of the king's younger sister, both approached the same exit from the palace grounds. The litter of the head of the *krom Kalahom*, in which also one of his minor wives was sitting, reached the exit first. They had not yet passed through the gate when they were jostled by the bearers of the litter of the head of the *krom Mahatthai*, who felt that they had precedence. In the scuffles that broke out, the *Kalahom's* men managed to snatch away the official sword of state belonging to the chief of the *Mahatthai*, who thereupon alarmed a section of the Palace Guard (a section commanded by the minister's younger relative). These followed the *Kalahom's* party and forcefully recaptured the sword. The next morning the *Kalahom* lodged an official complaint against his colleague. A tribunal headed by *kromamu'n* Chetsadabodin was appointed to investigate the matter. The *Kalahom's* case was dismissed on a technicality, related to fact that he had been accompanied by one of his minor wives.[61]

The incident itself is trivial, yet it is indicative of some jealousy and hostility among the chief executives. The minister of the *Kalahom*, *chaophraya* Mahasena, had only recently been appointed to the post, and etiquette would probably have demanded that he make way for the minister of the *Mahatthai*, *chaophraya* Aphaiphuthon. The fact that he allowed his men to carry away his colleague's sword of state also indicates a distressing lack of statemanship. Bearing these aspects in mind, it becomes clear why the tribunal was pleased to be able to brush aside the minister's complaint. It also explains why *kromamu'n* Chetsadabodin dismissed *chaophraya* Mahasena the following year when he succeeded his father.

More disturbing was the death of two white elephants.[62] While the finding of such an elephant was generally regarded as an auspicious omen, as a sign that the gods looked favorably upon the reign, the death of such a 'heavenly sign', let alone the death of two of them, was an indication that some great evil was about to happen to the reign.

By this time, *chaofa* Mongkut had reached his twentieth year and, following established custom, he entered the order of monks. After his Lenten season he could have expected to be given his first duties, and his father would then have had the opportunity to decide whether the eldest *chaofa* prince would be worthy of the status of *Uparat*, which would have made him a strong candidate for the succession. However, Mongkut had been in the monastery for only a few weeks when his father became ill and died on 21 July 1824.

The second reign lasted almost fifteen years. At his death, the king was only fifty-six (sixteen years younger than Rama I had been when he died). Compared with the reigns of Taksin and Rama I, that of Rama II is noteworthy as a period of relative peace and calm. This was partly due to the fact that Rama II's predecessors had already given battle so often: by 1809 Siam was firmly re-established among the independent nations of mainland South-East Asia. The relative peacefulness of the period 1809-24 also reflects a lack of belligerence directed against Siam by the neighboring countries. Between 1812 and

[61] *PKRt Song*, pp. 198-9.

[62] *Chotmaihethon*, pp. 37-8.

1819 Bodawpaya of Burma was occupied with troubles at the western and north-western sides of his kingdom, disturbances that led to increased hostilities between the Burmese and the British. In the south, British power became firmly established in Penang, Singapore, and Malacca, while the Siamese felt that they had the traditional overlordship in Kedah, Perak, Kelantan, and Trengganu. They were not so certain about their rights in Pahang and Selangor, Negri Sembilan and Johore were free of Siamese intrusion. Siam's intervention in the affairs of Kedah and Perak between 1818 and 1821 caused anxiety in Penang over Siamese territorial rights. The Europeans had, in contrast to the Siamese, an 'all-or-nothing' approach to the rights of influential countries over their vassals. The Siamese, however, still used their traditional system of letting their vassal states organize their own affairs as long as they sent tribute and allowed Bangkok to confirm the position of the local ruler. Only when the unwritten rules of vassalage were broken would Bangkok send a punitive force. One of Crawfurd's duties while visiting Bangkok was to assess Siam's actual military might and its ability to back up territorial claims in the south in the event of a clash between Britain and Siam. Crawfurd's conclusions and attitudes are worth noting:

> *Should the arrogance of the Siamese embarrass us in the manner I have pointed out as probable, it appears to me that it will unquestionably be the best policy to meet the difficulty at once. The military preparations for this purpose may be made on the most moderate and economical scale. A simultaneous attack by a few companies of sepoys from Penang and the blockade of the Menam [Chaophraya] by 2 or 3 cruziers of the smallest class, it appears to me, will be adequate to every object... The blockade of the Menam will be the easiest, safest and most effectual measure that can well be contemplated.*[63]

To the east, Siam's relations with Cambodia saw a reversal of the situation under the first reign. The Cambodian ruler, who had been closely watched by Rama I, asserted his independence soon after Rama II gained the throne by ignoring a Siamese request for troops. The Cambodian court was divided among pro-Siamese and pro-Vietnamese factions, and the Cambodian king chose to place himself under Vietnamese protection, at the same time continuing to send tributary missions to Bangkok. Rama II allowed the vassal state to fall more and more under Vietnamese control, accepting the yearly tribute as a sign that Siam was still master. The Siamese king's personal character seems to have played a role in this unusual complacency.

After the first spate of administrative measures, the king seems to have settled into a life of courtly splendor, preferring

---

[63] *Crawfurd Papers*, p. 151.

to compose poetry and supervise the building of the large pleasure garden to keeping a personal watch upon the affairs of state. These were largely delegated to the senior ministers and a few princes.

The second reign was a time when the court was often short of money. Probably this was a result of a slackening of the rules which allowed tax evasion to become so widespread as to seriously affect the State's income. It has been recorded that some years the king could pay the full *biawat* to his senior administrators, but in other years he paid them three-quarters or only half the amount.[64] All the king's efforts to raise more money seemed to be directed towards increasing the trade with China. By sending with the yearly fleet an ever-increasing number of royal ships, the king managed, in good years, to pay his court, or even give a bonus.

The internal revenue, where it was raised, seems to have been dissipated before it reached the Treasury. The laxity prevalent at the time is apparent from a statement in the *Dynastic Chronicles*, Second Reign, which can be translated as follows: 'In this reign princes and nobles sent out people to go to the secret meeting places of people who live in the forest regions in order to obtain forest products, and thus obtain *suai*. Runaway freemen and slaves secretly lived there and could not be arrested, because their leaders had great power.'[65] Little wonder that Crawfurd could report that the monarch was one of the mildest sovereigns that had ruled Siam for at least a century and a half. It appears that the government of Siam was slipping from Rama II's control, and this probably influenced the question of the succession which arose in July 1824.

---

[64] *PKRt Song*, p. 204.

[65] *Ibid.*, p. 205.

Plate 6. An engraving of a young prince probably a grandson of King Rama III with his attendant.

5

ECONOMIC DEVELOPMENTS
(1824-1851)

Although Rama II had died without officially naming an heir to the throne, the succession in 1824 was by far the smoothest thus far described. *Kromamu'n* Chetsadabodin, the previous king's eldest son, to whom much of the burden of government had been delegated during the preceding years, was unchallenged when *kromamu'n* Sakdiphonlasep, one of Rama II's half-brothers, proposed his name.

Gossip among foreigners would have it that the accession had not been a smooth affair, the legitimate heir having been deprived of the throne. Thus the American Edmund Roberts blithely relates the following account of the accession:

> *The present king, the illegitimate son of the late monarch, by the sudden death of his father, aided by bribes, placed himself on the throne, to the exclusion of the eldest legitimate son, who, on the death of his father, fled the palace, and became a Talapoin to save his life.*[1]

This view, which was widely held among foreigners, was confirmed whenever visitors from other countries met with *chaofa* Chuthamani, who would be eager to let them know that he and his brother were really of a higher rank than their elder half-brother. Indeed, according to the letter of the law, the eldest son of *chaofa* rank would be the first to be considered as successor to the throne. However, Mongkut's greatest supporter, his uncle *somdet chaofa kromaluang* Phithakmontri, had died two years before Rama II. The idea that Mongkut was being groomed for the position of *Uparat* is in itself quite feasible, but when his father died he was only nineteen years old, much too young and inexperienced for such a high office.[2] Chetsadabodin, on the other hand, was by no means illegitimate; he was the *king's* eldest son by a wife who was not queen. Chetsadabodin had been a prince of *krom* rank for ten years and had gradually become one of the most powerful men of Siam. Since the Siamese had never felt bound to the rule of letting the eldest *chaofa* prince ascend the throne, the choice of Chetsadabodin was the natural and expected one. In the Chronicles it is stated unequivocally that it was Chetsadabodin's past record, his proven wisdom, intelligence and experience, which decided the issue, and all available information fits in with this presentation of the facts.[3]

---

[1] E. Roberts, *Embassy to the Eastern Courts of Cochin-China, Siam and Muscat during the Years 1832-3-4*, pp. 247-8, and an even more garbled version on p. 300.

[2] For the date of birth of Mongkut I have relied upon Prince Damrong, *Phraratchaphongsawadan Krung-ratanakosin Ratchakan thi Song*, vol. 2, pp. 222-3.

[3] This is confirmed in *The Burney Papers*, vol. 2, pt 4, pp. 112-3.

The gossip regarding Mongkut's fleeing to a monastery in order to save his life is simply untrue. In accordance with established practice Mongkut had been ordained a Buddhist monk just before his father became ill.[4] He had no cause to fear for his life on account of his elder half-brother becoming the king; on the contrary, Rama III was well disposed towards *chaofa* Mongkut and occasionally helped to further his career.[5]

That the accession of Rama III was uncontested is strongly supported by the fact that all senior civilian appointments were carried over from the reign of Rama II to that of Rama III. Had there been dissent among some of the *krom* heads, a change in senior portfolios would have occurred. Rama III chose his uncle *kromamu'n* Sakdiphonlasep as *Uparat*. In addition, the Chronicles mention a general amnesty and orders to clear the courts of litigation cases, just as had been done at the king's father's accession in 1809.[6] Another measure, which would prove to be the first of many of its type, was the proclamation of a new tax, one on salt.[7] A further decree that appears indicative of the new king's style of government was the digging of a new canal, together with the construction of a bridge, at the edge of the capital city.[8] The new king's anointment, which took place in April 1825, necessitated an adjustment in the ranks of royalty. During Rama III's first year on the throne, he issued a list of royal appointments, in which eight relatives were elevated to *kromamu'n* rank. Interestingly, throughout his reign he refrained from elevating any of his children to *chaofa* rank.

Meanwhile, the news from Burma was disconcerting. The incursions of Burmese troops into Assam, Manipur and Cachar had caused the British to declare some of the small states Burma regarded as its vassal regions to be under British protection. Hostilities broke out. In March 1824 the British formally declared war against the Burmese; the Siamese were anxious about the outcome. If Burma defeated the invading troops, Siam would again have a strong and quarrelsome neighbor on her western borders. Already during the last months of Rama II's reign, the Siamese had been encouraged by the British to harass and threaten the Burmese. Siam had eagerly responded to the British strategy, and the new king continued to regard himself as Britain's ally in the conflict with Burma.[9] Rama III considered Burma likely to be the loser and hoped that Britain would accept Siamese help in return for Siamese control over all of Martaban and Tavoy.[10] However, after due consideration the British did not feel the need of a firm alliance and apparently did not wish to strengthen the position of a country that controlled some of the Malay states in which the British were becoming interested.

In December 1825 another British envoy arrived in Bangkok, again armed with a letter from the governor-general of Bengal. This was Captain Henry Burney, who spent almost

[4] *PKRt Song*, pp. 201-3.

[5] R. Lingat, 'La vie réligieuse du roi Mongkut', The Siam Society Fiftieth Anniversary Commemorative Publication, vol. 1, pp. 24-28.

[6] *Chaophraya* Thiphakorawong, *Phraratchaphongsawadan Krungratanakosin, Ratchakan thi Sam* (hereafter *PKRt Sam*), p. 11.

[7] *Chotmaihethon*, p. 39.

[8] *Ibid.*, p. 39.

[9] See the letter of the *chaophraya Phrakhlang* to John Crawfurd, dated 21 August 1825, reproduced in *Burney Papers*, vol. 1, pt 1, pp. 6-7.

[10] See the letter of Henry Burney to the governor of the Prince of Wales Island, dated 22 December 1825, *Burney Papers*, vol. 1, pt 1, p. 22.

eight months trying to persuade the Siamese to grant the British more favorable trading conditions. His mission was made difficult by the fact that he could offer no concessions to the Siamese other than the prospect of more trade if tariffs were lowered. The situation was further complicated when in February 1826 the envoy sent his ship southwards. This led to the rumor that it was fetching a large British fleet which would attack Bangkok. The resounding victory over the Burmese by the British made the Siamese courtiers wary and distrustful of them. When the formation of a British fleet of sixty ships was reported, Bangkok mobilized. As Burney reported:

> *Troops were called into the capital from the interior, the forts at Paklaat and Paknam were manned and additional defenses commenced. All was war and bustle. The situation of the Mission was now by no means comfortable. Not a word uttered by any of us received credit. The boatmen allotted to us were removed and we were evidently viewed with indignation as well as distrust.* [11]

This situation lasted for more than a month. Finally, at the end of July 1826, Burney left Bangkok with a less than satisfactory draft treaty.

The Siamese did not believe Burney's protestations regarding Britain's friendly attitude, so they proceeded to improve their defenses in order to be able to withstand an attack from those who had just defeated the Burmese with alarming ease. Three warships continuously cruised near the mouth of the river Chaophraya, and large sheds were erected in Bangkok to house the war boats. In the largest of these sheds were 136 boats, each one capable of carrying about thirty men, and a second shed contained another one hundred such boats. Other similar, smaller sheds had been constructed further along the banks of the river. As a further deterrent, the king ordered the casting of a truly massive brass cannon, weighing almost 2,500 kilograms. Almost two thousand men were occupied for two months with this work.[12]

D. E. Malloch, who had acquired much knowledge of life in Bangkok during three years' residence in Siam, provides further information about the court that neatly complements Thiphakorawong's chronicle. In contrast to his father, Rama III did not wish to be personally involved with trading, leaving much of this in the hands of the *Phrakhlang* and the deputy *Phrakhlang*, *phraya* Siphiphat. Apparently Rama III also intended to reduce the number of public holidays so that time could be given to more useful employment.[13] This information, meager and incomplete by itself, gains importance when it is seen in connection with the many other initiatives taken during the third reign.

Meanwhile, the rumor of an imminent British attack on Bangkok was seized by *chao* Anuwong, the ruler of Vientiane,

[11] From a report by Burney dated 2 December 1826, published in *Burney Papers*, vol. 2, pt 4, p. 41. Apparently these rumors had already been rife several months before, because they are mentioned in a letter dated 2 September 1825 by J. Gillies to J. Crawfurd (*Burney Papers*, vol. 1, pt 2, pp. 3-4), and serious distrust of British intentions must have undermined all negotiations at that time.

[12] D. E. Malloch, excerpts from his private journal, published in *Burney Papers*, vol. 2, pt 4, pp. 227-31.

[13] Malloch, Journal, p. 226.

as the best opportunity for a revolt against Bangkok. He apparently had been contacting the rulers of other Laotian vassal states with the aim of throwing off Siam's overlordship. *Chao Anuwong* had planned a raid deep into Siamese territory to the province of Saraburi, where some ten thousand Laotians were living, who had been deported from Vientiane more than four decades earlier. In a cleverly devised strategy, *chao* Anuwong sent a message to Rama III explaining that he was sending a large number of troops in order to fortify Bangkok against the imminent attack of the British. Apparently he hoped that thereby he would be able to move freely across Siamese territory without raising the alarm and collect the Lao families who had been forcefully moved into Siamese territory. Unfortunately for *chao* Anuwong, the ruler of Luang Prabang, instead of assisting him, actually warned the Siamese king of *chao* Anuwong's intentions and in late February 1827 the Siamese were able to move their troops up to Saraburi. They expelled Anuwong's troops and marched on to take Vientiane. The town was looted and all its fortifications destroyed. Large numbers of farmers were moved westwards, to settle in what is now north-east Thailand.[14] *Chao* Anuwong eventually was captured and died ignominiously in captivity.

The *Records of the Astrologers* note that in the year 1829 the *Huai Ko Kho* lottery was begun.[15] This grew rapidly to be a very popular State-sponsored gambling organization.[16] The introduction of a State lottery can be regarded as typical of the third reign. While Rama II often had insufficient cash to pay the traditional *biawat* in full, Rama III appears to have been more successful in raising funds. During 1829 he also ordered a nationwide survey of all taxable fruit trees, undoubtedly another measure intended to boost the State revenue.

Rama III's success in increasing revenue enabled the execution of several expensive projects. For example, a new fortress was built at the mouth of the river Tha Chin, some thirty kilometers south-west of Bangkok, the Chinese bricklayers being paid just over 3,800 *baht*.[17] This fortification was an extension to the defenses of Bangkok, because the mouth of the Tha Chin was directly linked with the capital by the old Mahachai Canal. Having fortified that strategic position, the king ordered a number of Mons to live there, under the leadership of *chaophraya* Mahayotha. At the same time, a large number of Chinese workers were hired to excavate approximately another thirty kilometers of canal to the mouth of the river Mekong, at a cost of more than 8,100 *baht*.[18] When these canals had been made, it was possible to travel by boat from Bangkok to Ratburi without having to cross stretches of open sea. Thus the south-western parts of the central lowlands were now firmly linked with the capital, and troops could be rapidly moved at all seasons via the canals and rivers. The recent fear

---

[14] The best account of this confrontation between Lao and Siamese, as well as the consequent devastation of the city of Vieng Chan is probably to be found in Martin Stuart-Fox, *The Lao Kingdom of Lan Xang: Rise and Decline*, Bangkok: White Lotus, 1998, pp. 117-27.

[15] *Chotmaihethon*, p. 44.

[16] For details on the lottery, see B. O. Cartwright, 'The Huey Lottery', *JSS* 18, pt 3 (1924), pp. 221-39. Cartwright gives a different date for the first organization of the lottery, namely 1835.

[17] *PKRt Song*, p. 92.

[18] *Ibid.*, p. 93.

of a British invasion could well have been the catalyst in making the decision to dig this canal.[19]

Rama III did not order *corvée* laborers to do the work, as had been customary during the reigns of Taksin and Rama I. Already in the days of Thonburi and the first building of Bangkok, massive tasks such as digging new canals had not been done by the regular *corvée* labor, that in principle always was available to the central authorities. Instead, such heavy work was performed by manpower from vassal states. This suggests that even in those early days people liable for regular *corvée* were usually otherwise employed. Many of them would have made up the regular standing armies. During the third reign there was again a continuing need for a large number of reliable troops, due to the above-mentioned uprising in Vientiane, and as the Siamese were still uneasy about the Burmese and distrustful of the British. The situation in the south also needed constant attention and Cambodia was a seat of potential trouble. Therefore many ordinary *phrai luang* may have served *corvée* by performing military duties. The length of time that people served varied according to military needs. Around the main palaces there were always many bands of permanent soldiers who received a small salary. Other less essential but still fairly important platoons consisted of men who served half a month and were free to earn their living the other half. Most *phrai luang* in and around the capital served one month and were free for two months to earn their living. Those who served part-time did not receive food or money during *corvée*. However, when there was a campaign, all who were under marching orders would receive their victuals and also a small amount of money. If the army was not on campaign, the king could allot it other tasks. It has been noted that many soldiers were employed in cutting timber and collecting sapan wood for the royal warehouses.[20]

This at least partly explains why Rama III decided to hire Chinese to build a new fortress and dig a long canal: he did not want to tie down his standing army in one small area of the kingdom, not be deprived of the valuable trading goods these troops provided him with. In addition, there was a large supply of Chinese labor as Siam was still regularly receiving Chinese immigrants eager to work, the annual intake of Chinese in the late 1820s estimated at more than two thousand.[21]

During the early years of the third reign, the position of the *Phrakhlang* was undoubtedly the most important one in Siam next to that of the king. This office was headed by Dit Bunnag, who had been closely allied to the king when the latter was still *kromamu'n* Chetsadabodin. During the first decade of the third reign he appears to have been the king's chief adviser and executive officer. It was Dit Bunnak who was in charge of the digging of the canal to the Mae Klong River. He had already

[19] For details, see Shigeharu Tanabe, 'Historical Geography of the Canal System in the Chaophraya River Delta', pp. 43-4 and fig. 4.

[20] From Captain Burney's notes, published in *Burney Papers*, vol. 1, pt 1, p. 180.

[21] Malloch's journal, *Burney Papers*, vol. 2, pt 4, p. 223.

been offered the post of head of the *krom Kalahom* once, but had declined it, probably because the *krom Phrakhlang*, though not as high in status as that of the *Kalahom*, gave the opportunity for many lucrative deals.[22] Later, in 1830, the offer was repeated and this time the *chaophraya Phrakhlang* was able to add the acting headship of the *krom Kalahom* to his existing position, a combination of offices unprecedented in Siamese history.[23] In his function of *Phrakhlang* he handled all matters regarding foreigners and so the matter of two enthusiastic Protestant missionaries came to his attention. They were Jacob Tomlin and Karl Gutzlaff, who had arrived in late August 1828 to preach Christianity in a manner different from that of the long-established Roman Catholics.

Gutzlaff relates how the British conquest of lower Burma had greatly impressed the Siamese populace; the fact that Christian soldiers had defeated Buddhist ones was interpreted by him as a sign of the superiority of the Christian way of life. He freely distributed literature regarding the imminent eclipse of false doctrines such as Buddhism.[24] This resulted in the *chaophraya Phrakhlang's* request to the British agent, Robert Hunter, to assist with the expulsion of the two missionaries. Hunter protested that neither had broken any law and that their presence was allowed under the treaties negotiated by Crawfurd in 1822 and renegotiated by Burney in 1826. Thereupon the Siamese let the date of the expulsion order lapse and proclaimed a new law prohibiting the distribution of Christian booklets.[25] Near the end of 1829 Gutzlaff left Bangkok for a visit to Singapore, where the first printing press using Siamese characters was established, so that he could have some of his biblical translations printed in Siamese. Meanwhile, he and Tomlin had sent a letter to America to ask for the speedy sending of more Protestant missionaries. Not long afterwards the first American missionaries began to arrive.[26]

In 1830 *phraya* Rachasuphawadi, an official who had shown leadership qualities during the Laotian campaign, was rewarded with the headship of the *krom Mahatthai*, receiving the new name of *chaophraya* Bodindecha. Until his death in 1849, he was to play an extremely important role throughout most of Rama III's reign.

In 1831 the rice harvest was largely lost because of disastrous floods, the price of rice rising to 400 *baht* for a cartload of paddy.[27] Edmund Roberts, who arrived two years later in Bangkok, reported that as a result of the food shortage the number of Buddhist monks had 'doubled'.[28] That year the *chaophraya Phrakhlang* led an army to the south. Several governors of *mu'angs* in the southern region had been feuding. It was felt that there could have been danger of further British involvement if Bangkok had not asserted itself. *The Records of*

[22] The fact that the position of head of the *krom Kalahom* had been offered to the *chaophraya Phrakhlang* before 1830 is mentioned in Captain Burney's diary, which was dispatched in February 1826 (see *Burney Papers*, vol. 1, pt 1, p. 65).

[23] *PKRt Song*, pp. 107-8; Vella, *Siam Under Rama III*, pp. 7-8.

[24] K. Gutzlaff, *Verslag van een Driejarig Verblijf in Siam, en van eene Reize langs de Kust van China naar Mantchou-Tartarije*, p. 2.

[25] K. E. Wells, *History of Protestant Work in Thailand, 1828-1958*, p. 12.

[26] Udom Poshakrishna, 'Geschichte der Chirurgie in Thailand, 1828-1922', *JSS* 51, pt 1 (1963), p. 60.

[27] A cartload *(kwian)* of paddy was reckoned to be equal to 16 *hap*, each *hap* weighing sixty kilograms. pp. 7-8.

[28] Roberts, *Embassy to the Eastern Courts*, p. 259.

Table 3. Siamese annual revenue as recorded by Edmund Roberts in 1833

Annual Revenue obtained by the Government of Siam from Farms and Duties				
Names	Annual quantity	Prices in ticals	Duties	Revenues
Paddy and rice	1,696,424 coyans of 23 *picul*	1st sort 16 ticals	}	Ticals
" "	" "	2d " 14 "		862,358
" "	" "	3d " 12 "		
Orchards	68,235 in No.			545,880
Samsoo or spirit	4,251			17,800
shops	Bangkok			104,900
" "	Sieuthaja			16,000
" "	Bangxang			8,000
" "	Suraburi			4,000
" "	Krungtaphan.			4,000
Bazaars	Bangkok			39,200
"	Sieuthaja			12,800
"	Suraburi			1,600
"	Bangxang			1,600
Duty on floating houses				36,000
Chinese gambling				64,000
Siamese, ditto				58,000
Treak wood	127,000 tress			56,000
Sapan wood	200,000 *piculs*	1st sort 3 1-2 to 3	}	
" "	" "	2d " 2 1-2 to 2		84,000
" "	" "	3d " 1 1-2 to 1		
Coconut oil	600,000 "	7 1-2 to 8	1 1-4 to 1 1-2	56,000
Sugar, 1st	10,000 "	8 1-2 to 9		
" 2d	60,000 "	7 to 7 1-2	}	
" 3d	20,000 "	6 to 6 1-2	1 1-2	40,000
" black	1,000 "	2 1-2 to 3		
" candy	5,000 "	16 to 17	1-2	
Jaggery	150,000 jars	18 tcls. p. 100 jrs.	2 ticals	8,000
Salt	8,000 coyans	2 1-2 to 3	6	32,000
Pepper	38,000 *piculs*	10 to 11	1 1-2	23,200
Bastard cardamums	4,000 "	32 to 40	6 ticals	16,000
Cardamums	1st. 100 "	360 to 380	"	
"	2d. 150 "	280 to 300	} 16 "	5,400
"	3d. 300 "	200 to 220	"	
Sticlac	8,000 "	12 13 14	1 1-4	9,500
Tin	1,200 "	24 26 28	3 ticals	18,200
Iron	20,000 "	4 5 6	"	54,000
Ivory	300 "	160 170 180	12 ditto	2,500
Gamboge	1st 50 to 60	75 to 80		
"	2d 150 "	55 to 60	} 6 ditto	1,200
"	3d 50 "	40 to 45		
Rhinoceros horns	50 to 60	800 per *picul*	32 per *picul*	1,600
Benjamin	100 "	50 to 55		400
Bird's-nests		1st srt. 10,000		
" " }	10 to 12	2d " 6,000	} 6 ticals	32,000
" "		3d " 4,000		
Young deers' horns	26,000 pairs	1 1-2 to 2	10 per 100.	3,600
Old, ditto, ditto	200 *piculs*	8 to 9 per *pecul*	1-2	
Buffalo, ditto	200 "	3 to 4 per *picul*	1-4	
Deers' nervers	200 "	16 to 20	1 1-2	
Rhinoceros skins	200 "	7 to 8	1-2	800
Tigers' bones	50 to 60	50 to 60	3 ticals	
Buffalo hides	500 "	8 to 10	1-2	
Deers' ditto	100,000 "	20,25, and 30	3 ticals	1,600
White dried fish	4,000 "	8 to 9	1-2	
Black, ditto	15,000 "	7 to 8	1-2	18,000
Small dried fish	60,000 "	3 to 4	1-4	
Dried shrimps	10,000 "	30 to 35	3 "	4,600
Balachang	15,000 coyans	50 to 60	12 "	8,000
Wood oil	15,000 *piculs*	3 to 5	1-2	5,600
Pitch	10,000 "	3 to 4	1-2	6,000
Torches	200,000 bundles	5 ticals per 100	1-2	5,600
Rattans	200,000 "	4 " "	1-2	14,000
Firewood				
Wooden posts	1st. 500 to 600 in No.	1 per 4 ticals	10 per 100	8,000
" "	2d. 3,000 "	1 per 2 do.	5 " "	
" "	3d. 200,000 "	100 per 25 30	" " "	
Bamboos	600,000,000 in No.	40	10 "	8,000
Attaps	95,000,000,000 "	3 ticals per 100	15 100	3,000
Rose wood	200,000 "	3 ticals per 1000	20 "	1,600
Bark	200,000 bundles	342 per *picul*	10 "	
		100 per 6 ticals		1,600

the Astrologers mention also that in this year taxes on bamboo and teak logs were introduced.[29]

In 1832 the *Uparat* died. Speculation was rife about who would be chosen to fill the post and thus automatically be dubbed heir-apparent. However, then, as later, the king saw nobody of sufficiently outstanding qualities among his close relatives to groom as his successor. Therefore he decided to leave the post open for the time being, but at the same time he promoted eight relatives to higher *krom* ranks. Three became *kromaluang* and four *kromakhun*, so that together with the remaining *kromamu'n* princes, a distinct hierarchy was created. One of the princes elevated was *chaofa* Chuthamani, who became *chaofa kromakhun* Itsaret. Among the princes singled out for promotion were several who hoped to be elevated even further to head the Front Palace.[30]

In 1833 Bangkok was honored by the visit of another envoy from a Western trading country, the American Edmund Roberts, who came to see whether, as the English had done, he could ensure more equitable trade terms. The American was given quite a warm welcome, not only because previous contacts had been amiable but also because his country prided itself on not contemplating territorial conquest in Asia. Roberts wrote a valuable account with information on the various important people in Siam at the time. He also described the continuation of a lively shipbuilding industry in Bangkok, estimating the number of war boats to be no less than five hundred, there being fifty or sixty sailing boats, the largest of which did not exceed a hundred tons.[31]

The most important historical document produced by Roberts was a list with the annual Siamese revenue from farms and duties, as well as some items of the king's expenditure (see table 3). Since Roberts appeared eager to attract American trade, he was unlikely to have underestimated the annual quantity of produce, or the Siamese government's revenue. Yet in many instances the figures given for both are only a fraction of Crawfurd's lowest estimate. Birds' nests, for example, are shown by Crawfurd to have given the Siamese government 100,000 *baht* in tax in 1822. A decade later Roberts makes this 30,000 *baht*. Tin in 1822, according to Crawfurd reputedly earned 60,000 *baht* (in another report, 54,000 *baht*), whereas Roberts estimates it in 1833 to have been only 18,200 *baht*. Even greater discrepancies can be found in the case of pepper, which appears to have dropped almost nine-fold in revenue.

It is tempting to account for these differences by rejecting Crawfurd's figures as deliberate fabrications, because he has been shown in many instances to have inflated his figures. However, the discrepancy may also have been wholly or partly the result of a comparative slackening of trade between 1822 and 1833. Rama II had invested heavily in the trade with China,

---

[29] *Chotmaihethon*, p. 46.

[30] Six years later, this led to considerable trouble at the court, see later in this chapter.

[31] Roberts, *Embassy to the Eastern Courts*, p. 311.

hoping to amass sufficient revenue thereby to pay for the court's expenses.

There is some evidence supporting the idea of a smaller amount of trade. Crawfurd estimates the size of the annual fleet to have been about 140 ships and is unlikely to have greatly inflated this number, because this could be readily verified. Rama III, on the other hand, had withdrawn the king's large private trade interests,[32] and this could, at least partly, account for a much lower estimate of the size of the fleet in the early 1830s. Gutzlaff, who was well acquainted with the Chinese junk trade, says the fleet that left for China every year between May and August comprised approximately eighty junks,[33] and this was confirmed in 1835, when the annual fleet was said to have from sixty to eighty seagoing vessels.[34]

Roberts's figures on the Siamese revenue may be regarded as the first fairly reliable ones to indicate the state and size of the Siamese economy. With the help of these figures it is possible to make an estimate of the area of arable land, the number of fruit trees, and the relative size of the country's largest marketplaces. The details of the tax on alcoholic beverages, the manufacture of which apparently was almost completely in the hands of the Chinese, may be compared with Finlayson's list.[35] From this it would seem that consumption increased in Bangkok but decreased in various provincial towns. The increased figure for Bangkok is easily explained by the steady increase in the Chinese population. The provincial figures are more difficult to understand. The decrease may reflect a relative lack of opportunity in the provinces, but the possibility of a high rate of Chinese assimilation must not be excluded. The list of 'farms and duties' provides the first estimate of the number of teak logs cut; a massive 127,000 trees were felled and processed in Siam. Another interesting aspect of the list is the fact that so many new taxes seem to have been added during the reign of Rama III.[36]

Roberts also provides an estimate of the revenue derived from the outer provinces. The northern provinces contributed 32,000 *baht* annually, the southern ones under the *krom Kalahom* 24,000 *baht*, and the coastal central provinces 12,000 *baht*. In addition, he gives estimates of the revenue of the *chaophraya Yomarat* (4,800 *baht*) and of the (king's?) tribunal (8,000 *baht*). As for the state gold revenue, *phrai suai* delivered approximately 3,600 grams, and the Malay gold mines paid a tax of just over 3,200 grams. Finally, there is a statement of the annual amount paid by the king to his officers. Out of a total of 618,800 *baht*, princes with or without *krom* rank received 47,400 *baht*, and the Front Palace 29,000 *baht*[37] These figures suggest that the rate of *biawat* was approximately half that reputedly paid in late Ayutthayan times.[38]

[32] Malloch's journal, *Burney Papers*, vol. 2, pt 4, p. 223.

[33] Gutzlaff, *Verslag*, p. 30.

[34] Extract from D. B. Bradley's journal, published in the *Bangkok Calendar*, 1870, p. 90.

[35] G. Finlayson, *The Mission to Siam and Hue, the Capital of Cochin China, in the Years 1821-2*, p. 248.

[36] Many more still were to be added; for details, see *PKRt Sam*, pp. 361-2.

[37] Roberts, *Embassy to the Eastern Courts*, p. 427.

[38] H. G. Q. Wales, *Ancient Siamese Government and Administration*, p. 236.

In 1833 the Siamese were drawn into a conflict with Vietnam. In July of that year rebels in Cochin-China sent a request for military assistance to Bangkok. A weakening of Annamese power would automatically increase Siamese influence in Cambodia. Therefore Rama III boldly decided to extend the Siamese umbrella over Cochin-China. In late 1833 a main force of some forty thousand men under *chaophraya* Bodindecha left Bangkok. At the same time a conscripted Laotian force was ordered to descend the Mekong River and invade Cambodia from the north. The *chaophraya Phrakhlang* went with a fleet along the coast to take the harbor of Ha Tien and then move inland. The Siamese forces overran Cambodia without encountering much resistance. However, in January 1834, moving further eastwards in the direction of Saigon, the Annamite forces brought the advance to a halt. The Siamese planned a simultaneous attack by the forces of Bodindecha and the *Phrakhlang*, but the *Phrakhlang's* troops were late in arriving at the scene of the battle. According to Bodindecha, this forced the Siamese to retreat, suffering heavy losses. The *Phrakhlang* would not agree to the immediate execution of his chief officers demanded by Bodindecha, nor could the two military leaders come to an understanding about a renewed attack. The invasion was therefore called off and all troops hurried back to Siamese territory. The plan had failed and Annam was able both to strengthen its dominance of Cochin-China and also occupy Cambodia and rule it for a period of seven years. Then a popular revolt against the Annamese gave the Siamese another opportunity to add Cambodia to its vassal territories.[39] The military debacle of 1833 and 1834 must have had a sobering effect upon the court. It was realized that there was no longer a buffer state protecting the eastern borders, so the coastal town of Chanthaburi was immediately fortified.[40] The finding of a white elephant in the Khorat region, interpreted as a sign that the invisible powers were happy with the king, must have been especially valued at this time.[41]

One of the American missionaries, the physician Dan Beach Bradley, arrived in 1835 armed with the Siamese printing press from Singapore mentioned above. Bradley was to become intimately involved with Siam during the course of his long life. He provides probably the liveliest and most informative picture of the annual fleet to China available for this period:

> *Junks in the China trade would then as now make but one voyage in a year, taking advantage of the favouring SW monsoon in June to sail from Bangkok, and of the NE monsoon to return the latter part of January and first part of February. From February to June there were annually from 60 to 80 of these monsters of the deep moored in the river, forming two lines, all heading down the stream,*

[39] Further details can be found in Vella, *Siam Under Rama III*, pp. 96-99, and D. P. Chandler, 'Cambodia's Relations with Siam in the Early Bangkok Period: The Politics of a Tributary State', *JSS* 60, pt 1 (1972), p. 162.

[40] Bradley's journal, *Bangkok Calendar*, 1870, p. 96.

[41] *Chotmaihethon*, p. 49.

*always ready as to position, to start on another voyage.
These two long lines of junks were practically a great
Bazaar for a period of two months or more from the time
of their arrival. Each junk was freighted with the goods of
several parties, each of whom occupied a part of the deck
for the display of his wares until they were all sold out. The
goods they brought from China were chiefly teas, silks,
crapes, cotton fabrics, paper, crockery, Chinese cutlery,
Chinese trunks, chests, betel boxes, Japan wooden ware,
mirrors and a thousand other similar articles of Chinese
manufacture.*[42]

Bradley reported on 8 September 1835 a remarkable incident between Siamese and Europeans. On that day the British
merchant Robert Hunter, regarded as the general agent of the
British and the unofficial consul and given the rank of *luang* and
an honorary name by the Siamese,[43] had as his guest Captain
Wellar of the bark *Pyramus*, which he had chartered. In the cool
of the evening, Hunter and Wellar had strolled out into the fields
with their guns, intending to shoot crows and pigeons. By
chance they met Bradley and Hunter fell into conversation with
the missionary, while Wellar strolled on. Wellar soon found
himself within the precincts of a Buddhist monastery where
evening prayers were going on, and there he shot two pigeons.
The Buddhist monks, alarmed at the unfamiliar sound of
firearms in their monastery, rushed out to find Wellar collecting
his dead birds. Wellar apparently had no idea of the enormity of
his act. When the Buddhist monks tried to wrest the birds from
his hands and take his gun, a scuffle ensued. This ended when
someone dealt Wellar a heavy blow on his head, stunning him.

Hunter ran to the captain's aid and found him badly
wounded. Bradley described the ensuing scene as follows:

*Mr. Hunter sent forthwith for the Port Captain and
demanded that the case should without delay be brought
before the government, threatening that if this were
refused, he would take the Pyramus in front of the Royal
Palace and let the King hear from the mouth of her guns.
The Port Captain appeared not a little alarmed and went
post haste to the acting P'ra K'lang to lay the matter
before him.*[44]

The affair caused great commotion, with Hunter making
heavy demands, threatening that if these were not granted he
would send for foreign troops and 'establish British rule in
Siam'.[45] Wellar recovered, however, and the king let Hunter
know that the monks had their own ecclesiastical judiciary in
which he could not interfere. It was quite clear to the Siamese
that the monks had been severely provoked, but at the same

[42] *Bangkok Calendar*, 1870, p. 90.
[43] According to *PKRt Sam*, p. 279, he had in 1831 been given the title of *luang* Awutwiset. Hunter had gained considerable power at the court, having by 1835 four vessels working for him (Vella, *Siam Under Rama III*, p. 126).
[44] *Bangkok Calendar*, 1870, p. 97.
[45] *Ibid.*, entry for 9 September 1835. This is the first of such incidents reported for Siam. Later, with the arrival of more Europeans such clashes were to occur from time to time. After the Europeans had gained extraterritorial rights, they were in a much stronger position. See on this topic, Henry Alabaster, *The Wheel of the Law*, pp. 266-7.

time they should not have resorted to violence. Eventually some monks were punished fairly lightly.

The incident illustrates Hunter's extraordinary position at the court. He was quite friendly with the *Phrakhlang*, with whom he often conducted business and traded jointly. At the same time the threat of a possible British invasion, which had seemed imminent less than a decade earlier, still carried weight. Hunter's high-handed attitude is also related to the fact that at that time he held the monopoly in Siam of square-rigged vessels of which the Siamese could make use. The days of this monopoly were coming to an end, however, because two European-type ships were being built under the *Phrakhlang's* supervision. Late in 1835 they were presented to the king, who, after a few trial runs, ordered more such boats to be built.

In 1835 the renovation of Wat Phra Chetuphon, popularly called Wat Pho, was begun. Rama III had already decided that the monastery, which had been built upon the ruins of an older one by his grandfather Rama I, was much in need of repair. In 1832 some of the monks' quarters had already been rebuilt. However, in 1835 it was decided to renovate the whole complex. Traditionally Siamese monarchs, members of the royal family and rich nobles were frequently involved with the building and restoring of monasteries. Wat Pho, however, was already an outstanding institution. Rama I had housed various famous Buddhist images and relics in the monastery and artists of that time had made many paper illustrations which hung from the walls.[46] Since then, many of these decorations had deteriorated. During the third reign it was therefore decided to make a more permanent record by supplying many of the images and mural paintings with inscriptions. Apart from the many inscriptions on religious topics, some, such as those found in the cloisters surrounding the central area of the monastery, provide secular, contemporary records. There are allusions to literary works of the period and a list of *mu'angs* of the kingdom, together with the titles of their governors. Unfortunately, many of the stone slabs on which the inscriptions were made have been lost and the record is now incomplete.[47] In addition, there are many maxims and exhortations conducive to proper moral conduct. Other inscriptions relate to the *Jatakas* (stories of the Buddha's previous births), contemporary moralist poetry and practical formulae to ward off evil. A fascinating series of statues and inscriptions composed by the court physician *phraya* Bamroe Rachaphaethaya[48] deals with medical matters.

During the decade or more that it took to restore and rebuild the monastery, it gradually acquired the status of an encyclopaedia, where the best moral literature was displayed, where court artists depicted the best-known Buddhist stories

---

[46] For a description of the monastery before its restoration, see J. Crawfurd, *Journal of an Embassy to the Courts of Siam and Cochin China*, pp. 163-7.

[47] The available evidence is enumerated by Prince Dhani Nivat in 'The Inscriptions of Wat Phra Jetubon', in *Collected Articles by H.H. Prince Dhani Nivat Kromamun Bidayalabh Brdihyakorn*, pp. 13-6.

[48] For details, see A. B. Griswold, 'The Rishis of Wat Pho', in *Felicitation Volumes of Southeast-Asian Studies Presented to His Highness Prince Dhaninivat Kromamun Bidyalabh Bridhyakorn*, vol. 2, pp. 319-28.

and where an extensive 'medical library' was permanently exhibited at this 'university in stone'.[49]

The Two Chaofa Princes

In 1836 Rama III arranged the appointment of his half-brother, *chaofa* Mongkut, to the position of abbot of Wat Bowoniwet,[50] a new monastery in the heart of Bangkok. During the years preceding this appointment, Prince Mongkut had resided many years in Wat Samorai, a monastery on the outskirts of the city. Mongkut had at that time become somewhat notorious in the Buddhist *Sangha* for his unorthodox opinions. Earlier in his career in the order, he had come under the influence of a learned Burmese monk who informed him of the great debate concerning pure ordination that had rocked the Burmese *Sangha*. As a result, Mongkut became convinced that the Siamese order of monks had unwittingly lost the proper way of ordaining. In the quiet atmosphere of Wat Samorai he had arranged a new, meticulously organized ordination. Moreover, not far from the Wat Samorai was one of the Catholic churches, where Mgr. Pallegoix had resided since 1830. Pallegoix was an intelligent, knowledgeable and observant man who enjoyed frequent contact with the young prince-priest. Mongkut, like many other progressive young men of his day, was fascinated by glimpses of European culture. He arranged regular meetings with the bishop, during which he learnt a smattering of Latin and frequently engaged in debates on the respective merits of Buddhism and Christianity. The bishop had little but contempt for the Buddhist faith, and Mongkut often appears to have been forced to admit that some of the beliefs and practices of the average Buddhist were incompatible with the new scientific facts brought from the West. As a result, Mongkut became intent on removing the mass of accretions and superstitions from what he knew to be the true deep core of Buddhism.

Admirable as this may appear to his twentieth-century admirers, especially those steeped in Western education, most leading Siamese of the 1830s found Mongkut's acceptance of a Burmese point of view regarding ordination, and his translation of this into a re-enactment of the ritual, extremely contentious and dangerous issues, implying doubt about the validity of the ordination of all other monks in Siam. At the same time, Mongkut's contact with Europeans had led him to reject as fables several of the most highly revered Siamese classics, such as the *Traiphumikhatha*. Rama III might have been sympathetic to a serious attempt to eradicate some lax practices that may have crept into the Siamese *Sangha*, but on no account could he view with equanimity the Burmese-inspired re-ordination.

---

[49] Prince Dhani Nivat, 'Inscriptions of Wat Phra Jetubon', p. 19.

[50] Lingat, 'La vie réligieuse', p. 33.

Rama III's motivation in arranging Mongkut's appointment as abbot of Wat Bowoniwet should not, therefore, be regarded as a sign of royal support for the reform movement.[51] It is more likely that the king had been informed of Mongkut's unorthodox activities and that he placed him in Wat Bowoniwet in order to draw him more into traditional Siamese life, away from the relative isolation of Wat Samorai, also away from the intellectual stimulus that might have come from the contacts with Pallegoix. He may also have expected that the responsibility of being abbot of such a large organization would help Mongkut to settle down in the *Sangha*. Mongkut was to remain just over fourteen years as abbot of Wat Bowoniwet, where he was able to put into practice many of the ideas he had developed earlier. There was a stricter adherence to the rules in Wat Bowoniwet and a great deal of intellectual inquiry, which set Prince Mongkut and his followers apart. Rama III may have been successful in that Mongkut did not develop his new approach into a direct confrontation with the rest of the *Sangha*. This movement did not break off and establish a separate *nikaya* with the name *Thammayutikanikaya* until after Mongkut's death.[52]

Prince Mongkut's activities may thus have been occasionally frowned upon by the king. The same can be said about those of his younger brother, *chaofa kromakhun* Itsaret, who had developed an even keener appetite for matters European. At the beginning of the decade, Gutzlaff had described him as follows:

> Chow-fa-nooi, *the younger brother of the late king and the rightful heir of the crown,[53] is a youth of about 23, possessing some abilities, which are however swallowed up in childishness. He speaks the English language; can write a little, imitate works of European artisans; and is a decided friend of European sciences and of Christianity. He courts the friendship of every European; holds free conversation with him, and is anxious to learn whatever he can. He is beloved by the whole nation, which is wearied out by heavy taxes; but his elder brother, Chow-fa-yay,* who is just now a priest, is still more *beloved.[54]*

In December 1835 it was rumored that Prince Itsaret was considered as a husband for Rama III's favorite daughter and that his appointment as *Uparat* was imminent. Bradley noted that the prince was treading lightly so as not to incur the king's displeasure. Other missionaries appear to have received the same impression.[55] It is not known whether Itsaret had been encouraged in this belief by some action of his elder half-brother, or whether this was the *chaofa's* way of giving a hint, in the hope it might be followed up. At any rate, after some twelve months the rumor died out and Itsaret remained in his old position at the court.

[51] If the king had been an enthusiastic supporter of Mongkut's ideas, he could have arranged much greater honors than an abbotship in Bangkok. It has recently been suggested, however, that Mongkut's behavior was not altogether exemplary and that he had repeatedly left the order for amorous reasons, only to be reordained again (see Ki Thanit, *Prawat Khana Song Thai kap Thammayutprakan*, pp. 96-106).

[52] Over time the *Thammayutikanikaya* gained privileges that were resented by many monks of the mainstream *Mahanikaya*. In the 1930s this led to widespread protests. For details, see Walter Skrobanek, *Buddhistische Politik in Thailand; mit besonderer Berücksichtigung des heterodoxen Messianismus*, Beiträge zur Südasien-Forschung, Südasien-Institut, Universität Heidelberg, Wiesbaden: Franz Steiner Verlag, 1976, pp.124-51.

[53] Gutzlaff is wrong in two particulars: Itsaret was not the brother of Rama II, but his son, and he was not the rightful heir to the crown. However, it is quite possible that the prince liked to give the impression to foreigners that he was the legitimate and rightful heir.

[54] Gutzlaff, 'Journal of a Residence in Siam', *Chinese Repository* 1 (1832), p. 19. Gutzlaff's journal was reprinted in Anthony Farrington (ed.), *Early Missionaries in Bangkok; The Journals of Tomlin, Gutzlaff and Abeel 1828-1832*, Bangkok: White Lotus, 2001, pp. 65-90.

[55] W. L. Cowan, 'The Role of Prince Chuthamani in the Modernizing of Siam and His Court Position During the Reigns of Rama III and Rama IV', *JSS* 55, pt 1 (1967), pp. 49-50.

Opium Suppression

Since the second reign the import of opium had been forbidden by the Siamese government, but at first the law forbidding its import was openly flouted.[56] It was not until the late 1830s that the Siamese government became active in the suppression of illegal opium trade and the robber bands conducting this trade. The first big concerted drive was in 1837, when many weapons and much opium were handed in to government officials in return for a free pardon.[57] The following year some of the *Phrakhlang's* men heard about a ship transporting opium. Soldiers were able to catch one Chinese smuggler red-handed. Through him, an intricate network of opium traders was discovered. In 1839 a final free pardon was offered to those who surrendered opium, and the penalty for being caught and convicted was increased from the traditional fine – ten times the value of the contraband articles found – to the death penalty. Four committees of senior officers were formed to clear up the evil of opium in specific regions. The clearing of the Bangkok district was given to the three most powerful Siamese of the day: *kromaluang* Rakronaret, the king's uncle and the highest-ranking prince in the country, *chaophraya* Bodindecha and *chaophraya Phrakhlang*.[58] This drive achieved some success. The *Records of the Astrologers* mention laconically that opium was found in the city and beyond.[59]

The American missionaries' printing press was used to print ten thousand copies of the royal edict against the sale and use of opium. Relations between the relatively newly arrived Protestant missionaries and the court had become very cordial. Apart from printing the royal decree, Bradley had been paid 240 *baht* for inoculating some ten thousand Siamese against smallpox between January and April 1839, 'principally in the palace and in the families of the nobles.'[60] The missionary account of the drive against opium trafficking is as follows:

For nearly two months, the king's officers have been scouring the country, and numbers have been thrown into prison for endeavouring to secrete the drug. The king seems determined to free the country of this drug, at all hazards. We pity the poor creatures who have been accustomed to use it, but cannot but rejoice at the prospect of the removal of so great an evil. His majesty, however, has permitted a very small quantity to be restored to those who cannot break off the use of it immediately, but gives them to understand, that when it is gone they are to have no more for ever. Two or three ships from Singapore, etc. happening to come up at the time having, as was said, opium were obliged to secrete it and take it back. The opium business is not yet completed; new discoveries are daily made, and for a number of days past, it is said the burning of the precious drug has gone on at a great rate.[61]

[56] Farrington, *Early Missionaries*, p. 144.

[57] *Chotmaihethon*, p. 52. This is the event alluded to in Rama III's proclamation of 1839, which appeared in the *Singapore Free Press*, 13 June 1839. It was reprinted in the July 1839 edition of *The Chinese Repository* (vol. 5, pp. 125-32) and again Bowring, *The Kingdom and People of Siam*, vol. 2, pp. 368-77. The translation is a remarkable piece of work in that it is practically unintelligible to those unfamiliar with the Siamese language; it is a literal translation by someone apparently unfamiliar with Siamese court language and legal terms.

[58] *Chinese Repository* 5, p. 131.

[59] *Chotmaihethon*, p. 53.

[60] *Chinese Repository* 8 (November 1839), p. 384. The king's interest in European technology caused *chaofa* Itsaret to indulge openly in European pastimes, impressing fellow-Siamese with daily sessions of 'watch-repairing' where he would sit with a pair of huge goggles protruding from his eyes, fixing some clock. Itsaret still liked to impress his European friends with the romantic fantasy that he was in fact a 'prisoner', someone jealously watched and guarded. At the same time this did not prevent him from organizing, at great expense, a noisy Christmas party in December 1840, where British sailors were encouraged to drink to excess, dance, play leap-frog and demonstrate a boxing match. For details see F. A. Neale, *Narrative of a Residence in Siam*, pp. 87-94.

[61] *Chinese Repository* 8 (November 1839), p. 384. Early 2003 there was a similar government-led drive to combat the use of drugs, this time concentrating on the widespread use of amphetamines.

The spate of robber-band and opium-trade suppression in the late 1830s can probably best be understood by taking the wider trade practices into account. Opium had been imported into Siam for a considerable time. Originally it had been almost exclusively consumed by Chinese, the great number of Chinese immigrants causing an increased demand for the product. At the end of Rama I's reign opium-trading and consumption was already felt to be a problem, hence Rama II's edict against the sale and use of the drug. In this the Siamese king followed the Chinese emperor's example of 1796.[62] Opium was being produced in various areas of British India and loaded onto British trading vessels at Calcutta. Traders sent the chests of opium to local dealers, mainly in China, but also directly or indirectly to those in Siam. By 1832, when the matter of Indian revenue was discussed in the British Parliament, mercenary interests outweighed considerations of morality and justice, hence the opium trade gained the semi-official approval of the British government. This was one of the factors involved in the rapid increase of opium production in India. In 1820 just over 4,000 chests of opium were sold in Calcutta, whilst by 1830 this had increased to more than 8,700 chests, by 1835 almost to 13,000 chests, by 1837 to circa 16,000 chests, almost all of this opium destined for the Chinese market.[63]

In China, as in Siam, the number of addicts rose, the central government issued harsher warnings, increasing the fines and punishment. One result of the severe legislation, coupled with increased supply and demand, was that in both countries the trade was forced 'underground': secret networks were set up to carry on this lucrative business. The big Siamese drive against the opium traffic in the late 1830s may be seen as the central government's realization that the illegal trade had reached such dangerous proportions that the use of opium had to be regarded as an endemic social evil. It is no coincidence that the Chinese emperor also decided in late 1839 to send one of his ablest and most trusted mandarins as special commissioner to Canton to suppress the opium trade.[64] However, while the Siamese were able to conclude their drive with limited success, the Chinese became involved in a series of confrontations with British merchants that led to the Opium War.

The Siamese opium problem was by no means resolved by the raids following the decree of 1839. By 1844, opium was being imported again with the tacit agreement of state officers. In addition, a large number of people had switched to using cannabis (kancha), which could be grown locally. The government's stance in protecting the people from the ill effects of opium was weakened by its lenient attitude to alcoholic intoxication, for the Treasury gained a large sum every year through tax-farming liquor licenses throughout the country. Finlayson had reported that the license for the Bangkok district brought the government a sum of 72,000 baht in 1822; this had risen by

[62] There are many sources dealing with the opium trade between India and China. The figures mentioned here are mainly drawn from E. W. Stoughton, 'The Opium Trade – England and China', Hunt's Merchants' Magazine 2 (1840), pp. 394-413.

[63] Apparently the Calcutta market was not the only source for opium, because the total number of chests brought in by the clippers is reported in a contemporary source to have been 34,000 (see 'The Opium Trade with China', Christian Examiner 24, no. 48 (1838), pp. 114-5).

[64] See A. Waley, The Opium War through Chinese Eyes.

1832 to 104,900 *baht*,[65] the trade in intoxicating spirits having become one of the largest sources of income.[66]

Renewed Expeditions to the Outer Regions

The southern dependencies were fairly restful after the expedition of the *chaophraya Phrakhlang* in 1832. Six years later, however, trouble began again in Kedah, which was attacked by supporters of the deposed sultan. The revolt spread into an anti-Siamese movement and at one stage even the Siamese stronghold of Songkhla was threatened. The governors of Nakhon Si Thammarat and Songkhla assembled all their forces, urgently asked for reinforcements from Bangkok, and gave battle. The Malay insurgents suffered defeat just before the advance troops from the capital arrived. Though the large army that arrived in April 1839 was too late to assist in the suppression of the revolt, the situation in the south remained tense, so it was not until 1842 that the Bangkok forces could be withdrawn.[67]

Late in 1840 the Siamese were again drawn into a conflict on their eastern borders. Cambodia had been a Vietnamese buffer state since 1834, but in 1840 there was a general popular revolt against Vietnamese rule. Cambodian representatives came to Bangkok to ask for the return of a scion of the Cambodian royal family residing in Siam, to become their new king, besides asking for assistance in throwing off the Vietnamese yoke. Various armies from Siam, mainly consisting of people of Cambodian descent,[68] rallied to liberate their country. After a few skirmishes, the Siamese advance came to a halt. For several years Cambodia was partly under Vietnamese control and partly under that of the Siamese, each side sponsoring their own candidate for the Cambodian throne. Gradually, the Siamese-backed candidate gained the upper hand, and in the late 1840s the Siamese could once more count Cambodia as their eastern buffer state.[69]

Hunter's Expulsion

It may be recalled that the *chaophraya Phrakhlang* had decided in 1835 to build square-rigged vessels. These proved seaworthy and further ships were commissioned.[70] Thus the *Singapore Free Press* on 27 July 1837 noticed the arrival of

> *his Siamese majesty's frigate 'Conqueror', a vessel of 600 tons, Just launched from the docks at Chantibun [Chanthaburi]. She is armed with forty guns, of what calibre it is not said; but, notwithstanding her warlike equipment and name, she is at present to be employed only as a peaceful carrier of the goods of his golden-footed majesty's subjects. Another vessel of 1,000 tons has*

[65] E. Roberts, *Embassy to the Eastern Courts of Cochin-China, Siam and Muscat*, p. 426. A missionary mentions a much larger sum for 1832, namely forty-five *piculs* of silver, or 180,000 *baht* (*Chinese Repository* 13 [April 1844], p. 202).

[66] *Chinese Repository* 13, pp. 215-7.

[67] Further details in Vella, *Siam Under Rama III*, pp. 71-73. For a view from the neighbouring State of kelantan, see Cyril Skinner, *The Civil War in Kelantan in 1839*, Monographs of the Malaysian Branch, Royal Asiatic Society, Singapore: Malaysia Printers, 1965.

[68] Possibly a reaction to the hostile reception of Siamese troops in 1834.

[69] Further details can be found in *PKRt Sam*, pp. 208-14; Vella, *Siam Under Rama III*, pp. 101-5; and Chandler, 'Cambodia's Relations', pp. 165-9.

[70] It is unlikely that anyone would still have remembered the unfortunate experiences with an earlier European-type shipbuilding in Siam, the building of a galleon in 1725, a joint venture of the Spanish of the Philippines and the Siamese king. That ship was apparently very badly built, made a few short runs, requiring extensive repairs after each journey, and was finally pronounced not seaworthy and condemned at a great loss to the owners. For details, see *Chinese Repository* 8 (1839-40), pp. 258-9. During the reign of Rama II, several square-rigged trading vessels had been built, and these were used especially as the king's vessels during the missions to China, but also for general trading purposes (see R. Adey Moore, 'An Early British Merchant in Bangkok', *JSS* 11, pt 2 [1914-15], p. 25).

been laid down, and is to be similarly equipped and employed.[71]

Rama III planned to create a royal fleet of Western-style ships which would be able to augment the king's income by trading and at the same time be heavily armed – by local standards – so as to increase Siamese might. Gradually new ships were added to this incipient merchant navy. According to reports, by 1847 the king had eleven to thirteen European-type ships, with his nobles owning another six.[72]

It was not long before the king gained confidence in the new venture, and by 1840 he became a serious competitor for Robert Hunter, who until then had a virtual monopoly of space in European vessels, which he rented out to Siamese traders. In 1841 a shipment of teak in the hands of the firm of Hunter and Hayes was seized and confiscated. Until then, the product had been allowed to be shipped openly. The next year, the king suddenly declared a new levy on sugar leaving the country, and by seizing part of the cargo being handled by Hunter's firm, managed to extract a large sum.[73] Hunter's remonstrations were to no avail, even though the Siamese had been deeply shocked to hear that the British had attacked China and were waging a war in which the Chinese suffered defeat after defeat. Hunter's firm provided Siam with chain cables which were drawn over the mouth of the River Chaophraya, where the forts were also repaired and partly rebuilt. At the same time Hunter, who had been supplying the king with arms, ordered 250 guns of small caliber from England, in anticipation of hostilities between England and Siam.

In this tense atmosphere the Siamese asked Hunter to supply Siam with a modern armed steamship, so that the country could be defended against the expected attack by the British when they returned victorious from China. However, when the British troops returned to India without stopping at Bangkok, the king, possibly feeling that Hunter had misled him about the situation, no longer wanted the arms or the vessel.[74]

The growing hostility between merchants and the Siamese government is demonstrated in a series of remonstrations and memoranda sent to the British authorities. Hunter and Hayes report a case of mishandling of a British subject by the Siamese authorities[75] and repeatedly accuse the Siamese of acting contrary to the treaty of 1826. They would have welcomed a show of power from a few British warships, and at least one influential senior officer sympathized with them and stated that 'such a measure would tend to do good throughout the Malayan Archipelago, where the Petty Chiefs have assumed a tone quite inconsistent with their insignificance'.[76]

Relations between Hunter and the Siamese government deteriorated further. It became known that Hunter had sold

---

[71] 'Journal of Occurrences', *Chinese Repository* 6, p. 256.

[72] Vella, *Siam Under Rama III*, p. 128, citing the *Bangkok Calendar* 1847, 1850.

[73] Letter from J. Hayes to the governor of Prince of Wales Island, Singapore, and Malacca, dated 1 November 1843, *Burney Papers*, 4, pt 2, pp. 92-4.

[74] Letter from W. B. Butterworth, governor of Prince of Wales Island, Singapore, and Malacca to the Government of India, dated 8 November 1843, *Burney Papers*, 4, pt 2, pp. 88-89; see also p. 162.

[75] In January 1844 the British authorities received a detailed statement from the *krom Phrakhlang* regarding their handling of cases of smuggling. This statement was detailed and convincing. The British authorities accepted that Hunter and Hayes had not informed them properly in this matter, and this was noted in the subsequent confrontation.

[76] *Burney Papers*, 4, pt 2, p. 91.

opium[77] thus knowingly breaking Siamese laws. Early in 1844 two Chinese traders were given the right to collect the new sugar levy for a prearranged fee, which made the new tax a more permanent feature of the state revenue. It seems that at this time the steamship ordered, a vessel called the *Express*, arrived, and Hunter learned that Rama III was no longer interested in buying it. Apparently Hunter declared that if the agreed price for the ship were not paid, he would sell it to the Vietnamese.[78] Thereupon he was ordered out of the country and left on the *Express* for Calcutta. Hunter tried hard to convince the British authorities of the need to send a punitive expedition against the 'ignorant and haughty despot', but the British authorities found that there was no flagrant breach of the existing treaties and also that Hunter had brought much of his trouble upon himself, and no action was taken. It was noted, however, that there were grounds for a revision of the international trade agreements between the two countries.[79] In July 1844 Hunter made a voyage to Bangkok, where he was coolly received. He obtained permission to remove his personal possessions. In December 1844 he finally left the country, ending a relationship which had lasted just over twenty years.

The events leading up to Hunter's expulsion from Siam demonstrate the deep impression China's defeat had made upon the court. Up until 1840 the emperor of China had been regarded as the world's most powerful person. From the Siamese point of view, the Chinese nation was on a different scale from 'ordinary' countries such as Annam, Burma, and until 1840, also countries such as the United States of America, France, and Britain. Britain's conquest of lower Burma in the 1820s had shaken this view, but the relative might of the European weaponry and European command of a new technology was definitely established in the eyes of the Siamese court during the Opium War.

The confrontation with Hunter had come about when the British merchants, probably wishing to pay back for the unexpected seizure of teak and for the sugar levy, had gladly helped spread the rumor that British troops would make a foray into Siam. Cashing in on Siamese ignorance regarding British intentions did not succeed when the king realized the merchants' duplicity. Hunter's loyalty was not to the British, as was shown by his supplying weaponry to Siam, but neither was it to the Siamese, as was proven by his threat to sell the steamer to Siam's greatest foe at that time: the Vietnamese.

Rama III's decision to expel Hunter was therefore not unjustified. At the same time it may be noted that Hunter and Hayes were not physically molested, never called before a tribunal, their possessions not confiscated, though Siamese law – which at that time applied also to British residents in Siam – would have called for severe punishment for some of Hunter's

[77] Letter from the *Phrakhlang* to the governor of Prince of Wales Island, Singapore, and Malacca, *Burney Papers*, 4, pt 2, p. 102. See also Vella, *Siam Under Rama III*, p. 129; C. M. Wilson, 'State and Society in the Reign of Mongkut, 1851-1868: Thailand on the Eve of Modernization', p. 180 and p. 187; and Adey Moore, 'An Early British Merchant', pp. 29-30.

[78] Letter from W. J. Butterworth, governor of Prince of Wales Island, Singapore, and Malacca to the Government of India, dated 13 February 1845, *Burney Papers*, 4, pt 2, p. 163 and p. 165.

[79] *Ibid.*, p. 162.

actions. At any time he could have been arrested for dealing in opium or for threatening the safety of the kingdom. On the whole, the Siamese acted with caution and restraint, no doubt aware of the fact that Hunter would attempt to call in an expeditionary force. However, Hunter seems to have brandished that weapon so often that his ability to call in troops must have been doubted. The Siamese action shows that in 1840 Siamese confidence was fairly strong and, no longer depending on Hunter's arms supplies, now preferred to act without him.

Meanwhile Hunter's case was soon overshadowed by local problems. In 1844 yet another opium-smuggling ring was discovered; it was clear that Chinese secret societies were deeply involved in the continuing opium trade. In this and the following year a series of raids was made by government forces to break up some of these secret societies.[80] This was also a year with a considerable rice shortage: the price of a cartload of unhusked rice rose to 18 *chang*, or 1,440 *baht* and there was widespread famine.

Hunter's hurried departure marked for the time being both the end of the merchant's position of power and influence at the court, and a cloud of suspicion that now surrounded all Westerners. Only the staunchest believers in European technology continued for a while to flirt with the West. Prince Mongkut in particular had been very friendly with the American missionaries, from whom he had obtained some good medical advice.[81] During the years when Europeans were favored, Mongkut had learnt something of printing techniques, and also commenced learning English. He continued his English lessons in 1845 and 1846 with Jesse Caswell, one of the American Protestant missionaries. However, upon a strong hint from the king that he disliked his subjects learning English, the classes stopped.[82] Late in 1845 Siam's first English language periodical, the fortnightly *Bangkok Recorder*, was discontinued after having been printed for just over a year. The main reason for its lack of success was apparently the fact that the news-sheet was too blatantly a vehicle for missionary propaganda.[83]

Chaofa Itsaret must have been the last high-ranking Siamese to demonstrate publicly pro-European leanings in the 1840s. With the help of his European friends, Itsaret had obtained a small steam-engine and had it fitted in a ship in which he traveled up and down the Chaophraya River. Eventually, however, even Itsaret sensed the mood at the court and in 1847 he abandoned his pro-Western display.

The Chinese Revolt

Early in 1848 riots broke out among the Chinese in the region between Nakhon Chaisi and Sakhonburi, west of Bangkok. A

[80] *Chotmaihethon*, pp. 60-1.

[81] D. B. Bradley's journal entry for 23 April 1836. An interesting account of the early days of Bradley's medical practice can be found in *Chinese Repository* 5 (1837), pp. 445-56. Prince Mongkut was treated for paralysis of a facial nerve, a condition affecting his physiognomy throughout his life.

[82] W. L. Bradley, 'Prince Mongkut and Jesse Caldwell', *JSS* 54, 1 (1966), pp. 31-2.

[83] See D. B. Bradley's remarks in his private journal on 12 May 1867, when the new publication the *Siam Weekly Monitor* is being discussed. Details regarding the *Bangkok Recorder* can be found in *Periodicals and Newspapers Printed in Thailand between 1844-1934, a Bibliography*, p. 3. The *Bangkok Recorder* was revived in 1865.

police force sent to establish order met with violence. Consequently, the *chaophraya Phrakhlang* took a large number of troops and suppressed the revolt, killing some three to four hundred Chinese and taking a few hundred prisoners. This was followed by the news of an even larger uprising east of Bangkok in the provincial town of Chachoengsao, where the Chinese rebels were reported to have taken the local fortress. This time the nation's two most senior generals, *chaophraya* Bodindecha and *chaophraya Phrakhlang*, took several thousand soldiers to Chachoengsao. Meanwhile, the folly of open revolt had been seen by a faction of the Chinese, who aided the Siamese in retaking the fort. In the aftermath of this rebellion thousands of Chinese were massacred. A great number of sugar plantations were also destroyed during the hostilities.

Both uprisings seem to have been caused by a rapidly worsening economic situation in the sugar plantations, probably the result of the imposition of a series of new taxes on sugar refineries and on the finished product. It might be argued that Rama III's policy of increasing the tax burden in order to raise state revenue had been pushed much too far with respect to sugar.[84] The ensuing massacre may be interpreted as a sign that enmity and feelings of aggression had developed between Siamese and Chinese.

The Case of Prince Rakronaret

For many years Rama III's uncle Prince Rakronaret, who in 1832 had been promoted from *kromamu'n* rank to that of *kromaluang*, had been the most senior relative of the king. He had been given many responsibilities, especially in the judiciary. In this respect his position resembled that of Rama III when he was still Prince Chetsadabodin, during the latter part of the reign of Rama II. Prince Rakronaret was disappointed in his hope of becoming *Uparat* in 1832 when Prince Sakdiphonlasep died. Nevertheless, he had retained his powerful position that entitled him to many perks of office. It was reported that Rakronaret and other powerful princes had indulged in abuse of power. Such princes were reported to have arrested members of the populace and influenced the judging of legal cases to their own advantage. For example, some princes would take attractive girls to be their concubines without obtaining the permission of parents or guardians.[85] Since the highest princes were involved in such cases, people dared not protest. However, in November 1848 the king received a formal complaint and an inquiry was made into the legality of the prince's actions. Rakronaret's personal life was investigated and it became clear that he had often acted immorally and dishonorably. In addition, his ambition to become *Uparat* was revealed, togeth-

---

[84] Vella, *Siam Under Rama III*, p. 18; G. W. Skinner, *Chinese Society in Thailand*, pp. 143-4.

[85] *PKRt Sam*, p. 361.

er with his opinion that he would stand a good chance to be Rama III's successor. Rakronaret was found guilty and Rama III ordered his execution.

Rama III and the Representatives of Western Culture, 1849-50

In June 1849 Bangkok was again ravaged by a serious cholera epidemic, reminiscent of the days of 1819 and 1822. In a few weeks an estimated thirty to thirty-five thousand people died. One of the victims was *chaophraya* Bodindecha, the head of the *krom Mahatthai*.[86] Rama III emulated the measures his father had taken to combat the disease, admonishing people to generate good *karma*. One of the traditional methods of doing so was by freeing all captive animals. However, the Christian missionaries at first refused to condone what they considered heathen ceremonies. A situation reminiscent of Taksin's confrontation with European priests developed – a Siamese king, already distrustful of Westerners, found that his measures intended for the good of the country were being opposed. In this case, however, both Protestant and Catholic missionaries, decided to ease their consciences by considering this releasing of animals to be a civil state ceremony rather than an act pertaining to a false religion, and cooperated with the king. However, as a result Rama III ordered an investigation into the activities of foreign missionaries, following which he had four Protestant converts arrested on several charges. First the missionaries had printed documents pertaining to Siamese laws without having obtained the necessary permission. Then the Siamese translation of the Bible contained sacred expressions borrowed from Buddhism. Finally the foreign missionaries persisted in depicting Siamese Buddhism as a false creed.[87]

This action of Rama III has been depicted as a reflection of the king's increasing distrust of foreigners as well as of his worsening health.[88] This view is not wholly supported by evidence. Rama III distrusted foreigners, but this was already apparent at the beginning of his reign. His wariness abated a little in the 1830s, but it returned when the most prominent Westerner, Hunter, who had been granted many favors at court, proved to be a grasping and selfish man with no loyalty to the country where he was making his fortune. The Western priests' refusal to help 'make merit' in order to combat an outbreak of cholera must have looked like further proof that Europeans had no concern for Siam's welfare.

At the same time, Rama III's reaction, understandable as it was, was not precipitate or hasty. When he discovered that the Protestant printers were acting in contravention of Siamese regulations, he did not force the missionaries to go to court and

---

[86] Letter by the American missionary S. R. House, reported in *Chinese Repository* 18 (September 1849). pp. 503-4. See also Wells, *Protestant Work in Thailand*, p. 1.

[87] *PKRt Sam*, pp. 330-1; Vella, *Siam Under Rama III*, pp. 36-7.

[88] *Ibid.*, p. 37.

listen to charges. Instead he vented his anger upon a few Siamese subjects who were close to the missionaries. From Rama III's point of view, the missionaries were offensive. He was a king, intensely proud of the best achievements of Siamese culture, as exemplified by the display at Wat Chetuphon, and the missionaries' public denigration of Buddhism must have offended him.[89]

The failure of two Western trade missions in 1850 has been depicted as a further sign of Rama III's choleric, stubborn anti-Western policy. Again, the circumstances in which the missions failed are not wholly in accordance with the view that the king and the 'conservatives' at the court obstructed more friendly relations between Siam and foreign powers.

The first mission to arrive was that of Joseph Balastier, the American consul at Singapore, who was sent to attempt to secure better trade conditions and obtain permission to establish an American consulate in Bangkok. Balastier came armed with a letter from the American president, but he arrived at the court bringing only a Chinese servant and a local missionary as his retinue. The Siamese had looked forward to receiving the delegation with all honors, but became suspicious of Balastier's credentials when he arrived so unceremoniously.

To make matters worse, Balastier's initial interview with *phraya* Siphiphat, the *chaophraya* Phrakhlang's younger relative and deputy, went very badly. Balastier cut straight through the traditional preliminary questions and answers and demanded an audience with the king. He and *phraya* Siphiphat could not come to an agreement regarding matters of protocol and the interview ended in an atmosphere of hostility. When the *chaophraya Phrakhlang* returned to Bangkok, from Chumphon, where he had been supervising a tattooing drive, attempts were made to reopen meaningful contact, but no progress was made and Balastier left Bangkok without having met any other high officials. His whole attempt had lasted less than a month.[90] The failure of the mission was clearly the result of Balastier's inability to adapt to Siamese protocol. The American envoy displayed such a lack of dignity and, to Siamese feelings, such a rude directness, that all Siamese who were involved were united in their efforts to shield the king from such an unpredictable and strange individual. The king never set eyes upon Balastier and he can hardly have been sorry to miss an audience with that American.

The second envoy to reach Bangkok in 1850 was Sir James Brooke, sent by Lord Palmerston to attempt to improve commercial relations between Siam and Britain. He arrived in August at the mouth of the Chaophraya River, and ominously, the larger of the two steamers on which the mission traveled became stuck in the mud. Brooke had to transfer to the smaller boat to proceed further. His preliminary meeting with the *chaophraya Phrakhlang* went smoothly, and by the end of

[89] The 'University in Stone' was officially opened in 1848 (*Chotmaihethon*, p. 61).

[90] A detailed account of Balastier's dealings with members of the court is given in '*Chotmaihet ru'ang Ballestier Thut Amerikan khaoma nai Ratchakan thi Sam mu'a pi cho Ph.S.2393*', *PP.* vol. 35 (1969), pp. 3-71.

August he had good hopes of securing a favorable result. However, suddenly at the end of August 1850 a marked change occurred in the conduct of the Siamese towards the mission: everybody became distrustful and cold. Brooke valiantly wrote several proposals for a new treaty, but received nothing but evasive replies. He too left Bangkok feeling insulted at not having seen the king.[91]

In Brooke's case the *chaophraya Phrakhlang* had advised the king to agree to a new treaty. The king, however, had Brooke's credentials examined and found them wanting. Even before Brooke had his meeting with the *chaophraya Phrakhlang* the king had already issued an order not to proceed with positive discussions. The available sources do not reveal what exactly decided the king to act against the *chaophraya Phrakhlang's* advice. He certainly was not alone in his view, because several other senior ministers also disagreed with the *chaophraya Phrakhlang* on this matter.[92]

When it was clear that his mission was not going to succeed, Brooke did not attempt to hide his ill feelings. To Lord Palmerston he wrote advising nothing less than a British take-over: 'The time for conciliation with this people never was; reasonable remonstrance will no longer be attended to, a blockade would aggravate and not cure – and intimidation will fail unless followed up to its legitimate consequences.'[93]

Brooke had been aware that there were people at the Siamese court who would favor a new treaty with Britain. When he was still preparing for his voyage to Bangkok and residing for a while in Singapore, he was told of the existence of two princes at the court who were generally favorably inclined towards Europeans. Rather prophetically he had written about *chaofa* Mongkut and his younger brother *chaofa kromakhun* Itsaret as 'worthy instruments' to bring about better relations between the two countries.[94] From this letter it is also clear that in Singapore the myth of Rama III usurping the throne and the *chaofa* princes being the legitimate heirs to the throne was generally believed.

In Bangkok, however, the problem of the succession looked quite different. In principle there was nothing to prevent Rama III from elevating his chief wife to be the queen and nominating a series of relatives to *chaofa* rank. However, he refrained from doing so, just as he had deliberately omitted to fill the position of *Uparat* when it had become vacant, possibly because he was himself full of vigor and did not find any of his relatives outstanding enough to merit an elevation to the Front Palace. However, speculation remained rife at the court, and as the king became older it seemed that the two *chaofa* princes had the best chances of succession to the throne, not least because of their friendship with members of the *chaophraya Phrakhlang's* family. The elder of the two himself liked to point

[91] For details, see N. Tarling, 'Siam and Sir James Brooke', *JSS* 48, pt 2 (1960), pp. 43-72.

[92] Vella, *Siam Under Rama III*, p. 135.

[93] Dispatch from Singapore, 5 October 1850, as cited by Wilson, 'State and Society', pp. 190-1.

[94] Tarling, 'Siam and Sir James Brooke', p. 49.

out to foreign acquaintances that his name was Mongkut, which meant 'crown', so that his name, could be rendered in English 'His Royal Highness the Crown Prince'.[95]

The End of the Reign

The king became ill in September 1850. At first the illness was treated as a temporary lapse of health. However, when his condition worsened, he was forced to discuss his succession. At first the king asked a committee to select a successor, a highly irregular procedure. The committee could not come to a conclusion and reported back that it was inappropriate to discuss such matters when the king was ill and that they hoped he would soon recover. Realizing that there was no one who would please all parties, Rama III reputedly discussed some of the candidates frankly with *phraya* Sisuriyawong, then *chang-wang* of the *Mahatlek*:

> *I cannot see any prince who can lead the country. For example,* kromakhun *Det [Detadison] is a gullible person, whatever people tell him, he will readily believe it, he cannot be the leader. As to* kromakhun *Phiphit [Phiphitphuben] he does not know how to work, he has not got an enquiring mind, he only thinks of his pleasure, he has not got the character to look after the country. That leaves us only the two* chaofa *princes about whom I have reservations, namely that the elder [prince Mongkut] holds Mon [Buddhist] beliefs, and if he became king he might order the* Sangha *to dress like the Mons throughout this country; whilst the younger* chaofa *prince does have knowledge about various matters concerning warfare, this is not sufficient to lead a government, he only loves pleasure and therefore he has not got my approval.*[96]

If this account is a faithful record of what was said, it is clear that the Siamese king dispassionately went through a list of possible candidates. It is interesting to note that the *chaofa* princes were not mentioned first and succession by them was not seen as the only legitimate course, a view often expressed in later literature. Of the four candidates, the king was enthusiastic about none, but of all the objections, the ones against Mongkut seem the least devastating. The statement demonstrates that Rama III was not wholly in agreement with Mongkut's reformist movement. The fact that Mongkut and his followers wore the Buddhist robes in a manner that differed from that of the rest of the Siamese *Sangha* evidently preyed on the king's mind, because in late February, after having donated large sums of money to many monks, Rama III had ordered all monks to dress in an orthodox fashion, and the 'reformists' were quite mortified to lose such a distinguishing feature.[97]

[95] As in his letter to G. W. Eddy, dated July 14, 1848. See M. R. Seni and M. R. Kukrit Pramoj, *A King of Siam Speaks*, Bangkok: The Siam Society, 1987, pp. 12-3.

[96] *PKRt Sam*, p. 365.

[97] D. B. Bradley, journal, 1 March 1851.

When the king's health further deteriorated, full executive responsibility fell upon the *chaophraya Phrakhlang* as the most senior and experienced administrator.[98] On 15 March, when it seemed that the king would not survive the night, the *chaophraya Phrakhlang* made the crucial decision regarding the succession. He formally invited Prince Mongkut to become heir to the throne and, when the latter accepted, ordered troops to guard the future king at his monastery. Not long afterwards, on 2 April 1851, Rama III died, aged sixty-three, having been in command for just over twenty-five years.

The third reign is often depicted as reactionary and conservative, probably as a result of the failure of Western powers to secure a firm trading base in Siam. However, as shown here, the Siamese were willing to renegotiate the existing treaties and more diplomatic and sensitive envoys could have secured much of what was being sought. At the beginning of Rama III's reign the Burmese had suffered a humiliating defeat by the British; and fourteen years later the Chinese had a similar experience. Throughout the reign, Europeans appeared everywhere to be increasingly aggressive and expanding their territorial domination. The Dutch strengthened their hold upon the Indonesian archipelago and the French felt obliged to stage several naval demonstrations against the Vietnamese. In these circumstances Rama III appears fully justified in his noncommittal and circumspect dealings. While keeping foreigners at a distance, he did not close off his country altogether. With laudatory prudence, Rama III usually avoided direct clashes with foreigners and when forced to react, as in the case of Hunter, he did so without provocative harshness. In so far as the policies of Siamese kings helped the country escape becoming a colony, Rama III certainly deserves to be recognized as a shrewd leader who managed to sail the ship of state through a stretch of turbulent waters.

---

[98] After the death of *chaophraya* Bodindecha in 1849, the *chaophraya Phrakhlang*, who still held simultaneously the position of *Kalahom*, was by far the most powerful man in the kingdom next to the king.

Plate 7. A drawing of Chinese junks by W. Alexander, London 1803.
(Courtesy The Old Maps & Prints, River City)

Plate 8. A drawing of King Mongkut and Queen Thepsisin, New York, 1882.
(Courtesy The Old Maps & Prints, River City)

6

THE BEGINNING OF WESTERNIZATION
(1851-1868)

The Succession

Prince Mongkut's succession to the throne was decided just before Rama III's demise. The best account of the events was written on 28 March, 1851 when Rama III was still alive.

> *All parties concerned in the question of the succession were preparing themselves with arms and troops for self-defense and resistance. There is no doubt that had it been determined that the King's sons should have the throne there would have been a fearful civil war here before now. It now appears that on the night of the 15th inst. when the King was very low, when the affairs of the Royal palace seemed to be on the very eve of a terrible outbreak, there was convened at the King's Palace, or at a place within its walls, a meeting of all the Princes, nobles, and chief rulers of the land to confer together on the all engrossing question who shall become the successor of the present king. Up to this time it would seem that no one of the three political parties had ventured to take any very positive steps to carry out its intentions. Each party maintained great reserve towards the others, and consequently they became suspicious of each other's intentions, and were ready at a word to come into fearful collision.*
>
> *As His Excellency the Phraklang, the prime minister of the foreign department, was one of the most powerful rulers of the land, he was vehemently pressed to declare his purposes touching the question before them. He had borne a conspicuous part in placing the present king on the throne, and he had ever been a highly favourite ruler under him. This minister, it is said, had the boldness to declare firmly that he saw no man in the kingdom, who had equal claims with his Royal Highness T. Y. Chaufat Mongkut with his brother Chaufat Krommakhun Izaret as his colleague to become successor to the Throne.[1]*

The presentation of Mongkut and his brother as a pair, to succeed their elder half-brother, is unusual. It would have been more in accordance with Siamese custom if Mongkut had been chosen king, and after his enthronement had formally announced who would be made *Uparat*. The proclamation of the head of the Front Palace at such an early stage in the

---

[1] Letter by D. B. Bradley, dated 28 March 1851, to the *Singapore Straits Times*, as published in W. L. Bradley, 'The Accession of King Mongkut', *JSS* 57, pt 1 (1969), p. 156.

proceedings was probably the result of a difficult compromise. The choice of Mongkut as the new king must have been a great disappointment to Itsaret, who had long regarded himself as the leader of the 'modernists'. He had many more connections with Westerners, spoke better English than did Mongkut and was known as a leading innovator with a passion for technical reform.[2] In October 1848 the *Singapore Free Press* had published a glowing account of his first steamboat, with its two-horsepower engine. 'This little phenomenon has made several trips up and down the river, his Royal Highness the Prince generally acting steersman himself, in full view of thousands of astonished and admiring spectators, who crowded the banks of the river on each occasion.'[3] Itsaret had a much more intimate knowledge of the workings of the administration than Mongkut. While Mongkut did not even hold *krom* rank, Itsaret had risen from *kromamu'n* rank to *kromakhun*.

Undoubtedly Itsaret had hoped to become king himself, and that Mongkut and the *chaophraya Phrakhlang*, aware of this ambition, attempted to overcome Itsaret's objections to being delegated to second place by giving an extraordinary amount of honor and attention to that office. This would explain why both brothers were formally invited to succeed Rama III, and why both received the oaths of allegiance.[4] Only a week after Rama III's death, D. B. Bradley, prompted by the king-elect Mongkut, wrote to the *Straits Times* about Prince Itsaret: '[He] is to have titles equally honourable though the part he will take in the government must necessarily be a little lower than that of his elder brother.'[5]

The honors bestowed upon Mongkut's younger brother were quite unprecedented. His regular income from the Treasury was doubled to 160,000 *baht*. After his formal investiture, he was given a royal tour of the city, and in his official name could be found the royal epithet *chao yu hua*, 'the Lord in Charge'. How much the 'Second King' valued the epithet is shown by the fact that he often used it as part of his signature. In his correspondence with Europeans and Americans Mongkut usually called himself *Somdetch Phra Paramendr Maha* Mongkut (which he abbreviated to S. P. P. M. Mongkut), but his brother signed letters 'S. Pin Klaw chau yu hua, Second King of Siam'. The words 'Pin Klaw' refer to names devised by Mongkut not long after ascending the throne.

In common parlance, people had often called the reign of Rama I *phaendin ton*, or 'the first reign' and that of Rama II *phaendin klang*, or 'the middle reign'. Already during Rama III's time these reigns had been officially named *Phraphuthayotfachulalok* and *Phraphuthaloetlasulalai* respectively, probably in order to avoid the implication that the third reign would be called 'the last'. Mongkut changed the appella-

---

[2] Details can be found in Somathat Thewet, *Chaofa Chuthamani*.

[3] A. L. Moffat, *Mongkut, the King of Siam*, pp. 49-50. A photograph of this eight-meter steamer can be found in Somathat, *Chaofa Chuthamani*, p. 123.

[4] *Chaophraya* Thiphakorawong, *The Dynastic Chronicles Bangkok Era, The Fourth Reign*, trans. Chadin Flood [hereafter *DC Fourth R*], vol. 1, p. 4.

[5] Bradley, 'Accession of King Mongkut', p. 160.

tion of his father slightly to *Phraphuthaloetlanaphalai*, and not long afterwards issued a decree in which he announced a name for the third ruler: *Phra Nangklao*. While it was traditional to give a king a name posthumously, Mongkut broke with tradition by himself devising specific appellations for himself and his younger brother: King *Phra Chomklao* and King *Phra Pinklao* respectively.

All these unprecedented honors bestowed upon the king's younger brother may have blinded some observers to the Second King's actual position in court. He was seldom involved in matters of state and he did not have the ear of the king or the king's chief advisers. The Second King was engrossed in enlarging his collection of European goods, which in 1855 was described as a 'museum of models, nautical and philosophical instruments, and a variety of scientific and other curiosities'.[6] He used his position as Second king to try to impress his English friends in particular, but in the Siamese court he increasingly became an isolated, somewhat ridiculous figure.[7]

The New Administration

The general populace appeared genuinely glad to celebrate Mongkut's accession. The military parade and royal procession after the formal anointment were such cheerful events that the new king abruptly decided to extend the festivities another day and to add a boat procession to the program. Palace attendants must have worked long hours to prepare the more than ten thousand wooden presents, in the shape of legendary fruit painted red and green, in which money was hidden. From the royal state barge, these gifts were dropped in the water as gifts to the well-wishing populace. During the following week yet another procession took place, this time with Phra Pinklao as the center of attraction, who at great personal expense also gave away money and gold and silver flowers to Siamese and foreign spectators.[8]

The long list of promotions in the royal family of 1851 can best be understood by considering Mongkut's personal position genealogically. The new king came to the throne at the ripe age of forty-seven, and although the royal family was quite extensive, there were not many alive who were older than Mongkut himself. Eight of these elderly relatives were given high ranks, often skipping several steps in the princely ladder of *krom* ranks, three being created *kromaluang*, three *kromphra*, and two *kromsomdetphra*. The two selected for the highest honors were Mongkut's uncle, the Buddhist monk who became *kromsomdetphra* Paramanuchitchinorot, and Prince Dechadison. Two of Mongkut's younger half-brothers were promoted to

[6] Sir John Bowring, *The Kingdom and People of Siam*, vol. 2, p. 449.

[7] Mongkut's sarcastic remarks in a letter to his envoys in London bear witness to this. See Moffat, Mongkut, pp. 56-8, citing a typescript by Seni and Kukrit Pramoj entitled 'The King of Siam Speaks', pp. 222-7. This letter was written in 1858. See also D. B. Bradley's journal entry for 19 October 1851.

[8] For details, see *DC Fourth R*, vol. 1, pp. 6-49.

kromaluang, one being Prince Wongsathirat, who was to become one of King Mongkut's closest advisers. One of Mongkut's older relatives became *kromakhun* and so did two of his younger half-brothers. Twenty-one younger relatives received the lowest *krom* rank of *kromamu'n*. These were five younger half-brothers, ten of Rama III's children, and six sons of the long-deceased *Uparat* of the second reign, Prince Senanurak.[9]

An interesting feature of the long list of promotions is the honor done to offspring of former *Uparats*. It is possible that Mongkut decided to include them to boost further the dignity of the office of *Uparat* and thus soothe his brother's injured pride. Mongkut's bestowal of posthumous titles on previous *Uparats* may also be seen in this light. By the fourth reign the *krom* titles had lost their former direct link with state duties. They had become primarily a princely honor, a sign of the king's approval.

There were many changes in the civilian ranks of the administration. By 1851 the chief state executives were the brothers Bunnak, who held the top position in the Treasury and the acting headship of the *Kalahom*, and *phraya* Racha-suphawadi, acting head of the *Mahatthai* ministry. Almost all senior posts, as well as many lower positions, had become vacant during the later years of the third reign. Mongkut had therefore ample scope to select a vigorous team. First and foremost came the *Phrakhlang* (Dit Bunnak) who had been a minister of state since 1822 and whose word had decided the succession. Since he already occupied the top of the civil honors scale, Mongkut, for the first time since the development of the *saktina* system, broke the rule that a commoner could not hold more than 10,000 *rai*. He awarded the *Phrakhlang* honors appropriate to that of a royal prince with *krom* rank, his *saktina* was raised to 30,000 *rai*, his title was raised to the new rank of *somdet chaophraya*, he was given a new name engraved on a golden nameplate, a special umbrella, palanquin, a new sword of state and a new seal, and his personal attendants were raised in rank. The *Phrakhlang* became Siam's 'senior statesman', with executive authority throughout the kingdom. Similar honors were given to the *Phrakhlang's* brother, *phraya* Siphiphat. The two brothers became known as the Elder somdet (*somdet ong yai*) and the Younger *somdet* (*somdet ong noi*). It has been recorded that, during the auspicious occasion of the Younger *somdet's* receiving a new name in September 1851, King Mongkut prostrated himself before the two *somdet chaophraya* officials.[10] Such a humble act would have been quite unthinkable in any Siamese king other than Mongkut, who during the first two or three years of his reign occasionally shocked the courtiers by breaking all protocol. Even taking Mongkut's unorthodox character into account, the king's public prostration

[9] *Ibid.*, pp. 49-57. The king's own two eldest sons and Phra Pinklao's eldest son, who are mentioned by Thipha-korawong in this list, were probably promoted to *kromamu'n* rank at some later date during the Fourth Reign.

[10] There can be little doubt as to the accuracy of this information, which derives from D. B. Bradley's personal journal (the entry for 9 September 1851), for Bradley was sitting quite close to the two men.

may be seen as the strongest evidence for the view that the Bunnak brothers were 'kingmakers', and that Mongkut felt he ought to express his gratitude.

The Elder *somdet's* son (Chuang Bunnak) was given the rank of *chaophraya*, and retained his name of Sisuriyawong. He was placed in charge of the *krom Kalahom* and had such a prominent place in the administration that Europeans and Americans referred to him from early 1852 as the 'Prime Minister'.[11] The king offered him princely insignia, which he apparently did not accept. Yet another member of the Bunnak family, one of Dit Bunnak's sons, Kham, was soon raised to *chaophraya* rank, with duties in the Harbour Department, a subsidiary of the Treasury.[12]

At no stage of Siamese history had one family been able to gain so many prominent positions in the administration. In the junior appointments, the key posts also went to members of the Bunnak family, *chaophraya* Sisuriyawong's son was given his father's old place in the *Mahatlek*, and one of the positions of *changwang* of the royal pages went to Yaem Bunnak, *phraya* Siphiphat's son, whilst another of Siphiphat's sons gained a place in his father's section at the Treasury.[13]

While various members of the Bunnak family occupied the most influential and lucrative posts, some gaining honors beyond that which could be traditionally expected, only one other official was singled out for exceptional honor: *phraya* Rachasuphawadi, the last member of the triumvirate who controlled Siam's administration at the end of the third reign. He was promoted to *chaophraya* Nikorabadin and also received his full new name on a golden nameplate.[14] All other appointments and insignia of rank were in accordance with the system in use during the previous reigns. The *krom Na* was given to *chamu'n* Sisorarak, who thus became *chaophraya* Phonlathep.[15] *Phraya* Phetphichai became *chaophraya* Thammathikon, head of the *krom Wang*.[16] A *phraya* Surasena became *chaophraya* Yomarat, leading the *krom Mu'ang*.

In 1851 the new administration was entrusted with its first major task: the enlargement of Bangkok's city area by the digging of a new canal parallel with the existing outer moat, but further out from the center. The new canal, more than five kilometers in length, was dug, just as in previous reigns, with the help of Chinese labor. The whole project was placed in the hands of *chaophraya* Sisuriyawong and his son *chamu'n* Waiworanat (Won Bunnak), who completed the whole work in ten months at a cost of more than 31,000 *baht*.[17] The expense was of little consequence to the king, because Rama III had left unprecedented funds in the Treasury, reputedly 3,200,000 *baht* in silver and 8,000 *baht* in gold.[18] The work also involved building forts approximately a kilometer-and-a-half apart along the canal, as well as constructing forts on the Chaophraya River, at the city

[11] D. B. Bradley journal entry for 7 February 1852.

[12] In this case, rank is not commensurate with position in the administration. It must be regarded as one of the ways of honoring the Bunnak family.

[13] C. M. Wilson, 'State and Society in the Reign of Mongkut, 1851-1868', p. 325.

[14] *DC Fourth R*, vol. 1, p. 65.

[15] He died soon afterwards (*DC Fourth R*, vol. 1, p. 48).

[16] This official died in August 1861, aged seventy-five (*DC Fourth R*, vol. 1, p. 243).

[17] *DC Fourth R*, vol. 1, p. 90.

[18] Wilson, 'State and Society', p. 609.

boundary. These forts were built to give the people of Bangkok a sense of security and to impress foreign visitors. In addition, a small stronghold was constructed solely for the purpose of firing salutes, which can be seen as a clear indication of the new Siamese administration's wish to accommodate itself to European customs. A European man-of-war visiting a foreign nation had to greet that nation's flag with twenty-one gun shots while hoisting the flag on the forward mast. A fortress or ship of the nation visited was expected to return the honor with an equal number of shots. This alien custom had caused anxiety and misunderstanding among many Asian states, where the firing of guns had invariably been interpreted as the crudest and most blatant token of aggression.

There were other signs of the new government's pro-Western stance. At the beginning of his reign, Mongkut ordered that all those attending the king's audience must wear an upper garment to complement the formal dress, a ruling intended to make the court 'more civilized' in the eyes of the world.[19]

During the first three years of Mongkut's reign the European and American trading and missionary community was especially favored. In July 1851 customs duty was almost halved, and during the first year of the reign restrictions on rice export were lifted and a state opium monopoly was established, to obtain some measure of control over its use.[20] In August a group of missionary women were admitted to the inner palace to set up a class, mainly to teach the English language.[21] On 18 October, the king's birthday, all Westerners were entertained in European style. During the cremation rituals for the late king, which were attended by many foreigners, King Mongkut espied Bradley and suddenly clambered down from his platform to shake the American's hand.

> *This mark of respect was regarded as being a great departure from the customs of all former kings of Siam. The Officers of Government of the highest rank skulked away from His Majesty in order to get as low before him as they could. One of them remarked after the king returned: 'Where has Siam ever heard of a king who was pleased to show so much respect to Foreigners'. Another said: 'He would not do this to sailors. He will do it only to foreigners of respectability like the Doctors'.*[22]

In July 1853 the king presented a plot of land to the Protestant missions to use as a cemetery. In January of the following year he decided to have his family vaccinated against smallpox.[23] However, all was not well in the kingdom and the great sometimes unreasonable expectations cherished by many Europeans at the time of Mongkut's accession were not fulfilled.[24] The first frustrations arose during the campaign in Burmese-controlled territory.

[19] *DC Fourth R*, vol. 1, pp. 5-6.

[20] O. Frankfurter, 'The Mission of Sir James Brooke to Siam', *JSS* 8, pt 3 (1911), p. 31.

[21] This class was set up on 14 August 1851, upon the repeated request of King Mongkut (see D. B. Bradley's journal entries for 13, 14, 16 and 30 August 1851.

[22] Bradley's journal entry for 6 May 1852. The cremation rituals were held between 25 April and 9 May of that year.

[23] Bradley's journal entry for 21 January 1854.

[24] D. B. Bradley, moved by sentiments not unlike those of the French missionaries in the mid-1680s, believed a massive conversion possible, and he used his greatly increased status as one of the court's regular physicians and husband of one of the teachers in the palace to go and preach all around town, in public places as well as in Buddhist temples. He was in these years so sure of himself that he did not bend to local customs. Witness his personal diary for 31 August 1851:

In the morning preached to a company of Siamese on a bridge over a canal out far from my house. The bridge had over it a cool cover and upon it comfortable seats. While preaching boatloads of priests came along in the canal and wished me to move off from the bridge so that they might pass under without contracting sin. It is one of the teachings of Buddhism that it is wicked to live or pass under any person, particularly if the person or persons are female, I kept my seat and told them that I did not believe in such foolishness - they replied. Then we cannot pass - Well, said I, be it so. I shall not humour such a notion as that. Presently they put their paddles in the water with unusual force and spray [and moved] through with all their might.

The Battle of Chiangtung

In 1851, not long after Mongkut had been elevated to the throne, a serious confrontation arose between Britain and Burma. Three British warships were dispatched to Rangoon in order to force the Burmese king to cease anti-British action. The Burmese met the challenge of a blockade with troops and a few cannon shots. Thereupon the British commander destroyed every Burmese war boat within reach and returned to Calcutta to report. During most of 1852 there was war between Britain and Burma. The British seized some coastal towns, and when the Burmese king did not negotiate for peace, the invading army continued its progress, gradually occupying most of lower Burma. Eventually, early in 1853, a palace revolution brought a new king, Mindon, to the throne, who immediately sued for peace. To his consternation he discovered that the British had resolved to annex the whole of lower Burma, which cut off Amarapura from the sea.

The Burmese involvement in a full-scale war and the subsequent loss of Burmese territory were major factors in Siam's decision to send an army to Chiangtung, one of the Shan towns traditionally under Burmese overlordship. The Burmese hold over towns such as Chiangtung and Chiangrung was only indirect, the local Shan *sawbhas*[25] managing their own affairs. However, Siam's attack upon Chiangtung was not merely an opportunistic gesture resulting from Burma's weakness. It was also provoked by a succession struggle in the town of Chiangrung, in which one of the contending parties had requested Siamese recognition. Rama III had decided to throw his support behind this faction and had ordered his northern vassal states of Chiang Mai, Lamphun, and Lampang to assemble an army and attack Chiangtung, so as to free the whole of the Tai-Lue area from Burmese control. This army had been duly dispatched and reached Chiangtung in February 1850. However, the various generals quarreled among themselves and supplies ran out, so that the troops had been withdrawn in July 1850.[26]

The chief ministers advised Mongkut to assist again Chiangrung, and since Chiangrung was subject to Chiangtung, it was necessary to make another effort to subdue the latter town. It was expected that the campaign would bring honor to the king and the country, and that both officers and men would gain skill in warfare. This time, the battle would be under direct Bangkok control. Mongkut's younger brother, *kromaluang* Wongsathirat, was given general command, with the *chaophraya Yomarat* as second-in-command. The latter left Bangkok in October, 1852, with authority to recruit troops from Chiang Mai, Lampang, and Lamphun. In the following month *kromaluang* Wongsathirat went to do likewise in Nan, Phrae,

[25] The Shan people of Burma speak Tai languages, and this title is related to the Siamese *chaofa*, or 'celestial prince'.

[26] *PKRt Sam*, pp. 339-40; see also *DC Fourth R*, vol. 3, pp. 69-70; W. F. Vella, *Siam Under Rama III*, pp. 92-3; and Wilson, 'State and Society', pp. 522-3

and Lomsak. In March 1853 the Siamese-led armies arrived before the walls of Chiangtung, where, however, leaders had long been forewarned and prepared their defense. The attackers soon suffered a lack of fresh water for the elephants and horses and they ran into gunfire from unsuspected fortified positions in the hills. Moreover, the Siamese generals found to their alarm that their troops were not in the least motivated to give battle to the Chiangtung defenders. When Wongsathirat reported to Bangkok that there was fraternization among his troops and the local populace,[27] Mongkut recalled his half-brother for consultation. However, Wongsathirat did not heed this command, replying that he wanted additional troops and was preparing to attack again after the rainy season was over. The king was displeased with Wongsathirat and in June 1853 asked him once more to return to Bangkok, an order again disobeyed.[28] At the same time Mongkut tried to persuade the rulers of Chiang Mai, Lampang and Lamphun to take up arms with more enthusiasm; he elevated all three of them from *phraya* rank to that of *chao* and gave them insignia and regalia commensurate with their position as semi-independent rulers of vassal states.[29] Mongkut finally seems to have agreed to let Wongsathirat attack Chiangtung for a second time. In late October that year, *chaophraya* Sisuriyawong went up north to meet Wongsathirat and *chaophraya* Yomarat in order to give instructions and hand over weapons and some troops.[30] By November the weather permitted large-scale troop movements, and a new expedition was formed. The recruiting of troops had not been as successful as expected and morale again was low, even though this time the army was better supplied than the year before. However, when Wongsathirat arrived before Chiangtung he found that he had to give battle to Burmese troops, because by this time the Anglo-Burmese war had come to an end and King Mindon had been able to send some reinforcements. Moreover, the ruler of Chiangtung had been able to enlist large numbers of local troops. During the ensuing skirmishes the Siamese ran low in ammunition and food. To make matters worse, the army under the leadership of the *chaophraya* Yomarat, which had taken a different route to Chiangtung, had run into severe problems and failed to arrive. Disease broke out among the beleaguerers and when the rainy season of 1854 began, the siege was broken off and the Siamese returned to Chiang Mai. When the news of the failed expedition reached Bangkok, Mongkut decided to call off the whole campaign.[31]

This expedition must have had a sobering effect upon Siam's leaders. In 1852 they had believed that a large number of troops combined with some rather sophisticated weaponry would be sufficient to give them an easy victory. However, the modern guns were heavy, and the troops were not trained in the use and positioning of artillery. There were many other factors

[27] Letter dated 15 May 1853, cited in Wilson, 'State and Society', pp. 527-8.

[28] Wilson, 'State and Society', p. 529.

[29] *DC Fourth R*, pp. 59-60.

[30] *Chaophraya* Sisuriyawong and a detachment of soldiers left Bangkok on 28 October 1853 (see Bradley's journal, 2 November 1853).

[31] Short accounts of the expedition can be found in *DC Fourth R*, vol. 1, p. 93-5, 109-10, and 118-9; King Mongkut's account has been published in Bowring, *Kingdom and People of Siam*, vol. 2, pp. 364-7; see also Wilson 'State and Society', pp. 525-33.

leading to the ignominious retreat; they included problems of supply, disease among men, elephants and horses, and the spirited defense by Chiangtung's leaders. Possibly the most important factors, however, were the lack of military discipline and morale among the Siamese-led soldiers.

Relations with the West, 1854-56

In most standard history books dealing with this period, the treaty between Britain and Siam dominates the scene. The fact that it may be called a successful treaty which had a great impact upon the development of the country makes it eminently suitable as a feather in King Mongkut's cap. In biographical accounts we find statements such as: 'When Sir John Bowring arrived at the head of a British mission, he [King Mongkut] received him with open arms and the two became firm friends. Within a relatively short time, they agreed upon a diplomatic and commercial treaty that was mutually advantageous to both countries.'[32] In reality, Mongkut's role in the drawing up of the treaty was not as prominent as such statements would lead us to believe.

In mid-1854 a rumor regarding the imminent arrival of an American punitive mission headed by the redoubtable Commodore M. C. Perry alarmed Bangkok; the forts at Paknam and Paklat were put in fighting order, and the chain cable purchased during the previous reign was prepared for positioning across the river to prevent the Americans from entering.[33] It is not clear what caused such a panic in the capital. Possibly it was the outcome of a confrontation between the king and a certain 'Captain' Trail, which had resulted in Trail's imprisonment. Trail was released and reinstated in his old command, but he had to atone for having displeased the king by undergoing a formal bathing ceremony in Ayutthaya.[34] These events were reported in the *Straits Times*, together with an account of the disastrous expedition to Chiangtung, and a note of disappointment that Mongkut's reign had not been able to improve matters for foreigners or for the Siamese people. Foreigners were greatly inconvenienced by Siamese customs officials, while the Siamese were oppressed by taxes. People were fined for not obeying the king's commands regarding the use of proper language.[35] Mongkut was accused of treating his officers more like dogs than human beings, of not consulting with his ministers and spending his time with his wives instead of looking after the country's welfare. This very critical report, apparently written by some irate Westerner, caused great consternation at court.

All European and American residents were summoned to the residency of *chaophraya* Sisuriyawong, where they were asked to give a written testimony that the statements in the

[32] J. Blofeld, *King Maha Mongkut of Siam*, p. 79. Similar remarks can be found in D. R. SarDesai, *British Trade and Expansion in Southeast Asia, 1830-1914*, pp. 89-90.

[33] Anonymous letter, dated Bangkok 12 July 1854, which appeared in the *Straits Times* on 12 September 1854.

[34] *Ibid*. No other information could be found on Trail. The name occurs three times in the 1894 Directory for Bangkok and Siam, E. Trail being the First Engineer H. S. M. S. Coronation, and J. and W. Trail, both employed at the Royal Dock Yard.

[35] King Mongkut apparently was very interested in the Siamese language, and he occasionally made a declaration on the use of words. In Proclamation 68, for example, he forbids the classifier *tua* to be used in connection with elephants. The author of the letter states that the word 'cupper' was forbidden by the king, who decreed that 'ca-cone' should be used instead. Apparently the king wished to ban the Burmese-derived word *kapi*, and advocated the use of the Siamese word *khoei*.

article were untrue. However, while there were some statements that might have been considered false, there were many 'which had much the appearance of being true.'[36] The Westerners decided to declare instead that they were 'in many respects more pleasantly situated under the reign of His Majesty Somdet Phra Chom Klao,'[37] an answer that could hardly have satisfied the king.

In subsequent inquiries it was found that not long before one of the American missionaries had a small altercation with Siamese customs officials.[38] Since rapacious customs men feature large in the article, the king decided for himself that this missionary was the author, or that at least he had furnished the author with details. To make matters worse, two months later, on 5 December 1854, while the king was travelling along the new canal around much of the city as part of the festive celebration surrounding its completion,[39] he noticed a new Western-style house being constructed much nearer the edge of the canal than the regulations allowed. Upon inquiring, he learnt that it was being built for the same missionary suspected of authorship of the critical letter. The king had not even given permission for that plot of land to be used by foreigners. Greatly enraged, he had the Siamese parties involved with the land-transaction thrown into prison and forbade Protestant missionaries to travel down-river. If they resisted the king's officers in the execution of their duties, they could be shot without warning. If the missionaries could find a ship in which to leave the country, he would be glad to have them go.[40] The Protestant missionaries who had harbored such high hopes at the beginning of the reign now found their projects suspended, their Siamese teachers arrested, their building program halted, their pupils remaining home and most of their servants absconding.

Subsequent inquiries showed that *chaophraya* Sisuriyawong himself had given permission for the house site on the canal to be rented to the foreigners and the people arrested were soon released. The interdiction against Protestant missionaries' going down-river remained in force until April of the following year, when Sir John Bowring, the governor of Hong Kong, interceded on their behalf. *Chaophraya* Sisuriyawong was embarrassed by the affair, since his seal had been attached to the documents. When Bradley visited the Bunnaks to prescribe medicine, he met Sisuriyawong, who declared frankly that he considered the whole case to be nothing but foolishness and that he was quite dissatisfied with this manner of conducting matters of state. During Rama III's time there had been a government, but at present there was no government.[41] Three months later he again criticized the state of affairs in Siam.[42]

Early in 1855 Sir John Bowring arrived in Bangkok to negotiate a new treaty between Britain and Siam. The failure of the Brooke mission in 1850 had been felt by Mongkut and

---

[36] Bradley, journal, 28 September 1854.

[37] *Ibid.*

[38] Apparently it was Samuel J. Smith, calling for the luggage of J. H. Chandler and Robert Telford, representatives of the American Baptist Missionary Union (see Bowring, *Kingdom and People of Siam*, vol. 1, p. 388).

[39] *DC Fourth R*, vol. 1, p. 123.

[40] Bradley, journal, entries for 18, 24, and 27 December 1854.

[41] *Ibid.*, 4 January 1855.

[42] N. Tarling, 'The Mission of Sir John Bowring to Siam', *JSS* 50, pt 2 (1962), p. 96; the tension between Mongkut and Sisuriyawong was visible even during an official audience, where Sisuriyawong knitted his brows and 'pished' several times at the king's words (see Tarling, 'The Bowring Mission: The Mellersh Narrative', *JSS* 63, pt 1 (1975), p. 118).

Sisuriyawong to be an unfortunate development, and as early as May 1851, on the day after his enthronement, Mongkut had written to the British authorities about resuming negotiations.[43] Britain undoubtedly had now supplanted China in Siamese eyes as the most powerful nation in the world. Although Mongkut had sent 'tribute-bearing' missions to China in 1851 and 1852, this time-honored custom lapsed after that.[44] Great efforts were made to receive the first foreign envoy in a proper manner. Robert Hunter's old residence was refurbished to house the mission. Lengthy and intricate deliberations took place between Bowring, his son John, and Harry S. Parkes, the consul at Amoy, on the one hand, and the four most powerful Bunnaks (the Elder *somdet*, the Younger *somdet*, the *Kalahom*, and his brother Kham, who was acting *Phrakhlang*) and Prince Wongsathirat on the other hand. Published and unpublished sources bear out the general conclusion of Bowring's personal journal, that Sisuriyawong played a greater role in the treaty than King Mongkut himself.[45] The four Bunnaks controlled much of the country's internal and external trade, and by agreeing to lower many specific taxes they appear to have been the first affected.

King Mongkut's contribution seems to have been largely ceremonial; during the private audience with Bowring the details of the proposed treaty were not discussed. The king appeared mainly concerned with the exchange of presents between Queen Victoria and himself. Subsequent events show that Mongkut was personally opposed to some articles in the treaty and acted to prevent their application. *Kromaluang* Wongsathirat had already warned Parkes and Bowring's son that the treaty was almost wholly Sisuriyawong's responsibility, that they could not always count on the king's support, adding that the situation might abruptly change through the king's sudden displeasure, hoping that should disagreement occur the British government would view the matter with indulgent consideration.[46]

However, in 1855 the Bowring treaty was still in draft form when the envoy departed on 23 April 1855. Three days later the court became preoccupied with local events. The Elder *somdet* (Dit Bunnak) died[47] leaving his brother the Younger *somdet* and his son Sisuriyawong as the most senior administrators in the country. In May the king wrote to Bradley offering a hospital site. This proposal, which earlier had won the support of Prince Wongsathirat, was received with some enthusiasm by the Younger *somdet* who offered to supply all the wood needed for such a building. Bradley let this moment pass, however, and it was not until the next reign that Bangkok's first hospital was erected. A white elephant which had been brought to Bangkok with great pomp and ceremony earlier in the year – and with which King Mongkut especially identified, since it had been

[43] Letter to the governor of Prince of Wales Island, Malacca, and Singapore, dated 22 May 1851, in 'English Correspondence of King Mongkut', ed. G. Coedès, *JSS* 21, pt 1 (1927), pp. 8-9.

[44] G. W. Skinner, *Chinese Society in Thailand*, p. 47; *DC Fourth R*, vol. 1, pp. 47-8 and 86-90.

[45] Tarling, 'Mission of Sir John Bowring', p. 93. See also B. J. Terwiel, 'The Bowring Treaty: Imperialism and the Indigenous Perspective', the *JSS* 79, pt 2, 1992, pp. 40-7.

[46] Tarling, 'Mission of Sir John Bowring', p. 110.

[47] Thiphakorawong (*DC Fourth R*, vol. 1, p. 129) places the death one day earlier. I have relied here upon Bradley's journal entry for 26 April 1855.

established that the animal had been born approximately at the beginning of his reign – died in September.

The year had also its more encouraging signs for Mongkut. In November the king's first steamboat was launched, a vessel of about forty tons with a twelve-horsepower engine, built for Sisuriyawong, with the assistance of J. H. Chandler, one of the American missionaries. The monarch astonished his people by suddenly boarding the vessel for a pleasure ride. The ship took pride of place in the royal procession to Ayutthaya, where the king toured until the end of the year. Almost immediately, enterprising families in Bangkok ordered steam engines for a timber mill, a rice mill, and further ships.[48]

During the year 1856 the relations between Siam and Western nations determined to a large extent the widening rift between the king and the most senior members of the administration. The first foreign envoy to arrive in 1856 was Harry Parkes, returning from England where he had spent much time explaining the background and significance of the various treaty articles. Apart from ratification of the treaty, Parkes also carried letters from Queen Victoria and many presents. However, when the presents were transferred onto another ship in bad weather in Singapore, a great number of them were accidentally saturated with sea water.[49] The letters were undamaged, however, and they provided Parkes with the means of getting into direct contact with King Mongkut and drawing him into the further negotiations necessary to make the treaty more effective in the eyes of the British authorities.

Parkes was well aware of the tension between Sisuriyawong and the king. Mongkut found that too many concessions had been made and held the opinion that the Japanese were making a more favorable treaty with the Americans.[50] Sisuriyawong complained to Parkes that his counsel was no longer sought or listened to by the king, who received more favorably those advisers who advocated a strong stance against British-imposed changes.[51] Mongkut was not, however, prepared to insult the British envoy and received him graciously, readily agreeing to ratify the treaty and promising to do his utmost to correct any misunderstanding that might arise from ignorance or lack of knowledge regarding the articles of the treaty. Mongkut's warning that his 'half-civilized' and 'half-barbarous' people might misunderstand the treaty provide a clue to his tactics. There is, namely, good reason to believe that he intended secretly to obstruct the treaty, while openly professing his greatest satisfaction with the new relationship between the two countries.[52] The king's real intentions are revealed in his handbill, distributed when Parkes arrived, forbidding any Siamese to sell land to foreigners. When Parkes demanded an explanation, it was denied that the king had anything to do with it.[53] When proclamations explaining the treaty had to be printed,

[48] Bradley's journal entries for 9, 10, 12 November and 25 December 1855. The vessel was named 'The Royal Seat of the Siamese Forces' (an example of Mongkut's habit of translating Siamese idiomatic expressions into their literal English equivalent).

[49] A list of the presents and the state in which they were received can be found in King Mongkut's letter to Queen Victoria, published in 'English Correspondence of King Mongkut', JSS 21, pt 1 (1927), pp. 18-20.

[50] Apparently the king had not seen the actual treaty, which had been concluded at the end of March 1854, and soon after the American envoy Townsend Harris arrived, the Phrakhlang asked him for a copy. Harris replied that he would send one later. See M. E. Cosenza, ed., The Complete Journal of Townsend Harris, p. 104.

[51] These revealing comments have been published in N. Tarling, 'Harry Parkes' Negotiations in Bangkok in 1856', JSS 53, pt 2 (1965), p. 168.

[52] For the exact words, see Tarling, 'Harry Parkes' Negotiations', p. 171. Tarling does not seem to read any duplicity into the statement, possibly because he was unaware of Mongkut's actions to obstruct the treaty.

[53] Bradley, journal, 20 March 1856.

the king obstructed the work upon a flimsy pretext.[54] Bradley, who noticed the duplicity, remarked that he was very glad that 'the king has such a man as Parkes to deal with. He will henceforth find it much more difficult to carry out his craftiness than he has done!'[55]

While Parkes was applying his dexterity to gain further concessions, on 13 April 1856 the American envoy Townsend Harris arrived at the mouth of the Chaophraya River carrying a letter from President Franklin Pierce and a good number of valuable presents. The Siamese were hoping to conclude their post-treaty negotiations with Parkes quickly, but the British envoy insisted on settling many detailed questions. It was not until 15 May that Parkes finally left the country. By this time the impatient Harris was fuming, so the Siamese acted with uncommon speed, appointing a committee and negotiating at such a rate that the treaty was agreed upon, copied, translated and ready for signing before the end of the month.[56] Harris left on 31 May, despite earnest efforts by the king to delay him further so as to give Mongkut time to write a personal answer to the American president.[57]

In July and August the French envoy, Charles de Montigny, negotiated basically the same agreement that Bowring, Parkes, and Harris had wrested from the Siamese; in the following years similar exercises were repeated with the Danish, Hanseatic Republic, Portuguese, Dutch and the Prussians. Meanwhile, however, probably under the influence of the rather conservative Younger *somdet*, the king proceeded to block European and American land purchases. Mattoon, the new American consul, found it impossible to effect a transaction. In July 1856 Bradley wrote: 'It is to be feared that the king is endeavoring to play two parts directly opposed to each other. That he is secretly infusing fear of selling into the minds of the land holders – and at the same time pretending to the foreigners that he will not only give them perfect freedom to sell but also strongly urge them to do so.'[58]

During that same month the king wrote to the newly appointed British consul, C. B. Hillier, that the land the British Consulate wished to purchase belonged in part to a servant of Phra Pinklao, and that he had not the right to compel the owner to sell.[59] Matters came to a head in late September of that year when the king found out that a Siamese employed by the British consul as secretary had placed his name as witness on an agreement to lease a plot of land to a European. The secretary, Seng by name, was arrested and given ninety-nine lashes in King Mongkut's presence. Since Seng had acted upon the consul's orders and the transaction was legal under the new treaty, this punishment had the makings of an international incident. The British expressed their indignation to Prince Wongsathirat, who had the unfortunate Seng moved to his palace, where an opium plaster was applied to his back. Apparently too much opium

[54] The king put his printers in irons because they did not work to his satisfaction (see Tarling, 'Harry Parkes' Negotiations', p. 174).

[55] Bradley, journal, 10 April 1856.

[56] Harris's growing impatience is responsible for many of his caustic comments on Siam and its king. They are admirably summarized in Moffat, *Mongkut*, pp. 76-87. Harris the private person thought Mongkut 'quite as weak-minded as pedantic', while Harris the diplomat praised his 'great acquirements in many difficult languages and in the higher branches of science' (J. Wook Moon, 'United States Relations with Thailand: The mission of Townsend Harris', *Asian Profile* 1, no. 2 (1973), p. 369).

[57] Mongkut complained in no uncertain terms about Harris's hurried departure (see his letter to Franklin Pierce, published in 'English Correspondence of King Mongkut', *JSS* 21, pt 1 (1927), p. 31.

[58] Bradley, journal, 8 July 1856.

[59] 'English Correspondence of King Mongkut', *JSS* 21, pt 2 (1927), pp. 127-8.

passed through the wound into Seng's body, because he fell into a coma from which he did not awake. The British consul drew up a protest demanding Seng's body and the release of the other persons unlawfully imprisoned. Bradley, who had been called to assist Prince Wongsathirat when Seng's condition showed cause for alarm, noted:

> *It would appear that the leading rulers in the land, we call them king's cabinet, are much displeased with the late shameful conduct of His Majesty and disposed to show their disapprobation of it by unmistakable signs, even to demand of him a promise that he will henceforth take council with them on all matters concerning their relations with the English. It is quite evident that the king fears their power to depose him and has humbled himself before them.[60]*

Three days later he added:

> *The king of Siam has humbled himself much in view of the late outrage against the foreign community which he committed a few days since. He said to Mr. Mattoon today that he was willing to make an expiation of his offence by purchasing with his own personal funds ground for the British Consulate in the city and then place there a perpetual monument stating his offence and that he had given the plot of ground for the Consulate as lasting memorial of his crime. ... He fears the displeasure of Queen Victoria.[61]*

A real crisis had developed, and the king's position was, for the moment, vulnerable. Throughout the year there had been an estrangement between the king and his 'Prime Minister'. Chaophraya Sisuriyawong had felt himself unpopular with the king and also with an important faction at the court, including his uncle the Younger *somdet*. He had hinted darkly to the American envoy that there was often a change during the fourth generation of princes of a dynasty,[62] so the thought of a *coup d'état* may have crossed Sisuriyawong's mind. However, since Sisuriyawong did not have the backing of all those who were critical of the king,[63] such a move would have been quite risky and possibly accompanied by much bloodshed. Sisuriyawong was a clever and cautious man, who appears to have decided he would rather strengthen his position relative to that of the king, than risk all in open conflict.

If these were his considered tactics, they were quite successful. The anti-treaty party became silent, especially when the awkward situation was exacerbated by Hillier's death from natural causes on 18 October, only three weeks after the provocative incident. Henceforth there was no high-level obstruction against the treaties, the various foreign groups acquired the

---

[60] Bradley, journal, 3 October 1856.

[61] *Ibid.*, 6 October 1856. See also the letter of Charles Bell, the acting British consul, dated 4 December 1856, referring to a proclamation 'stating that the land has been given as an atonement for the insult offered by the seizure and putting to death of a servant of the British Consul' (cited in Wilson, 'State and Society', p. 372).

[62] The full quotation runs as follows: 'On being asked if there were often changes in the dynasty, he uttered the real republican sentiment that kings who claim their title by right of birth, often forget they originated from the people, consider themselves as superior beings and don't lend an ear to the sufferings of their subjects, – so there was often a change at the fourth generation of princes of the same dynasty' (Cosenza, *Journal of Townsend Harris*, p. 115). See also Neon Snidvongs, 'Siam's Relations with Britain and France in the Reign of King Mongkut, 1851-1868', pp. 297-8.

[63] Sisuriyawong had to reckon with the active opposition of Phra Pinklao, who may have been against his brother but certainly would not have liked to see a Bunnak on the throne. Wilson ('State and Society', p. 373) mentions hostilities between soldiers under the command of these two. Moreover, the Younger *somdet*, though a Bunnak, was quite unhappy at the prospect of foreigners having such free access to Siam, and it is likely that he would have used all his influence to forestall any possible bid by Sisuriyawong for the throne.

right to trade under more favorable conditions than before, and the consuls were granted the power to protect the interests of those who wanted to take advantage of Siam's 'opening up'.[64]

First Effects of the Treaties

The treaties had a dramatic impact upon life in Bangkok. Early in 1857 it was noted that there was a remarkable influx of traders. In January Bradley counted thirty-three square-rigged vessels in port and about as many at the mouth of the Chaophraya River.[65] By 1860 the river offered a picture of lively activity, with 'many boats, sailing vessels, steamships, etc. plying thereon, at all times, from sunrise to sunset.'[66] This is borne out by the available statistics: in 1856 there were 141 vessels, other than junks, trading with Bangkok, in 1857 there were 204, and in the following years this number gradually rose to some three to four hundred vessels.[67] The Siamese themselves were getting their share of the increased trade, for by 1860 they already had a fleet of fifteen steamships, and the local dockyards were busy building more.[68] Mercantile houses vied with each other for good sites and from the outset large profits were made. A sign of the rapid changes taking place was the sudden shortage of minted *baht*:

> *The Royal Mint cannot nearly supply deals for the merchants who bring in dollars to exchange. It turns out only enough to exchange $20,000 a week. Merchants and other foreigners under consular jurisdiction are allowed to go and exchange their dollars every Monday. As there are not ticals [baht] enough to exchange all the dollars presented, there has been a law made which gives each man the privilege of exchanging his proportion of the whole amount of dollars brought in that day. He may bring in $20,000 himself alone – and if there was no other person at the exchange but himself he would have the whole of the $20,000 exchanged. But as there are some 8 or 10 others with each 10 or 20 thousand he can get only his proportion among them. As I only had $196, my proportion was $12 for which I got 20 ticals. The whole amount presented that day was about $335,000.*[69]

Since the government could not possibly produce sufficient 'bullet-shaped' silver *bahts*, it decided to accept the Mexican dollar as legal tender at the rate of three Mexican dollars to one *baht*. At the same time new machinery for minting Siamese currency was obtained from England, and in 1860 Siam's first flat silver coins were put into circulation.[70] The introduction of new copper and tin coins met with great difficulties, however, for the public was reluctant to accept the idea

[64] On the Siamese perspective of the treaty, probably the best source is the commentary on the chronicles by Chadin Flood (see *DC Fourth R*, vol. 3, pp. 96-7).

[65] Bradley, journal, 3 January 1857.

[66] U. Guehler, 'A Letter by Sir Robert H. Schomburgk H. B. M.'s Consul in Bangkok in 1860', *JSS* 37, pt 2 (1949), pp. 151-2.

[67] For details, see Wilson, 'State and Society', p. 984. Only in 1865 did the number of ships drop dramatically, but this was undoubtedly the result of the temporary rice export ban imposed because of a bad crop in 1864/65.

[68] 'Letter by Sir Robert H. Schomburgk', p. 152.

[69] Bradley, journal, 28 February 1858.

[70] For details, see Chaloem Yongbunkoet, *Thonabat Thai*, pp. 8-20 and R. Le May, H. A. Ramsden, U. Guehler and W. H. Kneedler, *Siamese Coins and Tokens*, London: Andrew Publishing, 1977, pp. 84-5. See also 'English Correspondence of King Mongkut', *JSS* 21, pt 2 (1927), pp. 150-1 and p. 173.

that the government could guarantee a price on bits of base metal which apparently had little intrinsic value.

The sudden influx of large numbers of traders and sailors also brought an unprecedented number of disturbances. There was sporadic fighting among ships' crews, for example. The most serious incident in the first years after the treaties were signed, however, was that of late November 1857, when a party of British and Germans was assaulted and seriously hurt by a group of Buddhist monks who attempted to stop them hunting in the monastery grounds. It was an incident very similar to that of September 1835 involving Wellar. As in the Wellar case, the Europeans' representative, consul Gingell, protested and asked that justice be done. This time, however, there was no need for threats and heated words. A fortnight later the matter was settled, the abbot of the monastery concerned having been fined 240 *baht* and a special law having been enacted forbidding the use of firearms in temple grounds.[71]

In the years immediately following Hillier's death. King Mongkut's position in relation to his 'cabinet' stabilized into a situation in which many policy matters were left largely to the senior ministers, who would confer with each other, come to a decision, and transmit this decision to the king for approval.[72] This manner of working constituted a fundamental change in court procedure. Mongkut's predecessors obtained advice on policy matters in public and private audiences and then decided for themselves whose advice, if anyone's, to follow.

The king appears to have been obliged to delegate much power in respect of both foreign policy and internal matters. Thus, when in 1857 he was worried about the state of the *corvée* system, instead of ordering the various departments to prepare for a major registration, he wrote a letter to the senior administrators complaining that the lists were out of date, explaining that he had not sufficient money to hire laborers for large-scale works, and asking them whether or not it was time for a new general registration.[73] Apparently the administrators agreed that it was, and major tattooing drives were held during the following years.[74]

Although the king's influence on government had thus decreased, it would be wrong to depict him as a mere figurehead. His ceremonial role appears to have been left unaffected by the confrontation with his senior administrators, and Mongkut developed this aspect of kingship. Thus he continued to make his annual round of monasteries during the month following the Lenten season to present robes to Buddhist monks. Every year on 18 October he presided at a lavish dinner party for Europeans and Americans in honor of his birthday. He made efforts to foster his image with the population at large, taking an interest in the occasional lawsuit and finding opportunities of winning the people's gratitude for his beneficence. Thus, in

---

[71] Bradley, journal, 14 December 1857.

[72] For example, *DC Fourth R*, vol. 1, p. 179; this may be a reason for the frequency of the word *pru'ksa* (to consult, ask advice) in the description of Mongkut's relationship with his administrators, which has also been noted by Wilson, 'State and Society', p. 710.

[73] Chatthip Nartsupha and Suthy Prasartset, *Socio-economic Institutions and Cultural Change in Siam, 1851-1910, Documentary Survey*, pp. 10-11.

[74] *Ibid.*, pp. 17-24.

the middle years of the reign he sometimes called together all old and disabled persons in a district and distributed food and money to them.

In 1858 Mongkut made a lengthy tour of the eastern provinces, accompanied by many members of the court and the year after he visited many southern towns. Certain places, especially Ayutthaya, Nakhom Pathom, and Phetburi were regularly included in his itinerary. In Ayutthaya he would occasionally ceremonially receive a white elephant or accompany visitors to see the ruins or attend a rounding-up of wild elephants. In Nakhon Pathom he instigated a gigantic project, the building of a monumental *chedi* on the ruins of what presumably was the oldest Buddhist shrine in the country. At Phetburi he began building an impressive palace high up on a mountain. All these travels and activities gave him opportunities to see and meet many people who under a more orthodox king would never have had a chance to catch a glimpse of the country's highest dignitary.

Another feature of ceremonial life developed by Mongkut in the years after the crisis was the correspondence with other heads of state. Not only did letter-bearing missions involve an exchange of presents, which brought a large number of prestigious and valuable objects to fill the king's palaces, but also the fact that King Mongkut had received letters from Napoleon III, from the president of the United States, and especially from Queen Victoria, strengthened his position at court. A friendly letter from Her Britannic Majesty showed the Siamese that the world's strongest power approved of King Mongkut as ruler of Siam. It is in this respect that Mongkut's unfulfilled request for a British decoration must be seen.

It would seem that the king needed all the support he could muster, because he had lost a number of allies and associates since the beginning of his reign. His uncle *kromsomdetphra* Paramanuchitchinorot had died in 1853, and his uncles *kromaluang* Phisetsisawat and *kromphra* Ramitsaret not long after. In 1856 the king's elder half-brothers *kromphra* Phiphitphuben and *kromaluang* Phuwanet had died, followed in 1858 by the Younger *somdet*. The death of the latter left quite a vacuum at court, for the Younger *somdet* had controlled vast resources and wielded great influence. He had become more and more conservative and anti-Western in his later years and did not attempt to hide his antipathy to the innovations they had caused. With his death, the staunchest defender of 'Old Siam' had passed away. In 1859 the king's elder half-brother *kromsomdetphra* Dechadison died.[75] This prince, undoubtedly the most experienced administrator in the royal family, had held high positions in the time of Rama III and after the death of Paramanuchitchinorot, had probably become Mongkut's closest confidant.[76]

With Phra Pinklao left rather isolated, playing with his European toys and gadgets and never holding a position of real

[75] Bradley, journal 15 September 1857 and 8 February 1858. There can be no doubt that the Younger *somdet* died in 1858, and not in 1855 as D. K. Wyatt has asserted ('Family Politics in Nineteenth Century Thailand', *Journal of Southeast Asian History* 9, no. 2 (1968), p. 221), and Wilson is wrong in the dates for both the Elder and the Younger *somdet* ('State and Society', p. 715.)

[76] Wilson, 'State and Society', p. 712.

responsibility, the Siamese political scene in the middle of the reign seems dominated by four clever men who had learnt to work as a team. First there was Mongkut, who displayed a distinctive flair for public relations (occasionally marred by a fit of temper) and who was sincerely revered by much of the populace. Secondly there was Sisuriyawong, the undisputed leader of the administrators, a wealthy, clever and progressive man.[77] The third was Mongkut's half-brother Wongsathirat, who, even after his stroke in August 1861, held the confidence of both the king and Sisuriyawong. *Kromaluang* Wongsathirat was a member of all the committees negotiating treaties with foreigners and represented the king in many other capacities. The fourth was Sisuriyawong's brother, Kham Bunnak, who by the middle of the reign held the title of *chaophraya* Rawiwong and had been appointed *Phrakhlang*.[78] He appears to have been a thoughtful, trustworthy man, enjoying the respect of the other three.

These four men headed an extremely intricate administration and held effective daily control over the central delta area. At the end of the 1850s and the beginning of the 1860s they not only supervised the internal tax collection system but much of their time and energy was taken up by matters arising from the extraordinary influx of Europeans and Americans. Such new tasks were, for example: creating the post of harbor-master; drawing up of new laws; determining a satisfactory exchange rate; taxation of foreign residents and the creation of new roads to accommodate the newcomers.

However, these four were all in their fifties, an aging and vulnerable group. It was remarkable that no effort seems to have been made at the time to fill positions of power left vacant by the death of members of the royal family. Bradley remarked upon the situation as one of despondency in face of the recent changes.

> ... the usual thought among the Siamese rulers is that Siam is destined to pass into the hands of the English. They seem almost instinctively to think so and so to express themselves. And it is a remarkable fact that they are training no one for the Throne as if they really expect he will be called to it after the present incumbents shall have left it. My mind cannot light upon a single individual whom God seems in any way to be preparing for a future Sovereign in Siam. If I could see either of the present kings taking measures to educate some of their sons for the Throne as they themselves have been educated, I should by that providence be inclined to expect that the present Dynasty would be prolonged much beyond the days of the present sovereign. But they are doing no such thing. They seem to me to be wonderfully careless in educating their sons.[79]

---

[77] For a description of Sisuriyawong's European lifestyle and palace in 1861, see Philipp zu Eulenburg-Hertfeld, ed., *Ost-Asien 1860-1862 in Briefen des Grafen Fritz zu Eulenburg*, p. 350.

[78] This man was later to be appointed *chaophraya* Thiphakorawong, the compiler of many of the chronicles cited in this book.

[79] Bradley, journal, 7 November 1858.

This comment, by a man who had lived more than twenty years in Siam and who had regular access to the palaces, cannot lightly be dismissed. The surrounding world seemed to be changing rapidly into one dominated by colonial powers; the chances of Siam escaping the fate of all other traditional Asian nations must have appeared slight.[80] At the time Bradley wrote the above, the eldest *chaofa* prince, Chulalongkorn, was just five years old, much too young to be groomed for future kingship.

Siam's leaders may have been pessimistic about the country's long-term prospects of independence, but this did not prevent them from appreciating the marvels of modern technology. Late in 1858 the machinery for milling rice with the aid of steam power and a steam sawmill arrived in Bangkok from the United States. At that time King Mongkut already owned four or five steamboats, and the engines of two or three much larger ones had just arrived. *Kromaluang* Wongsathirat had his steamboat, Phra Pinklao had one or two and the engines for two or three more, and Sisuriyawong had a most elegant propeller-driven steamship and engines for several more. One enterprising missionary had imported several further steamship engines to sell to the Siamese.[81]

All this new enterprise had visible effects upon the educated youth of Bangkok. In the early 1860s the *Bangkok Calendar*[82] reported that the number of highly educated Buddhist monks had fallen dramatically since King Mongkut had come to the throne, allegedly because:

> *His present Majesty invites and allures out into secular life many of the smartest men in the Priesthood, and ... in the present reign there are many extraordinary openings for such men to enter into business, and seek pleasure and honour in the way of wealth and state preferments. The treaties of friendship and commerce which have, in this reign, been made with many western nations, thus opening Siam widely to western enterprise, and developing unlooked for native resources, have had great power to this end. This is doubtless one grand cause for the great diminution in the number in the Priesthood, which is thought to be about one-half since the beginning of the present reign.*[83]

One of the bright young men who left the shelter of monastic life, attracted by the new prospects in trade, was Thien, a novice at Wat Bowoniwet, who later became well-known as the innovative and controversial Siamese author, Thienwan. Young Thien was, according to himself, the first Siamese to adopt Western customs; he abandoned the short hair-style common in Bangkok, grew a moustache, refused to chew betel-nut, and began to wear shoes and socks.[84]

[80] It has become commonplace to endow Mongkut with extraordinary powers of foresight and depict many of his actions as part of a battle of wits to save his country from colonial domination. Evidence disproving this view is brought forward later in this chapter.

[81] Bradley, journal, 29 October 1858; see also the entry for 15 July of that year.

[82] The *Bangkok Calendar* was the first English-language annual, edited by D. B. Bradley between 1860 and 1874. In 1844 Bradley had already attempted to establish the Thai-language fortnightly *Bangkok Recorder*, a project abandoned after one year, taken up again in the English language in 1865 and abandoned in 1867. For details see *Warasan lae nangsu'phim nai Prathet Thai su'ng tiphim rawang Ph. S. 2387 - 2477, Bannanukrom, Nuai Warasan, Hosamuthaengchat.* Bangkok: Kromsinlapakon, 1970.

[83] *Bangkok Calendar*, 1863, pp. 84-5. The editor (D. B. Bradley) adds that another reason may be the diminishing faith in Buddhism, but this coming from a man who devoted many years to discrediting the worship of idols and 'false doctrines' may safely be attributed to wishful thinking.

[84] K. Rosenberg, *Nation und Fortschritt: Der Publizist Thien Wan und die Modernisierung Thailands unter König Culalongkon (r. 1868-1910)*, p. 34.

The French, Cambodia and the Succession

Britain dominated the international political scene, and the British consul therefore automatically became the senior diplomat in Bangkok. Immediately after the Bowring treaty was signed, the Siamese sent an embassy to London. The French also were rapidly becoming a formidable power in the region, and the king suggested that the French send a ship to carry a mission to Paris. The embassy arrived at its destination in June 1861; it was cordially received by Napoleon III and enabled to visit major industrial complexes and dockyards.

These friendly gestures served little to disguise an uneasy relationship. The French had conquered Cochin-China in 1850 and were casting their eyes towards Cambodia, a country upon which the Siamese believed themselves to have firm claims. In 1861 a struggle for the succession led to serious disturbances in Cambodia; Siam asserted its dominance by once more sending troops to quell the disorders. The French protested against this incursion, initially taking the attitude that Cambodia was traditionally ruled by Siam and Vietnam concurrently, and as the successors to Cochin-China's rights, they had acquired part-jurisdiction over Cambodia.[85] Soon afterwards the government in Paris instructed their army commander in the region not to recognize Siam's claims over Cambodia.[86] The Siamese, by then fully aware of French expansionist policies, launched a campaign to prevent further French incursions.[87] However, in July 1863 the French persuaded the Cambodian ruler to sign a treaty accepting Napoleon III's protection. The Siamese attempted to counter this action by drawing up a treaty of their own with Cambodia, which left no doubt as to Cambodia's subordinate status.[88] The full text of this treaty appeared in the *Bangkok Press* and was reprinted by the *Singapore Straits Times* in August 1864.

Since the Siamese-Cambodian treaty denied many of the French ambitions, the French consul, Aubaret, was instructed to negotiate a new treaty between France and Siam that would allow French influence in Cambodia. During the first half of 1865 Aubaret made strong demands, threatening that France would take punitive action against the Siamese if they did not agree to joint supervision over Cambodia. Aubaret's condescending and hostile attitude became widely known in Siamese circles[89] and may have played a role in pushing the Siamese more towards the British. It appears that when the British consul was secretly contacted in June 1865, he advised the Siamese to give no further concessions, intimating that the French consul was acting somewhat beyond his instructions from Paris. The British consul appears in fact to have drafted the Siamese 'final reply' maintaining Cambodia's subordinate status.[90] The plan was successful when Aubaret accepted this version.

[85] See, for example, the reports in the *Straits Times* for 12 October, 23 November, and especially 14 December 1861.

[86] Pensri (Suvanij) Duke, *Les relations entre la France et la Thailande (Siam) au XIXe siècle d'après les archives étrangères*, pp. 26-7.

[87] Some of the letters to the *Straits Times* were apparently inspired to put the Siamese government's point of view to the English-speaking world. King Mongkut was quite active in this respect, and this article to the popular *Quarterly Review* in London was inspired by a wish to make Siam's position widely known (see *Quarterly Review* 116 (1864), p. 303).

[88] Wilson, 'State and Society', pp. 549-51.

[89] Aubaret's hostility towards some of the Siamese is commented upon in the *Siamese Recorder* of May 1865. When the consul's request to have M. Lamache appointed representative for the Portugese was denied, Aubaret reputedly had the senior government servant who came to tell him this violently expelled from his house. See Bradley, journal, 31 August 1865 and 2 September 1865; see also the reference in Pensri Duke, *Les relations*, p. 43.

[90] Confidential correspondence was published in the *Siam Daily Advertiser* of 21 June 1870 and reprinted in the *Straits Times* of 16 July 1870. There can be little doubt about the authenticity of the documents. The confrontation with France drove the Siamese to seek British help, as can be seen from the letters sent by Mongkut in 1866 mentioned below.

However, when he presented the new treaty for ratification, the French government sent him back to extract further concessions.

The renegotiations took place in late 1866, resulting in little-disguised hostility between the two parties. Sisuriyawong told Aubaret outright that he was not prepared to concede any further points. The French consul thereupon demanded that Sisuriyawong be taken off the negotiating committee. Aubaret insisted that King Mongkut himself should take over in order to prevent a direct clash between France and Siam. Some ugly scenes allegedly took place between the two men, Mongkut threatening to write to Napoleon III personally about the consul's conduct, and Aubaret telling the king such a letter would have no effect as the consul was acting with the full backing of the French government.

It was during these protracted and difficult negotiations that Mongkut wrote confidentially to the British consul, suggesting that he would welcome a British take-over. In this letter of 18 December 1866, Mongkut says his opinion is a personal one made without the Siamese government's knowledge and continues: 'if the British protectorate is necessary, he [Mongkut] and his family would accept it.'[91]

The negotiations between Aubaret and Mongkut finally broke down, and the king decided to send a new embassy to Paris in order to settle the matter. In his instructions to the Siamese envoy, Mongkut expressed the view that the British were inclining towards extending their territory over Siam. Then he authorized his envoy, apparently overruling Sisuriyawong in this matter, to make as many concessions as were needed to come to an agreement with the French. Finally, he told the envoy to press for Aubaret's replacement:

> *If, however, they refuse to remove Aubaret from Bangkok but insist on keeping him here with full power, then the matter would be beyond my endurance. If you fail to get Aubaret removed, then you may cross over to Britain and ask for whatever assistance that you may think fit from the responsible ministers, from the English lords both in and out of office and from Sir John Bowring. I have my own reasons for this decision.*[92]

The letter to the British consul and the one to the Siamese envoy reinforce each other. At this point in time Mongkut had undoubtedly reconciled himself to Siam in some form becoming more closely linked to, or even becoming part of, the British Empire. These remarks should not be regarded as a sudden whim or irresponsible action arising from a moment of uncontrollable anger against the French consul, for the two letters are spaced more than two months apart. If one views these communications in the light of Bradley's earlier statement about the atmosphere of despondency and of the acceptance by many

[91] Letter from the king of Siam to Knox, dated 18 December 1866, cited in Pensri Duke, *Les relations*, pp. 54-5. Those who believe modern simplistic and chauvinistic depictions of King Mongkut as incessantly concerned to preserve Siamese independence will have difficulty to accept the veracity of this letter. However, the force with which colonial expansion was driven might at the time well have appeared irresistible.

[92] This letter was translated by Seni and Kukrit Pramoj, in *The King of Siam Speaks*, a typewritten manuscript, cited extensively in Moffat, *Mongkut*. This quotation is on page 124 of Moffat's work.

Siamese leaders of the idea that the country sooner or later would end up subject to a European power, Mongkut's two letters are a clear declaration of his preference for Britain over France in the event of Siam becoming a European protectorate. As it was, the envoys did not feel it necessary to contact the British on this matter, for they were quite honorably received, and were able to negotiate the new treaty. Not long after their return home Aubaret was replaced.

The first letter, which had been immediately passed on to London, does not appear to have caused much excitement. It was clear that the suggestion was only the king's personal opinion, and probably also because an implementation of the king's suggestion would have fuelled anti-imperialist agitation. At any rate, no action was taken. This episode had few international repercussions. What Mongkut's handling of the case does demonstrate is that his position *vis-à-vis* Sisuriyawong had changed since the late 1850s, when the king appears to have been forced to accept whatever Sisuriyawong and his advisers decided. In the years between 1861 and 1867 the political scene seems to have become more and more dominated by Sisuriyawong and Mongkut, the other chief actors either leaving the scene or being relegated to the background. Phra Pinklao, for example, after a long period of ill health, died in January 1866 without having played a prominent role in the country. Prince Wongsathirat still nominally held great power, but he was ill and virtually confined to his bed. Sisuriyawong's half-brother *chaophraya* Rawiwong, elevated to *chaophraya* Thiphakorawong in 1865, held the senior position of *Phrakhlang*, but he suffered from cataracts and his progressive blindness caused him to resign his post at the beginning of 1867.

The personal relationship between Mongkut and Sisuriyawong, at first rather cool, improved as they apparently found ways of co-operating and as the king's confidence grew. During the early 1860s the two seemed quite amicably disposed towards each other. By 1866 the king was asserting himself more and more, and he now boldly took ultimate responsibility in matters concerning Siam's relations with other countries as well as in some domestic affairs.[93]

The king's new confidence was visible not only in his letter to the British consul and in the freedom he gave his envoys in settling a treaty that had been opposed by Sisuriyawong, but also in several other measures. Thus, when *chaophraya* Thiphakorawong resigned his post as *Phrakhlang*, everybody expected one of the Bunnak family to replace him, for a Bunnak had been the head of the *Phrakhlang* since 1822. However, Mongkut made one of his younger half-brothers, *kromakhun* Worasak, the new *Phrakhlang*.

Another matter about which Sisuriyawong and Mongkut disagreed, and where the king's opinion prevailed, was the

[93] Like Mongkut, Sisuriyawong also travelled, including a little-known visit to Singapore from 17 July to 30 August 1861, the main reason for which was apparently an official call upon the authorities in Kedah (see the *Straits Times*, 3 August and 14 September 1861).

appointment of someone to take the late Phra Pinklao's place. In July 1867, to Mongkut's great sorrow, his eldest son, *kromamu'n* Mahesuan, died, and since he had been a possible candidate for the position of *Uparat*,[94] it was probably not long after his death that Sisuriyawong suggested that *kromamu'n* Wichaichan, Phra Pinklao's eldest son, who was twenty-nine years old, should succeed his father.[95] Sisuriyawong apparently considered Prince Wichaichan the ablest member of the next generation of the royal family. The appointment of an *Uparat* when the king himself was already sixty-two was significant because, as the highest-ranking prince after the king, the *Uparat* would automatically be a serious candidate for the throne. By this time, King Mongkut had begun to pin his hopes on his first son of *chaofa* rank, Prince Chulalongkorn, who had become his favorite. In January 1866, when the prince was twelve, his official tonsure ceremonies had lasted seven days and were unprecedentedly elaborate. Napoleon III, who had heard through his consul that Mongkut had a favorite son, had presented the young prince with a sword at the same time that he gave one to Mongkut.[96] In 1867 Chulalongkorn was much too young to be seriously considered for the position of *Uparat*, so the king, who was in excellent health,[97] decided to leave the position open for the time being.

Mongkut and Anna Leonowens

Early in his reign Mongkut had requested American missionaries to organize teaching the women in the inner palace.[98] Three of the missionaries' wives, Mrs. Bradley, Mrs. Mattoon, and Mrs. Jones, thereupon had taken turns teaching a morning class of more than twenty palace ladies. Inevitably the initial enthusiasm waned and soon only a few of the king's concubines remained. These were able to learn a certain amount of English, but in doing so they were exposed to a regular diet of Christian tracts. The missionaries' wives undoubtedly also expressed their deep-felt disapproval of the custom of polygamy. There are indications that this criticism caused some commotion, and it is quite possible that this eventually led to such revolutionary measures by the king as increasing the facility with which concubines could resign from the inner palace and take up a life outside the court.[99] It is quite likely that the Christian content of the course was the reason for the king's decision to put a sudden halt to the teaching. Mongkut's increasing distrust of Europeans and Americans during the middle and late 1850s explains why the subject of an English education within the palace was not broached again until the early 1860s, when the numerous offspring born to Mongkut since his enthronement began to grow up. By then Bangkok was undergoing rapid and

[94] Wilson, 'State and Society', p. 713.

[95] This prince was originally named George Washington after the first president of the United States. The name 'George' was pronounced 'Yot' by most Siamese, and the prince was often referred to as *'phra'ongchao* Yot'.

[96] *DC Fourth R*, vol. 2, pp. 380-81.

[97] In July 1867 King Mongkut in a jesting manner boasted to Bradley about his strength (Bradley, journal, 18 July 1867).

[98] *Ibid.*, 13 and 14 August 1851.

[99] Moffat, *Mongkut*, pp. 164-65; Bradley, journal, 25 January 1856.

fundamental change as a result of the ever-growing number of Europeans and Americans trading and seeking residence in Siam. The king himself had acquired a fair knowledge of English and was quite fascinated with the steady stream of innovations and inventions coming from abroad.[100] A progressive and forward-looking king such as Mongkut could no longer neglect to give his children an opportunity to learn the most important European language.

When the king made inquiries about a good woman teacher, Anna Leonowens, who ran a small school in Singapore, was recommended to him. In his instructions, the king expressly forbade her to preach Christianity in the palace: 'We hope that in doing your education on us and on our children ... you will do your best endeavour for knowledge of English language, science and literature, and not for conversion to Christianity.'[101] Anna arrived on 15 March 1862, accompanied by her small son, Louis. She was to stay a little over five years as governess at the Siamese court, leaving Siam on 5 July 1867.[102] As a result of her experiences, Anna wrote several books, two of which were widely distributed[103] and which later formed the basis for a film, *The King and I*, that deeply offended many Thais because of the way King Mongkut was portrayed. Anna's books provided a highly romantic, sometimes deliberately distorted, and occasionally totally false picture of daily life at the Siamese court. Most scholars have therefore discredited or summarily discarded her works. Recently, it has been established that Anna took liberties with the truth even before she went to Siam and that her claims to a genteel background and being the widow of 'an officer and a gentleman' were false.[104] Just as Bradley's diary is colored by his religious beliefs, but should not prevent the historian from learning valuable facts about Siam, so Anna's account is not completely worthless. Her books occasionally provide snippets of information that cannot be obtained elsewhere or that confirms events recorded elsewhere. Anna's graphic description of her arrival at Sisuriyawong's palace and her first interview with King Mongkut is amusing, and the reactions of both these men to Anna's petulant and haughty behavior may well come close to something that actually happened:

Suddenly his Majesty, having cogitated sufficiently in his peculiar manner, with one long stride halted in front of us, and, pointed straight at me with his forefinger, asked, 'How old shall you be?'

Scarcely able to repress a smile at a proceeding so absurd, and with my sex's distaste for so serious a question, I demurely replied, 'One hundred and fifty years old.'

Had I made myself much younger, he might have ridiculed or assailed me; but now he stood surprised and

[100] For example, an early form of photography was introduced with the visit of 'Mr. Alfred's Exhibition of Dissolving Views' (Bradley, journal, 12 and 16 April 1859).

[101] Letter from King Mongkut to Anna Leonowens, in W.S. Bristowe, *Louis and the King of Siam*, p. 22, citing H. Longhurst, *The Borneo Story, The First Hundred Years of the Borneo Company Limited*. See also Moffat, *Mongkut*, pp. 167-8.

[102] Bristowe, *Louis and the King*, p. 23, states that Anna held the position until 22 July 1867. Actually she left Bangkok for Singapore on July 5 of that year, never to return.

[103] First published as *The English Governess at the Siamese Court: Being Recollections of Six Years in the Royal Palace at Bangkok* and *The Romance of the Harem*.

[104] Bristowe, *Louis and the King*, pp. 23-31. Anna's shortcomings as a historian and her occasional flagrant plagiarism have been exposed by A. B. Griswold, 'King Mongkut in Perspective', *JSS* 45, pt 1 (1957), pp. 1-41.

embarrassed for a few moments, then resumed his queer march; and at last, beginning to perceive the jest, coughed and laughed, coughed again, and in a high, sharp key asked, 'In what year were you borned?'

Instantly I struck a mental balance, and answered as gravely as I could, 'In 1788.'

At this point the expression on his Majesty's face was indescribably comical.[105]

During this first interview with his new employee, Mongkut, no doubt unaware of British feminine coyness about their age, did not perceive the jest and may well have doubted the woman's sanity.

In another passage, Anna reveals the little scraps of knowledge remaining from American missionaries' wives' teaching: a bit of a Sunday-school hymn and various English sentences which had lost their meaning.[106] Probably the most valuable information that can be extracted from her works concerns the description of the personal habits of the Siamese leaders. Sisuriyawong's bright intelligence, remarked upon by many contemporary authors, is confirmed, but at the same time, some personal details are added which others have failed to see or mention. A careful reading of *The English Governess* reveals not only Mongkut's short temper but also the king as a scholar and as a father doting on many of his children.[107]

Astronomy and the Death of the King

The king had long been convinced that the Copernican perspective provided a satisfactory view on the make-up of the solar system. Even before his accession to the throne, Mongkut had accepted that the old Buddhist *Traiphumikhatha* cosmogony depicting Mount Meru as the center of the universe could no longer be regarded as an adequate guide to heavenly bodies and their movements. Rejection of the fabulous aspects of the *Traiphumikhatha* was one of the features of the reform movement in which Mongkut had been so active during his years in the Buddhist order.

This movement did not totally reject all things magical and miraculous, however. The subtle debate on the adjustments in Buddhism in the light of the new scientific information can be gleaned from *Kitchanukit*, probably the first printed Siamese book written by *chaophraya* Thiphakorawong, which appeared in 1867.[108] Thiphakorawong's views are not necessarily the same as Mongkut's, but they arise from the same intellectual questions, and they appear in general to be quite in accordance with the views of other 'modernists' of that time. Thiphakorawong rejects the *Traiphumikhatha's* explanation of the passing of the seasons,

---

[105] Leonowens, *The English Governess*, pp. 57-8.

[106] *Ibid.*, pp. 62-3.

[107] A series of impressions of the Thai leaders at this time by Dutch visitors has been collected by Zoomers. See Henk Zoomers, 'De Siamese elite in de perceptie van Nederlandse bezoekers van Siam: 1857-1863', in Raymond Feddema (ed), *Wat beweegt de bamboe? Geschiedenissen in Zuidoost Azië*, Amsterdam: Het Spinhuis, 1992, pp. 41-69.

[108] An abbreviated English translation was made by Henry Alabaster and forms a large part of his book *The Wheel of the Law*.

the origin of wind and rain, the cause of epidemics, and the movement of tides. He maintains that the Buddha never intended to make statements on these natural phenomena. While adhering to the latest scientific explanations regarding these matters, Thiphakorawong – and many others with him – accepted numerous miraculous stories, especially those connected with the immense powers of the Buddha, and occasionally he was able to suggest a reconciliation between the scientific world-view and the old legends. Thus it is said that the Buddha spent one rainy season away from the world, preaching in the Tavatimsa heaven in order to honor his mother. Thiphakorawong suggested that this heaven was one of the far-away planets which the Buddha, with his exceptional powers, managed to visit.[109]

The arguments for and against a European view of the cosmos found an excellent test case in the description of eclipses. Traditionally, every eclipse was seen as an act of Rahu, a black and ominous sky dragon who from time to time suddenly attempted to devour the sun or the moon. When the evil Rahu opened his mouth and began consuming the heavenly body, it was the duty of all those who perceived the danger to discourage that monster, and customarily the Siamese did so by making a tremendous din. Gongs were beaten, pots and pans were clashed together, the government would order big guns to be fired, so that before long Rahu would desist. With modern scientific explanation it was possible to predict the day on which an eclipse would take place, in itself not so noteworthy, for some traditional astrologers could do the same. Western astronomers could do much more: they actually predicted, with the aid of their theories, the exact minute a given lunar or solar eclipse would take place and the degree and precise direction of the shadow cover.

King Mongkut had long been aware of the force of this aspect of modern astronomy. He had come across the computations of eclipses for 1850 and used these to predict their occurrence,[110] and when they happened as foretold his reputation as being in touch with progressive science grew. Even the royal court astrologers could not say exactly when Rahu would bite or how far his attempt to swallow the heavenly body would go. In the following years Mongkut kept an interest in the results of various branches of science and technology, ordering impressive instruments from Singapore and letting it be widely known to foreign envoys that in the case of an exchange of gifts between Siam and a European power, the latest gadgets relating to the fields of physics and chemistry as well as books on physiology, natural history and technical innovation would be greatly appreciated. He also ordered the construction of a small observatory in his palace grounds at Phetburi.

Mongkut was thus quite well informed and his inquisitive mind ranged widely, yet it would be false to depict him as a

[109] *Ibid.*, p. 17.

[110] Bowring, *Kingdom and People of Siam*, vol. 1, p. 44.

competent linguist, historian, archaeologist or astronomer; he had a superficial acquaintance with these and other fields. Occasionally he wrote short essays on some aspect of them and used snippets of scientific information as conversational opening gambits when meeting Europeans. Thus he is reported to have said: 'You have two terms, – one, the vulgar – leap-year, and another, the classical – bissextile.'[111] This statement appears to have been uttered with no other intention than to draw admiring comment from his audience.

It may safely be assumed that the king's wish to help organize an expedition to the southern part of Siam to observe a total eclipse of the sun in August 1868 was not inspired by a genuine scientific curiosity. Mongkut could follow the calculations determining that the event would take place and that the path of the total eclipse would cross a certain region of southern Siam, but that was as far as his astronomical abilities went. His interest in the event was firstly to publicize the event widely and prove the 'modernists' right in rejecting certain aspects of legendary explanations of natural phenomena and secondly to foster his image as an enlightened monarch both in Siam and abroad. He invited a party of French astronomers, British diplomats, court astrologers, and a large number of members of the royal family as well as nobles, to travel south to Hua Wan, where the total eclipse could be viewed. His trust in the accuracy and methods of Western science was vindicated when the eclipse duly occurred as predicted.

At the same time, it may be doubted whether the expedition succeeded in convincing many Siamese of the fact that the old Siamese perception of the demonical Rahu was false. It so happened that many members of the royal family who had attended the event, including Prince Chulalongkorn, eight of the ten French scientists and also many of the nobles, became ill. To the consternation of all, Mongkut himself also fell seriously ill. By late September 1868 eight people who had attended the scientific expedition had died; the king himself expired on the evening of 1 October 1868, aged almost sixty-four, after having reigned for more than seventeen years.

Economic Changes During the Fourth Reign

The fourth reign was a period during which many changes were instigated that eventually fundamentally affected the country. The most spectacular was Siam's abrupt lowering of the trade barriers that had prevented most Europeans and Americans from working in Bangkok. With the signing of the Bowring treaty, and with Siam's adherence to its provisions under the supervision of *chaophraya* Sisuriyawong, a European quarter developed in the south of the city where a long row of wharves

[111] M. L. Manich Jumsai, *King Mongkut and Sir John Bowring*, p. 197.

marked the Western presence. Consulates, churches, shipyards, warehouses, a sawmill and a customs house soon changed Bangkok in European eyes into a city that had finally joined the race towards becoming a 'civilized' country.[112] This greatly increased Western presence acted as a catalyst in bringing about further changes: new harbor laws had to be written, a new and efficient system of coining money had to be set up, some government proclamations were printed in large numbers and distributed over the country. Steam-engines were imported for ships, rice mills, saw mills and sugar mills. The fourth reign saw the printing of books in both Siamese and English, as well as an impressive number of periodicals.[113]

In the light of all these innovations, the signing of the Bowring treaty is often regarded as a turning point in Siamese history, before which traditional Siam prevailed, while afterwards progressive forces held sway. While it cannot be denied that the Western presence added a new and stimulating dimension to Bangkok, its effects upon the country as a whole have probably been overestimated. Partly this has come about by a rather naive acceptance of Bowring's own estimates of what the treaty would achieve. Bowring promised a 'total change in the whole system of taxation' and that the agreement 'uprooted a great number of privileges and monopolies'.[114] A critical examination of the data shows that neither of these expectations was fulfilled.

Adherents of the 'watershed' view also assume that prior to 1855 Siam was an economic backwater, its economy was hardly developed, its farmers existed mainly at subsistence level and the rural population was self-sufficient except for occasional bartering. In fact, there are contemporary accounts that point to quite the contrary. Near the end of the third reign, the central plain and the eastern provinces appear to have become the scene of some spectacular economic development. The south-western part of the central plain had become a major source of palm sugar and salt production, and the eastern provinces saw the further development of large pepper and sugar-cane plantations.

The case of sugar production illustrates the vigor and strength of the pre-Bowring economy as well as the consistently effective administration in the 1830s and 1840s. Edmund Roberts tells us that in 1832 the Siamese exported some 96,000 *piculs* of sugar, to a value of approximately 760,000 *baht*.[115] By 1850, the value of the sugar export is estimated to be 708,000 *baht* in the most reliable source available for that time,[116] a decrease possibly reflecting the effects of new and higher taxes.[117] It is therefore somewhat deceptive to write about people predicting that after the Bowring treaty sugar would become one of the major exports.[118] In 1850 sugar was already the most valuable item in the list of exports, and it

[112] This is illustrated in an article that appeared in 31 August 1861 in the *Straits Times* under the heading 'Progress of the Eastern World'. Siam was assessed as follows: 'Siam, though comparatively small in territory, and but new in the race of civilization, has yet advanced in some respects beyond the larger kingdoms of Asia, and is unequalled in having a sovereign who is accessible to all and who is a lover and promoter of literature, science and the fine arts.'

[113] Apart from Bradley's *Bangkok Calendar* and *Bangkok Recorder* mentioned above, there appeared at some time during the reign issues of the *Siam Times*, the *Bangkok Press*, the *Bangkok Summary*, and the Siam *Weekly Monitor*. The latter appeared in 1867 and 1868 and was edited by E. d'Encourt and not by Bradley, as the official bibliography states (*Periodicals and Newspapers Printed in Thailand*, p. 4).

[114] Bowring, *The Kingdom and People of Siam*, Vol 2, p. 226.

[115] E. Roberts, *Embassy to the Eastern Courts of Cochin China, Siam and Muscat*, pp. 316-7.

[116] J. Homan van der Heide, 'The Economical Development of Siam During the Last Half Century', *JSS* 3, pt 2 (1906), p. 81, citing D. E. Malloch.

[117] *PKRt Sam*, p. 361.

[118] J. C. Ingram, *Economic Change in Thailand 1850-1970*, p. 123.

had been so for some time. While the Bowring treaty may have sparked off an initial added interest in sugar manufacture, there was no sign of a 'sugar boom'. It is even more deceptive to state that between 1849 and 1859 the sugar export rose from just over 100,000 *piculs* to almost double that amount.[119] The year-by-year accounts show that 1859 was an exceptionally good year for sugar, and that sugar exports actually began to decline rapidly from 1860 onwards, in 1863 dropping below the 100,000-*picul* mark and in 1866 to almost 60,000 *piculs*, only to rise again in 1867, which generally was a good year in the Siamese economy.[120]

Western technological innovations such as steam-powered sugar mills and later even a steam plough do not appear to have had any positive effect during the reign. The first steam sugar mill was set up in 1862, but capital-intensive experiments such as these often proved less flexible than the traditional methods and like many innovations, carried the risk of becoming liabilities.[121]

The decline in the sugar industry appears to have begun in 1860 and continued during the fifth reign until sugar virtually disappeared from the export market in the 1880s. One contributing factor was undoubtedly the gradual drop in the price of sugar on the world market. Another may be found in the Siamese taxation system. Under the Bowring treaty, sugar was made exempt from export duty and inland transit duties were fixed at one and two *salu'ng* per *picul* for brown and white sugar respectively.[122] However, there were no provisions restricting taxation of sugar in the earlier stages of manufacture and, to make up for the loss of export revenue, fairly heavy taxes were levied on the land on which sugar-cane was grown, the cane, mills, boilers and on the boats used for transport.[123] Many of these taxes were fixed, regardless of the actual yield and the state of the market, which increased the cost of manufacture and the economic risk involved.

These observations on the sugar production are relevant also to the production of cotton. In 1821 Crawfurd mentioned Siam's export of cotton;[124] in 1833 Roberts estimated the exports to be between 30,000 and 40,000 piculs,[125] and D. E. Malloch's figures, which generally are held to refer to the year 1850, give the value of the cotton export as 450,000 *baht*, and another 211,500 *baht* worth of cotton-filled pillows and mattresses were exported that year. The quantity and value of the yearly export demonstrate that Siam possessed an intricate network of trade and industry which ensured that products from home industry and small-scale industrial complexes would find a market.

If the total value of import and export is taken as an indication of Siam's 'openness' to international trade, the figures show a remarkable pre-Bowring activity. Siam's exports in

[119] *Ibid.*

[120] Wilson, 'State and Society', p. 985.

[121] In February 1869 the new steam-powered sugar mill at Nakhon Chaisi was in great financial difficulties. For details, see Bradley, journal, 5 February 1869.

[122] Bowring, *The Kingdom and People of Siam*, vol 2, p. 225; Manich Jumsai, *King Mongkut and Sir John Bowring*, p. 137.

[123] Each palm-tree was taxed, and a tax of one *baht* was placed on each hundred pots. Every boiling establishment of two kettles had to pay six *salu'ng* per year (see Bradley, journal, 28 March 1861; and Wilson, 'State and Society', p. 993).

[124] J. Crawfurd, *Journal of an Embassy to the Courts of Siam and Cochin China*, p. 383.

[125] Roberts, *Embassy to the Eastern Courts*, p. 317.

1832 were estimated at a value of not less than 7,500,000 *baht*, though only about five million *baht* worth appears to have been sent through the official channels.[126] Malloch reports for 1850 an export of just over 5,500,000 *baht*, and imports worth some 4,331,000 *baht*. By 1867, just over a decade after the Bowring treaty, and after an exceptionally profitable year of trading, the *Bangkok Summary* reported the total volume of export to be some 7,660,000 *baht* and the imports about 6,350,000 *baht*.[127]

Before the Bowring treaty, Siam's trade with China, Singapore, and Java was lively and lucrative,[128] and the changes after it appear to have led not so much to a sudden opening up of new markets and new sources of wealth as to an abrupt alteration in direction and a series of developments in the local taxation system. Europeans gained an increasing share of the international trade and European ships largely supplanted the fleet of trading junks that used to reach Bangkok around January and returned to China in July each year. The new limitations on Siamese export tax and the inland transit duties were intended to make international trade more profitable for Europeans. In practice, although many taxes were levied at fixed amounts and a few abolished, the treaties did not provide a comprehensive taxation model; the Siamese government was able to increase other taxes and levy many new ones to make up for the concessions.

Taxation

While import and export figures may provide an indication of Siam's economic role in the region, they reflect only an aspect of the Siamese economy as a whole. State revenue data from various sources reflect much more the size, scope, and character of the Siamese economy. The scanty information available on taxation during the third and fourth reigns shows an increasingly complex system. Roberts enumerated more than seventy separate taxes on floating houses, paddy, orchards, gambling, vegetables, alcohol and a vast array of other products.[129] Some time during the third reign, taxes were added on the transport of some goods, iron pans, cotton-growing lands, tobacco, jute and indigo, sugar-boiling establishments, timber used for the boat-building industry, stearin candles, cakes, lime, bullock carts, hire boats and on towing boats.[130]

During the first five years of the fourth reign, a few taxes were lowered for the specific purpose of attracting overseas trade. However, this relaxation applied only to foreign traders; the general populace was taxed as heavily as before, if not more so.[131] While the income from various farms and duties amounted in 1833 to some 890,000 *baht*, by 1851 this had risen to some 1,294,000 *baht*, a figure that slowly rose in the following

[126] *Ibid.*, p. 318.

[127] As copied in the *Straits Times*, 27 March 1869.

[128] A short description of the types of vessels that controlled the trade can be found in Sarasin Viraphol, *Tribute and Profit: Sino-Siamese Trade, 1652-1853*, pp. 227-31. For a picture of the continued share of Siam in regional trade, the figures in G. F. de Bruijn Kops, *Statistiek van den Handel en de Scheepvaart op Java en Madura sedert 1825*, give an impression of Siam's vigorous economy (see vol. 1, p. 394 and p. 461, and vol. 2, p. 228 and p. 543).

[129] Roberts, *Embassy to the Eastern Courts*, pp. 426-7.

[130] *PKRt Sam*, p. 361.

[131] In her study of the Siamese tax farming system Lysa Hong writes extensively about King Mongkut apologizing for decreeing new taxes. She specifies new taxes on fish, crabs and prawns, beeswax, silks, gunny sacks and cane baskets and assumes that these were an attempt to counteract the effects of the Bowring treaty. All these taxes were announced in C.S.1216, which does not correspond with the year 1857. C.S. 1216 corresponds with 1854-55, so that this part of her analysis is absurd. See Lysa Hong, *Thailand in the Nineteenth Century: Evolution of the Economy and Society*, Singapore: ISEAS, 1984, pp. 78-81.

years to 1,318,000 (in 1855) and 1,334,000 (in 1856).[132] The Bowring treaty established a fixed scale of export duties for fifty-one articles, stipulating that these be free of all other production, inland, or transit duties, and provided a further list of twelve articles on which transit duties were allowed but which would become free of all export duty.[133] The Siamese team of negotiators themselves controlled large sections of the taxation system, and it is unlikely that they would have agreed to a great cut in their personal income simply to accommodate European traders. As a matter of fact, it seems that the Bowring treaty had little or no immediate effect upon the revenues derived from all government farms; during the years between 1853 and 1868, the amount of Siamese revenue increased by an average of some 39,000 *baht* annually.

The system of taxation had become almost wholly dominated by tax-farming, with persons handing over a prearranged sum of money considered appropriate for a tax to a particular government *krom*. For example, the tax on carts pulled by buffaloes was set at 2 *baht*; on those pulled by oxen, 1 1/2 *baht*. During the first ten years of the fourth reign, the Siamese government could expect to receive 2,000 *baht* yearly from these particular taxes.[134] The tax-farmers would set up their own organization in order to collect the moneys, and in normal circumstances they expected to receive much more than the 2,000 *baht* which had been paid. If the tax-farmer had difficulties meeting his obligations, he could propose to pay the government a lower sum; if the tax-farmer was making too large a profit, the government could demand a higher tax for the following season or force the price up by inviting tenders.[135]

In contrast to what Bowring had predicted, neither the plethora of tax farms, nor the tax burden upon the people was fundamentally changed. Almost forty years after the Bowring treaty Kettlemann, the German Minister Resident reported:

> ... the people have to carry a tremendous tax burden, that in the wealthier provinces especially in the Malay Peninsula gradually has caused widespread dissatisfaction, so that England begins to take note of the circumstances in that region. There is hardly a necessity of life on which the state has not imposed a tax, mainly in the form of monopolies that have been leased to Chinese.
>
> Even the miserable palm hut in the middle of the rice fields in which the poor farmer and his dependents find shelter against the heat and storms is for the state an important taxable good. The state taxes the leaves, the bamboo poles and the twine, thus the building material as well as the earthen pots, containers and jugs that form the humble household contents.[136]

[132] Roberts, *Embassy to the Eastern Courts*, pp. 426-7, and Wilson, 'State and Society', p. 999. Roberts's assessment of the tax on rice land and orchards appears to be quite unrealistic, and these have been left out of the calculation.

[133] See Manich Jumsai, *King Mongkut and Sir John Bowring*, pp. 136-7.

[134] Wilson, 'State and Society', p. 989 and pp. 995-6. She enumerates more than eighteen treasuries.

[135] Wira Wimoniti, *Historical Patterns of Tax Administration in Thailand*, pp. 94-5.

[136] The original German text is as follows. 'Und dabei hat das Volk ungeheure Steuerlasten zu tragen, die in den reicheren Provinzen aber, namentlich auf der malayischen Halbinsel, allmälig so große Unzufriedenheit hervorgerufen haben, daß England beginnt den dortigen Zuständen seine Aufmerksamkeit zuzuwenden. Es giebt kaum noch ein Lebensbedürfniß von dem der Staat nicht eine Abgabe erhebt, meistens im Wege von Monopolen, die er Chinesen verpachtet. Selbst die elende Palmhütte inmitten der Reisfelder, in welcher der arme Bauer mit seinen Angehörigen gegen Hitze und Unwetter Obdach findet, ist für den Staat ein wichtiges Steuerobjekt. Er besteuert die Blätter, die Bambusstangen und die Bindefasern, d.i. das Baumaterial, und die irdenen Töpfe, Gefässe und Krüge, die den ärmlichen Hausrath ausmachen'. (P. H. I. G. M. Kempermann, in his Report No. 82, dated 27 August 1893, Politisches Archiv des auswärtigen Amts, R 19230, foll. 13 and 14).

As there had never been a centrally organized treasury; the original chief government departments had always had their own sources of income: the *krom Kalahom* from the south, the *krom Tha* from certain coastal towns, the *krom Na* from land tax and the *krom Mu'ang* from tribunals. With the proliferation of new taxes in the third and fourth reigns, the system of passing tax moneys on to the many separate treasuries of government departments became increasingly complex.[137] The two most important treasuries were the *Phrakhlang Mahasombat* (the Great Treasury, which during the fourth reign seems to have been controlled by *chaophraya* Sisuriyawong in his capacity as head of the *krom Kalahom*) and the *Phrakhlang Sinkha Phra Borom Maharatchawang* (the Royal Warehouse, supervised by Sisuriya-wong's brother *chaophraya* Rawiwong).[138]

The system of tax-farming worked so conveniently for the Siamese administration, who handed over all the problems of tax evasion, bribery and corruption to the tax-farmers, that it was adopted by the *krom Na* to collect rice-land tax in the central provinces. For an annual sum of 160,000 *baht* the state gave the full powers of collection to the head of the *krom Na*, making the whole *krom* into a tax-farm and legalizing the profits made by its officials. Tax on rice land was still levied directly in some of the 'outer provinces'. Thus the *krom Kalahom* was responsible for this tax in many of the southern provinces in a region that began at Ratburi and ended in Songkhla, and the *Mahatthai* officially had the right to levy the rice-land tax on the belt of northern provinces such as Phitsanulok, Angthong, Saraburi, and Nakhon Nayok.[139]

Apart from tax-farms and direct taxation, which formed the bulk of the government's income, throughout the fourth reign the State still had various other sources of wealth. One of these was the poll tax on Chinese, another the goods and services which could be commanded by State officials under the old *corvée* system. The *corvée* system was being changed by allowing people to pay a sum of money and thus free themselves from having to perform three months of onerous duties.[140] Some ceremonial remains of *corvée* still existed, mainly in connection with major state ceremonies, when large amounts of wood, bamboo and workers were needed to create temporary pavilions and ceremonial objects, and also during some of the great building programs instigated by the king and the senior nobles. At the same time, some of the outer provinces paid their taxes largely in kind by sending shipments of *suai* for the royal warehouses. Finally, some of the vassal states would regularly send tribute, but the value of the tribute varied from time to time and from vassal state to vassal state.[141]

The general picture appears to be one of increasing state control over various sources of revenue and over sections of the

---

[137] Wilson, 'State and Society', p. 1003.

[138] *Ibid*., p. 1001-43, and Wira Wimoniti, *Historical Patterns*, p. 93.

[139] Wilson, 'State and Society', pp. 1056-7.

[140] In 1868 Henry Alabaster spoke to some villagers, who reported being much relieved by being able to pay a sum of money in lieu of serving *corvée*. See *The Wheel of the Law*, pp. 267-8.

[141] For details, see Wilson, 'State and Society', pp. 533-55 and pp. 875-9.

populace, especially in the central plains area. Large numbers of households paid a yearly tax on firewood and often one-tenth of the value of the goods they sold in the market; also their home-industries were taxed. While some of these taxes dated from a previous reign, it may safely be assumed that their collection was more efficient during the fourth reign. For some there were opportunities to make a deal with a tax collector or even avoid paying any tax at all. Not far from Phetburi there were, for example, many woodcutters who

> cut timber free of duty as the forests have no owner but the king and He does not know where they are, they sell their wood to the Laos[142] and others who come with carts for it and pay them for it in rice and other merchandise at the rate of about 1 tical a picul. The cartsmen take it, a journey of two days, to Ratboree about 3 piculs to a load, and sell it for 2 ticals per picul and these [the buyers] carry it to Bangkok in boats and sell it for 2 1/2 to 3 ticals per picul.[143]

Not everyone lived as carefree and unfettered an existence as the illegal woodcutters. For this same region there are glimpses of various other conditions under which sections of the populace labored. There is a report of farmers who had to pay 2 1/2 *baht* yearly for the right to burn firewood in their houses. In 1859 it was mentioned that the people lost in tax one-fifth of the value of all the produce they took to market. In order to raise the cash for these taxes, the people mainly worked cutting wood.[144] In the Phetburi region there were also many people employed in the palm-sugar industry and in potteries. They also appear to have been heavily taxed: 'I had no idea that the manufacture of palm sugar is attended with so much labor and that so little profit is made by the manufacturer. They get but a very lean subsistence and pay heavy taxes on the palmyra trees and on their places for boiling'.[145]

Phetburi was also exceptionally busy with the building of a palace on a mountain not far from the town, on which large numbers of *corvée* workers were engaged. Some, apparently from the north, worked one month and then were free for three months to follow their own pursuits. Their *corvée* was quite heavy. Bradley talked with a few from a party of some five hundred of them:

> These 8 or 10 whom I conversed with are employed in drawing brick in ox carts 1 1/4 miles, that is from the river up to the foot of the mount and their daily task is 10 loads, as much as 2 men can draw and one push by the outlay of nearly all their strength. This is equal to 12 1/2 miles which they have to draw their loads daily and add to this the return trips each 1 1/4 miles, making 25 miles which

[142] The term *Laos* was used for all people from the north and north-east, and it was not limited to those living in the region at present known as Laos.

[143] Bradley, journal, 15 March 1865.

[144] *Ibid.*, 4 February 1859. Apparently the heavy market tax was replaced that year by one on boats, buildings, and rafts (Wilson, 'State and Society', p. 991).

[145] Bradley, journal, 10 February 1859.

they are obliged thus daily to travel or get a severe flogging for failing to do so.[146]

Not all groups of workers had such hard tasks, for Bradley had remarked when he visited that same site a few years earlier that there were several hundreds of *corvée* workers who mostly worked by the hour and who did not seem to expend much energy in their work. Moreover, they could always hire a substitute at prices ranging from six to eight *baht* per month.[147]

Many local inhabitants could not be drafted for *corvée*. Thus all those who labored full-time in the king's rice-fields near Phetburi gained exemption from *corvée*; they were allowed to use an area of 4 3/4 *rai* of rice-field for their own support, and also obtained a yearly sum of six *baht*. Some 260 families were thus employed in the king's fields.[148]

From these and a few other glimpses of life outside Bangkok it would appear that during the fourth reign there was a large measure of control over the various social groups of ordinary people. However, the region around Phetburi may not be representative of the rest of the central plains. It was an area of the specialized palm-sugar industry and in addition, the town was the focus of much attention because the king had selected it for a holiday retreat. In areas further away from the gaze of the king and senior members of the court, life may well have been easier.

Plate 9. A section from The Illustrated London News, *1856 showing the various types of the royal seal of King Mongkut and a copy of the letter to the editor in his own handwriting. (Courtesy The Old Maps & Prints, River City)*

---

[146] *Ibid.*, 1 September 1862.

[147] *Ibid.*, 3 November 1859. Bradley states that this group worked every alternate month and it is possible that they represented a special sub-category in the Siamese system of bondage, such as the offspring of prisoners of war.

[148] *Ibid.*

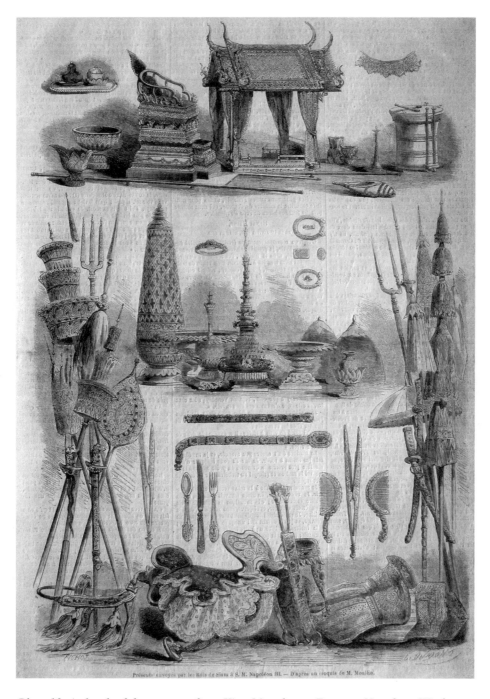

Présents envoyés par les Rois de Siam à S. M. Napoléon III. — D'après un croquis de M. Moulin.

Plate 10. A sketch of the presents from King Mongkut to Emperor Napoleon III of France, L'illustration Journal Universel, *Paris, 1865.*
(Courtesy The Old Maps & Prints, River City)

Plate 11. King Chulalongkorn in his coronation robes, London, 1874.
(Courtesy The Old Maps & Prints, River City)

7

THE REGENT, NEW SIAM AND
CHULALONGKORN
(1868-1883)

The Succession

I n matters concerning the Siamese succession, it is usually
not possible to reconstruct exactly how the various individuals involved interacted and what was decided in informal
meetings. It is possible, however, to make at least a plausible
reconstruction of the sequence which led to Prince
Chulalongkorn's elevation to the throne.

King Mongkut's final illness had lasted throughout the
month of September 1868. All who visited and treated him
agree on the fact that he was mentally clear. Therefore, when he
realized that death was imminent, the king had been able to discuss his succession with members of his family and senior
nobles. At that time *chaofa* Chulalongkorn was just fifteen.[1] He
had apparently already impressed various parties other than the
king, for the prince had a good bearing and displayed a good
measure of charm and intelligence. Moreover, it had become
quite clear to the Siamese that the idea of the succession
moving to a minor constituted no obstacle in the eyes of the
Europeans.

Apparently Sisuriyawong was able to accept Mongkut's
reasoning, and before the king died he had agreed to support
Chulalongkorn; in return for his support he was offered the
regency. It has been suggested that Sisuriyawong's support was
only half-hearted and that he only agreed because the boy was
at that time seriously ill and he expected him to die.[2] However,
by the time Mongkut knew he himself was dying, the young
prince had already passed through the feverish stage and was no
longer regarded as dangerously ill.[3] It is not justified to surmise
hostility between Sisuriyawong and Chulalongkorn at this
period or even to surmise disagreements at such an early stage
in their relations.

At the time of King Mongkut's illness, there was no single
Siamese who could rival Sisuriyawong in power. Sisuriyawong
commanded most of Siam's army, supervised much of the
government's income and expenditure and he and members of
his family occupied many key positions in the administration.
His situation was remarkably like that of his father's at the end
of the third reign in that the decision with regard to the succession could not be made without his consent. One might ask why

---

[1] Prince Chulalongkorn's fifteenth
birthday fell on 21 September 1868.

[2] D. K. Wyatt, 'King Chulalongkorn the
Great: Founder of Modern Thailand',
Asia, supplement no.2, 1976, p. 6.

[3] D. B. Bradley's journal, 3 October
1868.

Sisuriyawong did not use the opportunity of Mongkut's death to proclaim himself king. This reputedly was asked of him by a younger relative years later, and at that time the elder statesman answered guardedly: 'Why should I bother? I have everything a man could desire.'[4] In the light of Sisuriyawong's earlier statements made during the period when there was much tension between him and Mongkut,[5] the thought of becoming monarch must have crossed his mind. Sisuriyawong had only weak candidates opposing him and he realized that he could relatively easily have staged a *coup*. After an initial period of adjustment the international world would no doubt have accepted such a move. It is impossible to decide what held him back. Perhaps it was the embarrassment of the label of usurper, the difficulties inherent in dealing with members of an extensive royal family or some other consideration. A mere three weeks after King Mongkut's death, Sisuriyawong affords us a little glimpse of what had been on his mind when he suddenly asked Bradley in a playful manner 'if it would not be practicable to elect a president over this people and have a republican government.'[6] Bradley replied that he thought the Siamese people were as yet far too ignorant and ill-informed for such a form of government. Since this remark was made more than a month before Chulalongkorn's official inauguration – a most crucial time – it would not be too far-fetched to deduce that Sisuriyawong was pondering over the question of taking formal power, but at the same time he may have found the office of king, with all its pomp and ceremony, not really attractive.

Whatever Sisuriyawong's private thoughts may have been, it is a fact that a few hours after King Mongkut's death, on 1 October 1868, Siam's Great Council assembled and the most senior member of the royal family, *kromaluang* Thewetwacharin, proposed to offer the throne to *chaofa* Chulalongkorn. All agreed to this choice. Immediately thereafter, Sisuriyawong was elected regent. It was quite unorthodox to have someone who was not a member of the royal family appointed regent. A member of the *khunnang* ought not to command princes. In order to deal with this situation, *kromakhun* Bamrap (also known as *chaofa* Mahamala), brother of the late king, was chosen to be 'regent of palace affairs'. During the same meeting, Sisuriyawong proposed to appoint Prince Wichaichan as head of the Front Palace. *Kromakhun* Worasak, a senior prince who had much administrative experience and who outranked Wichaichan, criticized this proposal and suggested that the choice of the head of the Front Palace be left to the new king. Before Worasak could elaborate on the legal aspects of the case, Sisuriyawong demonstrated his power and openly accused Worasak of angling for that position himself. The meeting decided to accept Sisuriyawong's proposal and Wichaichan was thus elected to the position once held by his father, Phra Pinklao.[7]

[4] D. K. Wyatt, 'Family Politics in Nineteenth Century Thailand', p. 224.

[5] See above pp. 133 ff.

[6] Bradley, journal, 22 October 1868.

[7] The standard account of the meeting is in Prince Damrong Ratchanuphap, *Phraratchaphongsawadan Krungratanakosin Ratchakan thi Ha*, pp. 15-25. See also Chula Chakrabongse, *Lords of Life*, pp. 216-7.

The New Government

Probably it was the thought that all old currency could lose its value with the issue of new coins at the beginning of the reign that caused a renewal of the coin panic that had accompanied the first introduction of copper and tin currency during the previous reign. For a while buying and selling virtually stopped in the Bangkok markets. The government decided to exchange the copper coins for their full face value during a period of fifteen days only. After that, they would be exchanged at a reduced rate. In other words, the tin and copper coins of the fourth reign ended up being drastically devalued. The coin panic, and the resulting rush to have copper and tin coins exchanged for silver, lasted from some time during October until at least the beginning of December 1868. It forced the government to revert to a system whereby the appearance and weight of the metal would correspond more closely to the token value.[8]

The government appointments of 1869, at the beginning of the fifth reign, were headed by Sisuriyawong, who gained authority over policy-making throughout the country and was elevated to a *saktina* of 30,000 *rai*, equal to that which his father had been given upon Mongkut's accession. His retired brother, *chaophraya* Thiphakorawong, was formally honoured as 'senior statesman' and his *saktina* was increased from 10,000 to 20,000 *rai*.[9] The post of *Kalahom*, which became vacant with Sisuriyawong's elevation to regent, was given to the regent's son Won Bunnak, who became *chaophraya* Surawongwaiyawat. Prince Worasak was replaced as *Phrakhlang*, a rather unorthodox step in Siamese history and one that may be interpreted as an indication of the power of the Bunnak family, for his post was given to *chaophraya* Phanuwong, Sisuriyawong's brother Thuam. The remaining senior ministries were left in the hands of other families: the *Mahatthai* remained headed by *chaophraya* Phutharaphai of the Bunyarathaphan family, who had held the post since 1863; the *krom Mu'ang* stayed under the direction of one of the Singhaseni family, and the *krom Na* went to a certain Bunlong, whose mother, however, was a Bunnak.[10] The Bunnaks thus continued to dominate the administration. Members of the family were spread over various departments in the capital, and in addition a beginning was made of the Bunnak control of key coastal towns with the appointment of a younger scion, Sut Bunnak, to the governorship of the coastal town of Samutsakhon.[11]

At the beginning of the reign another general registration of the populace was held. The last had been carried out between 1858 and 1860. Thus, during 1870 large numbers of people, many of whom were ordinary *phrai luang*, whose masters resided in Bangkok, had to travel to the capital to receive new tattoo marks and be put down on the rolls. Many paid from nine

---

[8] Further details on currency problems at the beginning of the Fifth Reign can be found in Bradley's journal of 26 October and 3 December 1868, and in Prachoom Chomchai, ed. and transl., *Chulalongkorn the Great*, pp. 76-7.

[9] *Siam Repository* 1 (1869), pp. 319-23.

[10] Wyatt, 'Family Politics', p. 228.

[11] *Kantaengtangkhunnangthai nai samai Ratchakan thi Ha*, p. 12.

to twelve *baht* each year to buy themselves a certificate exempting them from *corvée* duties.[12] The tattoo marks indicated the *krom*, administrative region and master. People whose master belonged to a right-side *krom* were tattooed on the right wrist, or on the inside of the arm not far from the wrist. If a person's master was attached to a left-side *krom* the left wrist or arm was used for the marks.[13] The royal bodyguard was tattooed on the chest, just below the left armpit.[14]

Apart from the large contingent of general *phrai luang*, many other categories of people were classified and marked: the *phrai som* were directly attached to a particular master rather than to the government, and the *thanai*, personal assistants to men of power, who were given exemption from *corvée*. There were free men serving members of the royal family. Some categories had to serve fifteen days each month, some served nine months and some were permanently in government service. The latter invariably received a yearly sum of money and other benefits such as housing and food. Yet others had accepted debt-bondage by borrowing money and working for their creditors in lieu of paying interest, being registered as debt-slaves. In 1870 they were exempted from *corvée* provided their creditor paid a tax of one *baht* two *salu'ng* per slave per annum.[15] The general registration of 1870 apparently was quite all encompassing; many *phrais* were forced into one category or another. Avoidance was widespread. Some attempted to hide in the hope that their cases would be overlooked, others considered obtaining a debt-bondage certificate. In Bangkok many Malays and Burmese tried to register themselves as aliens so as to escape this burden. The Chinese immigrant could buy himself an exemption by paying his triennial poll tax, which then stood at four *baht* and one *salu'ng*.[16]

During the 1870 registration the government made a special effort to advertise the possibility of registering for the army:

> There is just now special effort being made to create an army. Proclamations have been issued to prevail upon young unmarked men from 15 years old and upward to present themselves for this branch of government service.

> Those who like this prospect are voluntarily being marked for this service.

> Others not liking a soldier's life are concealing themselves in hopes they may escape impressment and eventually be marked for some other department of Government service, that is, the department to which their father belonged.[17]

Apparently the central government had realized the need for a professional army, and the recruitment drive of 1870 may be seen as the first formal move in the direction of creating such a force.

[12] Siam *Repository* 2 (1870), p. 363.

[13] *Ibid.*, p. 362.

[14] *Bangkok Calendar*, 1871, p. 70.

[15] Siam *Repository* 2 (1870), pp. 363.

[16] *Ibid.*, pp. 363-4.

[17] *Ibid.*, p. 364.

Chulalongkorn during the Regency Period

When the young king was formally anointed on 11 November 1868, there lay before him almost five years of tutelage before his twentieth birthday would release him from his minority. Meanwhile, Sisuriyawong and his team were responsible for governing the country. This group consisted of men who neither needed nor asked for the king's opinion when making decisions. Some twenty-five years later. King Chulalongkorn recalled his feelings of isolation and powerlessness:

> *When I ascended the throne I was only fifteen years and ten days old. My mother [had long ago] died. Of my maternal relatives, they were either unreliable or they were in unimportant positions. My paternal relatives in the Royal Family had fallen under the power of the Regent, and had to protect their own interests and their own lives, and most did not support me in any way. As for government officials, although there were some who were very close to me, most of these were but minor officials. Those who had important positions did not have the ability to support me in any way. My brothers and sisters were all minors, younger than I, and not one of them was able to do anything. As for myself, I was but a boy. I had no great knowledge or ability in government affairs by which I might carry out my duties except for what my father had been able to give me. I was sick almost to the point of death. I grieved constantly because of my father's death. At that time I was like a headless person, my body propped up as a puppet king ... and there were enemies whose intentions were openly bared around me, both within and without, in the capital and abroad, and my bodily illness was afflicting and tormenting me beyond endurance.*[18]

This statement expresses well what the young king may have felt, though it appears somewhat exaggerated for dramatic effect. By the time King Mongkut died, young Chulalongkorn was recuperating from the 'jungle fever' contracted two months earlier. In the beginning of October he was still weak, but not so ill as to prevent him from attending the oath-taking ceremonies when thousands of civil servants pledged their allegiance, or from receiving delegations of foreigners. At the time of the coronation he seemed quite well and was able to make public appearances.[19]

It was true that the king had no close friends among those who held most power, and gossipy tongues pointed out that during the Ayutthaya period a young king had been assassinated by a regent who carried the same name as the present one.[20] However, such gossip only alluded to a peculiar coincidence,

[18] Wyatt's translation in '*King Chulalongkorn the Great*', pp. 6-7.

[19] Bradley, journal, 3 and 12 October and 11 and 18 November 1868.

[20] Chula Chakrabongse, *Lords of Life*, p. 219.

and it may not be taken as a reflection of existing hostilities. Sisuriyawong was a perfectly honorable man who had agreed to let Chulalongkorn become king, and he encouraged the boy to assume the royal role. The young Chulalongkorn presided at cremation rituals for members of the royal family; he gave public audiences whenever a foreign envoy came to Bangkok, and when one of Queen Victoria's letters reached Bangkok, it was Chulalongkorn who accepted the missive while a salute of twenty-one guns was given. Every October or November the young king would make official presentations to Buddhist monasteries in connection with the *Kathin* festival, and around 18 November there would be a large fireworks display in honor of the anniversary of his coronation tour. Early in 1870 he traveled to Nakhon Pathom, because at that time the gigantic pagoda his father had begun building was completed.[21] Thus the young king was able to become used to the regal role, and he often formally appeared in public as Siam's head of state.

In 1870, one year and five months after King Mongkut's death, the great ceremony of the cremation of his remains took place. This was a major state ceremony, a time when traditionally all the heads of vassal states would come to Bangkok in order to pay respect to the deceased and pay homage to the new king. The cremation may be seen as the formal farewell to the previous king, and it was a tradition that major decisions and innovations were best postponed until after the ritual. That is why the general registration of the populace in central Siam began immediately afterwards.[22] This appears also to have been the time when the young king began to show signs of wanting to be involved in the nation's affairs and to play an active and innovative role.

This was the year when the young king recruited among relatives, friends and acquaintances for the *Mahatlek*, the corps of royal pages. He created as part of that department a subsection, the *kong Thahan Mahatlek Raksa Phra'ong*, or the *Mahatlek* Royal Bodyguard Troops, with himself taking the position of commander, with the rank of colonel.[23]

On 19 September 1870, during the festivities for the king's seventeenth birthday, there was a grand illumination. According to one of the capital's oldest foreign residents, this was by far the most glorious illumination Bangkok had seen thus far. Two days later, on the king's actual birthday, some fifty Europeans and Americans were entertained with a banquet at the palace of the *chaophraya Phrakhlang*.[24]

Early in 1871 the young king went on his first voyage overseas, to Singapore and Batavia. This travel in foreign parts had been planned by the regent, in whose considered opinion it would be good to let the king observe the British and Dutch systems of administration. On 9 March 1871 the king, accom-

[21] Bradley, journal, 28 May 1870.

[22] *Ibid.*, 11 June 1870.

[23] *Prawatkitchakanthahan samai Krung-ratanakosin*, p. 44.

[24] Bradley, journal, 19 and 21 September 1870.

panied by the senior Bunnak members of the 'cabinet' and a number of others, left Bangkok, to return on 15 April. Everywhere abroad the king was lavishly entertained, and at the same time the educational aspect of the journey was not forgotten. Chulalongkorn visited 'post-offices, jails, hospitals, schools, telegraph offices, fire stations, lighthouses, botanical gardens and museums, theatres, shops and stores, orphanages, railways and factories.'[25] On his tour, Chulalongkorn attended a performance of a travelling American circus and invited the show to Bangkok, pledging a sum of money to persuade them to include Bangkok in their itinerary. Thus, a few days after the king returned, probably for the first time in Siam's history a circus performance took place at the Royal Palace.[26] This may be taken as a clear sign of the young king's independent and original turn of mind. Having greatly enjoyed his study tour, Chulalongkorn asked the regent to arrange a visit to Europe. However, Sisuriyawong decided that a European tour was out of the question and suggested instead a visit to India.

Meanwhile, at the Royal Palace the king reorganized his troops again, this time to form a separate *krom*, named *krom Thahan Mahatlek Ratchawanlop Raksa Phra'ong*, or Faithful Royal Bodyguard, consisting of six companies of ninety-two men each.[27] Some of the officers were officially given a monthly salary in their letters of appointment. This represents a departure from the system of yearly *biawat*. It indicates that the young king intended to offer, at least to some men of rank, financial security. For the time being, only four appointments in the *Mahatlek* were singled out for this honor, and other royal appointments during 1871 and 1872 were made according to the time-honored principles of mentioning only the person's name at the time of appointment, his new name, his *krom*, his *saktina* rating and the date of appointment.[28]

The military character of the six new companies may have been partly the result of wishing to imitate the 'Second King's' body of troops, the late Phra Pinklao's pride and joy, troops which had been drilled on European lines. At the same time, Chulalongkorn's ambitions were more comprehensive. To the military training the young boys received was added a program of general instruction directed towards a career in the government administration. At the king's instigation, a series of new textbooks was written with which the students could gain a grounding mainly in literary expression. It was intended to make English part of the curriculum, but no suitable instructor could be found on short notice. The king decided therefore to enroll fourteen of his relatives, all boys of *momchao* rank, at the Raffles Institution in Singapore.[29] He used the opportunity of his Indian tour to deliver this batch of Siamese students. Chulalongkorn's second journey abroad lasted more than three months and during that time he visited Singapore, Malacca,

[25] D. K. Wyatt, *The Politics of Reform in Thailand: Education in the Reign of King Chulalongkorn*, p. 40; see also N. A. Battye, 'The Military, Government and Society in Siam 1868-1910: Politics and Military Reform during the Reign of King Chulalongkorn', pp. 119-21.

[26] Bradley, journal, 29 April 1871.

[27] *Prawatkitchakanthahan*, p. 45.

[28] *Kantaengtangkhunnangthai*, p. 176-7.

[29] Wyatt, *The Politics of Reform*, p. 70 and *Prawatkitchakanthahan*, p. 45. This was the second group of high-ranking youths sent abroad. Already in 1871 some young students were sent to Singapore and England. The most notable among the first group were probably *momchao* Pritsadang, who successfully completed a course at King's College, London, and *phra'ongchao* Sawat, one of Chulalongkorn's brothers.

Penang, Moulmein, Rangoon, Calcutta, Delhi, Agra, Lucknow, Kanpur, Bombay, and Benares.

The young king appeared greatly stimulated by his experiences abroad. He was now one of Siam's most traveled men and eager to apply all he had learnt in the improvement of the palace, Bangkok and the country as a whole. During the welcoming reception upon his return, at the young king's express wish, not one of the guests was allowed to crouch or prostrate himself.[30] The military school in the palace was further built up with a section where English, French, and mathematics were taught under the supervision of F. G. Patterson, who was engaged for a period of three years, even though he had no previous knowledge of the Siamese language. Just as in the early experiments of this kind when King Mongkut organized English instruction for the women's section of the palace, after an initial period of enthusiasm the number of pupils rapidly declined, and by 1873 only five princes, all younger brothers of Chulalongkorn, still attended.[31]

During the year 1873 King Chulalongkorn would reach his majority, and he began preparing for the moment when he would gain formal control over Siam's destiny. By this time it had become quite clear that he was a bold and daring young man, and also that in the course of the five years preceding the 'second coronation'[32] no feelings of cordiality had developed between him and Sisuriyawong. The two appear to have avoided each other quite studiously, and nobody dared go near the king lest he should be taken as an informer against the regent.[33] A topic that was frequently broached in the houses of many powerful men during 1873 was what the king would do after gaining full power. Some time in late 1872 or early 1873 the king submitted a formal program for reform, proposing to abolish the *corvée* system, slavery and gambling, to reform the law courts and develop a salaried bureaucracy, police force and a regular army.[34] Quite understandably, these plans were rejected by the council of ministers as being impracticable, and it is with this background in mind that we must understand Bradley's conversation with one of the young princes, the gist of which was 'that the young king was fully prepared to make great improvements in his administration when he comes into full power, but that now he meets with much opposition from the old fogies in high places or power, and hence he judges it best to wait quietly for his full power.'[35]

The First Reforms

In November 1873, almost two months after the king's twentieth birthday, he was formally re-anointed and the period of regency came to an end. The king's first decree could have

[30] Bradley, journal, 19 March 1872. Apparently the king had begun training the members of his Royal Bodyguard with regard to the European custom of moving freely about during a reception for his birthday, not long before his departure for India; for details see Battye, 'The Military', p. 122.

[31] Wyatt, *The Politics of Reform*, pp. 70-71.

[32] By this time, under European influence, the moment of crowning had gained considerable symbolic value so that one is more justified in speaking of a coronation rather than an anointment.

[33] Prachoom Chomchai, *Chulalongkorn the Great*, p. 16.

[34] For details, see Battye, 'The Military', pp. 137-8.

[35] Conversation with Prince Sai Sanitwong, one of Prince Wongsathirat's sons (Bradley, journal, 4 April 1873).

caused little surprise, because he had indicated his views quite clearly on previous occasions. It was an order that henceforth his subjects were not permitted to prostrate themselves before him. He had come to view this time-honored Siamese practice with distaste, aware of the discomfort Europeans felt when confronted with these outward signs of a system of inequality. Possibly the king hoped that by doing away with the custom he would encourage people to stand up for themselves, to speak more openly and with more forth-rightness. If those were his intentions, the measure cannot be regarded as very effective outside the group of the king's personal friends.

Almost immediately upon assuming formal control of the government, the king made a series of appointments strengthening the *Mahatlek* and its military branches. Most of these carried monthly salaries, an expansion of the first four salaried positions given in 1871, so that the number of people receiving money every month was raised to thirty-two. All these positions were held within the palace organization, and for the time being the experiment was not extended over the *kroms* beyond. It is also clear from the list of appointments that the leading positions were given to young men from influential families, such as the Chuto, Kanlayanmit, Singhaseni, Khochaseni, Khridet, Buranasiri and Amatayakun families. The Bunnak family was also well represented. Among the first batch of appointments young Thuy Bunnak was promoted to lieutenant in the first company and Thomya Bunnak to ensign. Also remarkable honors were accorded to Phon Bunnak, who became lieutenant-colonel in the *Mahatlek* with the title of *phraya* Phatsakora-wong and a *saktina* of 3,000 *rai*.[36] The strong representation of the regent's family in these appointments should not be seen as an attempt on the regent's part to enlarge his influence at the king's palace, because the Bunnak family ought not to be regarded as a unified group. *Phraya* Phatsakorawong appears to have been a very independent character. He was the youngest son of the late Elder *somdet*, and therefore the regent's youngest half-brother. When he was fifteen Sisuriyawong had sent him for four years' education in England and at the time of King Mongkut's death he had already become a junior official in one of the king's palace departments. Probably he was the only Siamese of his time who was completely fluent in both written and spoken English. During the regency period he became a close friend of the young king and shared and stimulated some of Chulalongkorn's reformist ideas. Apparently he was loyal to the king and did not hesitate to defend him strongly when the regent voiced some criticism.

Phraya Phatsakorawong aided the king in finding a solution to the problem of the large measure of control over senior ministries still exercised by the Bunnaks, even after the king had formally taken on responsibility for ruling Siam. In early

[36] Further details can be found in *Kantaengtangkhunnangthai*, pp. 197-202.

May 1874, Chulalongkorn announced the appointment of a State Council to advise the monarch in making laws. All members of the State Council were of *phraya* rank; none of the senior *chaophraya*-ranking officials were included, nor did the council have any representatives from the royal family. All its members appear to have been fairly senior officials, scions of influential families whom the king trusted as knowledgeable, reliable and progressive men. Naturally, *phraya* Phatsakorawong was included as a member. Siam's senior ministers were invited to attend the new council's deliberations. The ex-regent did not attend, although it is likely that he was invited. The appointment of a State Council was generally seen as a measure intended to diminish the power of Sisuriyawong's faction. At first many members did not dare to attend meetings for fear of offending the ex-regent.[37] Gradually, however, as no drastic revenge was taken, confidence grew.

The State Council bravely began its deliberations with two major items. The first was the question of the control of the country's finances. It was the council's intention to begin collecting all forms of taxation and paying all state revenue into a central treasury. It was not long before the council met with a direct refusal to co-operate. In July 1874 the head of the *krom Na, phraya* Ahanborirak, a nephew of the ex-regent, was reprimanded for being unwilling to disclose details regarding the collection of land tax.[38] Later that year one of the council's committees found him guilty of misappropriation of government funds. He was dismissed and imprisoned, whereupon one of the members of the State Council, *phraya* Ratchaworanakun (Rot Kanlayanmit) was put into the vacant position. A second item for deliberation concerned the gradual abolition of slavery. After lengthy discussion, it was decided to proclaim an act providing for a new scale for the valuation of 'absolute' slaves' children, a law acting retrospectively and including all children born as 'absolute' slaves from the beginning of the fifth reign onwards. These children had a legal maximum value, which under the new law was to diminish gradually so that by the age of twenty-one they would automatically have lost all value and become free.[39]

In August 1874 the king created a second committee, the Privy Council, the members of which were to be personal advisers to the king. At first forty-nine men made up the Privy Council. Among them were thirteen members of the royal family, the head of the *krom Mahatthai* (*chaophraya* Phutharaphai) and the head of the *krom Phrakhlang* (*chaophraya* Phanuwong), and many officials in less exalted positions, including some as low in the official hierarchy as *luang*.[40] All members of the State Council were *ex officio* Privy Counselors. Sisuriyawong was invited to become a member, but he declined firmly. So did his eldest son, head of the *krom*

[37] Prachoom Chomchai, *Chulalongkorn the Great*, p. 37.

[38] Battye, 'The Military', p. 155.

[39] Prachoom Chomchai, *Chulalongkorn the Great*, pp. 50-65.

[40] *Ibid.*, p. 40.

Kalahom. Unlike the State Council, from which members could resign, the Privy Council was thought of as 'permanent', and all Privy Counselors had to swear a special oath of allegiance to the monarch. The Privy Council was created to guarantee a constant flow of information to the king and to provide a wide debating ground to discuss the ways and means for major reforms.

The fact that the king proceeded rapidly with major and fundamental reform measures that threatened to deprive the largest *kroms* of their financial independence and impinged upon their judicial powers, combined with the fact that Sisuriyawong and his eldest son took no part in the deliberations, made for an ominous situation. Sooner or later, it seemed, the ex-regent and his party would find themselves in open conflict with the king and the reformers. This situation was to a large extent the result of Chulalongkorn's youthful impatience and inexperience. The ex-regent was not in principle against many of the proposed reforms, but he resented the fact that he was not given a prominent role in the process of policy-making and he decided for the time being to remain aloof.[41] However, before the situation developed into a confrontation between the young radicals and the established interests, a completely different conflict, between Chulalongkorn and the *Uparat*, decided the fate of the reformers.

The 'Palace Incident' and its consequences

When Prince Wichaichan was installed as head of the Front Palace, he did not receive the quite extraordinary honors that had been given to Phra Pinklao in 1851. His title reverted to that of *Maha Uparat*, and the details of his anointment demonstrate clearly that his position was not as exalted as his father's had been.[42] Nevertheless, he was able to act, especially with respect of Europeans and Americans, in the manner that had become customary during the fourth reign. Thus he placed his seal as 'Second King' upon treaties with foreign powers, gave receptions to foreign dignitaries and freely distributed a photograph of himself, crowned and seated on a throne flanked by regalia. He received his father's income of 160,000 *baht* per annum from the Royal Treasury, and with that amount of money he was able to maintain an entourage comparable in size to that of Chulalongkorn. It included a number of troops, some two thousand infantry and four hundred artillery, all well armed, drilled and trained.[43] The following account of one of the parades at the Front Palace, held early in 1872 to entertain an American visitor when Chulalongkorn was in India, provides an idea of their high standards:

[41] On the ex-regent and his attitude towards the reformers, see the correspondence published in the *Straits Times*, 28 May and 18 and 27 July 1874.

[42] Battye, 'The Military', pp. 161-2.

[43] *Ibid.*, p. 164.

There were two companies of troops, which marched in quick time from their barracks. The Second King has two thousand soldiers; but these were picked men (or rather boys, for such they were), who guarded the palace and its royal occupants, and of whose proficiency in military tactics His Majesty is especially proud. They have had various instructors (drill-masters) at different times - French, English and German; the orders which we heard given were in broken German. Their uniform of white duck is patterned after that worn by the British troops in India; they wear also (mirabile dictu!) shoes and socks. The companies, in turn, went through the manual of arms, and performed some skirmishing in remarkably good style; the musket drill was better than that of many of our so-called "crack" regiments at home. After the parade His Majesty's own brass band played for us.[44]

The *Uparat* was a busy man during the regency period. He traveled and was actively involved in the drawing up of the most accurate maps of Siam at that time.[45] He was interested in European technology and the modernization of the country, and the few accounts of him show him to be an attractive, well-educated, and mature person. Sisuriyawong could get along with him, and possibly the regent would have liked him to have occupied the position of monarch, a situation which was not unthinkable during the first five years of the 1870s. If a fatal accident had befallen Chulalongkorn, who had as yet no descendants, the *Uparat* would have been in an excellent position for consideration for elevation to the throne.

Chulalongkorn was envious of the *Uparat's* impressive little army, which outdid that of the *Mahatlek*. Prince Wichaichan bought two Armstrong guns with his own funds. The royal edict of September 1874, in which it was prohibited to buy or accept as a present the redoubtable Gatling gun, was directly aimed at preventing the *Uparat* from obtaining this weapon 'with which one man would dare to fight an army.'[46] Possibly the king saw the *Uparat's* presence as a threat to his own authority while the process of reform was meeting with its first opposition. When T. G. Knox, the British consul-general and a close friend of the *Uparat*, left for six months' leave in Europe in late 1874, he asked W. H. Newman, who would be acting British consul, and F. Garnier, the French consul, to watch over Prince Wichaichan.[47] During December of that year it seemed that the king was planning to either abolish the position of *Uparat* altogether or to replace Wichaichan. Rumors of the king's intentions reached the Front Palace, and Wichaichan's people felt exceedingly apprehensive. In late December the king heard that the *Uparat* was arming an unusu-

[44] F. Vincent, *The Land of the White Elephant*, pp. 151-2.

[45] Bradley, journal, 19 April and 31 May 1869.

[46] Battye, 'The Military', p. 169.

[47] *Ibid.*, p. 172. The following account of the 'Palace Incident' is based on Battye's dissertation, as well as the study by Xie Shunyu, *Siam and the British, 1874-75: Sir Andrew Clarke and the Front Palace Crisis*, Bangkok: Thammasat University Press, 1988.

ally large number of men and before the veracity of the report could be tested, some of the king's guards were alerted. No direct communication took place between Chulalongkorn and Wichaichan regarding the tense situation.

On the night of 28 December 1874, a fire broke out in the gasworks of the Grand Palace, a dangerous spot not far from the gunpowder magazine, the armory and an oil storage. When the fire was being extinguished, it was noted that the troops from the Front Palace had been tardy in coming to the rescue. It was assumed that the *Uparat's* men had been responsible for the fire and when they arrived later in the night to offer assistance, they were refused entry. Chulalongkorn treated the event as a direct assault upon himself and ordered a full alarm. On 29 December, some five or six thousand men were armed to protect the king,[48] and the Front Palace was besieged during the early hours of that day. Chulalongkorn wrote a letter to Sisuriyawong, who was at his private residence in Ratburi, asking him to return to Bangkok for consultations, but before the ex-regent had time to come, the king invited Wichaichan to discuss the matter in a private audience, during which he planned to have the *Uparat* arrested. However, Wichaichan declined the invitation.

On 31 December Sisuriyawong arrived upon the scene and advised the king to negotiate a settlement. Sisuriyawong himself became the go-between, and he presented Wichaichan with Chulalongkorn's terms, which were that the *Uparat* should abandon the Front Palace, disband its personnel and assent to a ritual purification as amends for any offence to the king's person. He would then be allowed to retain any personal servants who chose to stay with him and would be assured of sufficient income to keep them. The prince considered the proposals and eventually decided that they were unacceptable. No longer certain of Sisuriyawong's protection, and in the face of the massive number of troops pitched against him, the unfortunate Wichaichan decided to flee. During the night he managed to leave his palace unseen and reach the British consulate, where the acting consul-general granted him asylum.

The *Uparat*, not wishing to be sacrificed for the sake of national unity, had in his despair forced an international incident. All efforts to persuade Wichaichan to leave the consulate failed. There were rumors that the British would invade the country and many people prepared for flight. It was not long before a British and a French man-of-war arrived at Bangkok. New proposals were made to Wichaichan, offering him the Front Palace and a certain amount of power, but the prince, probably aware of the widespread opinion that his flight was a treacherous act, refused to leave the safety of the British consulate. Three weeks after his arrival there, the acting consul requested Sir Andrew Clarke, the governor of the Straits

---

[48] *Straits Times*, 16 January 1875.

Settlements, to come and assist in breaking the deadlock. A month later, the affair was settled. Clarke had decided, in accordance with general British opinion,[49] to support Chulalongkorn in his attempt to dismantle the *Uparat's* military establishment and at the same time he arranged for Wichaichan's safe return to the Front Palace. While Chulalongkorn had succeeded in asserting himself towards the *Uparat*, it cannot be said that he had gained a clear victory over his opponent. During January 1875 it became quite clear that the crisis was seen by many as the outcome of the king's extraordinary pace in reforming the country. The pro-Western clique around Chulalongkorn was widely blamed for encouraging the king to act hastily. A petition was circulated in Bangkok addressed to Sisuriyawong, asking him to drive out the king's associates, abolish the State Council, dispense with newfangled ideas such as allowing people to wear shoes in sacred precincts, and abandon the recently introduced modes of address and salutation.[50] Sisuriyawong had witnessed with growing disapproval how members of the State Council and the Privy Council, in their youthful zeal, had antagonized many people, including members of the *senabodi* (ministerial committee, or 'cabinet') whose co-operation was necessary for efficient government. He was quite happy to lay the blame upon the reformist faction. Probably Chulalongkorn himself became convinced by the popular reaction against the new councils that he had been too hasty and he asked the members of the councils to show restraint. In 1875 the Bunnak-dominated *senabodi* regained its authority.

During the years immediately following the 'Palace Incident' both the State Council and the Privy Council continued to exist, but the king no longer attempted to force major changes by means of these institutions. It may be tempting to depict the abrupt halt in major reform measures as a triumph for the conservative factions, with Sisuriyawong, in his late sixties, as the 'arch-conservative' again in power. However, such a view would do justice neither to the king nor to Sisuriyawong. Chulalongkorn appears to have been penitent and contrite. Events had shown a widespread resentment of some of his fondest ideas; his actions had been instrumental in creating a crisis that had threatened the national peace. At the same time he had noted how many people had spontaneously rallied behind him, even though they considered his clique of modernizers a bad influence. The king reconsidered his position and decided that he was king of Siam 'by consent of all', and that he ought to avoid actions that would make the people unhappy.[51]

At the same time, Sisuriyawong should not be seen simply as an intransigent reactionary. It is true that he had no sympathy with the State Council and the Privy Council, which he considered dominated by juveniles, but this does not preclude his broad-mindedness in other respects. Sisuriyawong had always

---

[49] *Ibid.*, editorial.

[50] Battye, 'The Military', pp. 194-5.

[51] W. S. Bristowe, *Louis and the King of Siam*, p. 45, citing an account of a dramatic confrontation between Knox and Chulalongkorn in 1879. Similar sentiments were expressed on other occasions during the years immediately after the 'Palace Incident' (see Battye, 'The Military', pp. 209-10).

been in the vanguard of reformation: he had pioneered the introduction of Western technology, and had an intelligent appreciation of the insights that could be derived from comparing foreign customs with those of one's own country. He shared many of the ideals of the group that surrounded Chulalongkorn in 1874, disagreeing with its members largely over the means they chose and the speed with which they wished to attain their goals. He also had a good grasp of international developments, in particular the immense power of the British Empire. In 1876 Sisuriyawong again had an opportunity to travel abroad when he chose to attend the large Delhi durbar on the occasion of Queen Victoria being proclaimed Empress of India. On his way to India he spent some time in Singapore, where he was received with great honor.[52]

King Chulalongkorn was still a reformer and he let it be known that he hoped to instigate many changes. However, in contrast to the year immediately after his coming of age, he now moved with great circumspection, encouraging innovation only when he had ascertained there would be no opposition from the more conservative factions. New initiatives ascribed to the king during the years immediately following the 'Palace Incident' were relatively minor ones, such as a decree encouraging all royal monasteries to use the textbooks that had originally been devised for the palace school.[53] During 1877 he waxed enthusiastic over a proposal that had been put forward by Samuel McFarland for the establishment of a college of education in Bangkok. This would give both princes and nobles a chance to receive a modern education. It would be an institution where they could learn European arts and sciences. This school proved initially much more successful than the earlier one in which Patterson had taught.[54] In addition to founding this college, the king reputedly was personally involved in ordering a 'floating fire engine' to protect Bangkok port,[55] and he described himself as having been active in encouraging the digging of new canals and the opening up of new rice land.[56]

Towards Firmer Control of the Outer Regions

Siam's leaders were aware of the dangers inherent in the ancient system of vassal states. France's incursion into Cambodia had demonstrated the necessity for consolidation of the nation's strength in the outer regions to forestall other powers' expansionist programs. Bangkok's control was fairly strong in most of the southern provinces. Towards the east the Siamese rule was accepted in Battambang and Angkor provinces; however, in Vientiane, Luang Prabang, Chiang Mai and many smaller *mu'angs*, Siamese overlordship was largely a matter of ceremony. From time to time a formal tribute

[52] *Straits Times*, 9 December 1876.

[53] D. K. Wyatt, 'Samuel McFarland and Early Educational Modernization in Thailand, 1877-1895', *Felicitation Volumes of Southeast-Asian Studies Presented to His Highness Prince Dhaninivat Kromamun Bidyalabh Bridhyakorn*, vol. 1, pp. 1-2.

[54] *Ibid.*, passim.

[55] *Straits Times*, 3 March 1877.

[56] From King Chulalongkorn's 1877 birthday speech, as reported in the *Siam Weekly Advertiser*, 25 October 1877, and reprinted in the *Straits Times*, 10 November 1877.

mission would be sent to Bangkok, and while the Siamese government had the formal right to appoint local chiefs, these *mu'angs* remained for all practical purposes independently governed territories. During the regency and the early years of Chulalongkorn's reign, this situation continued in the Laotian states of Wieng Chan (Vientiane) and Luang Prabang, but it changed considerably in Chiang Mai and its surroundings *mu'angs*. Already during 1870, in order to protect some American citizens resident in Chiang Mai, the regent had been forced to send a 'royal commissioner' to the north, empowered to command Kawilorot, the lord of Chiang Mai, to leave the resident American missionaries in peace.[57] Sometime around 1874, taking advantage of the fact that the man who had succeeded Kawilorot was mild and rather indolent, Chulalongkorn appointed a permanent representative at Chiang Mai, complete with a bodyguard co-opted from troops attached to the Grand Palace.[58]

The commissioner, *phraya* Thepworachan, had the unenviable task of being the king's representative without a clearly formulated brief. His task appears to have been mainly limited to dealing with cases involving international rights. Usually these concerned complaints by Burmese, who professed to be British subjects, regarding infringements upon teak-felling contracts that they had signed with local chiefs. Whenever the Siamese decided a lawsuit in favor of the Burmese, hard feelings were aroused among the local leaders, and some resentment against Siamese 'meddling' was apparent. A challenge to Siam's authority came in 1878 when the commissioner adjudicated a case between the senior administrators of *mu'ang* Lampang. In this instance his decision was not respected by one of the parties, namely the ruler of Lampang himself. Soon afterwards, the king strengthened his hand by changing his appointment from 'commissioner' to 'governor', nominally bringing the north under direct Siamese control.[59] However, it would take several far-reaching measures more than a decade later before this nominal control was backed up by an administrative reform that would effectively bring Chiang Mai under Bangkok's sway.

Meanwhile, the Siamese leaders had been able to reassure themselves regarding their authority over the region controlled by Vientiane and Luang Prabang. In these northeastern parts there had been an insurrection caused by Chinese 'Ho gangs', who had mustered an army of some four thousand men. The problem was handled effectively in a traditional manner, the northern region falling under the *krom Mahatthai*. In late 1875 its officials raised a small army in the northern provinces and marched up to meet the enemy. The Ho chiefs decided to avoid a direct military confrontation and tendered their submission. The campaign was concluded in April 1876, apparently without a shot having been fired.

[57] D. McGilvary, *A Half Century Among the Siamese and the Lao*, pp. 102-29.

[58] Battye, 'The Military', p. 146.

[59] McGilvary, A *Half Century Among the Siamese*, p. 220.

186

In the following year, large-scale rioting broke out in the southern provinces of Ranong and Phuket. The central government sent *chaomu'n* Samoechairat (Chun Bunnak) to rally forces from various southern provinces and put down the disturbances at Phuket. The governor of Ranong, assisted by troops from a neighboring province, managed to restore order in his own region.[60] By the end of 1877 the government had demonstrated its ability to maintain its hold over outer provinces and vassal states, being able to do so by following the time-honored methods. Chulalongkorn played only a minor role in these affairs; the responsibility for the day-to-day decision-making had reverted to the Bunnak-dominated *senabodi*. The case of the ill-fated *phra* Pricha clearly illustrates in whose hands most power lay.

Phra Pricha, Chulalongkorn and Sisuriyawong

The case against *phra* Pricha was in itself not very important and it would have run its course unnoted by historians, had it not been for the passionate intervention of the British consul. *Phra* Pricha was a middle-ranking government official, a member of the Amatayakun family, one of the leading influential families of that time. An Amatayakun (Mot) had been appointed to the State Council, one (Khlip) was governor of Prachinburi, another (Phlap) was one of Siam's chief judges,[61] yet another held a senior position in the *krom Phrakhlang.*[62] *Phra* Pricha was not as high-ranking as all these relatives, yet he wielded more influence than his rank would suggest, because he knew the king personally. Early in 1879 *phra* Pricha was in great trouble, for he had been formally accused of embezzling funds. The accusation came from members of the Bunnak family, at that time undoubtedly by far the most powerful in the country. In a bid to save himself, *phra* Pricha married Fanny Knox, the eldest daughter of the British consul-general. The newly forged links with the leader of the consular corps did not prevent his arrest, which took place in March 1879 not long after the marriage,[63] by which time *phra* Pricha had given Fanny all his property.

In April, knowing that his daughter was expecting a child, Consul Knox made a bold attempt to help *phra* Pricha. He went to Chulalongkorn and asked him to intervene. Meanwhile, however, the investigations into *phra* Pricha's past had uncovered serious malfeasances relating to the management of the Kabin gold-mine in Prachinburi province. In addition he was now charged with having murdered some of the prisoners working there. The case had developed into a full-scale scandal and apart from the main culprit, *phra* Pricha, other members of the Amatayakun family were arrested and held in

---

[60] For details, see *Prawatkitchakanthahan*, p. 47, and the *Straits Times*, 10 November 1877.

[61] *Kantaengtangkhunnangthai*, p. 6 and p. 184.

[62] Bristowe, *Louis and the King of Siam*, p. 44. Probably this refers to *phraya* Charoenratchamaitri, mentioned in *Kantaengtangkhunnangthai*, p. 217 and p. 219.

[63] Manich Jumsai, *Prince Prisdang's Files on His Diplomatic Activities in Europe, 1880-1886*, p. 238.

custody. Knox reminded the king of the friendship that had existed between him and *phra* Pricha and requested that the king appoint unbiased judges to examine the charges. Chulalongkorn assured the consul that he did not wish *phra* Pricha to be punished unless he was found guilty. Realizing that the king was not willing to risk the displeasure of most of the cabinet by appointing new judges, Knox did his utmost to provoke the king to action. He depicted the charges as weapons in the hands of the Bunnak family to destroy a rival power, and described Sisuriyawong and his eldest son as the king's enemies. Siam itself was enslaved to Sisuriyawong. Knox is reported to have continued as follows:

> *I should like to see it [Siam] free for once. If Your Majesty will dismiss the* Somdetch Chao Phraya *[Sisuriyawong] and the Minister for Foreign Affairs, I will help you in every way. And Siam will be free. ... I know for certain that that party wish to wrest the Sovereignty from Your Majesty and destroy you. If you do not act now, you will in future have no-one to help and no authority.*[64]

In addition, Knox told the king that he had summoned a warship that could be of assistance. Chulalongkorn did not take the bait and insisted that *phra* Pricha would stand trial, reassuring Knox that he saw no imminent danger to his throne. Knox, a man with a formidable record in Siam,[65] clearly had no business interfering officially on behalf of *phra* Pricha, and his spirited attempt not only was firmly rejected by Chulalongkorn but also was repudiated in London and caused him to be recalled and retired. *Phra* Pricha was duly tried and found guilty. Not long before his execution Fanny left the country, taking her newly born baby, two of *phra* Pricha's children by another marriage, and a large amount of money and valuables.[66]

The confrontation between the British consul and the king reflects also on the relations between the king and the Bunnak family. Knox tried to turn the enmity between Sisuriyawong and Chulalongkorn to his own advantage. It was now four years since the 'Palace Incident', and the king had not established cordial relations with the *senabodi*. The affairs of the Grand Palace were left to Chulalongkorn, while the government of the country remained largely in the hands of the senior ministers. Legally, Chulalongkorn had immense powers and he was gradually regaining some confidence in himself. However, he clearly felt in no position to act of his own accord and provoke a direct conflict over *phra* Pricha's case.

The Tug-of-war for Manpower

Although King Chulalongkorn may outwardly have demon-

---

[64] As recounted by Bristowe, *Louis and the King of Siam*, p. 45. A much more dispassionate account of Knox's interview can be found in Chulalongkorn's diary for 1879-80. See *Chotmaihet Phraratchakitraiwannai Phrabatsomdet Phrachunlachomklao Chaoyuhua Pi Tho Chunlasakarat 1241*, the entry for 21 April 1879, pp. 30-1.

[65] Thomas George Knox had served in the Siamese army between 1851 and 1857. During that time he had married the daughter of a high Siamese official. In 1857 he left the army and became interpreter at the new British Consulate. From 1887 he had been the British consul-general in Bangkok.

[66] Bristowe, *Louis and the King of Siam*, p. 46, and Manich Jumsai, *Prince Prisdang's Files*, pp. 238-45. A rather romantic, but fairly well-researched account of the whole affair can be found in R. J. Minney, *Fanny and the Regent of Siam*, London: Collins, 1962.

strated a united front with the *senabodi*, he retained and expanded his circle of 'progressive modernists' and occasionally managed to favor his trusted friends with appointments. Thus, when in 1879 a mission was sent to England to conclude an arrangement regarding the status of Siam's northern vassal states, the honor of leading the mission was given to Phatsakorawong. Prince Sai Sanitwong had been put in charge of the Royal Arsenal and in 1879 he also gained the command of the Royal Yachts.[67] Choem Saengchuto, another of Chulalongkorn's close friends, became an officer of the First Foot Guard, and when the commander was replaced on account of gross negligence,[68] Choem rose to be deputy-commander. He had direct access to the king and was thus able to suggest and implement reforms over the head of his commanding officer. Having been trained in the king's personal bodyguard, Choem found the First Foot sadly lacking. Its enrolment had dropped over the years until it had only about three hundred men under arms at any one time.[69]

> *The officials tucked away the fees the commoners paid not to serve and padded the registration lists when they drew funds and supplies; with one hand they cheated their subordinates and with the other they misappropriated funds from the Royal Treasury. Many of them were incompetents who had purchased their posts which were investments made to pay by corrupt practices. The men in the ranks were poorly trained by the best Siamese standards of the day.[70]*

With the king's full knowledge and backing, Choem began to reform the First Foot Guard. Corrupt officers were delegated to a reserve force and more enthusiastic ones put in their positions. In order to boost the number of troops, Choem proposed to attract young men who were not officially registered and tattooed as being *phrai luang* or *phrai som*. The king agreed and posters were put up asking for volunteers to join the First Foot Guard. Those prepared to enlist for five years were offered four *baht* in cash and a piece of cloth and permitted to remain free of administrative tattoos.[71]

The recruiting drive was immensely successful. Over five thousand men, mainly from the Ratburi and Phetburi regions, flocked to Bangkok. The gains to the reconstituted First Foot Guard were, however, at the expense of the old system of *phrai som* and *phrai luang*, and state officials in Ratburi and Phetburi were faced with an acute shortage of manpower. Sisuriyawong, who had a large estate at Ratburi, came to intercede with the king, asking him to allow the volunteers to return. The king pointed out that most of his recruits had been unregistered under the old system and therefore they automatically fell into the category of king's men. He agreed to return the few men

[67] Battye, 'The Military', p. 216.

[68] The First Foot Guard was responsible among other things for the safety of all those taking part in royal processions. In mid-1880 there was a boat accident near the king's palace at Bang Pa-In in which one of Chulalongkorn's senior queens, his half-sister Queen Sunanda, was drowned. The accident has been wrongly taken as having occurred in 1881 by Chula Chakrabongse (*Lords of Life*, p. 221), because he took the date of the monument commemorating the event as the date for the accident. For the exact date, see *Ratchasakunwong*, p. 59.

[69] Battye, 'The Military', p. 223.

[70] *Ibid.*, pp. 223-4.

[71] *Ibid.*, p. 226.

who had been firmly employed in Ratburi and kept the remainder.

The king's firm stance towards the ex-regent may be seen as a sign that by 1880 he had ceased to be subservient to the *senabodi* and that he was beginning to assume a greater share of responsibility. He was able to do so for several reasons. In the first place many of his half-brothers were reaching maturity; some of them were able and diligent men who were happy to serve their elder brother. Outstanding among these was young Prince Thewan, who assisted the king as private secretary.[72] Secondly, over the course of time the king had been able to change the composition of the *senabodi*. Whenever a vacancy occurred, he had been able to fill the post with someone in whom he could place trust. In 1876 the twenty-year-old *kromamu'n* Phutharet was appointed to head the *krom Mu'ang*, and in 1878 the king's uncle, *kromphra* Bamrap (*chaofa* Mahamala), became the head of the *krom Mahatthai*. Thirdly, Sisuriyawong was growing rather old and feeble. Fourthly, the three most senior Bunnaks – the ex-regent, the *Kalahom*, and the *Phrakhlang* – by no means formed a united family group. *Chaophraya* Surawongwaiyawat, the ex-regent's eldest son, who had been placed in the best position to maintain Bunnak dominance in Siamese politics, had been a great disappointment to his father. He apparently lacked his father's integrity and administrative ability.[73] *Chaophraya* Phanuwong, Sisuriyawong's half-brother, fell into disgrace in 1880 when he was unsuccessful in negotiations with the British government regarding a new treaty.[74] Sisuriyawong, who was not altogether unsympathetic towards the idea of a more professional army, but who did not wish to see the *corvée* system severely undermined, obtained permission to update the *corvée* lists and instigate tattooing drives. Thus many men who had not joined the new volunteer army were forced to enroll under the old system.[75] The king's innovation in allowing his new volunteers to remain without a tattoo on their wrist caused problems, because these soldiers could now be caught and tattooed under the old system if they could not prove exemption. On the other hand, volunteers with exemption papers could desert and escape all their obligations.

Throughout 1881 there were several clashes of interest between the First Foot Guard and various provincial authorities. In that year a cholera epidemic broke out in Bangkok; hundreds of volunteers died, and thousands were allowed to flee to the provinces.[76] Later it was difficult to round them up and regroup them. In Ratburi province it was discovered that Sisuriyawong's grandson To Bunnak, who was in charge of the local registration, had incited soldiers of the First Foot Guard to desert and register under the old system. One of the king's pet schemes was being undermined by a young Bunnak, as the king was duly informed by officers of the First Foot Guard. Those

[72] Better known under the name of Prince Thewawong, a name he acquired in 1881 (*Ratchasakunwong*, p. 55).

[73] See, for example, C. Bock, *Temples and Elephants: The Narrative of a Journey of Exploration Through Upper Siam and Lao*, p. 15.

[74] Bristowe (*Louis and the King of Siam*, p. 46) asserts that Phanuwong was dismissed from office. This was not the case; he retained his post until his retirement in 1885.

[75] A tattooing office was set up almost immediately at Ratburi (Battye, 'The Military', p. 231), and by December 1881 a traveller reported the arrival of a tattooing official in the northern town of Raheng (Bock, *Temples and Elephants*, p. 133) – undoubtedly part of the same drive.

[76] Battye ('The Military', p. 233) places the epidemic in 1882, but Bock's account (*Temples and Elephants*, pp. 60-61) would suggest that it was in 1881 that the outbreak took place.

who may have hoped for a direct clash between Chulalongkorn and the Bunnaks underestimated Sisuriyawong's political skill and the king's caution. Young To Bunnak was sent to the king to offer his apologies and the king in return waived punishment.[77] In order to prevent further competition between Bangkok and the provinces over the volunteers, it was finally decided to create a new tattoo design for all members of the First Foot Guard, including officers.[78]

Towards Curbing the Consular Powers

Because of the Bowring treaty, Europeans could import a large number of articles at only three per cent duty. Consequently, Siam was opened up as a market for goods produced cheaply abroad, and the results of this could be seen all over the country. Cheap calico and various items of metal, the 'Birmingham ware', found their way to provincial markets.[79] Since European wines and ardent spirits were generally much more costly than the alcoholic beverages manufactured under government licenses, the Siamese had not thought to make a special provision for alcohol. However, rice wines from Java and from Cochin-China could be obtained at comparatively cheap prices, and already during King Mongkut's reign the Siamese government was alarmed at the thought of foreign traders undermining the State's liquor monopoly. The consuls insisted on their rights in this matter, however, and not only imported rice wine but also issued licenses to foreign nationals to trade in this commodity. Each license created a new outlet for selling liquor, and each caused the Siamese government to suffer a reduction in income. In the 1867 treaty with France a clause had been inserted giving the right of issuing licenses to the Siamese authorities. However, none of the other consuls would agree to have their powers thus curbed, and the French consul eventually did not feel obliged to heed the clause since it was prejudicial to the rights of a single country.[80]

The consuls had wide judicial powers, and they could extend their protection not only over foreign nationals but also over locals in their employ. As many consuls had little or no training in legal affairs, it was inevitable that their decisions would often encroach upon what was felt, by the Siamese authorities, to be their own domain. The liquor licensing, however, epitomized in Siamese eyes the inequalities that had emerged from the treaties, and in 1881 a major drive was launched to stop the consuls from issuing these permits. The consuls were advised of the appointment of a Siamese envoy to negotiate with the various European governments a revision of the treaties with particular reference to the sale of spirits. The person appointed was *phra'ongchao* Pritsadang, who, after

---

[77] Battye, 'The Military', pp. 234-35.

[78] *Ibid.*, p. 235.

[79] Bock, *Temples and Elephants*, p. 137. On the effect of cheap imports on some of Siam's local industries, see J. C. Ingram, *Economic Change in Thailand 1850-1970*, pp. 113-21.

[80] Pensri Duke, *Les relations entre la France et la Thailande (Siam) au XIXe siècle*, pp. 58-60.

completing his education in London, had assisted Prince Thewan and been sent back to Europe to guide another group of young Siamese students[81] and carry messages and presents from King Chulalongkorn to various European heads of state. Pritsadang spent many months traveling and negotiating, but all hopes of a quick settlement foundered when France insisted on introducing various political issues and on making political concessions on the part of Siam a condition for an agreement on the sale of spirits.[82]

The Kra Canal

A question that occupied many minds was the possibility of digging a canal through the Isthmus of Kra in southern Siam. The first serious estimate of the amount of work required to cut through the isthmus took place in 1843.[83] Undoubtedly it was the spectacular success of the Suez Canal, which was opened in November 1869, that rekindled interest in the possibility of creating yet another short cut in shipping routes, albeit on a much smaller scale than the Suez Canal. When in 1881 a British firm requested assistance from the British government in its application for a concession to construct the canal, the response was rather discouraging: Her Majesty's government could not recommend any particular applicants for the concession to the Siamese government.[84]

The matter became one of much greater moment when it was learnt that a French concern was interested in the scheme. By 1882 Britain and Siam were the chief powers in the Malay Peninsula; a French concession would introduce a third major party into the region. Moreover, a French-built canal would provide France with control over the shortest shipping route between Europe and China. Furthermore it would greatly stimulate French expansionist drives, one of which had just begun in Tonkin. Thus the British representative in Bangkok was instructed to ensure that a concession would only be granted to a British firm, and only after previous communication with Her Majesty's government.[85] By this time a French emissary was already on his way to Bangkok, and both *chaophraya* Surawongwaiyawat and *chaophraya* Phanuwong were supporting the French move.

In June 1882 the pressure upon the Siamese government was intensified by the arrival of François Deloncle, employed by the French Ministry of Foreign Affairs, who offered the Siamese the services of the famous Ferdinand de Lesseps.[86] Eventually the Siamese government decided to allow the French to make a survey of the terrain where the canal was planned. To prevent international rivalry, the project was handled by the international Suez Canal Company, and the British government agreed not to offer opposition to the concession so long as British subjects

[81] Among them Prince Sawat, the only one of Chulalongkorn's brothers to be given an education abroad.

[82] Details can be found in Manich Jumsai, *Prince Prisdang's Files*, p. 28ff., and Pensri Duke, *Les relations*, pp. 85-9. While from Manich's account it would appear that the negotiations ended successfully in August 1885, it is clear that at the last moment the French refused to implement their ratified treaty, pending further clarification of matters relating to the protection of Annamites and the establishment of a vice-consulate at Luang Prabang.

[83] The 1843 survey was made by G. B. Tremenheere and E. A. Blundell. For references to this and subsequent efforts to examine the question of a canal, see H. B. Smith, 'Historic Proposals for a Kra Canal: Their Impact on International Relations in Southeast Asia with Emphasis on British Perspectives', *Asian Profile* 3, no. 1 (February 1975), pp. 43-58.

[84] *Ibid.*, p. 48.

[85] *Ibid.*, p. 47.

[86] Antoine Benoit François Deloncle was *chef de cabinet* to the undersecretary of state at the French Ministry of Foreign Affairs from 1881 to 1888. See R. d'Amat and R. Limouzin Lamothe, ed., *Dictionnaire de biographie française*, vol. 10, p. 874.

and British vessels would enjoy the same rights as those granted to any other nation.[87] The survey began in January 1883, but
its findings were of such a nature that they effectively put an
end to the French proposal.[88]

The French had demonstrated, however, that they possessed the power and drive to force the issue, notwithstanding
the king's opposition and the British moves to forestall them.
The French proposal may be seen as one of the moves related
to a French expansion of interests in mainland South-East Asia
and China, one that would threaten Siam's very existence in the
years to come.[89]

The Bangkok Centenary

During 1882 the capital was the scene of large-scale festivities
in order to mark the hundredth anniversary of its foundation by
Rama I. It was a time to stress the nation's accomplishments, to
rejoice and to perform ceremonies designed to enhance the
country's chances in the future. The king, now twenty-eight
years old, had devised various ceremonies to celebrate the
event. The most important was probably the official opening of
Wat Phrakaew, or the 'Temple of the Emerald Buddha' as it
became known in foreign circles. This monastery had first been
inaugurated at the beginning of the first reign, but for this occasion it had been completely renovated. Chulalongkorn had
decided upon this scheme in late 1879 and the work was done
at his expense and that of his near relatives. The various buildings in the monastery were decorated in a most lavish style so
as to make the *Wat* a fitting symbol during the celebrations.[90]

Chulalongkorn used the opportunity of the centenary to
complete one of his father's projects: the creation of a fully-
fledged system of European-style decorations to be added to the
array of traditional Siamese marks of ranking. The Most Noble
Order of the Royal House of Chakri was reserved for senior
Siamese princes and members of foreign royal families. The
Order of Chula Chomklao was for presentation to Siamese
princes and nobility. The Order of the White Elephant and the
Order of the Crown of Siam were created for members of the
wider public, for services to the State.[91]

The centenary was also an occasion for setting up a large
national exhibition. The idea of such a spectacle was undoubtedly drawn from foreign examples. Ever since the first 'universal exhibition' in London's Crystal Palace, great cities had vied
with each other in surpassing previous displays. The Siamese
National Exhibition of 1882 consisted of more than fifty
sections illustrating the country's handicrafts, natural resources
and fine arts.[92] The following year a large part of this exhibition
was sent to the international fair at The Hague.[93]

[87] Smith, 'Historic Proposals', p. 51.

[88] It was by no means the last time that
the idea of a canal was put forward.
From time to time the matter was
raised again. For some literature on
more recent proposals, see H.
Cucherousset, *Quelques informations
sur le Siam*, pp. 97-9; J. L. Christian,
'The Kra Canal Fable', *Amerasia* 1
(February 1938), pp. 559-63; and M.
Rajaretnam, *Thailand's Kra Canal:
Some Issues*.

[89] Probably the best background article
on Siam's international politics at this
period is V. G. Kiernan, 'Britain,
Siam, and Malaya: 1875-1885', *The
Journal of Modern History* 27, no. 1
(March 1956), pp. 1-20.

[90] For details, see Bock, *Temples and
Elephants*, pp. 385-91.

[91] One of the first foreigners to be
awarded the Grand Cross of the
Order of the Crown of Siam was
Ferdinand de Lesseps, who received
this honor in 1884, probably for
having been willing to supervise the
digging of the Kra Canal (see Manich
Jumsai, *Prince Prisdang's Files*, pp.
72-3).

[92] Details can be found in Bock,
Temples and Elephants, pp. 392-9.

[93] Manich Jumsai, *Prince Prisdang's
Files*, pp. 117-19.

The Bangkok festivities were an appropriate moment to sum up the king's accomplishments during the fourteen years after his father's death. In a felicitation address five achievements were mentioned: the gradual emancipation of certain classes of slaves, the abolition of prostration before the king, granting permission for all government officers to submit written opinions to the king on any point they thought proper, the improvement in relationships with foreign countries and the construction of Wat Phrakaew.[94] Considering that the State lacked the means of enforcing the proclamation on the gradual emancipation of certain classes of slaves,[95] that the British had not yet made up their minds whether or not they ought to dispute Siam's rights in the Malay Peninsula,[96] and that France was threatening Siam's northeastern vassal states, the list of accomplishments is rather meager. However, it is only fair to add that the king had encouraged educational reform, actively sponsored the opening up of new rice-fields and stimulated economic life by having new canals dug.

It had been the intention to mark the centenary by the inauguration of at least one telegraphic link with the international network, but the lines had not yet been completed. Similarly, a Siamese postal service to supplant the consular services which used Hong Kong and Straits Settlements stamps had been planned for this time. A general post office had been erected and all houses had been numbered in preparation for this service,[97] but it was not until August 1883 that the Siamese postal department finally began selling its own stamps and delivering its own letters.[98] The establishment of the Siamese postal service was organized by the young *kromaluang* Phanuphantuwong (Prince Phanurangsi).

The Bunnak Decline

In January 1883 *somdet chaophraya* Sisuriyawong died at the age of seventy-four. All first-hand accounts agree in describing him as one of Siam's greatest men who possessed a keen intelligence and great statesmanship. In order to assess his role in the Siamese political system, it is necessary to take into account his position in the Bunnak family as a whole.

Sisuriyawong was the son of the Elder *somdet*, the man who had played a decisive role in Siamese politics from the early 1820s until the mid-1850s. The Bunnak family had been one of the families supplying the State with administrators since Ayutthayan times, but at the beginning of the nineteenth century they surpassed all other noble families in power and influence. The Bunnaks secured for themselves and their relatives the best positions, because they had great influence on Rama III and Rama IV; at the beginning of the fifth reign their hold upon the State's decision-making was supreme.

[94] For an account of the address, see Bock, *Temples and Elephants*, pp. 379-80.

[95] A somewhat emotional account of the condition of Siam's slaves during the 1870s can be found in W. H. Senn van Basel, *Schetsen uit Siam*, pp. 85-99.

[96] Kiernan, 'Britain, Siam, and Malaya', pp. 7-8.

[97] Bock, *Temples and Elephants*, p. 384.

[98] P. P. Lindenberg, 'The Early Postal History of Thailand', *Journal of the Thailand Research Society* 35, pt 1 (1944), p. 87.

The late-Ayutthayan and early Bangkok period system of administration was one whereby many noble families vied for lucrative appointments and the king would select from a large field of candidates. Quite often a minor official would manage to have one or more of his sons accepted in the junior ranks of the administrative hierarchy. The positions of great power were usually given to men who had much influence, including the right family connections. As far as can be determined, there were at that time about a dozen leading families who competed for the top appointments. Although the king had the right to dismiss any officer, in practice this was not often done, and under normal circumstances senior officials enjoyed the prerogatives of their office until death. In this system of competition and checks, the rise of a single family to dominate the chief executive posts must be seen as an extraordinary event.

In retrospect, it is possible to determine the set of circumstances that allowed the Bunnaks to manipulate the system in their own favor to such an extent that an imbalance was created. These arose during the third reign. Rama III came to depend upon two men in whom he could trust, upon whom he could rely implicitly, namely *chaophraya* Bodindecha (Sing Singhaseni) and *chaophraya* Phrakhlang (Dit Bunnak). When Rama III became ill, it was apparent that nobody had been groomed for the succession. Therefore it seems that Rama III's failure to stimulate the development of a full cabinet, the sudden death of one of his trusted executives, and the succession struggle all combined to place Dit Bunnak in the position of king-maker.[99] He himself, his brother That and his two sons Chuang and Kham gained the most powerful positions. After Dit and That's death, Chuang (*chaophraya* Sisuriyawong) became the most senior member of the Bunnak family. The Bunnaks then had great wealth; they possessed extensive lands, controlled a large work force, managed many lucrative tax-farms and invested in trade. It has been remarked that Sisuriyawong's power was also partially based upon deals with various Chinese secret societies.[100] Mongkut's personal wish to be succeeded by *chaofa* Chulalongkorn played into Sisuriyawong's hands and, in a masterly move, the head of the Bunnak family became regent.

At the beginning of the regency period, the 1851 situation seemed to be repeated: the cabinet was stacked with Bunnaks and their men; many promising younger Bunnaks entered government service, so yet another generation could be trained. It would seem at first sight that the regency period marked the zenith in the fortunes of the Bunnak family.[101] Yet in reality the situation was not without ominous signs. In the first place, a feeling of cordiality and trust between Sisuriyawong and Chulalongkorn failed to develop. During the first years of the fifth reign, when the king was still inexperienced, this did not

[99] In his seminal article on the Bunnak family, D. K. Wyatt places the crucial point in their history early in the Second Reign ('Family Politics', p. 219). Clearly I disagree here with Wyatt. Even though Dit Bunnak was very favorably placed in 1810, there were many scions of other families in the administration who could be elevated to senior positions. Dit's appointment as head of the *krom Phrakhlang* did not take place until 1822, and at that time he was no more than an able member of a team of state ministers.

[100] Sisuriyawong's involvement with Chinese interests may have dated from the negotiations surrounding the Bowring treaty. His links with secret societies appear to have been widely known. The British consul-general reported on this in 1882 (as quoted in Bristowe, *Louis and the King of Siam*, p. 135).

[101] Wyatt, 'Family Politics', p. 222.

threaten the Bunnak fortunes, but as the king gradually became more sophisticated it became a matter of concern. A much greater problem for Sisuriyawong was the fact that his son Won Bunnak, who had been groomed to succeed his father as Siam's most powerful man, turned out a great disappointment. Won has been described as a man who blatantly used his powerful position for his own private advantage, enriching himself at the cost of his subordinates,[102] and as being 'a man without talent or strength of character, whose unfitness to keep up the prestige of the Sisuriyawongs was a source of unconcealed anxiety to the ex-Regent.'[103] The most outstanding adult Bunnak of the 1870s was probably Sisuriyawong's youngest brother Phon, but he was firmly on Chulalongkorn's side and occasionally even spoke up against his brother Chuang. In addition, the Bunnak family had been too conspicuous for too long a period and a downturn in their fortunes would not have displeased many of the other noble families. However, if these latter expected to gain from the setbacks of the Bunnak family they were to be disappointed, because the king generally no longer gave new senior appointments to members of the nobility, preferring to select members of the royal family for such posts.

Right: Plate 12. A page from The Graphic Magazine, *London, 1883 showing from left to right: Queen Sawang, King Chulalongkorn and The Regent. Below is a sketch of the funeral of the late Queen Sunanda and her daughter who died after a boat accident at Bang Pa-in, Ayutthaya.*

---

[102] Battye, 'The Military', pp. 138-9.

[103] Report by E. Satow to the Earl of Granville, dated 26 June 1885, as reprinted in Chatthip Nartsupha and Suthy Prasartset, *The Political Economy of Siam, 1851-1910*, p. 322.

Plate 13. An engraving from L'illustration *showing the Temple of the Emerald Buddha and the procession on the occasion of the crown prince's ordination as a novice, 1893. (Courtesy The Old Maps & Prints, River City)*

3ᵉ année. — N° 333   HEBDOMADAIRE — O FR. 10 LE NUMÉRO   12 mai 1907.

LA CROIX ILLUSTRÉE

ABONNEMENT D'UN AN

La Croix Illustrée (France et colonies)... 6 fr.
La Croix Illustrée (Union postale)...... 7 fr.
La Croix quotidienne (Grand format).. 20 fr.
La Croix quotidienne et la Croix Illustrée. 24 fr.

RÉDACTION ET ADMINISTRATION
5, RUE BAYARD, PARIS, 8ᵉ
Les manuscrits non insérés ne sont pas rendus.

ABONNEMENT GLOBAL

Pour 35 fr. 50 par an, on reçoit la Croix, la Croix Illustrée, le Pèlerin illustré en couleurs et le Pèlerin-Supplément, la Vie des Saints, les Contemporains et les Questions actuelles.

LE ROI DE SIAM VISITE LA FRANCE

Plate 14. *Front page of* La Croix Illustrée, *1907, showing the arrival of King Chulalongkorn in France during his second visit to Europe being greeted by the French President. (Courtesy The Old Maps & Prints, River City)*

8

HUMILIATION AND THE PATH TO AUTOCRACY
(1883-1910)

Problems in the North-East

In 1881 the French parliament had authorized renewed attacks on Tonkin. They managed to capture Hanoi in April 1882, but also met with unexpectedly violent resistance. The Vietnamese, aided by Chinese warlords, seriously threatened the French garrison and substantial reinforcements had to be sent to the region. In 1883 the Vietnamese emperor died and the French took advantage of the ensuing dynastic crisis to conclude an armistice, whereby Vietnam became a French protectorate. Thus by late August 1883 the French had gained for themselves the right to establish forts to pacify and control the whole of Vietnam. Further reinforcements were sent in and the slow and painful conquest of the region continued, hampered not only by the fierce resistance of the local population but also by the continued presence of the warlords.

These Chinese troops, who, as noted earlier, were known in Siam as Ho soldiers, terrorized the countryside of the upper reaches of the Red River, the Black River, and the Song Ma, where many Tai-speaking groups lived. That region was not under the firm control of any of the surrounding powers, the local chieftains recognizing Hue's might, but not denying that of Luang Prabang. The Ho troops found the Laotian states an easy prey, and they 'roamed or settled in their stockades, plundering, killing, enslaving, sometimes levying taxes and virtually ruling.'[1] King Chulalongkorn and his advisers were now reminded of their role as nominal overlords in Vientiane and Luang Prabang, and in 1883 the king announced a military expedition against the Ho.[2] While in the days of Rama III such a call to arms would automatically have resulted in the sending of a large expeditionary force, in the 1880s various new options were debated. Instead of a full-fledged army, it was decided this time to send a team of surveyors accompanied by some two hundred soldiers to explore and map this region where Siamese power was weakest. When the surveying team left Bangkok in January 1884, the Ho deftly avoided a confrontation. Most of the Siamese contingent came down with malaria and the expedition was recalled.[3]

During 1885 the French suffered heavily under attacks from Ho troops. The power of the Laotian princes was so deeply

[1] Battye, 'The Military', p.251.

[2] *Ibid.*

[3] Details of the survey can be found in *An Englishman's Siamese Journals 1890-1893*, Bangkok: Siam Media International Books, n.d.

undermined that the Thai rulers considered a strong show of force necessary. This time it was decided not to rely upon untrained *corvée* forces, but to send most of Bangkok's professional army, drawn from the First Foot and the Royal Household Guards, armed with the most modern weapons available at that time. In November 1885 this model force, divided into two separate columns, one under the command of Chulalongkorn's younger brother *kromamu'n* Prachak and the other led by *chamu'n* Waiyaworanat (Choem Saengchuto), set out for the north. The campaign began very promisingly. Waiyaworanat ventured deep into what had become Ho country and used his superior weapons and supplies to dislodge some Hos from their strongholds. During the wet season, however, the column was forced to be on the defensive and at one stage it was hard pressed. When the rains eased, Siamese forces again took the initiative and managed to cause many Ho troops to seek shelter further east and others to negotiate a truce.[4] It was not until the beginning of May 1887 that the Siamese troops returned to Bangkok, carrying with them some of the captured Ho leaders and some thirty young Laotian princes and noblemen as hostages, to guarantee the future submission of the region.[5] The army was given a triumphant welcome back at the capital.

The military operation had taken place during a critical period when the French expansionist mood had been demonstrated, not only by her tightening grip in Cambodia, Annam, and Tonkin, but also by fervent diplomatic activity. In 1885, after two years of negotiations, a commercial treaty was signed between France and Burma, and a French consul was sent to Mandalay. The French consul in Bangkok negotiated a new treaty with Siam, in which provision was made for a French consul at Luang Prabang. This treaty was submitted to parliament in 1886, but was not ratified. Had it been, the French would have implicitly recognized Siam's suzerainty over the Laotian region.[6] The Siamese must have realized that the French were now aiming towards a greater control over some of the Laotian territories.

Much more sudden and alarming, however, was the conflict that arose between the British and the Burmese. A court case against a British firm was the stated cause of the British invasion of upper Burma, but the French activities in Mandalay and British fears that the French might soon control all southern routes to China may well have been the real cause to take immediate military action. As a result, at the beginning of 1886 the territories that had formerly been governed by King Thibaw were formally annexed and became part of the British Empire.[7] Thus, between 1882 and 1886 two major South-East Asian kingdoms, Annam and Burma, had been forced to accept European dominance. By 1886 Siam was the only self-ruled

[4] Battye, 'The Military', pp. 251-9, and *Prawatkitchakanthahan samai Krung-ratanakosin*, p. 50.

[5] A. Pavie, *Eine friedliche Eroberung, Indochina 1888*, p. 98.

[6] Pensri Duke, *Les relations entre la France et la Thailande (Siam) au XIXe siècle*, p. 121. *Luang* Vichitr Vadakarn, *Thailand's Case*, pp. 31-32, gives the details of the 1886 convention but omits to mention that this treaty was never ratified and that neither country ever felt bound to adhere to its provisions.

[7] For details, see Muang Htin Aung, 'Three Unpublished Papers by Harvey, Introduced, Explained and Commented Upon', *Journal of the Burma Research Society* 63, pt 1 (1975), pp. 1-52.

country remaining in the whole of Southeast Asia. Many people considered this an ominous state of affairs; it did not need much imagination to foresee further encroachments upon Siam's traditional sphere of influence.

The Search for Reform

Siam's precarious position was noted with alarm by the Siamese legation in London, and the senior officials debated among themselves about the strategies to be followed in order to maintain the country's independence. They drew up a lengthy document, dated 8 January 1885, which they submitted to the king.[8] In broad outline their suggestions were that it would be futile to rely upon Siam's military power or upon the strength of diplomatic links with European countries to avoid colonization. The best way to counter European expansion was to deny Westerners the opportunity to denounce Siam's government as archaic and oppressive. Therefore the signatories (four princes and seven other members of the legation's staff) argued that drastic internal reform was needed, reform of a much more fundamental nature than the few steps hitherto undertaken. They proposed the introduction of a constitutional monarchy in conjunction with a cabinet of ministers who would carry full responsibility for their departments. Also they suggested clarification with regard to succession to the throne so that the choice of a new monarch would become more predictable and less likely to cause an upheaval. In addition, they boldly suggested the eradication of corruption in administrative circles and the overhaul of the taxation system. They pointed out that promotions ought to be given on the principle of merit rather than being determined by family connections. Other ideas brought forward were the introduction of universal suffrage and the establishment of legal rights such as equal justice and freedom of the press. In order to make these drastic changes possible, the reformists suggested that the king first institute military reform, bringing all troops under a single high command consisting of trustworthy officials.[9]

This frank, revolutionary proposal has been described as '*lèse-majesté*'[10] and as a 'treasonable challenge'.[11] However, Chulalongkorn had specifically invited written proposals for change and the signatories had simply taken him at his word, probably recollecting the spirit of 'Young Siam' of the first half of the 1870s. In his reply, Chulalongkorn first thanked them for their patriotic interest and assured them that questions of reform had often been in his mind during the past eighteen years. Also he told them that he lacked the manpower to carry out such drastic changes:

[8] D. K. Wyatt (*The Politics of Reform in Thailand*, p. 89) dates the document 8 January 1887. However, other sources (Battye, 'The Military', p. 263; Manich Jumsai, *Prince Prisdang's Files on His Diplomatic Activities in Europe*, p. 257) place it two years earlier, while Chula Chakrabongse (*Lords of Life*, p. 261) says 1886. The document carries the date Thursday the 8th day of waning moon, second month C. S. 1246, which corresponds to 9 January 1885.

[9] The text was published by Chai'ainan Samutwanit and Khattiya Kannasut, eds., *Ruam Ekasan Kanmueang Kanpokkhrong Thai, B.E. 2411-2475*, Bangkok: Social Science Association of Thailand, 1974, pp. 47-75. A full translation into the German language can be found in Hung-Guk Cho, 'Die thailandische Denkschrift des Jahres 1885 und ihre historische Bedeutung (Mit einer vollständigen Übersetzung des Originaltextes)', unpublished M.A. thesis, Hamburg University, 1987.

[10] Chula Chakrabongse, *Lords of Life*, p. 261.

[11] Wyatt, *The Politics of Reform*, p. 90.

That we need in this country a reform of the whole system of government I entirely agree, but then members of an effective legislative council must be independent men. Where are we to find such men? ... The older ministers, who know their limitations, now hardly ever dare to speak. What should they do? Should they resign en bloc? ... I, too, want political reforms, but at present there are other matters more pressing.[12]

While the tone of this letter is calm and reconciliatory, there can be little doubt that the petitioners had misjudged the king. In his reply the king made clear that he did not consider a more democratic form of government a feasible option: instead, a strong captain was what Siam needed to weather future storms. The king knew of course that *phra'ongchao* Pritsadang was the instigator and author of the document and released him of his diplomatic duties. The promising career of Prince Pritsadang was abruptly terminated.[13]

Gradually, as senior posts had become available, Chulalongkorn had filled the ministry with men of his choice, often members of the royal family. He had begun to take away some of the senior administrator's lucrative perquisites, and felt sufficiently confident to remove from *chaophraya* Surawong-waiyawat (Won Bunnak) the control over the opium tax-farm and the administration of liquor licensing.[14] In 1885 his position was strengthened further when the retirement of *chaophraya* Phanuwong (Thuam Bunnak), enabled him to appoint his close associate and trusted younger brother *kromaluang* Thewawong to the post of Minister of Foreign Affairs.

In 1885 the *Uparat*, Prince Wichaichan, died. During the ten years after the dangerous confrontation with the king his powers had been so drastically curbed that in the event of the king's premature demise he would have had little chance of election to the throne. With his death, the office of *Uparat* was abolished and Chulalongkorn took the opportunity to implement one of the reforms suggested in the 1885 petition. He announced the appointment of Siam's first *sayam makut ratchakuman*, or crown prince, who would bear the title of *somdetphraborom-orotsathirat*. The eldest of Chulalongkorn's sons of *chaofa* rank, Prince Wachirunhit, at the tender age of nine, was chosen to be the heir to the throne and his investiture took place in January 1887.[15]

The appointment of an official heir was one of the many fundamental changes that swept Siam during the late 1880s. Notwithstanding the king's formal rejection of the reform program that had been suggested by his legation in London, it was clear that he was actively altering Siam's system of government. It is in this context that his request for a report on the working of the *corvée* system must be considered. In June 1885 *chaophraya* Mahinthon presented his assessment of the

[12] Chula Chakrabongse, *Lords of Life*, pp. 262-3.

[13] Pritsadang first was degraded to supervise relatively unimportant tasks in Siam, went into exile and spent some years in Perak, became a Buddhist monk in Ceylon and returned to his own country after Chulalongkorn's death in 1911. See Nigel Brailey, *Two Views of Siam on the Eve of the Chakri Reformation*, Whiting Bay: Kiscadale Publications, 1989, pp. 19-24.

[14] See Satow's letter to the Earl of Granville, dated 26 June 1885, reprinted in Chatthip Nartsupha and Suthy Prasartset, eds., *The Political Economy of Siam, 1851-1910*, p. 322.

[15] For details of the ceremony, see *Somdetphraboromorotsathirat Sayammakutratchakuman*, pp. 31-3.

administration of *corvée*. From the report it is clear that various classes of people were charged different amounts. Some *phrai luang* paid twelve *baht* per year, some ten *baht*, some eight *baht* and some six *baht*. Since the fourth reign the general rate for *phrai som* had been fixed at six *baht*, whilst those registered as slaves were liable to pay one *baht* and two *salu'ng*. The lowest ranks of government servants were taxed at a rate of four *baht* per annum. The government kept a register, noting for how many slaves, *phrai luang*, *phrai som* and minor officials each prince and nobleman was responsible. It was thus possible to calculate how much money these notables ought to collect and hand over to the government. Already during the fourth reign the king had decided not to press his officials for payment of these sums and this had remained so during the fifth reign.[16] The 1885 report showed that many high officials and princes regarded the poll tax payable for all members of the lower classes under their jurisdiction as one of the perquisites of their rank and status, and the king must have realized that he could only change the *corvée*-linked taxation system in conjunction with a major financial restructuring of the whole civil service.

The Politics of Gradual Reform

The changes that were to take place in 1892 have been called the 'great transformation,'[17] and a 'general reorganization of government',[18] statements that give the impression of a sudden metamorphosis. In actuality, the reform edict of 1892 was the culmination of a series of changes that had begun approximately five years earlier. Already in April 1887 the king had created the *krom Yutthanathikan*, or Department of the Military, which united all Siam's army and navy units. He gave his brother Prince Phanurangsi the acting command of this new government unit.[19] The new commander was assisted by the king's brothers Damrong and Narit, by Choem Saengchuto and Prince Sai Sanitwong,[20] a team the king could rely on; thus yet another of the reforms suggested in 1885 was established. The military reformation was largely at the cost of the power of the *krom Kalahom*, and there can be little doubt that this led to Won Bunnak's resignation from the *senabodi*. During May 1887 Chulalongkorn created the Department of Education, and soon added a Department of Public Works, a Department of Justice and a Department of the Privy Seal, each of them headed by a prince.

The increasing prominence of princes in Siam's administration represents a fundamental deviation from the traditional Siamese system of government. Earlier kings had occasionally selected a prince to head an army or to supervise a particular task, but in general princes were not allowed to do the work

[16] The report has been translated and printed in Chatthip Nartsupha and Suthy Prasartset, eds., *Socioeconomic Institutions and Cultural Change in Siam, 1851-1910*, pp. 12-6, and reprinted in their Political Economy, pp. 249-55.

[17] F. W. Riggs, *Thailand, The Modernization of a Bureaucratic Polity*, p. 117.

[18] Rong Syamananda, *A History of Thailand*, p. 130.

[19] *Prawatkitchakanthahan*, pp. 51-53.

[20] For details, see Battye 'The Military', p. 276.

customarily performed by senior nobles, thus lessening the danger of challenges to the throne from within the royal family. By 1888 it had become clear to the Thai nobility that Chulalongkorn had no hesitation in training his brothers as civil servants and in assigning them to all the major executive posts, thus excluding all but a few trusted young nobles from their traditional work sphere. Chulalongkorn could choose from no less than twenty-six younger brothers, now all adults, who generally looked up to him as the man who decided their future careers and who was now leading Siam cautiously towards a promising future.

The 1887 December decree against gambling illustrates Chulalongkorn's style of gradual reform. As early as the 1870s, opium and gambling had been singled out by 'Young Siam' as evil practices that ought not to be fostered by the government. Yet opium and gambling licenses constituted the largest sources of state revenue. While the king still espoused an abolitionist cause, he decided to leave the opium problem alone and tackle gambling dens and lotteries first. In his decree of 1887 he gave warning of the decision to close a large number of licensed gambling houses, leaving only sixty-seven dens open in and around Bangkok. Provincial gambling was not yet affected by this first measure. Other decrees, each of them further limiting certain types of games of chance, were issued in the years to follow.[21]

Between 1887 and 1892 reorganization is apparent in many departments, with a spate of decrees and effective measures. Thus the new Department of the Military founded a cadet school and a school for non-commissioned officers. The infantry was re-equipped with rapid-firing Mannlicher guns.[22] A uniform code of military law was drawn up, an officers' club created and a military journal, *Yutthakot*, established.[23] These and other reforms were inspired by both the wish to imitate the colonial powers and fear of those same powers. The addition of these newly trained troops made it possible to send small garrisons to support Siamese high commissioners in the vassal states. By sending commissioners to Chiang Mai, Luang Prabang, Nakhon Ratchasima, Nongkhai and Ubon Ratchathani, Bangkok asserted its might by establishing a degree of control and opening regular channels of communication, making it more difficult for foreign powers to challenge Siamese rights there. Chulalongkorn's decision to have the terrain between Bangkok and various places in the north surveyed in preparation for the establishment of railway lines was also inspired largely by strategic considerations.

In April 1892 the protracted search for a new government structure and the creation of new *kroms* at the cost of established ones culminated in the appointment of a new cabinet consisting of twelve men, nine of them Chulalongkorn's broth-

[21] Prachoom Chomchai, *Chulalongkorn the Great*, pp. 66-72.

[22] Mannlicher (1848-1904) designed many guns. In 1885 he invented the cartridge clip with which a soldier could load a box of ammunition with a single movement. *The New Encyclopaedia Brittannica, Micropaedia*, Vol. 7, 1995, p. 786, col. 3, Art. 'Mannlicher, Ferdinand, Ritter von'.

[23] Battye, 'The Military', pp. 291-96.

ers. Many of the new ministries were continuations of the previous major *kroms*. For example, the *krom Wang* simply changed its title to Ministry of the Royal Household, and the *krom Na* became Ministry of Agriculture. The main administrative innovation was the installation of a powerful Ministry of the Interior to supersede the old *krom Mahatthai* and the *krom Kalahom* and to absorb some of the functions of the previous *krom Phrakhlang*. All revenue collection was centered in the Ministry of Finance, military affairs in the Ministry of Defense and legal affairs in the Ministry of Justice, in accordance with the structural changes brought about earlier in the reign.

While creating a new cabinet the king did not delegate any of his powers: none of the ministers could make policy decisions without his formal approval. The whole cabinet consisted of 'king's men' chosen because Chulalongkorn trusted their personal loyalty. They could be seen primarily as extensions of the king. When Thewawong was sent to England as the king's representative at the celebrations for Queen Victoria's jubilee, he had to collect ideas about government administration for submission to his elder brother. Similarly, Prince Damrong's visit to Europe in 1891 and 1892 was to gather ideas on various ways of organizing an education system. To Damrong's consternation, he learnt upon his return that he had been transferred to the new Ministry of the Interior, because the man who by rights ought to have inherited the office, *chaophraya* Ratanabodin (Rot Kanlayanmit), had become seriously ill.

Loyalty to the king appears to have been the overriding criterion for allocation of cabinet posts; little thought seems to have been given to other qualifications. The result was an ill-assorted group of people who had little experience in co-operating with each other and with working as a team. The cabinet formed in 1892 'proved to be not a deliberative and administrative body which could forge a common policy of internal modernization and united resistance to Western pressures, but rather a battleground for personal, intra-family 'cabals and recriminations'.'[24] Several serious disputes did in fact mar the atmosphere within the cabinet. Tension had arisen between *chaophraya* Phatsakorawong (Phon Bunnak), since 1888 in charge of the *krom Na*, and the Siam Land, Canals and Irrigation Company, a private enterprise that had obtained the rights virtually to all canal and land development projects in the country. The company accused the chief of the *krom Na* of being more interested in his relatives' speculation than in Siam's development, and Phatsakorawong was moved to the Ministry of Public Instruction. Choem Saengchuto, now *chaophraya* Surasak, replaced him.[25] Some time earlier, Surasak had resigned angrily from his army command after he had lost a dispute with the Treasury over army expenditure.[26] Prince Narathip, the Treasurer, quarrelled with Prince Phanurangsi, the new Minister

---

[24] Sir Henry Norman, *The Peoples and Politics of the Far East* (New York, 1895), as quoted by Wyatt, *The Politics of Reform*, p. 95.

[25] D. B. Johnston, 'Opening a Frontier: the Expansion of Rice Cultivation in Central Thailand in the 1890's', *Contributions to Asian Studies* 9 (1976), pp. 32-3.

[26] Wyatt, *The Politics of Reform*, pp. 96-7.

of Defense, on matters concerning the future of *corvée* and conscription, and Phanurangsi threatened to resign. Chulalongkorn backed Phanurangsi, who was given the right to prepare a draft conscription law. When in September 1892 this draft was ready for discussion, *chaophraya* Surasak found much to criticize, and the cabinet could not come to a decision on the matter.[27] Meanwhile, it became increasingly apparent that Prince Narathip was not a good Treasurer and early in 1893, after an audit of the accounts by four of his brothers, he was dismissed and replaced by Prince Narit.[28] This was not the type of cabinet to be helpful in a serious crisis. The squabbling among the king's senior advisers may have contributed to some of the ill-thought-out decisions of 1892 and 1893 in response to the French expansion westwards.

The Crisis of 1893

In the late 1880s several French colonialists noted with dismay how the Siamese were proceeding to consolidate their hold upon the Laotian vassal states. The regions known as the Sibsong Chao Thai and the Hua Phan Tang Ha Tang Hok threatened to fall under Siamese rule, at least in the eyes of the French consul.[29] Some sort of delineation between the French and the Siamese sphere of influence had to be made, also with respect to the territory more directly ruled from Luang Prabang and Nongkhai. The idea that the whole region east of the Mekong River could be brought under French control had passed through the minds of many officials convinced of the superior blessings of French culture.[30] In 1887 the French and the Siamese each had sent commissioners to explore the border regions. The Frenchman, Auguste Pavie, used the opportunity to make contact with local chiefs and to consider the possibilities of 'pacification' under the French flag.[31] The Siamese heard that a French occupation of *mu'ang* Theng (Dien Bien Phu) was imminent and hastened to send reinforcements. In December 1888 French and Siamese troops confronted each other and the Siamese were forced to retreat, leaving the Sibsong Chao Thai in French hands. This event pushed Tonkin's border deep into Laotian territory.

The French consul in Bangkok had asked the Siamese to recognize that the Annamite empire[32] used to dominate the whole region up to the Mekong River, but this claim was dismissed by Prince Thewawong. The two governments agreed, however, to establish a joint committee to collect evidence upon the basis of which a border could be fixed. Meanwhile, the Siamese set up many military posts between the Mekong River and the Annamite Cordillera, and the restoration of Luang Prabang became a matter of priority. The French

[27] Battye, 'The Military', pp. 306-8.

[28] Wyatt, *The Politics of Reform*, p. 97.

[29] Dispatch by the French consul, 2 July 1887, quoted in Pensri Duke, *Les relations*, pp. 122-3.

[30] The idea was part and parcel of the French proposals to Britain in 1889. See Jeshurun Chandran, *The Contest for Siam 1889-1902: A Study in Diplomatic Rivalry*, pp. 5-6.

[31] See Pavie's diary, 27 June 1887, *Eine friedliche Eroberung*, pp. 136-7.

[32] In 1884 the French revived the name Annam ('pacified South') with which the Chinese had indicated the country of the Viet, to designate the central region of modern Vietnam. The term Annamite was often used rather loosely to indicate the whole of Vietnam.

proceeded with establishing trading posts along the Mekong River and asked the Siamese to cease collecting taxes on certain products in that region, an issue the Siamese relegated to the frontier question.

Siamese tempers rose when a French member of the joint commission appointed a Laotian as French representative of one of the Mekong River posts. When the official protest did not have the desired effect, the Laotian was arrested and his post's flag and weapons were captured. In another incident, which took place in 1892, two French traders who refused to wait for local Siamese travel permits and had not obeyed Siamese tax regulations were arrested and their goods confiscated. Late in 1892 the French agent at Luang Prabang died; it was rumored that he had committed suicide as a result of the tense political situation.[33] Such problems were the inevitable outcome of the differing aims of the French and Siamese agents entering the disputed region. Some of the incidents caused alarm and consternation in France and demands were made that the Siamese be taught a lesson.

The Siamese were quite aware that a dangerous situation had developed. It may be asked why they were not more willing to accommodate the French and suggest certain territorial concessions in exchange for a more secure border. In the first place the Siamese were convinced of their rights in this matter: Siam had a much better claim on Lao territory than Annam because Siamese suzerainty had been reaffirmed many times during the previous hundred years. Secondly, the Siamese military appeared stronger than ever before. This had been demonstrated by the second expedition against the Ho troops, and again later in the suppression of Chinese riots in Bangkok, Ratburi and Nakhon Chaisi.[34] Thirdly, France's position did not appear to be very strong. France had virtually no troops in the disputed territory, and the French demands were not very forcefully expressed. Fourthly, the Siamese were actively engaged in proposing a treaty in London whereby Great Britain would agree to protect Siam against the dangers of losing territory by annexation on the part of any foreign power.[35] They did not realize that British anxieties mainly centered upon what was going to happen further north, in the upper reaches of the Mekong, where Burmese, Chinese, and Siamese interests met and where a French expansion in the region was rapidly complicating the problems of an unsettled border.[36]

The British reluctance to become involved with Siam's border dispute, combined with Siamese 'provocations', provided the French with the opportunity to press their claims vigorously. In April 1893 Prince Thewawong, the Minister of Foreign Affairs, again offered to submit the whole border question to international arbitration, but the French rejected that offer, asking for immediate concessions. They increased

---

[33] For these and other conflicts, see Pensri Duke, *Les relations*, pp. 133-9.

[34] Battye, 'The Military', p. 297.

[35] Chandran, *The Contest for Siam*, p. 33.

[36] C. Hirshfield, 'The Struggle for the Mekong Banks, 1892-1896', *Journal of Southeast Asian History* 9 no. 1 (1968), pp. 25-31; Chandran, *The Contest for Siam*, pp. 52-4.

the pressure by adding the ship *Cométe* to the man-of-war *Lutin* already stationed at the mouth of the Chaophraya River. At this stage the Siamese became seriously alarmed. The French were informed that they did not have the right to proceed up-river, and the fortresses at Paknam were alerted and reinforced. Once again the Siamese beseeched the British to intervene and they also sent an emissary to Washington for help; meanwhile, a brave front was shown at home. In May skirmishes broke out at Khong, an island in the Mekong River near the border with Cambodia, in which several French officers were killed and a senior officer captured. From then on the situation worsened; clashes broke out at various points along the left bank of the river, and reinforcements were sent. By June a formal declaration of war seemed imminent. As the Siamese did not seem prepared to back down, they provided the French with an opportunity to press their case even further. Pavie wrote on 28 June 1893 to the French Foreign Minister: 'Events have taken a turn which permits us to make the greatest demands and which makes even the foreigners envisage the inevitable solution as being the establishment of our Protectorate over the whole of Siam.'[37] The Siamese government, however, still hoped to dissuade the French by raising a daunting force, and a general mobilization of the masses was ordered.[38]

On 10 July Pavie reported to Thewawong that he planned to call two gunboats, the *Comète* and the *Inconstant*, to Bangkok to join the *Lutin* already there in order to protect French subjects during the emergency. The Siamese protested that the French were exceeding the provisions of the Franco-Siamese Treaty, and the king warned that the fortress would fire upon warships attempting to cross the bar at Paknam. For a moment it seemed that the Siamese protests were effective, for the French government sent assurances that the gunboats would not cross the bar of the Chaophraya River. For reasons that are not absolutely clear, however, the chief officers on the French boats did not receive clear instructions on this matter. The possibility that Pavie deliberately enticed the commanders to proceed, thus provoking an incident, may not be ruled out. The Frenchmen had brought their own pilot, the captain of the small steamer *Jean-Baptiste Say*, and during the evening of 13 July, when the tide and weather were favorable, a small convoy, consisting of the *Jean-Baptiste Say*, the *Inconstant*, and the *Comète* went over the bar and proceeded up-river. The Siamese fired warning shots from a fortress. When these had no effect, Siam's largest warship, the *Coronation*, which lay in mid-stream, opened fire. However, when the second projectile was launched, its largest gun exploded, and in the ensuing confusion the *Inconstant* narrowly avoided colliding with it. Meanwhile, the batteries on the river bank fired and the French returned fire, all the time moving full-speed further up-river. Eventually the

[37] In Pensri Duke, *Les relations*, p. 152, the letter is quoted: '... les évenements ont pris une tournure qui nous permet les plus grandes exigences et fait envisager la question par les étrangers même, comme devant avoir pour solution fatale l'établissement de notre Protectorat sur le Siam tout entier.'

[38] For details, see Battye, 'The Military', pp. 338-55.

two French gunboats joined the *Lutin* at anchor opposite the French consulate; the *Jean-Baptiste Say* lay in the mud at the side of the river with a large hole in her side.[39]

The leaders in Bangkok were in a quandary over how to react. Some contemplated attacking the three ships in front of the consulate; others argued for caution. The Bangkok populace was deeply perturbed and there was some looting of shops. Many feared that the Chinese would revolt.[40] Eventually caution prevailed, and an uneasy calm reigned while people awaited further French reaction.

Circumstances had played into France's hands. Siam could be accused of having violated the 1856 treaty and of having fired at French ships, killing some of the crew. Moreover, the failure to stop the ships from entering the river greatly assisted in demoralizing the Siamese military, because they had proudly believed that the renovated fortress at Paknam was indomitable.[41] A British offer to mediate was rejected by the French. The French consul was authorized to present the Siamese with an ultimatum on 20 July 1893, asking the Siamese to withdraw from east of the Mekong River, punish all those who had caused belligerent incidents, pay two million *francs* indemnity, deposit a further three million as guarantee, or instead of the latter clause, allow France to appropriate the customs revenue of Battambang and Siemreap provinces. If the Siamese did not agree within twenty-four hours, France would close Bangkok harbor by a naval blockade. When the Siamese attempted to negotiate, France proceeded with the blockade until 29 July, when the Siamese agreed not only to all the terms of the original ultimatum but also, during the following days, to a temporary French occupation of Chanthaburi, to the Siamese withdrawal of military posts from Battambang and Siemreap, and to the Siamese withdrawal from a twenty-five-kilometer zone along the west bank of the Mekong River.

Probably afraid that even more terms would be added, and not aware that British diplomats, alarmed at the extent of French gains in a country where the British had large trade interests, were negotiating more favorable conditions,[42] the Siamese abruptly signed their new treaty with France in October 1893. The treaty still did not satisfactorily determine the border between French and Siamese territory, and it extended the status of 'French subject' to numerous residents of Vietnamese, Cambodian, and Lao origin, which created the likelihood of many further 'incidents' involving the two countries.

After the Debacle

It was quite clear that the Siamese government had not handled

[39] For details, see O. J. A. Collet, *Étude politique et économicque sur le Siam moderne*, pp. 26-30; and especially Chaen Patchusanon and Sawat Chanthani, ed., *Koraniphiphat rawang Thai kap Farangset lae Kanrop thi Paknam Chaophraya samai r.s. 112*.

[40] L. Weiler, *Anfang der Eisenbahn in Thailand*, p. 49; Battye, 'The Military', pp. 350-2; and B. A. Smith, 'The King of Siam', *Contemporary Review* 71 (January-June 1897), p. 891.

[41] Some contemporary accounts can be found in H. Warrington Smith, *Five Years in Siam, From 1891-1896, Volumes 1 and 2*, Bangkok: White Lotus, 1994, Chapter 12 and P. H. I. G. M. Kempermann, the German Minister Resident in his Report No. 82, dated 27 August 1893, Politisches Archiv des auswärtigen Amts, R 19230.

[42] Chandran, *The Contest for Siam*, pp. 82-3.

the situation well. There had been an under-estimation of the French appetite for conquest, coupled with an over-optimistic view of Siam's own military might. At the same time too much hope had been placed on Britain's power and on the idea that justice was on the side of the Siamese. Chulalongkorn could now see that he should have been more prudent and not have relied upon those who had advocated military resistance. He realized that he was personally responsible for Siam's humiliation and for the excessive loss of territory.[43] Before the confrontation he was already ill, but at the time of the ultimatum and blockade he collapsed and left the country's daily affairs in the hands of his cabinet. He took matters so to heart that he refused to eat and to meet people. It was widely expected that he would die, his spirit broken. The king's grave illness caused a serious succession crisis.

The crown prince was still a teenager, and it was difficult to decide who ought to be regent in the case of Chulalongkorn's death. The king's brothers could not agree upon a candidate for that important office, some rallying behind Prince Phanurangsi, others preferring Prince Thewawong.[44] Late in 1893, however, the king's health began to improve and the king's brothers could stop wrangling over the position of regent.

Meanwhile, the cabinet, urged on by Phanurangsi, reacted in its own way to the disastrous confrontation with the French. It was clear that Siam needed a complete overhaul of its defense system. A plan was drawn up by which army and navy would fall under a single command and the provinces would be included in the defense plan of the country as a whole; various other administrative changes were also proposed.[45] This plan was submitted to the king in April 1894, but before it could be discussed the king caught a fever and in his weakened state he was not expected to recover.[46] Again the court was divided over whom should be called upon to become regent; again the king rallied. By late 1894 he was beginning to emerge from his deep depression and to show signs of interest in the debate on how best to safeguard Siam's independence. Many people feared at that time that sooner or later the country would become a French colony.[47] While accepting some of Phanurangsi's proposals for military reform, the king was no longer interested in creating a major modern army. He saw more merit in plans put forward by Damrong and Gustave Rolin-Jaequemyns, a Belgian lawyer who in 1892 had been appointed as Siam's General Adviser and had rapidly established himself as a man with Siam's interests at heart.[48] Damrong's plan consisted of a series of government priorities for the years to come, namely, the maintenance of peace and order in the whole territory that remained under Siamese rule, the strict avoidance of conflicts involving foreigners and foreign interests, and the drawing up of plans for internal administrative reforms. A modern army

---

[43] During these days of turbulence the king did not forget his children's welfare and he secretly deposited a large sum of money in England on their behalf (W. F. Vella, *Chaiyo!: King Vajiravudh and the Development of Thai Nationalism*, p. 12).

[44] Battye, 'The Military', pp. 372-4.

[45] The full text of the proposal can be found in *Prawatkitchakanthahan*, pp. 58-63.

[46] Weiler, *Anfang der Eisenbahn*, p. 68; the author's diary entry for 28 March 1894 mentions that the king could hardly move about without help and that there were grave doubts whether he would ever recover. See also J. MacGregor, *Through the Buffer State: A Record of Recent Travels through Borneo, Siam and Cambodia*, p. 56.

[47] Chandran, *The Contest for Siam*, p. 125; Weiler, *Anfang der Eisenbahn*, p. 79. MacGregor, *Through the Buffer State*, p. 56.

[48] For details see C. de Saint-Hubert, 'Rolin-Jaequemyns (*Chao Phya* Aphay Raja) and the Belgian Legal Advisers in Siam at the Turn of the Century', *JSS* 53, pt 2 (1965), pp. 181-90, Kanlaya Chunnuan, comp., *Chao phraya Aphairatchasayamanu kunkit (Khutsatap Rolin Yakhmin)*.

was no longer regarded as an effective means of halting foreign incursions. In January 1895 the court was shocked to learn that the crown prince had died, but the king rapidly appointed fourteen-year old Wachirawut to the position.[49]

The Creation of the Buffer State

The French territorial conquests in the region had caused some anxieties about safeguarding British interests. The problem of French-held territory coming uncomfortably near that under British control had led to much diplomatic activity. In July 1893, at the end of the French blockade of the Chaophraya River, the French and the British 'agreed to recognise the necessity of constituting, by means of mutual sacrifices and concessions, a neutral zone between their possessions.'[50] The subsequent negotiations centered upon the Shan state of Keng Cheng, which straddled the Mekong River. Throughout 1894 it was not clear what Keng Cheng's fate would be. Although Britain maintained it had inherited the state as part of Burma's sphere of influence, France claimed at least that part of the state which lay east of the Mekong River, a part which, incidentally, included Keng Cheng's capital town, *mu'ang* Sing. At the same time Siam hoped to be given Keng Cheng, and thus create a neutral zone between the French and the British. Britain, however, was discouraged by the news of Chulalongkorn's ill health and Siam's apparent instability. In early 1895 the British decided to leave no doubts about their superior claim to Keng Cheng and set up a military post at *mu'ang* Sing, but soon afterwards they withdrew again when agreement had been reached to split up Keng Cheng between themselves and France, making the Mekong River the actual border. In return for this concession, the way was opened for a more satisfactory arrangement regarding the status of Siam.

The British perceived three options: they could leave Siam to be taken by the French, in which case they would have to ensure that the whole Malay Peninsula would come under British control; they could declare Siam to be a British protectorate, whereby they would face the French along a vast stretch of the Mekong River; or they could negotiate for an internationally guaranteed, independent Siam.[51] The latter option was considered preferable, and after further negotiations this was achieved. In January 1896 an agreement was reached which guaranteed the inviolability of the Chaophraya River basin; a stretch of Siamese territory, ranging from Chiang Rai in the north to a point not far south of Prachuap Khirikhan in the south, was designated as the guaranteed portion of Siam. Not included in the portion was the whole of the Khorat plateau, the provinces neighboring Cambodia, and most of the Siamese

[49] Prince Wachirunhit died on 4 January 1895 and not in 1894 as Battye would have us believe ('The Military', p. 377 and p. 394). Rong Syamananda also wrongly took Wachirawut's appointment to have occurred in 1894 (A *History of Thailand*, p. 146); in fact it was 17 January 1895. See *Somdetphraboromorotsathirat Sayammakutratchakuman*, p. 88; *Ratchasakunwong*, p. 76 and pp. 78-9; and Smith, 'The King of Siam', p. 887. His formal installation took place on 8 March.

[50] Chandran, *The Contest for Siam*, p. 71.

[51] *Ibid.*, p. 116.

portion of the Malay Peninsula. Naturally, after the traumas of 1893, the Siamese initially regarded the declaration as a direct threat to all the territories not guaranteed and feared that soon they would be left only with the Chaophraya River basin. In due course, however, it became clear that the British and French had indeed agreed to allow Siam to remain independent. Siam's leaders began looking more hopefully to the future.

Renewed Initiatives

Throughout the period of almost three years of uncertainty about Siam's status and prospects, ordinary life had largely resumed. The Siamese economy went on expanding, and various major projects continued. The Siam Land, Canals and Irrigation Company proceeded with the opening up of large stretches of land to the east and northwest of Bangkok. In 1888 the surveyor James McCarthy had been just east of Bangkok and had reported 'no cultivation' to the north of the Saen Saeb Canal. In 1895 he noted: 'I was astonished at the change that had taken place. In every direction the land was cleared of the heavy jungle grass which afforded shelter to wild elephants.'[52] It has been estimated that during the 1890s more than a hundred thousand people came to farm in the Rangsit area alone,[53] and it can thus be said that although the central government was incapable of effective leadership, a 'quiet revolution' took place in the countryside that began to have a major effect upon Siam's economy by the turn of the century.[54]

Similarly, the years of despondency between 1893 and 1896 should not obscure the fact that Siam's first railway was steadily being constructed. The contract for the Khorat line from Bangkok to the northeast had been signed in December 1891 and, notwithstanding considerable problems, large stretches of this 'pioneer railway of Siam' had been completed. In November 1895 King Chulalongkorn, though showing signs of having suffered deeply, traveled several sections of the new line still under construction.[55] This line was built with German technical personnel and large numbers of Chinese laborers.

During the early 1890s there were more than a hundred foreign technical specialists in Siam assisting with a wide range of development projects. Most of them were British, Danish, and Germans. Other nationalities were represented in much smaller numbers. The French had some missionaries and consular representatives in Siam, but no technical advisers.[56] In 1897 the foreigners in state service were: fifty-four Englishmen, twenty Danes, eighteen Germans, nine Belgians, seven Italians, and a few Dutchmen, Austrians, Americans, Portuguese and Swiss.[57]

[52] Letter from McCarthy to Surasak, 6 April 1895, quoted by Johnston, 'Opening a Frontier', p. 35.

[53] *Ibid.*

[54] The standard source on Siam's economic change, Ingram's *Economic Change in Thailand 1850-1970*, depicts a consistent and steady growth in Siam's rice exports between 1880 and 1895, and accelerated growth between 1895 and 1905 (see pp. 38-39). The table and graph tend to obscure the fact that there seems to be an abrupt change in 1900. According to Dilock's figures, Siam's rice exports for the years between 1896 and 1900 were 7.6, 9.8, 8.6, 7.1, and 6.8 million *piculs* respectively, while in the subsequent five years the figures were 11.1, 13.0, 9.5, 13.5, and 13.2 million *piculs* (Dilock, *Die Landwirtschaft in Siam: Ein Beitrag zur Wirtschaftsgeschichte des Königreichs Siam*, p. 191.

[55] Weiler, *Anfang der Eisenbahn*, p. 85.

[56] *Ibid.*, pp. 76-7.

[57] As reported in the *Siam Free Press* quoted by Weiler, *Anfang der Eisenbahn*, p. 102.

In 1896 the king resumed active control over the senior administrators and reshuffled cabinet. The chief posts were given to
the king's brothers Damrong (Interior), Mahit (Finance and
Agriculture), Phithayalap (Palace and Public Works),
Thewawong (Foreign Affairs), Narit (Army), and Naret (Local
Government). A new face in the Siamese administration in
1897 was young Prince Ratburi (Ratchaburidirekru't) freshly
returned from his studies in Oxford, the first of
Chulalongkorn's sons to gain ministerial rank. Most of the
king's advisers were progressive reformist in outlook, and
under the by now experienced hand of the king, many new
initiatives were broached. Thus during 1896 plans for the new
King's College, an English school for the country's prominent
youth, gained cabinet approval. It was given Sisuriyawong's
old residence as its temporary quarters.[58]

The king's renewed interest in administrative reform is
also apparent in the fact that he asked his newly appointed
Financial Adviser, Alfred Mitchell-Innes,[59] to make a report on
the nature of Siam's financial system and suggest alterations
and improvements. The Mitchell-Innes report provides an
excellent means by which to note how the system of taxation
had developed since the fourth reign.[60] The range of taxable
goods and property was at least as wide as that under Mongkut.
There were more than twenty different types of land tax, more
than twenty types of fruit trees upon which taxes were levied,
more than seventy types of excise, as well as house tax, boat
tax, fishing tax, and other taxes. Many of these were still being
collected by intermediaries – the tax-farmers, usually Chinese
– a system considered particularly odious by Mitchell-Innes. In
general, the role of the tax-farmers seems less prominent than
during the fourth reign. In the fifth reign the Ministry of
Finance, the Ministry of the Interior and the Ministry of
Agriculture, sent out their own tax collectors.

From the Mitchell-Innes report it is possible to obtain a
fairly clear picture of the state of the *corvée* system. This
appears to have hovered between being a poll tax and a forced
labor system. The amount *a phrai* would pay in order to be
exempt from *corvée* varied greatly and was usually determined
by what his father had paid and whether he was attached to a
certain *krom* as a *phrai luang* or to a private person as a *phrai
som*. Whenever the tax was not paid, it was converted into
corvée. For an ordinary man it depended greatly, therefore, on
the type of *krom* or master to whom he was assigned. If a man
belonged to the *thahan ru'a*, or navy, it was likely that he would
have to serve the state. If he belonged to a *krom* not in need of
manpower, he could pay the poll tax.

An interesting development was taking place with regard
to the collection of the tax on rice land. Until 1896, officers of
the Ministry of Agriculture would be sent out every year to

---

[58] The school was officially opened in
early 1897 and turned out to be
Siam's most successful venture in
this type of education. For details, see
Wyatt, *The Politics of Reform*, pp.
183-4.

[59] Mitchell-Innes, with four years
experience in Egypt, took up his
duties in Siam in June 1896. See I.
Brown, 'British Financial Advisers in
Siam in the Reign of King Chulalongkorn', *Modern Asian Studies* 12,
no. 2 (1978), p. 196.

[60] The full text of Mitchell-Innes's
report is reproduced in Chatthip
Nartsupha and Suthy Prasartset,
Political Economy of Siam, pp. 269-
90; further details can be found in
Piyachat Pitawan, *Kanyok-loekra-
bopphrai nai Ratchasamai Phrabatsomdetphra Chulachomklao rawang
Ph. S. 2411-2453*.

collect moneys due on the rice lands. They were paid 6 per cent on the amount they brought in, and another 6 per cent went to various other officials. However, in 1896, by way of experiment, the rice-land tax collection was transferred to the Ministry of the Interior, which gave the responsibility for the tax collection to the provincial administrators. This, undoubtedly, was one of the measures devised to bring all parts of the kingdom under effective control.

During the year 1896 Siam's government moved to prevent a recurrence of the shameful breaching of Bangkok's outer fortifications. With the assistance of Rolin-Jaequemyns, the services of the famous Belgian defense specialist General Brialmont were secured and plans for three new fortresses at the first bend of the Chaophraya River were drawn up and handed over to the Siamese envoy in 1895.[61] By 1896, engineers had arrived to examine the site and prepare a draft of a project that would bring Bangkok's defense up to modern standards.[62]

Chulalongkorn's First European Visit

By late 1897 the situation in the region appeared relatively stable. Siam's position in the Malay Peninsula was being clarified with Britain. The hostilities between Siam and France were mainly concerned with the vexed problem of the status of people of Cambodian, Laotian, and Annamite descent.[63] In fact, the problem of identifying French *protégés* was one of the reasons for Chulalongkorn's European travel in 1897. He hoped that a state visit might be an opportunity to ask for the abrogation of the clause concerning Laotians, Cambodians and Annamites.

The king had always been keen on travelling. In 1871, upon his return from Singapore and Batavia, he had attempted to persuade Sisuriyawong to send him to Europe on a study tour. Later, in 1880, a state visit to America and Europe had been organized, but this had had to be cancelled when Sisuriyawong was suddenly taken ill.

In 1896, at the age of 43, he had revisted Singapore and Java, travelling with an impressive retinue that included four of his brothers, thirteen officers and some ladies-in-waiting. The success of this second visit to the Dutch Indies prompted the fulfilling of his old plan to visit Europe the year after. At the last moment the king was able to clear his desk, sign the secret convention with Britain[64] and officially open the first part of the Khorat railway[65] before embarking once more in early April 1897 on the royal steamer *Mahachakri*. This time the journey would last nine months. During his absence, Queen Saowapha was appointed regent, an unprecedented move in Siam's history. The queen had to undergo a ceremony similar to that of the

[61] Saint-Hubert, 'Rolin-Jaequemyns', p. 185.

[62] Weiler, *Anfang der Eisenbahn*, p. 93.

[63] *Revue Politique et Parliamentaire* 12 (April, May, June 1897), pp. 658-9.

[64] Thamsook Numnonda, 'The Anglo-Siamese Secret Convention of 1897', *JSS* 53, pt 1 (1965), pp. 45-60.

[65] *Annual Register*, 1897, p. 366.

installation of a crown prince; she had to take an oath of allegiance, and during the regency she was entitled to be addressed as *chao phaendin* (the country's overlord). It is not known for certain why Chulalongkorn decided to elevate his queen to the regency. It is likely that the choice was prompted by the fact that there was no suitable elderly member of the royal family who could fill the post. In addition, the choice of a woman absolved the king from the difficult task of singling out one of his able brothers. Throughout the long voyage the king kept regular contact with his regent by telegram and letter.[66]

After a fairly uneventful journey via Colombo, Aden and Port Said, the king and his entourage arrived in Venice on 14 May 1897. During the following months the king visited Geneva, Turin, Florence, Rome, Vienna, Budapest, Warsaw, Saint Petersburg, London, Hamburg, Essen, The Hague, Brussels and Paris, as well as many smaller cities. A sovereign of an Asian country was a rarity in Europe, and Chulalongkorn's travels aroused considerable interest. He was quite warmly welcomed by European royalty, Although he was received at Buckingham Palace by the Prince of Wales, Queen Victoria excused herself,[67] a circumstance which must have distressed King Chulalongkorn. In September he was treated with full honors by the French, but unfortunately was unable to obtain abrogation of the troublesome clause regarding people under the French consul's protection.[68] After a final visit to European health and holiday resorts, an invigorated king, enriched by a first-hand knowledge of a wide range of European cultural traditions, began the long voyage home on the *Mahachakri*. His arrival in Bangkok on 16 December was the occasion of a splendid welcome.[69]

The king's improved health and vigor, and the stimulus of returning after a prolonged stay abroad, are reflected in some of the decisions of 1898. An assessment was made with regard to the effectiveness of earlier measures that had been intended to draw the northern semi-independent states of Chiang Mai, Lampang, Lamphun, Nan, and Phrae closer into the Siamese administrative system. The local traditional rulers had been discouraged from using Chinese tax-farmers and invited to use the services of state employees instead. When this plan failed, it had been decided in late 1895 or early 1896 to give the responsibility for collecting state revenue to committees comprising both local leaders and the Siamese commissioner. Some local leaders resented this intrusion and there were signs of a growing hostility against Bangkok.[70] Up till 1898 the Siamese had attempted gradually to introduce changes in the north, treating the northern rulers with great respect and heeding their interests. From 1898 onwards, however, a firmer line was taken after a thorough tour of inspection by the Minister for the Interior, Prince Damrong himself. A missionary likened the

[66] See *phrabatsomdetphra Chulachomklao chaoyuhua Phraratchahatlekha mu'a Sadetphraratchadamnoen Praphat Yurop Ph. S. 2440.*

[67] Chula Chakrabongse, *Lords of Life*, p. 254.

[68] *Annual Register*, 1897, p. 366; Pensri Duke, *Les relations*, p. 228.

[69] Weiler, *Anfang der Eisenbahn*, pp. 105-6.

[70] For details, see Tej Bunnag, *The Provincial Administration of Siam, 1892-1915: the Ministry of the Interior Under Prince Damrong Rajanubhab*, pp. 116-7; J. A. Ramsay, 'The Development of a Bureaucratic Policy: The Case of Northern Siam', pp. 164-77.

effect this tour had on the local nobles to that of 'a whiff of ozone'.[71] The inspection tour resulted in a deeper awareness in Bangkok of the need to win the local nobles' co-operation. It was decided to create consultative bodies comprising both Siamese and 'Lao' and to increase the salaries of the local chiefs. In 1899 a special commissioner for the north was appointed to implement the reforms.[72]

When the king was in Europe, he had personally inspected the schooling of many younger members of the royal family and had discovered that they were usually ill prepared to benefit fully from a Western education. The king asked *phraya* Wisut, the Siamese ambassador in London, to prepare a report on foreign education. *Phraya* Wisut suggested sweeping reforms of the whole system of Siamese education, including the translation and distribution of large numbers of simple foreign textbooks, the introduction of English as part of the curriculum in many schools, and the adjustment of the Siamese system to fit in better with that of the British. In April 1898 the report was submitted and the king demanded a speedy reaction from *chaophraya* Phatsakorawong, the Minister of Public Instruction. The minister responded with the complaint that his officials had in the previous six years come up with innovative plans, many of them along the lines suggested by Wisut, which had had to be abandoned because of lack of funds. There had thus far been little enthusiasm for education, but now suddenly reform appeared to be coming at too great a speed: 'Education is not like the construction of buildings, which can be quickly accomplished. It is rather like the planting and felling of trees. Education is like the slow growth of the great tree of the forest. If it is properly nourished with foods, it will yield its fruit in due course.'[73]

In September 1898 the king convened a meeting with senior officials of the Ministry of Public Instruction to which his brothers Damrong and Wachirayan were also invited.[74] The latter was a Buddhist monk, abbot of Wat Bowoniwet, and he had proved himself to be an able administrator and organizer of the Mahamakut religious academy.[75] The king openly criticized the Ministry of Public Instruction for having failed to raise the standards of Siamese schools, and listened with approval to Damrong and Wachirayan, who proposed to set about providing all existing monastery schools with modern textbooks, not books translated from foreign sources, but written by Siamese and from a Siamese perspective. The king ended the ensuing discussion by handing over the responsibility for curriculum development for all schools in the provinces to Damrong and Wachirayan. Only Bangkok schools would henceforth remain under the Ministry of Public Instruction; the bulk of the nation's educational institutions were transferred to Damrong's Ministry of the Interior.

[71] L. J. Curtis, *The Laos of North Siam*, p. 128.

[72] For details, see Ramsay *'Development of a Bureaucratic Policy'*, pp. 178-83.

[73] A letter from Phatsakorawong to the king's secretary, dated 21 June 1898, translated and quoted by Wyatt in *The Politics of Reform*, pp. 213-4.

[74] For a detailed discussion, see Wyatt, *The Politics of Reform*, pp. 217-29. See also Wuthichai Munsin, *Kanpatirupkansu'ksa nai Ratchakanthi 5*, pp. 121-3.

[75] A background to Prince Wachirayan's early life can be found in C. J. Reynolds, transl. and ed., *Autobiography: The Life of Prince-Patriarch Vajirañana of Siam, 1860-1921*.

The king's decision became law in November 1898 and for a period of four years the administration of Siam's education remained split between two separate organizations. The provincial schools were given to the Buddhist monks and a program was devised to standardize and improve the thousands of existing monastery schools. In Bangkok, however, educational reform was modeled on the British education system. Each of the systems had its merits and faults. In 1902 the whole of Siam's educational goals were again re-examined and a completely different administrative structure was devised. This episode serves to illustrate the king's almost unlimited power. Not since the time of Taksin had a king been able to act so freely. After his first European journey, Chulalongkorn was fully in command and his word was law. Inevitably this situation stifled debate and encouraged the writing of reports that were drafted with the specific aim of pleasing the monarch.

The king's confidence was further boosted by the fortuitous discovery in India of a stone coffer containing what was accepted to be the bones and ashes of the Buddha himself. The king of Siam, as the only remaining Buddhist monarch, was invited to receive the relics, provided he was willing to share them with Buddhists in Burma and Ceylon. Naturally this was a great honor, and to commemorate the occasion it was decided to erect a monument at Bangkok's highest point, the mount near Wat Saket.[76] Apart from this welcome event, there were signs that the government would have much more money to spend than foreseen. In 1898 state revenue had increased greatly to more than 34 million *baht*, and after taking into account an increased expenditure, the surplus for 1898 was still a healthy 4.5 million *baht*.[77]

Administrative reform affected most government departments. Apart from the changes mentioned above, there was an improvement in the police service and in post and telegraph services. An important aspect of the reform movement was the implementation of the 1896 Law of Provincial Courts, which reorganized the workings of the entire judiciary at the provincial level.[78] A committee of senior men had been appointed to direct the implementation of the provincial law reform. In the late 1890s most of the country's legal processes were gradually brought under direct Bangkok supervision.[79]

With so many features of Siamese administration under review, it should not come as a surprise that in 1900 Chulalongkorn reassessed Siam's military forces and decided that a larger share of the budget ought to be spent on Siam's defense. The king still feared the imperialistic aims of Britain and France, aptly illustrated by the manner in which they took advantage of China's weakness to gain 'concessions'.[80] The king was inspired by his young son Prince Chiraprawat, who had successfully completed a course at a Danish military academy and

---

[76] *Annual Register*, 1898, p. 341; Prachoom Chomchai, *Chulalongkorn the Great*, p. 102.

[77] Figures taken from the *Annual Register*, 1898, pp. 341-2, and converted to *baht*, taking one pound sterling to be worth 17.40 *baht* for the year 1898 (Ingram, *Economic Change*, p. 337).

[78] D. M. Engel, *Law and Kingship in Thailand During the Reign of King Chulalongkorn*, p. 70.

[79] *Ibid.*, p. 72.

[80] Battye, 'The Military', pp. 401-2.

who now was rapidly promoted to be Siam's army commander-in-chief.[81] By 1901 Chiraprawat, Damrong and the king had agreed to move in the direction of developing a large army based on universal conscription. It was decided to begin conscription in Nakhon Ratchasima and Ratburi, provinces where the government was conducting an experiment relating to the abolition of *corvée*. In these two provinces, notwithstanding the local nobles' opposition, a flat poll tax was levied upon all eligible men and personal service had officially been abolished. If the government were reasonably successful in collecting the universal poll tax, the plan was then to proceed with universal conscription, whereby the government would supply and pay the serving conscripts.[82] When the king decided to go ahead with the formation of a conscripted army to defend Siam against foreign aggressors, he had chiefly the French in mind, with whom protracted negotiations were in train for the settlement of various matters arising from the agreement of 1893. However, before these negotiations were concluded, domestic crises broke out which placed a completely different perspective upon the question of Siam's military power.

The 1902 Uprisings

Early in 1902 a growing excitement swept through many villages and towns in northeastern Siam. A cataclysmic disaster was expected in the middle of the fourth lunar month (March-April), to be followed by evil times. Messages were circulated in which people were exhorted to take magical precautions. A holy man who claimed to be the intermediary for the god Indra would lead the faithful during the predicted troubles. He promised great wealth to all those who would follow his instructions.[83] Other documents of a similar kind were passed around,[84] but because of their mystical and vague character they did not unduly alarm the authorities.

However, in March a certain Ong Man claimed to be the awaited prophet and followed by a band of armed men, began a march upon Ubon Ratchathani, the seat of government of his region. On the way, the party met a local garrison and put it to flight, killing two officials and capturing the governor of Khemmarat. The king's commissioner at Ubon, Chulalongkorn's brother *kromakhun* Sanphasit, telegraphed the army post at Nakhon Ratchasima and reinforcements were sent. Meanwhile, more people joined Ong Man's band, and by the time he had won another skirmish his force had increased to several thousand. Sanphasit set up artillery at a strategic point and when Ong Man walked into the ambush more than three hundred rebels were killed and four hundred captured. The leaders escaped into French-held territory, where they contin-

---

[81] Also known as *kromamu'n* Chaisi (*Ratchasakunwong*, p. 75). King Chulalongkorn, imitating an aspect of the British system of peerage, had established the custom of attaching the name of a Siamese province to his sons' titles when he elevated them to *krom* rank.

[82] Battye, 'The Military', pp. 403-11.

[83] Chatthip Nartsupha and Suthy Prasartset, *Political Economy of Siam*, pp. 361-5.

[84] J.B. Murdoch, "The 1901-1902 'Holy Man's' Rebellion", *JSS* 62, pt 1 (1974), p. 57; and Yoneo Ishii, 'A Note on Buddhistic Millenarian Revolts in Northeastern Siam', *Journal of Southeast Asian Studies* 6, no. 2 (1975), pp. 121-2.

ued organizing resistance.[85] These events were viewed with some concern in Bangkok as they occurred close to the demilitarized zone between Siam and French Indo-China. Had the Siamese not been able to demonstrate their ability to quell the uprising, it would have detrimentally affected the Siamese-French negotiations on a new treaty. Almost at the same time there were reports of rebellion in the Malay provinces, but these proved to be of no great concern for the central government.[86]

Much more important was the 'Shan Rebellion', which broke out in late July of that year. It began when a large police force failed to apprehend and arrest a band of Shan robbers and abandoned their weapons and ammunition.[87] Many Shans joined the outlaws and more than a hundred men attacked *mu'ang* Phrae, sent the Siamese troops fleeing and seized the town. Looting took place and government property was seized. The Shans obtained the co-operation of some local leaders in arresting and killing Siamese government officials who had attempted to hide. The idea of routing all Siamese caught their imagination. In a few days a large group of rebels marched up to Lampang, the town halfway between Phrae and Chiang Mai, while another moved in a southern direction in order to forestall possible Siamese reinforcements. At Lampang, however, local police and hastily armed farmers, under the command of the Danish adviser H.M. Jensen, made a stand. On 3 August they drove off the Shans, killing the rebel leader. Soon afterwards, on 14 August, the rebellion was totally crushed by large numbers of locally mustered troops and subsequently by a royal army of some two thousand men sent up under the command of *chaophraya* Surasak.

Altogether the Shan rebellion had lasted less than three weeks. Notwithstanding Bangkok's successful suppression of the civil disturbances, the events created apprehension among many administrators. Most of the Bangkok standing army was used in the occupation of the north in the aftermath of the rebellion, and it was clear that Siam's military resources would be insufficient to handle a larger-scale emergency. As a result of the 1902 uprisings, the conscription experiment was extended to the north and northeast. The Siamese tightened their control over the northern states, especially over Phrae, which was henceforth administered like an 'inner province'.

The disturbances in the northeast may also have served to hasten protracted negotiations with France regarding a 'definitive' border settlement. In October 1902 a document was signed in which Siam agreed to allow France rights over the trans-Mekong part of the old kingdom of Luang Prabang as well as a portion of land along the border with Cambodia. In return the French would retreat from Chanthaburi, they would no longer insist on a demilitarized zone along the Mekong and would limit the classes of people who would be able to claim French

---

[85] Murdoch, 'Holy Man's' Rebellion', p. 60.

[86] Battye, 'The Military', p. 415.

[87] Accounts of the Shan rebellions can be found in Ramsay, 'Development of a Bureaucratic Policy', pp. 217-34; *Prop Ngiew Ton Thi 1, PP*, pt 75; Battye, 'The Military', pp. 416-18, and Bristowe, *Louis and the King of Siam, pp.* 107-21.

legal protection.[88] The October agreement met with opposition in France and was never ratified. New negotiations were begun, and a treaty that was still more favorable to France was drawn up and signed in February 1904. Even that proved insufficient to satiate the colonialists' appetite for expansion.

The Shan rebellions may also have served to spur on the central government to proceed with the long-planned railway to Chiang Mai.[89] In each of the following years several million *baht* were set aside for its construction. In January 1908 the king opened the first half of the line reaching Phitsanulok.[90]

Rice and Irrigation

For as long as people could remember, the price of rice had remained remarkably stable, especially when compared with sugar, pepper, cotton and other commodities.[91] A growing farming populace, abundant land, an ever-increasing system of canals, roads and railways, combined with an efficient class of traders, middlemen, millers and merchants, provided the circumstances under which jungle was cleared and marshland was transformed into rice-producing land. Though the yield varied from year to year, there was a steady increase in the amount sold on the international market. The annual growth rate of rice exports in the half-century between 1860 and 1910 was approximately 5.2 per cent.[92] In the first decade of the twentieth century, rice exports formed some 80 per cent of the total value of the nation's export; teak accounted for another 10 per cent, while all other products made up the remainder.[93]

Meanwhile, however, the grand plans for opening up new tracts in the Chaophraya Delta, undertaken by the Siam Land, Canals and Irrigation Company during the 1890s, were proving less successful than originally hoped. On the Rangsit project, for example, newly dug canals had been silting up, and by the turn of the century less than 40 per cent of the entire area opened up by the project had been cultivated.[94] In line with Chulalongkorn's general policy of obtaining the services of foreign technical experts, a Dutchman, J. Homan van der Heide, was persuaded in 1902 to become adviser to the Ministry of Agriculture. He and a team of Dutch engineers compiled a comprehensive report, proposing the construction of a large dam across the Chaophraya River near Chainat, as well as a network of irrigation canals and a great number of additional water-control measures. The government decided that in principle future hydraulic works had to be constructed in such a manner that they would fit in with the proposed overall scheme. However, the adoption of the whole plan would involve a massive capital investment, estimated to be 47 million *baht* over a period of twelve years, a cost comparable to that of the current

[88] Pensri Duke, *Les relations*, pp. 239-51; M.F. Goldman, 'Franco-British Rivalry over Siam, 1896-1904', *Journal of Southeast Asian Studies* 3, no. 2 (1972), p. 218.

[89] Apparently the decision was taken in late 1902 (see I. Brown, 'British Financial Advisers', p. 218).

[90] *Volkswirtschaftliche Chronik für das Jahr 1908*, p. 125.

[91] N. G. Owen, 'The Rice Industry of Mainland Southeast Asia, 1950-1914', *JSS* 59, pt 2 (1971), p.91.

[92] *Ibid.*, p. 95.

[93] See, for example the export figures in Dilock, *Die Landwirtschaft*, p. 191; and *Volkswirtschaftliche Chronik für das Jahr 1906*, pp. 212-3.

[94] L. E. Small, 'Historical Development of the Greater Chao Phya Water Control Project: An Economic Perspective', *JSS* 61, pt 1 (1973), p. 2. The problems of the Rangsit scheme are well illustrated by the report dated 4 May 1906, published in Chatthip Nartsupha and Suthy Prasartset, *Political Economy of Siam*, pp. 333-7.

railway-building program. A newly appointed British Financial Adviser to the government flatly rejected the scheme:

> *Before we can think of a great Irrigation scheme we must provide funds for the strategic Railways which are essential if the outlying Provinces are to be properly governed. Those Railways must be constructed out of borrowed capital and I am altogether averse to borrowing money for Irrigation at present in addition to money for Railway Construction. Such a course would be rash in the extreme.*[95]

At that time the king and his ministers were adjusting themselves to the idea of borrowing money for the railway, rather than financing it from government revenue. In addition, it had just been decided to base Siam's currency upon the gold standard, and the ensuing revaluation had caused some financial problems.[96] Van der Heide's proposal therefore came at an awkward moment. He proceeded to develop several less expensive alternative plans and fought hard to have them adopted. In 1906 and in 1908 the whole question was reviewed, but the scheme failed to pass the council of ministers, it could not see a way of raising the necessary money. In 1909 all plans for large-scale irrigation works were abandoned and van der Heide resigned.[97]

The restraining and conservative advice of financial advisers played a role in the rejection of this imaginative plan,[98] the adoption of which would have benefited millions of Siamese.[99] Yet it seems wrong to assign the full responsibility to such advisers. The council of ministers and the king were not convinced of the merits of the scheme. If Chulalongkorn had shown enthusiasm for the irrigation plans and had wished them to be implemented, special loans could have been raised, especially when the 1905 and 1907 loans in Europe were oversubscribed and it had been proved that Siam was able to raise foreign capital for its development.[100] Siam's reform measures during this period showed little imagination. One of the reforms was the 1905 extension to the provinces of the limitations on gambling.[101] To make up for the accompanying loss in government revenue, a heavier land tax was established.[102] This was also the year during which the general conscription edict was proclaimed, formally abolishing the remnants of the *corvée* system.

The Monarchy

At the beginning of the twentieth century King Chulalongkorn held sway over Siam as no Siamese monarch had done before. Most of the key executive positions were occupied by the

[95] Memorandum by the Financial Adviser, 1903, quoted by J. C. Ingram in *Economic Change in Thailand 1850-1970*, p. 197.

[96] For details, see I. Brown, 'Siam and the Gold Standard, 1902-1908', *Journal of Southeast Asian Studies* 10, no. 2 (1979), pp. 385-6.

[97] Further details in H. C. F. ten Brummelhuis, 'De Waterkoning; J. Homan van der Heide, staatsvorming en de oorsprong van moderne irrigatie in Siam, 1902-1909', Ph.D. Dissertation, Amsterdam University, 1995.

[98] Ingram, *Economic Change*, p. 198; Brown, 'British Financial Advisers', p. 202.

[99] Van der Heide's plans seem to have much in common with the Greater Chaophraya River Irrigation Project, which was adopted after the Second World War.

[100] Brown, 'British Financial Advisers', pp. 205-6.

[101] Prachoom Chomchai, *Chulalongkorn the Great*, p. 71.

[102] Brown, 'Siam and the Gold Standard', p. 388.

king's younger brothers and sons. All policy decisions first had to gain the king's approval before they could be implemented, any time he could overrule existing legislation and introduce new ideas. At the same time the king controlled a large proportion of Siam's revenue, an amount estimated to have been as large as one-sixth of the nation's annual income.[103] During his long reign the royal family had attained more than a good measure of financial security. The king also invested money, especially for the benefit of the higher-ranking princes and princesses.[104]

Although the king's power was unparalleled in Siamese history, this did not diminish his popularity. Chulalongkorn was revered by large sections of the populace and in general he was considered an enlightened monarch, a king who, like his father, had the nation's welfare at heart and was guided by high personal standards. There was no sign of public opposition to the king's spending, even when it concerned projects such as the creation of the Dusit pleasure grounds, which cost many millions of *baht*, and through which large tracts of productive rice-fields were converted into a park.[105] To begrudge the king his lavish lifestyle would have been felt tantamount to denigrating the nation's wealth and prosperity. The country was stable, many people were earning more than before, and this was seen to be directly linked to the fact that the country had a virtuous king. His display of wealth was a symbol of Siam's well-being. The king was aware of this general feeling and rejoiced in it.[106]

Some Siamese intellectuals, especially those who had studied abroad or otherwise had first-hand experience of foreign attitudes, occasionally had ambivalent feelings towards the monarchy. On the one hand, most prosperous, leading countries did not allow a monarch to have such a measure of influence; in this respect, Siam appeared to have an outmoded form of government. On the other hand, the king was widely acclaimed as an able monarch who managed the country in an admirable fashion. The most intellectuals such as Thienwan could do was hint at the possibility of other forms of government.[107] Clearly, the initiative for a system of shared responsibilities should have come from the king himself, because Chulalongkorn was quite knowledgeable about various systems of government. In fact, he decided to strengthen rather than weaken his own position. He relied on the argument that the Siamese were not ready for a constitution and that a long period of education was still needed before any fundamental changes could be contemplated. Meanwhile, he actively fostered the idea that the king occupied the position of 'father of the nation'.

Publicly the king was enjoying both great power and a wide popularity, yet in his private life all was not well in the years between 1904 and 1907. In the first place it had become clear that the young man who had been elevated to the position

[103] See C. J. Rivett-Carnac's memorandum on the expenditure of the royal household, Chatthip Nartsupha and Suthy Prasartset, *Political Economy of Siam*, pp. 291-4.

[104] A full picture of the royal finances is not available. Glimpses of the king's investments are given in Chatthip Nartsupha and Suthy Prasartset, *Political Economy of Siam*, pp. 305-7 and M. Collis, *Wayfoong, the Hongkong and Shanghai Banking Corporation*, p. 91. In 1889 the king deposited 960,000 Mexican dollars with the Hongkong and Shanghai Bank in the understanding that this money would not be withdrawn for many years. See Paul Sithi-Amnuai, *Finance and Banking in Thailand: A Study of the Commercial System, 1888-1963*, p. 139. The king's personal wealth was such that he could buy Queen Saowapha a necklace valued at £100,000 (M. Smith, *A Physician at the Court of Siam*, p. 111). The king bought tracts of land for his dependents. Queen Saowapha's income was estimated to have been between £80,000 and £90,000 a year (*ibid.*, p. 109), and Prince Chakraphong apparently received £20,000 annually from 'his Bangkok estate' (Chula Chakrabongse, *The Twain Have Met, or An Eastern Prince Came West*, p. 64).

[105] Weiler, *Anfang der Eisenbahn*, p. 122.

[106] Sir Josiah Crosby, *Siam: the Crossroads*, p. 32.

[107] K. Rosenberg, *Nation und Fortschritt*, pp. 103-4.

of crown prince in 1895 was not altogether living up to his father's expectations. When Prince Wachirawut returned in 1904 from England, where he had completed his education, he did not conduct himself fully in the manner expected of the heir to the throne. He shunned court life and did little to make himself liked in the royal family; he limited his personal contacts largely to a circle of intimate friends who shared his artistic tastes.[108] If at this stage the king had felt free to choose a different crown prince from among the *chaofa* princes, he would probably have selected Chakraphong, who was lively, intelligent, gregarious, and displayed an easy charm.[109] In 1906 this favorite prince finally returned to Siam, having successfully completed his military education in Russia. Soon, however, gossip would have it that Chakraphong had secretly married a Russian woman who was being kept in hiding in Singapore. When the fact emerged that the Russian bride really existed, Chulalongkorn was very angry with his son, whom he regarded as second in the line of succession.[110] During the remaining years of his life, Chulalongkorn refused to meet the foreign woman. These family troubles regarding the succession were further compounded by the king's ill health. The king suffered from diabetes and chronic interstitial nephritis,[111] so his doctor suggested a sojourn in a different climate. This took the shape of a new tour in Europe, Chulalongkorn's second one, which lasted almost eight months, from March to November 1907.[112]

When it became known that the king was preparing for a long voyage, all urgent state business was quickly settled. It was during this period that the French plenipotentiary, Colonel F. Bernard, contacted the king and asked him to discuss the final settlement of border problems between Siam and French Indo-China. A joint committee had been preparing reports on these since the treaty of 1904. A few days later an agreement was reached. France would cede a small strip of land north of the village of Dan Sai, near the Laotian border and also return the strip of coastal land near the town of Trat. In addition, France would relinquish judicial rights over French *protégés* while retaining full jurisdiction over French nationals. In return for these concessions, Siam ceded the provinces of Battambang and Siemreap.[113] The extraordinary haste with which the 1907 treaty was drawn up and the ease with which Siam had made great land concessions took everybody, including the French consul, by surprise.[114] The French were delighted to receive Battambang and Siemreap in return for two small strips of land and some legal concessions.[115] Bernard had taken advantage of the king's illness and his wish to clear his agenda thus achieving a great diplomatic success. For Siam it was a disadvantageous step, closely watched by Britain. Soon after the king's return from Europe, the British emulated the French and offered to relinquish some of the British consul's extraordinary

[108] Vella, *Chaiyo!*, p. 8.

[109] Smith, *Physician at the Court*, p. 115. A detailed account of the life of this prince can be found in Eileen Hunter and Narisa Chakrabongse, *Katya & the Prince of Siam*, Bangkok: River Books, 1994.

[110] Chula Chakrabongse, *The Twain Have Met*, p. 62.

[111] M. Smith, 'The Families of the Kings of Siam of the House of Chakri', *Annals of Eugenics* 12 (1943-45), p. 153. See also *Physician at the Court*, pp. 93-4.

[112] For an account of the king's travel observations, see Ampha Otrakul, *König Chulalongkorns Reisetagebuch, 'Glai Baan' (Fern von Zuhause)*, Bonn: Deutsch-Thailandische Gesellschaft, 2001.

[113] Further details in Pensri Duke, *Les relations*, p. 266 and pp. 294-5.

[114] Weiler, *Anfang der Eisenbahn*, pp. 149-50.

[115] *L'Asie Française*, 1910, p. 418.

legal rights in return for Siam's abandoning all claims on Kedah, Perlis, Kelantan and Trengganu, as well as the adjacent islands.[116]

During Chulalongkorn's second European tour, Crown Prince Wachirawut was appointed regent. However, just as during the voyage of 1897, Chulalongkorn did not really delegate his authority; all policy decisions had to be submitted to him telegraphically for approval.[117] The king's return in November 1907 was the occasion of festivities on an unprecedented scale. The parkway that led from the river to the Dusit palace was decorated with the help of some fifteen thousand soldiers, and half a dozen beautifully embellished 'gates of honor' were erected for this occasion. There were speeches, blessings from a chapter of Buddhist monks, processions, a general illumination, fireworks, a military parade, and large-scale parties.[118]

The negotiations for the new treaty between Siam and Britain lasted through most of 1908. Britain obtained Siam's withdrawal from the above-mentioned Malay states, a Siamese promise not to cede or lease any territory south of Ratburi (a clause inspired by fears of the creation of a Kra Canal), and the rights to build a railway through the remaining Siamese part of the Malay Peninsula.

The latter clause was prompted by intense international rivalry between the three largest European countries for a share in Siam's imports. After 1904, the French had partly succeeded in overcoming the Siamese government's reluctance to develop closer contacts. They had gained an advisory position in the sanitary department and had opened a bank in Bangkok. The Germans controlled the railway department and thus were able to secure many contracts for their compatriots. Moreover, German shipping was competing seriously with that of the British. Britain still had most advisers in Siamese government service. In 1908 there were altogether 110 Englishmen employed by the Siamese. They dominated the Siamese departments of survey, mining, police, education, justice and customs. In that same year there were forty-five Germans, mostly railway engineers; forty-two Danes dominating the naval section; thirteen Italians mainly in public works; eight Dutchmen in irrigation; seven Frenchmen who were judges and civil engineers, and three Americans, one of whom was the nation's General Adviser.[119] The Siamese-British treaty, which was ratified in 1909, effectively split up the railway department into a northern and central section still under German control, and a southern one supervised by the British.

Apart from the painful concessions to the British, in 1908 there were also financial difficulties. During 1906 and 1907 the Ministry of Finance was headed by *phraya* Suriya, who abandoned his predecessor's cautious policies and pressed for a series of rapid revaluations of the *baht*. While in November

[116] Weiler expressed his dismay in his diary entry for 7 April 1907 and rather prophetically wrote that it would not surprise him after this to hear soon of the cession of some of the Malay sultanates to England (*Anfang der Eisenbahn*, pp. 149-50).

[117] Vella, *Chaiyo!*, p. 3.

[118] For details, see Weiler, *Anfang der Eisenbahn*, pp. 156-8.

[119] *Ibid.*, pp. 169-70.

1905 one pound sterling was worth 16 *baht*, in December 1906 it was worth only 13 *baht*.[120] This massive revaluation caused export trade problems, and the ministry was forced to sell a major portion of its sterling reserves in order to support the *baht*.[121] The king asked his General Adviser, Edward Strobel, to suggest what action should be taken. Strobel replied that devaluation at that moment would severely undermine trust in the currency and that the government ought to assert its intention to maintain the going rate. In 1906 an alternative course of action existed – to reduce the silver content of the *baht*, a measure that had been taken in the Philippines and in the Straits Settlements that year. However, *phraya* Suriya rejected that alternative because he feared a general loss of faith in the *baht*, which would have become a mere token coin.[122] *Phraya* Suriya resigned early in 1908, and the king appointed his son Prince Chanthaburi as the new Minister of Finance. The run on the *baht* continued during that year, and the ministry again had to spend large sums to support the currency.[123]

On the suggestion of the Financial Adviser, it was decided to reaffirm the government's position. In November 1908 this was demonstrated by the promulgation of the Gold Standard Act, whereby the value of the *baht* was determined in centigrams of gold.[124] Bolstered by a buoyant economy, Siam weathered the storm.[125]

While it is true that Siam would have been better served by a drastic reduction in the *baht's* silver content, the ministry's reluctance to countenance this is quite understandable. The government had repeatedly been forced to withdraw or amend measures intended to change and streamline the nation's currency. At the very beginning of the reign, as has been mentioned above, the there had been widespread panic with the introduction of new copper and tin coins. Paper notes had been introduced in September 1902. Initially these had had a good reception, especially in the business world. However, in 1903 forged twenty-*baht* and hundred-*baht* notes began to appear, and for many months the public refused to put trust in the paper money.[126] At the same time the government had attempted to simplify the system of small coins by introducing a decimal system, creating the *satang*, one-hundredth of a *baht*. That attempt failed, mainly because people did not take to the newfangled coins. The old system had been based on the *at* (one sixty-fourth of a *baht*). People were used to copper half-*at* and two-*at* pieces, as well as silver eighth and sixteen-*at* coins. In conjunction with the gold-standard edict of 1908 came a renewed drive to introduce *satangs*, and great amounts of one-, five-, ten-, twenty-five and fifty-*satang* pieces were put into circulation.[127]

In June 1908 the king had the satisfaction of promulgating Siam's new Criminal Code, the culmination of many years'

[120] Brown, 'Siam and the Gold Standard', pp. 389-91.

[121] *Ibid.*, p. 392.

[122] *Ibid.*, p. 395.

[123] *Ibid.*; see also Weiler, *Anfang der Eisenbahn*, p. 163.

[124] According to Brown ('Siam and the Gold Standard', p. 396), the gold *baht* was set at 56.25 centigrams of gold; Weiler (*Anfang der Eisenbahn*, p. 169) mentions 55.8 centigrams.

[125] For the general state of the Siamese economy between 1908 and 1911, see *L'Asie Française*, 1911, p. 463.

[126] Prachoom Chomchai, *Chulalongkorn the Great*, p. 83.

[127] Weiler, *Anfang der Eisenbahn*, p. 175.

experimenting and drafting, an undertaking likened by the king himself to that just over a century earlier during the first reign.[128] It was, however, essentially the result of quite a different type of inquiry. The legal revision under Rama I was intended to provide the most authoritative version of the ancient Siamese code; the 1908 laws were an attempt to provide a modern set of rules which could be applied in Siam's changed circumstances. The legal code was drawn up with the assistance of foreign experts, and its promulgation was loudly heralded so as to convince foreigners of Siam's ability to rule itself and thus pave the way for future action against the iniquitous extraterritorial rights of foreign consuls and their charges.

In November 1908, a year after his return from Europe, there was yet another massive ceremony in honor of the king, this time the celebration of his fortieth anniversary as a ruler. Apart from a military parade and a festive ball, the occasion was marked by the unveiling of an equestrian statue of Chulalongkorn, paid for by voluntary public subscription.[129] On this occasion the king gave a speech in which he looked back on his long reign. As the major feature of his times he chose the political transformation of the whole region, where all independent states except Siam had been changed into colonies. It was the king's duty to retain his country's independence. In order to do so he had opened up Siam to Western innovation, while at the same time not denigrating long-established Siamese customs. He felt that by doing so he had followed the right path.[130] This speech seems to have set the pattern for general assessments of Chulalongkorn's reign: that of a wise man steering deftly, playing off one nation against another, sacrificing the outer regions in order to preserve the nation's independence.[131]

It has been seen that Siam's independence was primarily decided by the 1896 agreement between France and Britain: Siam's fate was discussed and determined without Siamese being present to influence the course of events. The crisis that arose in 1893 could have been prevented; Siam appears to have lost considerable tracts of land by being obdurate and attempting to fight the French, giving them a chance to press for more than they had originally envisaged taking. After the 1893 debacle the king proceeded with laudable caution, but it has been shown that the final settlement of 1907 was unnecessarily generous towards his adversaries and this had a detrimental effect on the ensuing negotiations with Britain. While there can be no doubt about King Chulalongkorn's good intentions, or that he must be regarded as a leader who kept Siam's interests at heart, in face of the available evidence it is difficult to maintain the image of a skilled diplomat.

During the year 1908 there were many other events that needed the king's personal attention. A new section of railway

---

[128] Engel, *Law and Kingship*, p. 75.

[129] Vella, *Chaiyo!*, p. 141; Chula Chakrabongse, *Lords of Life*, p. 266.

[130] Weiler, *Anfang der Eisenbahn*, pp. 167-8.

[131] See, for example, Rong Syamananda, *A History of Thailand*, p. 144.

had to be opened; one journey had to be made in the southern provinces and another to the northern part of the central plain. Every major problem that required cabinet action eventually reached the king. Probably 1908 was an exceptionally heavy year for Chulalongkorn because there had been a backlog of work upon his return from Europe. The financial difficulties that arose must have involved many meetings and reports. Even during an ordinary year the tasks of an absolute monarch were immense. With the country rapidly adopting innovations, an ever-expanding economy and increasingly complex problems, the duties probably became too onerous for a single person to carry.

A government decree in March 1909, which changed the triennial poll tax on Chinese into a yearly capitation tax, in line with that applying to the Siamese, caused unexpected troubles.[132] The 1909 collection proceeded without undue stress, but when in 1910 it became clear that government officials would proceed to tax the Chinese again just like other members of society, there was widespread dissatisfaction in the minority group. The Chinese secret societies decided to force the Siamese government to desist. In order to bring this about, a general strike was organized for 1 June 1910. At first it seemed that the strike was a resounding success; all Chinese business came to a halt for several days and food became expensive. However, Siamese police, reinforced by troops, managed to make their presence felt; when disorders occurred arrests were made. After three days some shops reopened, and by the fifth the strike was over, leaving the government in a stronger position than before. Once again it had been demonstrated that the Siamese could handle a local emergency. At the same time, the strike served as a warning to the Siamese, for it showed that many Chinese were not integrated into Siamese society, and they formed a potential danger to the nation. The strike also strengthened anti-Chinese feelings among certain groups, especially some of the Western-educated nationalistic Siamese. Chulalongkorn himself did not agree with anti-Chinese views; his policy was always to guide them into becoming an integral part of the nation.[133]

The king's health remained poor. His second European trip had not succeeded in restoring him to full vigor. He began, therefore, to prepare for his retirement and made known his intention to step down in 1913, when he would be sixty, in favor of the crown prince. He built himself an estate where he hoped to spend his later years, imagining that he could still be of use to the country by breeding leghorn chickens and helping improve the country's poultry stock.[134] Before these plans could be put into action, however, the king fell sick, his kidneys failed and on 23 October 1910 he died of uremia, at the age of fifty-seven. He had been Siam's king for almost forty-two years.

[132] G. W. Skinner, *Chinese Society in Thailand*, pp. 162-3.

[133] *Ibid.*, pp. 161-2.

[134] Chula Chakrabongse, *Lords of Life*, pp. 260-1, and *The Twain Have Met*, p. 64.

The fifth reign thus encompasses a very long period. It may be assessed from various angles. The Siam of 1910 was a very different country from that of 1868. The population in the central region had increased greatly and the country's wealth was much augmented. Siam had lost nominal control over large tracts of land, but the remaining region had been more effectively brought under Bangkok's suzerainty. While in 1868 the Bunnak family held the chief executive positions, in 1910 it was royalty who filled the most important posts.

General assessments of this reign often stress the positive and laudable aspects, and in retrospect the fifth reign has assumed the glow of a golden age. In this and the preceding chapter several of the well-intended, helpful, and progressive governmental reforms have been described. Chulalongkorn attempted to be a 'father of the people', a wise and autocratic figure who acted in the interest of the community at large. When growing older and more experienced, he played that role very well indeed. Chulalongkorn became an able administrator and an admirable head of state. During the years he won the respect and loyalty of a great number of people. Yet these and other rare personal qualities ought not to blind us to the fact that the concentration of power and responsibility in a single individual carried severe risks. Even a king as experienced as Chulalongkorn could make hasty decisions. It is likely that his unsatisfactory health contributed to his making some ill-considered resolutions of far-reaching consequences. Finally, the king's refusal to create a system in which he would have to delegate a measure of his authority put an extraordinarily heavy burden upon his young successor, to whom he handed over all the power and prestige it had taken him a lifetime to accumulate.

Plate 15. *Front page of* Le Petit Parisien, *August 1893, showing French warship blockading the mouth of the Chaophraya River, near Paknam. (Courtesy The Old Maps & Prints, River City)*

1. Le nouveau roi de Siam, Chowfa Maha Vajiravudh; 2. La barque sacrée transportant le trône au lieu du couronnement; 3. Le Cortège Royal à la Cérémonie religieuse; 4. Le Palais Royal à Bangkok; 5. Un Arc de Triomphe sur le passage du Cortège Royal.

Les Monarchies Asiatiques. — Le Couronnement du Roi de Siam

Plate 16. Front page of the Belgian newspaper, Le Patriote Illustré *of 10 December 1911, showing the new king, Wachirawut and various scenes of his coronation. (Courtesy The Old Maps & Prints, River City)*

9

NATIONALISM, AND THE REORGANIZATION OF THE BUREAUCRACY

(1910-1925)

Not long after Chulalongkorn's death the cabinet met and confirmed Wachirawut's succession to the throne. For more than fifteen years this prince had been officially recognized as Chulalongkorn's successor. At the time of his investiture as crown prince in 1895 he was a student in England, so the ceremony of investiture took place at the Siamese legation. After some years of private tuition the Siamese crown prince qualified for admission to the Royal Military College at Sandhurst, where he followed several courses. Then for a while he went to Oxford University, but left without a degree and returned to army training. Altogether, Wachirawut spent just over nine years abroad from the age of twelve to twenty-one. He was one of many who had been sent abroad by Chulalongkorn.

Although Wachirawut had become intimately acquainted with European culture and acquired much military knowledge, two other *chaofa* princes who were almost his contemporaries had distinguished themselves more. *Chaofa* Boriphat (Prince Nakhon Sawan) had gone to school in Germany and graduated from the military academy at Kassel. *Chaofa* Chakraphong had been sent to Saint Petersburg, where he studied successfully at the military academy, gaining great distinction.[1] Upon their return to Siam, these three princes had been given high ranks and titles: Wachirawut was given the post of Inspector-General of the Army, Boriphat became Chief of the General Staff and Chakraphong, several years his junior, became Deputy Chief of Staff.

On 11 November 1910, Wachirawut was solemnly crowned King of Siam and became officially known as *phrabatsomdetphra* Mongkutklao *chaoyuhua*. He reaffirmed Chulalongkorn's policy by proclaiming Queen Saowapha's male children to be in line for the succession, at least until he himself had sons. At the age of twenty-nine Wachirawut was still unmarried, an oddity at the Siamese court. Therefore his younger full brother Chakraphong automatically became heir-apparent, but it was understood that the prince's children by his Russian wife would not be eligible for the throne.[2] During the previous reign, the monarchy of Siam had gained immensely in both power and popularity. Wachirawut had never been very popular, was rather shy and retiring and particularly deficient in social graces. Unable to make many people feel at ease, he was

---

[1] Battye, 'The Military', pp. 509-16.

[2] L. Weiler, *Anfang der Eisenbahn in Thailand*, pp. 197-8.

expected to have difficulties living up to his father's reputation.[3]

The Wild Tiger Corps

During the first months it was not immediately clear how Wachirawut would adjust to the role of monarch and what changes he would bring about. They were taken up with routine matters of state and the new king was also preoccupied with preparations for his father's cremation, which took place in March 1911. Not long after this ritual farewell to the previous king, Wachirawut made his first major original contribution to the Siamese political scene when he created the Wild Tiger Corps (su'a pa)[4] in May 1911, an organization of Thai citizens of good character united to further the nation's cause. The king and some of his intimate friends who had worked out the idea drew up a list of prominent Siamese who might wish to join – men who would gladly sacrifice the entrance fee of fifty baht[5] and regularly take part in exercises designed to strengthen the body, inculcate a team spirit and pride in the nation. Each member had to swear allegiance to the king and purchase a spectacular uniform in black and yellow with a wide-rimmed black felt hat.[6] The king spent much time on the development of the Wild Tiger movement, setting up this paramilitary organization, devising badges, signs, mottoes, drills, marching orders and war games. Three months later he founded the Tiger Cub (luk su'a) branch, almost a replica of the Wild Tiger organization: 'Boys in their adolescent years should also receive both physical and mental training of the sort given Wild Tigers so that when they become older they will know their proper duties as Thai men. Everyone should do what is useful to the nation and country, to the land of one's birth.'[7]

W. F. Vella, who studied Wachirawut's Wild Tigers and Tiger Cubs, has stressed that Wachirawut's movement ought not to be confused with Baden-Powell's Boy Scout organization. 'Baden-Powell's organization came too late to have been responsible for the Wild Tiger idea, and the Wild Tiger concept was certainly not a literal or even a close approximation of the entirely youth-directed, essentially non-military concept of the Boy Scouts.'[8] This view, which assigns an extraordinary high degree of originality to the Siamese king, can be challenged. Baden-Powell's organization dated from January 1908 and it had become a widely publicized, internationally known movement. By 1911 the non-military nature of the Boy Scout movement had not yet been determined. On the contrary, the original idea had evolved from the paramilitary duties given to young boys in India and South Africa. Baden-Powell, the Chief Scout, was a lieutenant general in active service until May 1910. In

---

[3] Ibid., p. 187 and p. 199.

[4] The inauguration is described in The Souvenir of the Siamese Kingdom Exhibition at Lumbini Park B.E. 2468, pp. 149-50.

[5] W. F. Vella, Chaiyo!: King Vajiravudh and the Development of Thai Nationalism, p. 36.

[6] For posed photographs of Wild Tigers in full uniform, see The Souvenir of the Siamese Kingdom Exhibition, pp. 149, 185, and 237; and for a rare action picture of Wild Tigers on parade, see I. de Schaeck, S.A.I, le grand-duc Boris de Russe aux fêtes du Siam pour le couronnement du roi, opp. p. 120.

[7] As cited by Vella, Chaiyo!, p. 42.

[8] Ibid., p. 29.

Baden-Powell's original draft of Scouting for Boys he had written, 'So long as war remains possible, it is the duty of every man and boy to prepare himself to defend his country in case it should unfortunately become necessary.' While this sentence did not appear in the printed version,[9] in 1910 it was still not certain how far there was a military side to the Scout movement.[10] The king, who regularly kept himself informed of British news, must have been aware of Baden-Powell's Scouts, who frequently came before the public eye during the early years. Boy Scouts were on duty at the funeral of Edward VII in 1910 and during the coronation of George V in 1911.

While the inspiration for organizing Thai Scouts must have come from England, it cannot be denied that King Wachirawut incorporated many of his own ideas into the Siamese Wild Tiger movement and deliberately stressed its military aspect. The king saw it as an opportunity to create a bond between himself and loyal citizens; a volunteer corps willing to make sacrifices for the king and the nation. With a keen sense of the theatrical, the king proclaimed that the concept of staunch and loyal Wild Tigers was one that went back to olden times when the ordinary citizen was trained for warfare and belonged to detachments used to guard Siam's frontiers.

All people of good name and standing could volunteer for the corps, but rank and position did not automatically lead to an appointment to officer rank in the Wild Tigers. The king conferred status in this new organization according to his personal inclination. Among the first 122 appointments in May 1911 there were nineteen officers, of whom only one was a prince of *krom* rank, the others being various nobles with titles below *chaophraya*. The lower ranks, however, boasted one *chaophraya* and nine *krom* princes.[11] *Chaofa* Boriphat and the heir-apparent *chaofa* Chakraphong, probably the country's highest-qualified military leaders, were only given the status of subalterns in the Wild Tigers, part of a deliberate plan of the king to break through the traditional class divisions.[12] The king made the Wild Tigers his personal concern and in Bangkok he commanded the Wild Tigers' first company, an elite group often on parade when the king performed public duties.

While at first the Wild Tigers were drawn from the king's personal entourage, and it is likely that many joined in order to gain favor with Wachirawut, the idea rapidly caught on. A genuine widespread enthusiasm for the Wild Tigers and the Tiger Cubs arose. In September 1911, just over five months after the inauguration of the scheme, Weiler described them:

This is a troop of volunteers in black uniform, drilled in a more or less military fashion, but without weapons. The British Scouts are apparently the paradigm for the Tiger Corps. In the whole country, at the most far-away places,

[9] E. E. Reynolds, *Baden-Powell: A Biography of Lord Baden-Powell of Gilwell*, pp. 157-8.

[10] *Ibid.*, p. 154.

[11] Vella, *Chaiyo!*, pp. 36-37.

[12] De Schaeck, *Fêtes du Siam*, p. 119.

units of this corps are being set up. One would hardly recognize the quiet and phlegmatic Siamese. The oldest people, of high and low status, join the corps and take part in the exercises, which have been changed to the evening hours from 4 to 6 p.m. in order not to clash with the ordinary duties of life. The king himself prefers to appear in the Wild Tiger uniform. The princes must, of course, follow his example.[13]

What originally had been a local idea, directly emanating from the king and his entourage, had rapidly evolved into a nationwide movement. Old and young joined in the regular drill and were proud to swear their new oath of allegiance to the king, the nation and religion. Both Mongkut and Chulalongkorn had gained strength through creating links between the monarch and the common people, but Wachirawut established a truly nationalistic organization that made people feel that they were part of the Siamese nation and bonded to the monarch himself.

The Second Coronation

The king was an accomplished actor and playwright. Between 1903 and 1910, while living at Saranrom Palace, he had written at least four full-length plays and had directed and written texts for his own troupe of classical dancers. He shocked some people, notably his mother, Queen Saowapha, by taking roles and appearing on stage.[14] Acting, it was widely felt, was a fine and honorable art form, but not one a *chaofa* prince ought to practice. Wachirawut, however, was not to be discouraged and persisted in taking part in dramatics, even after he became king. This taste for drama can be seen in the king's preoccupation with the Wild Tigers, for whom he designed uniforms, flags and banners, as well as maneuvers and war games. It was the same gift for drama that inspired him to order the preparation of a second coronation, one that would surpass all previous coronations and impress the international aristocratic circle.

A second, more formal inauguration had once been organized for Wachirawut's great-great-grandfather, the founder of the dynasty. The coronation of November and December 1911 was such a traditional event, beginning with the consecration of *abhiseka* water in seven shrines, lighting the victory candle and rituals guided by court Brahmans and Buddhist monks. It included the ritual on the octagonal throne, a royal procession and vows of allegiance by palace servants. It was concluded on 4 December by a royal procession around the city and a formal boat procession.[15] This elaborate Siamese ritual lasted almost four weeks and was followed by another six days of festivities

---

[13] Translated from Weiler, *Anfang der Eisenbahn*, p. 199.

[14] Vella, *Chaiyo!*, p. 7.

[15] *Programme of the Coronation of His Majesty Vajiravudh, King of Siam.*

234

devised by the king. Apparently inspired by European royal accession ceremonies, which Wachirawut had attended when still a crown prince, invitations to attend the coronation festivities from 5 to 10 December were personally delivered by Prince Chakraphong to heads of state and royalty around the world. As a result, a large number of countries sent high-ranking representatives. There was Prince Hiroyasu Fushimi from Japan, a Mr. Hamilton deputizing for the President of the United States, and a virtual constellation of princes, princesses, a grand-duke, a duke, a count, a baron and a marquis, together with their suites, from a dozen European countries.[16] No expense was spared to receive the foreign guests in European style; some 750 tons of furniture was bought from abroad 'to provide the guests with nothing but the best.'[17] During the European part of the coronation festivities the king himself provided ample entertainment. There was a formal reception, a presentation of new colors to the army, a grand troop review, an excursion to the royal palace at Bang Pa In and to Ayutthaya, and a great muster of the Wild Tiger Corps. One evening there was a theatrical and classical dance performance; on another, fireworks.

The ceremony was hailed as a great success. The foreign guests had been well entertained. At the same time, it had been extremely costly. In fact, the king had grossly overspent. While some 450,000 *baht* had been allocated in the budget for this purpose, more than 4 1/2 million was used, or nearly eight per cent of the national budget of just over 60 million.[18] The lavish spending may have served to impress many people with the new monarch's grandeur, but if the king had entertained the thought that it would make him universally liked, he was suddenly made aware of considerable opposition, which became apparent when in late February 1912 a plot to overthrow his regime was discovered.

The Abortive Plot

Since the beginning of February 1912 the king had been on maneuvers at a camp near Ban Pong with his Bangkok Wild Tigers, who, reinforced by the Ratburi contingent, contended with the Nakhon Chaisi Wild Tigers. The king's party were declared victors, even though at one stage the king had been 'taken prisoner' by the opposing group.[19] While Wachirawut was thus engaged, Prince Chakraphong was informed by an army officer that many people were preparing to stage a *coup d'état*, Chakraphong acted fast, and 106 conspirators and sympathizers were arrested.

There was indeed a group of young army officers discussing ways and means of overthrowing King Wachirawut. They had only recently begun sounding out officials in various

[16] A list is given in *The Souvenir of the Siamese Kingdom Exhibition*, pp. 175-76.

[17] Vella, *Chaiyo!*, p. 19.

[18] *Ibid.*, p. 25 ('nearly 8 per cent of the national budget'). On the size of the budget, see *L'Asie Française*, 1911, p. 463.

[19] *L'Asie Française*, 1912, p. 124.

government departments and had met with quite a positive response. Although the arrests took place on 1 March 1912,[20] it was not until 4 March that the *Bangkok Times* noted that there had been an attempted 'mutiny'. After the press had revealed the plot, Prince Chakraphong issued a formal statement disclosing that there were three separate parties who had been formally in contact for less than two months. One was led by a medical officer and consisted of Siamese of Chinese descent, another was led by an officer in the Judge Advocate's Department and the third by an officer on the General Staff. The first group advocated changing Siam into a republic, with Prince Ratburi as Siam's first President. The second group wanted a constitutional monarchy under *chaofa* Boriphat, while the third also aimed at a constitutional monarchy, but under *chaofa* Chakraphong. At the moment when the plot was revealed, the first group seemed to have been strongest, and in order not to dissipate the initial thrust, all parties had agreed to pursue the first group's aims.[21]

When the plot was discovered, the conspirators had just reached the stage of deciding upon practical measures. The best moment, it was thought, would be the April ceremony of the swearing of the oath of allegiance, when all important people would be at the Temple of the Emerald Buddha. All key members of government would be arrested. However, long before any member of the government was in danger, the whole affair was over. Prince Chakraphong, who was in charge when the plot was uncovered, decided to downplay it as a problem of minor importance, caused by a group of misguided young men who did not really understand grave matters of state. However, it must have been noticed that the movement appeared to have rapidly gained support among young and progressive government officials and that there was a keen interest in the idea of a change of government.

There were both external and domestic factors that stimulated such a movement. Abroad, there was the example of Turkey, where in 1908 young army officers, the so-called 'Young Turks', had overthrown Sultan Abdul Hamid II's regime. Even more important was Sun Yat-sen's revolutionary republican movement in China, which in 1911 had led to the formal secession of various southern provinces and, on 1 January 1912, to the proclamation of the Republic of China. At home, Siamese intellectuals had for some time been considering alternatives to the absolute monarchy. King Chulalongkorn had once favored a more broadly based form of government, but with increasing age and experience had decided to retain personal control of all policy decisions. The accession of a new king, the first to have received his education in a country with a system of parliamentary democracy, was in itself sufficient reason to reopen the debate on Siam's form of government.

---

[20] Thamsook Numnonda, 'Khabuankan R.S. 130', *Warasan Thammasat* 8, pt 2 (October-November 1978), pp. 2-7. Hunter and Narisa Chakrabongse write that the arrests took place on February 27 (*Katya and the Prince of Siam*, p. 129).

[21] See Prince Chakrabongse's interview, reported in the *Straits Times*, 18 March 1912. This is basically also the version in Weiler's diary, dated 28 March (see *Anfang der Eisenbahn*, pp. 208-9).

All these factors played a role, but the chief impetus for a revolutionary movement in Siam was no doubt a widespread disenchantment with the new king. The fact that of the three 'branches' in the movement, two subscribed to a constitutional monarchy headed by a king other than Wachirawut, testifies to antipathy against the man who succeeded Chulalongkorn. Some young military officers held a grudge against Wachirawut because in 1909, when he was still crown prince, he had insisted upon a humiliating public flogging of some military men, among them two junior officers who had been involved in a fight with several of his personal pages.[22] Others feared that Wachirawut lacked statesmanship, for he had bestowed rank and honor on personal friends who were widely held to be unworthy of such an increase in status.[23] Among the military in particular there was resentment of the king's manifest preoccupation with the quasi-military Wild Tigers. In addition to these factors was the king's strangely undignified personal behavior. Instead of settling down to a traditional royal family life, he remained a bachelor and, together with his bachelor friends, engaged in artistic pursuits, including appearing on the stage in a wide variety of roles. At the time of the plot it was also quite clear that the king had a strong and willful character and that he was not willing to consider seriously any fundamental change in the system of government.

The king realized that the plot was partly directed against his person and his way of governing. When he returned from some two months of the Wild Tiger exercises he did not wear his customary Wild Tiger uniform.[24] In a move apparently designed to protect himself and to counter criticism against his personal lifestyle, the king issued a decree stating that all palaces and palace grounds were the king's private domain and that access to the king was restricted. In an oblique reference to the plot he stated:

> ... the number of government servants is increasing, but their awareness of the fact that they are servants of the king has been decreasing. For one thing, they have the false idea that their places of work are public property and from this they proceed to take the king's palaces also to be public places. This, however, is a completely wrong idea. The king still has absolute power and it is he who shall allow or forbid people to enter royal palaces. He may even refuse all access.[25]

Just over two months after the plot had been discovered, a special court passed sentence. Three men were sentenced to death and twenty to life imprisonment, thirty-two received jail sentences of twenty years, seven fifteen years and thirty twelve years. The king commuted the sentences, however, so that only the first two categories (involving twenty-three men) were put

[22] Rian Sichan and Net Phunwiwat, *Kabot R.S. 130 (Kanpatiwat khrang raek khong Thai)*, pp. 2-5.

[23] Weiler, *Anfang der Eisenbahn*, p. 209.

[24] *Ibid.*

[25] *Phraratchaniyom nai Phrabatsomdet Phramongkutklao Chaoyuhua*, pp. 14-5.

in jail.[26] The king regarded the episode as a serious warning and for the time being gave heed to his personal security. The daily Wild Tiger exercises were reduced to once a week. With respect to placing himself under the guidance of a parliament, Wachirawut considered the time inopportune. He continued to be the final authority in all matters of state and liberalized only to the extent of frequently following the recommendations brought forward by the chief advisory committees.

The King's Style of Government

It has often been remarked how Wachirawut's style of government differed from that of his father, and that a main feature of his reign was that he decided no longer to rely upon his many brothers and uncles who had been placed in executive positions.[27] While there are grounds for this general statement, what is usually overlooked is that the shift away from the princes occurred only gradually. At the beginning of 1912 the cabinet of twelve still included seven princes of *krom* rank, and several of the remaining posts were also occupied by men who had been appointed by Chulalongkorn.[28] Notable among the latter was the head of the Ministry of Municipal Government, *chaophraya Yomarat*, under whose unassuming, but at the same time firm leadership, various schemes to improve Bangkok were completed. New roads were built, a tramway was set up and a large number of wooden bridges were replaced with reinforced concrete ones. During 1912, 1913 and much of 1914, Bangkok was provided for the first time with a regular water-supply system. *Yomarat* has been described as Bangkok's most popular personality.[29]

Wachirawut continued to use Chulalongkorn's team and there was no sudden break in the daily routine of government; nor was there widespread anxiety about tenure of office. It was only when a vacancy occurred through death, retirement, or resignation that the king would fill a senior post with one of his *coterie*. Much of the running of daily affairs was therefore in the hands of experienced men. To them and their staff Siam owed many progressive steps, such as the development of a national plan for the education of the whole populace, the setting up of clinics in Bangkok and some of the provinces where free vaccination was given against smallpox, and the continuing investment in the building of railways. During 1913 the northern line reached as far north as Ban Pak Tha in the province of Lampang and the construction of a southern line was proceeding satisfactorily.[30]

In 1913 the Siamese government managed to control and overcome a serious financial crisis that began when the Chino-Siam Bank collapsed. This bank, established in 1908, was

---

[26] Thamsook Numnonda, 'Khabuankan R.S. 130', p. 7.

[27] For example, Phra Sarasas, *My Country Thailand (Its History, Geography and Civilisation)*, p. 131.

[28] Prince Chakrabongse (Defense), Prince Boriphat (Navy), Prince Thewawong (Foreign Affairs), Prince Naret (Public Works), Prince Damrong (Interior), Prince Sanphasit (Palace), Prince Chanthaburi (Treasury), *momchao* Charun (Communication), *chaophraya* Yomarat (Municipal Government) *chaophraya* Wongsa (Agriculture), *momratchawong* Piya Malakun (Justice) and *phraya* Surasena (Chamberlain). Source: *Phraratchaniyom nai Phrabatsomdet Phramongkutklao Chaoyuhua*, pp. 21-22.

[29] Weiler, *Anfang der Eisenbahn*, pp. 214-5.

[30] *Souvenir of the Siamese Kingdom Exhibition*, pp. 180-1.

under Chinese management and had been engaged in financing much of the rice trade with Hongkong. It had also been providing funds for the Chinese revolutionary forces; the 1913 split among the revolutionaries and Sun Yat-sen's flight to Japan were undoubtedly related to the bank's failure. The government-sponsored Siam Commercial Bank came to the rescue, but when various malpractices were uncovered, not only did the Chino-Siam suspend payments, but there was also a run on the Siam Commercial Bank itself. The government had to intervene and spent large amounts of money to restore a measure of confidence in the Siamese banking system.[31]

The king's personal style of government can be seen most clearly in his decree of 22 March 1913 regarding the use of sur-names. Up until 1913 most Siamese were known only by their personal name, often a monosyllabic 'nickname', but mostly among the prosperous, a pleasant-sounding polysyllabic 'real name'. Both 'nickname' and 'real name' referred to the individual and it was impossible to decide from these names who was related to whom. Family names had long been in use, but generally only by the *phudi*, people of rank and refinement. There were signs that the number of people adopting surnames had been steadily increasing, but they remained limited to those who had distinguished themselves somehow and had achieved a measure of wealth and influence. In the 1913 decree, it was stipulated that all heads of families were given six months from 1 July in which to choose and register their surnames. The king, who was of no mean literary talent, devised lists of well-sounding names from which the general populace might choose.[32]

The measure was obviously inspired by European prac-tices. Like many other measures that were directed 'from above', the decree did not immediately achieve the intended results. The idea of choosing a surname seemed unnecessary to many farmers who would have no need to distinguish them-selves in this manner and who felt that, even if a surname were chosen, it would soon be forgotten. Throughout the reign the central government, prompted by the king, made various efforts to implement the decree, but the universal adoption of surnames was not achieved during the sixth reign.[33]

In his public review of the year 1914, the king was happy to mention many projects which were helping Siam along the path of progress, such as the completion of the capital's water-supply system, opening of a government electrical power station, continuation of work on the northern and southern railway lines, and educational and legal reform. Meanwhile, war had broken out in Europe and, though it seemed unlikely to affect Siam directly, this stimulated Wachirawut's interest in Siam's defense. In a move reminiscent of establishing the Wild Tigers, he devised a scheme by which the general public would

[31] Further details on the financial crisis can be found in W. A. Graham, *Siam: A Handbook of Practical, Com-mercial, and Political Information*, vol. 1, pp. 342-43; G.W. Skinner, *Chinese Society in Thailand*, p. 158; *Souvenir of the Siamese Kingdom Exhibition*, p. 182; and especially Chatthip Nartsupha, Suthy Prasartset, and Montri Chenvidyakan, eds., *The Political Economy of Siam, 1910-1932*, pp. 19-20 and 125-38.

[32] Vella, *Chaiyo!*, pp. 128-36.

[33] The Personal and Family Names Act was finally enforced in 1941. See the *Bangkok Chronicle*, 16 October 1941, p. 5. It is interesting to note, however, that surnames never achieved the same status as European ones. The Siamese still generally prefer to be addressed personally by their 'real names', and the Bangkok telephone directory lists people under these.

be given a chance to be personally involved in the nation's defense. He founded the Royal Navy League of Siam.[34]

> *the first object of which is to invite the Siamese people to subscribe for King and country money for acquiring a warship for the Navy to serve as a protection for King, country and religion. I am happy to associate myself with and to take a deep interest in the success of this laudable object, which is an evidence that the Siamese people are determined, like their ancestors, to show their affection and loyalty to their Sovereign, to preserve the independence of the nation, and to uphold our Holy Religion, which has been the precious emblem and moral support of the Siamese race for many generations.[35]*

The king's rhetoric knew no bounds when it came to an attempt to rouse the nation into participating in this scheme. He set his heart upon acquiring a light cruiser and in the following years he instigated many campaigns to raise funds. State officials throughout the country were ordered to cooperate. Writing under a pseudonym, Wachirawut praised the cruiser-fund; he wrote several plays intended to increase people's enthusiasm, caused street signs to be erected exhorting people to contribute and placed large advertisements in the papers. Helped by large donations from the king himself, the fund got off to a grand start, but soon the rate of contributions slowed down, and it was not until 1920 that it was used to help buy a Siamese warship.[36]

By 1915 Wachirawut's style of government was clearly established. This is apparent, for example, from an examination of the composition of the cabinet. In 1912 this had consisted almost wholly of King Chulalongkorn's appointees; three years and several shuffles in senior positions later, half the cabinet consisted of new faces. Notable was Prince Damrong's absence. He resigned in 1915 from his post as Minister of the Interior, officially because of ill health, but in actuality because of friction between himself and the king. From the very beginning of his reign Wachirawut had whittled sections away from the Interior Ministry.[37] In addition the king proved to be a difficult leader, a man who discouraged personal contact with many of his chief administrators, preferring to keep them at a distance. His shyness caused him to avoid speaking directly to people and he often resorted to sending written instructions. On some of the rare occasions when he had to receive European guests, this awkwardness was 'distressing to witness'.[38]

Commentators have attributed Waichirawut's strained relationship with most members of the royal family to the fact that he had spent many of his 'impressionable and formative years' abroad.[39] These commentators politely omit to mention that Wachirawut returned from England with a decided preference for male company and demonstrated this by refusing to

---

[34] Officially it was stated that others came and persuaded the king, but there can be little doubt that the whole idea was Wachirawut's (see Vella, *Chaiyo!*, p. 97.)

[35] *Souvenir of the Siamese Kingdom Exhibition*, p. 189.

[36] Vella, *Chaiyo!*, p. 120.

[37] Greene, *Absolute Dreams*, Chapter 5.

[38] M. Smith, *A Physician at the Court of Siam*, p. 114.

[39] *Ibid.*, and Vella, *Chaiyo!*, pp. 264-5.

marry, not even agreeing to a *pro forma* marriage. In 1915 he was already thirty-four years old and still a confirmed bachelor who relaxed only within a circle of intimate male friends who readily accepted him. While shunning contact with his relatives, he lavished favors and gifts to his personal friends. There can be little doubt that many of Wachirawut's personal communication problems stemmed from his awareness of criticism of his personal life style.

The resulting stress and isolation must at least partly account for his attempts to reach out to 'his nation', to appeal directly to the general public, to lead and direct the Siamese people. Wachirawut's nationalism, his writings under the name Asvabahu in the *Siam Observer*, his fervent speeches to the military and his setting up of a warship fund, were all measures that seemed to have been devised largely by the king and his circle of personal friends. One of Wachirawut's more popular programs was his encouragement of sports and athletics, at first within the Wild Tiger movement, but later also in schools and among the military. From 1913 onward the king went once a year to Suan Kulap School to view athletic events and award prizes, and other schools began to emulate these sports days. By late 1915 sporting events had gained some passionate support, as witnessed by an indignant European resident:

> On 4 November, going for an evening drive, at the great Pramaen Place in front of the Maha Chakri Palace I came across a disorderly mass of maybe a hundred sailors and marines who were pushing their way through the streets, lifting their caps and hurling them in the air, cheering, followed by half a dozen cars packed with navy officers. I had to make my way to the side of the road and stop my car in order to let the mass of people pass. At first I could not imagine what could have caused this unusual occurrence. The next day I read in the court news that the king had personally handed over a gold cup to the navy cadets as a sports trophy, and that this had been carried in triumph by the champions to the navy school.[40]

This gold cup was Siam's first football trophy. The king had himself organized that year's competition, which proved a resounding success.[41]

In yet another respect Wachirawut influenced the lives of a great number of Siamese, namely in proclaiming public holidays. To the traditional holidays such as Siamese New Year in April, and holidays related to the yearly cycle in the nation's Buddhist monasteries, the king added various nationalistic festivals which were widely celebrated, at least in Bangkok. The twenty-third of October was Chulalongkorn Day, commemorating that king's death. The eleventh of November was Wachirawut's accession day, sufficient reason for three days of

[40] Translated from Weiler, *Anfang der Eisenbahn*, p. 273.

[41] For details, see Vella, *Chaiyo!*, pp. 144-51.

festivities. The first of January was the King's Birthday, and that needed another three days' holiday, complete with a great illumination of the city.[42] On 11 November 1916,[43] the sixth anniversary of his accession, the king announced a simplified, Western-style system for referring to the various kings in the Chakri dynasty. The well-established names, such as Phraphuthayotfa, Phraphuthaloetla, and Phranangklao, were still to be recognized, but the whole dynasty was given the name of Ramathibodi. Wachirawut himself therefore became King Ramathibodi VI. It was permitted to abbreviate the dynastic name to Rama. The practice never became popular among the Siamese, but it was readily adopted by Western authors, often troubled by the elaborate Siamese terminology.

Another Wachirawut brainwave was his scheme for radical reform of the Siamese system of writing, proclaimed in April 1917. Instead of the existing method of placing vowels in various positions around consonants, they were to be written immediately after the appropriate consonant. In addition, Wachirawut suggested that spaces be left between words. The Wachirawut system would have simplified Siamese for those learning for the first time to read and write it, notably Europeans and young children.[44] The abolition of cumbersome obsolete practices is in the interest of future generations, and this scheme would have been a most suitable one for a benevolent absolute monarch to execute. However, Wachirawut did not possess the measure of control over his administrators needed to implement the idea. He relied upon the hope that the reform would trigger off a broadly based supporting movement, just as the Wild Tigers and football competition had done. In this case, however, he soon discovered that the general public did not clamor for spelling reforms and his system was soon forgotten.

Siam and the World War

From a Siamese perspective, the First World War initially was simply a European conflict and in August 1914 the Siamese government readily proclaimed its strict neutrality. Although the British constituted the leading foreign community in Bangkok, the Germans had established themselves as a major force. At the beginning of the war the Germans had by far the largest shipping interests, carrying much of Siam's imports and exports.[45] Throughout the first years of the war, this proclaimed neutrality was maintained.

The suggestion to consider joining the allied forces came from Prince Thewawong, Siam's experienced Minister of Foreign Affairs, as late as February 1917, after the United States had broken off diplomatic relations with Germany.

---

[42] Weiler, *Anfang der Eisenbahn*, p. 278.

[43] Vella, *Chaiyo!*, pp. 136-7; H. Cucherousset, *Quelques informations sur le Siam*, p. 32, gives the date a week earlier, 4 November.

[44] Vella, *Chaiyo!*, pp. 241-2.

[45] See, for example, the table in *L'Asie Française*, 1911, p. 465.

Should the United States declare war, Siam might consider doing the same, Prince Thewawong thought. However, he advised caution and preferred Siam to sever relations rather than declare war. After April, when America did enter the war, Siam's position was further debated between Prince Chakraphong and Prince Thewawong; Chakraphong advocated war, but Thewawong argued for continued neutrality. Realizing that the Germans were now likely to be defeated and that Siam might derive benefits from joining the winning side, the king decided on a declaration of war, but waited for an opportune moment to make his decision public. Throughout June and most of July preparations were made, which included plans to seize German ships and arrest and intern German nationals. The king himself, under the pseudonym Ramachitti, published in a newspaper a series of articles setting out the moral reasons for entering the war.[46]

The official declaration of war, on 22 July, therefore came as no surprise. This should not imply, however, that it was a popular decision. The Germans had a good record in Siam. Unlike Britain and France, Germany had never threatened Siamese-held territory. Some prominent princes, notably Boriphat and Dilok, had completed their education in Germany. While most ordinary Siamese had little interest in the war, among Siamese intellectuals there was debate on whether or not a declaration of war was the right decision. Prince Boriphat was clearly distressed at the move to abandon neutrality, and he showed his disapproval by being absent from cabinet meetings in May and June 1917. There even developed a plot on the part of some army and naval officers to overthrow Wachirawut and replace him with Prince Boriphat, a plot that was suppressed and long kept secret.[47]

The arrest and internment of the new 'enemies' went smoothly; with one stroke Siam cancelled the existing unequal treaties with Germany and Austria. There are several reasons why Siam declared war. French and Russian diplomats had assured the Siamese that Siam would be greatly helped in future by entering the war, that treaty revisions and restrictions on customs duties might be lifted.[48] Apart from these legal benefits, there was for King Wachirawut a great attraction in that he could forge a closer link between himself and his people by personally leading them on a course towards battle. Before announcing that Siam had entered the war, he underwent the appropriate state ceremony for a king about to lead an army, and then, dressed in the appropriate scarlet robe, he made the public declaration.[49] In September 1917 it was decided that an extraordinary force should be dispatched, consisting of some thirteen hundred men, representing the most modern developments in the Siamese army. Siam decided to send a flying squadron and an ambulance corps with drivers and mechanics.

[46] Vella, *Chaiyo!*, pp. 104-10; *L'Asie Française*, 1917, pp. 124-5.

[47] B. A. Batson, 'The End of the Absolute Monarchy in Siam', p. 22.

[48] Vella, *Chaiyo!*, p. 106.

[49] *Souvenir of the Siamese Kingdom Exhibition*, p. 181. Details can be found in Edward M. Young, *Aerial Nationalism; A History of Aviation in Thailand*, Washington: Smithsonian Institution Press, 1995, pp. 8-21. See also Stefan Hell, 'The Role of European Technology, Expertise and Early Development Aid in the Modernization of Thailand Before the Second World War', *Journal of the Asia Pacific Economy*, 6 (2), 2001, pp. 158-178.

A call for volunteers was issued. The response was quite gratifying, and between October 1917 and June 1918, under the personal supervision of the king, the troops were selected, equipped and trained in such a manner that they would do honor to Siam.[50]

The Siamese expeditionary force arrived in France in late July 1918, when the final offensive under Marshal Foch was already under way. When the Siamese motorized unit finally arrived at the front in September, they were just in time to witness the end of the hostilities. A newly formed German government began negotiating for peace on October 4. In November King Wachirawut could proudly announce that Siam belonged to the victorious nations, leading thousands in chanting prayers of thanksgiving. The general public was reminded of Siam's victory in the king's birthday speech, by the festive reception given to the returning aviation corps (who had not had a chance to go into action), and by the fact that Siamese troops marched in three gala victory parades, in Paris, London and Brussels. In September 1919 the victorious ambulance corps finally returned and received a true hero's welcome, with three days of banquets, decorations, fireworks and nationalistic speeches. Though Siam had not lost any troops in battle, there had been nineteen casualties. These dead soldiers were solemnly honored by having their ashes placed in a large monument.[51]

All the speeches and pathos could not, however, hide the fact that Siam had entered the war at a rather embarrassingly late stage, that its role had been largely ceremonial, and that the troops had gained no military experience. In addition, it soon became clear that Siam was not accepted as an equal partner in the post-war international negotiations. It had been hoped that the inequitable foreign treaties would rapidly be revoked. Only the United States, whose president had been an ardent advocate of the rights of smaller nations, was willing to draft a new treaty; the negotiations with other nations proceeded slowly. It was only near the end of the sixth reign, six years after the end of World War I, mainly through the able work of the American adviser Francis B. Sayre, that treaties were renegotiated and Siam gained international autonomy. Sayre's success was not based upon Siam's participation in the war; arguably it would have been no more difficult to achieve had Siam remained neutral. To a large extent the 'joining the cause of justice' was intended for home consumption. It was used by the king to enhance nationalistic feelings and to strengthen the ties between monarch and people.

Dusit Thani

While the Siamese expeditionary force was on its way to

---

[50] A series of statements issued by Wachirawut regarding the great heroic role of the troops being sent to Europe can be found in Prayut Sitthiphan, *Phramahathiraratchao*, pp. 117-49.

[51] Vella, *Chaiyo!*, pp. 119-20.

Marseilles in July 1918, the king began the construction of a miniature town in his private gardens behind the royal palace. 'It contained houses, palaces, temples, roads, rivers and canals, trees and parks, fountains, waterfalls, and electric lights – an enchanted fairyland by more than one account.'[52] The king and his circle of personal friends created there a world of their own, called Dusit Thani, or 'Dusit City'.[53] They devised their own system of government, under a *nakhonaphiban* or 'town care-taker'. On 7 November 1918 they drew up an elaborate town constitution with fifty-one provisions.[54] The town caretaker would govern for a period of one year only, and he would not be eligible to stand again until another person had served.[55] The miniature town was organized along modern lines, with a fire department, an electric company, a sewage department and a health department. Dusit Thani was an elaborate game, where courtiers could express themselves on matters of language and society, on government and modernization, stimulated by the setting of the miniature city. Dusit Thani also provided tremendous fun. During 1919 there were frequent boat-races with miniature boats on the miniature river.[56] Before the end of 1918 Dusit Thani had its own fortnightly paper,[57] the *Dusit Samit* (Dusit United) and before long it also boasted a daily.[58]

When Queen Saowapha, the queen mother, died in October 1919, Wachirawut decided to move to her palace. As he enjoyed his miniature town so much, he decided to transfer it to his new residence, and in December 1919 the ceremony of the placing of a founding 'city pillar' took place.[59] In the miniature city, with his few hundred associates, Wachirawut instituted an elaborate political game, he himself being the leader of one of the two parties formed.

Authors sympathetic to Wachirawut have suggested that the ultimate purpose of Dusit Thani was to provide a testing-ground for democratic experiments on the national level.[60] As Vella rightly points out, there is little or no evidence for this idea.[61] At first sight Dusit Thani resembles the *Suan Khwa* (the Garden on the Right) during the reign of Rama II. The *Suan Khwa*, like Dusit Thani, was built for the king's pleasure; it was a place where the king and his artistic courtiers could write, recite and act. Dusit Thani, however, was not just a setting for plays; it was a Utopian model world, where beauty and friendship flourished. In spite of all its constitutional rules and regulations, there was never any doubt that it was Wachirawut's creation. At any time he could overrule decisions by the elected 'town caretaker'.

For an assessment of the role of Dusit Thani, it is necessary to make a judgement regarding Wachirawut's personality, his position in relation to senior administrators and his relationship with various members of the royal family. Wachirawut's strained relationship with many people of experience and rank led him to

---

[52] *Ibid.*, p. 75.

[53] Dusit is the Thai pronunciation of the Pali word Tusita, the name of one of the heavens recognized in Buddhist cosmology.

[54] The full text of the constitution can be found in Prayut Sitthiphan, *Phramahathiraratchao*, pp. 182-92.

[55] *Ibid.*, p. 185.

[56] Vella, *Chaiyo!*, p. 75.

[57] Vella (p. 75) appears to be mistaken in calling it a weekly; see Prayut Sitthiphan, *Phramahathiraratchao*, pp. 201-4.

[58] There were two dailies, the *Dusit Samai, and the Dusit Sakkhi*. The *Dusit Samai* appeared in B.E. 2462 (1919/20). The National Library in Bangkok has no holdings of *Dusit Sakkhi*.

[59] Vella, *Chaiyo!*, p. 288.

[60] For example, Amon Darunrak, *Dusit Thani*, quoted by Vella, *Chaiyo!*, p. 76.

[61] *Ibid.*, p. 76.

withdraw gradually from matters of administrative routine which would have brought him in contact with his critics.[62] By creating a friendly and harmonious Dusit Thani, where he was appreciated and where he was the undisputed leader, Wachirawut was able to fulfil the role of absolute monarch. The fact that it was a world of make-believe, a fairly secret and sheltered world, suited Wachirawut's thespian inclinations. Dusit Thani complemented the king's personal interest in his ceremonial role. In the outside world, Wachirawut continued to make speeches and design uniforms and insignia, but the number of his public appearances declined.

Siam's Financial Crisis, 1919-23

As early as 1916, when the price of silver began to rise, the Financial Adviser warned that Siam's silver coins soon could become worth more than their face value and the danger would arise of people melting down the coins and exporting the silver. He recommended debasing the *baht* by reducing its silver content,[63] a measure that had been adopted as early as 1906 in the Philippines and the Straits Settlements.[64] The Siamese government, in line with earlier decisions with respect to the *baht*, refused to act other than by moving officially to prohibit all export of silver.

As a result, in 1919 a serious financial crisis developed. In the first place the price of silver, which had been steadily rising since 1916 and long since pushed the actual value of silver coins above their face value, went much higher, hence it became increasingly profitable to smuggle silver out of Siam. The government decided to revalue the *baht*. Late in 1919 the exchange rate was gradually raised from 13 *baht* per pound sterling to 9.54 *baht*. Further, earlier in the year, an unprecedented increase in the price of rice had caused a shortage of currency and the Siamese Treasury had printed massive amounts of banknotes.[65] By the end of the year it also became apparent that Siam's rice crop was failing. The king was forced to prohibit all export of rice, take measures to prevent smuggling, intervene in the crisis and buy and distribute rice.[66]

This combination of factors proved very damaging to Siam's economy. In 1920/21 the value of the export trade dropped to almost half that of the previous year, a direct result of the ban on rice export. At the same time the value of imports rose to an unprecedented level, much of the increase caused by the revaluation of the *baht*. The price of silver rose even higher, but the government could no longer follow its policy of increasing the value of the *baht* at a time when only a massive devaluation could have prevented a run on the currency. With the exchange rate not high enough to make smuggling of silver

[62] V. Thompson, *Thailand, the New Siam*, p. 55.

[63] J. C. Ingram, *Economic Change in Thailand, 1880-1970*, pp. 156-7.

[64] I. Brown, 'Siam and the Gold Standard, 1902-1908', p. 395.

[65] Ingram, *Economic Change*, pp. 156-7.

[66] For details, see the king's anniversary speech, 1 January 1920, as reported in *The Souvenir of the Siamese Kingdom Exhibition*, pp. 224-5.

unprofitable, and too high for the international currency market, Siam's wealth was eroded on several sides.[67] Siam's administrators decided to weather the storm and hoped that the next crops would be abundant, the price of silver would drop and the financial troubles would soon disappear.

The rice exports were resumed and the price of silver finally dropped, but as time went on it became clear that the exchange rate of 9.54 *baht* per pound sterling was too high. Throughout 1920, 1921 and 1922 the Treasury had to shore up the *baht* by purchasing sterling. Thus Siam's external debt had to be increased by borrowing two million pounds sterling at, for that time, the high interest rate of seven per cent. Finally, on 3 January 1923, the decision was taken to devalue the *baht* to the rate of 11 *baht* per pound sterling; for a while it would appear that a recovery was possible.

The financial crisis had cost the country massive amounts of revenue, foreign loans had to be raised, imports became more expensive, and the revaluation costs were partially borne by the rice farmer. King Wachirawut, in theory, had the power to change the nation's financial policies and he could have decreed a lessening of the silver content of the *baht*, a measure that would have freed the Treasury to determine a realistic currency rate. There is no evidence that the king even considered such a step. He retreated more and more into his fantasy world, leaving government affairs to the administrators. Moreover, he tended to regard foreign advisers with suspicion and had reduced their numbers and influence,[68] so that he may not have given the Financial Adviser's warnings the consideration they deserved.

The King and the Government

In the early 1920s it became more and more clear that the king wished to have little to do with administrative routine.[69] The leadership of the cabinet rested largely upon *chaophraya Yomarat*, who in 1915 had been appointed to the Ministry of the Interior, but retained the post and title of Minister of Local Government, which he had been given at the end of the fifth reign. A man with even longer experience in the cabinet was Prince Thewawong, who remained responsible for Siam's foreign affairs, whilst in 1922 he was given the power to supervise the Treasury as well.[70] Not long before his death in June 1923 he was given a special honor which – the king not being in good health and seldom attending cabinet meetings – amounted to that of being appointed Prime Minister. Prince Thewawong's death came at a time when the country's financial situation, notably the continuing budget deficit, was causing some alarm. Early in 1924 a committee consisting of the princes Damrong,

[67] Graham, *Siam*, vol. 1, p. 348; Ingram, *Economic Change*, p. 157.

[68] Thompson, *Thailand, the New Siam*, p. 54. The king's attitude towards foreign advisers was quite clear. See W. F. Vella, 'Siamese Nationalism in the Plays of Rama VI', p. 5; and S. Greene, 'King Wachirawut's Policy of Nationalism', in Tej Bunnag and M. Smithies, ed., *In Memoriam Phya Anuman Rajadhon, Contributions in Memory of the Late President of the Siam Society*, p. 255.

[69] Thompson, *Thailand, the New Siam*, p. 55.

[70] *Ratchasakunwong*, p. 56.

Narit, and Phanurangsi was appointed to study the situation. During 1924 another massive loan of three million pounds at six per cent interest was floated. Early in 1925 Siam's economic position seemed weaker than ever. The cabinet met repeatedly to consider the situation. It demanded a report from the new Financial Adviser, Sir Edward Cook. The government was spending too much and was using up its international reserves. Cook pointed out that an excessive amount was spent on defense (23.3 per cent of the national budget) and on royal expenditure (10.7 per cent). As a matter of fact, even the official amount of royal expenditure did not cover all that was used by the king, several items of Wachirawut's spending being placed under various other headings in the regular budget.[71]

The cabinet, fortified with these figures, decided to approach the king and ask him to curb his expenses as part of the measures to improve the country's finances. In July 1925 Wachirawut flatly refused to accept their recommendation. He reminded cabinet that he was the head of government and that the budget committee was only advisory; he had no intention of handing over any of his powers and was not willing to show restraint regarding royal expenditure. Indeed, the king would soon need more funds than ever for the preparation of the Siamese Kingdom Exhibition. Apparently it did not concern him that there was no money for public works.[72] Clearly, an impasse had been reached between the king and almost all his senior administrators. A situation developed in which at least part of the king's powers were likely to be stripped away. However, before long Wachirawut died a natural death, which, from the cabinet's point of view, provided an easy way out of the stalemate.

While the king had abandoned many of his responsibilities, he was by no means an idle man. He maintained his direct and indirect links with the general public. He was still the leader of the Wild Tigers and the Tiger Cubs. The Tiger Cub organization had gradually grown into a separate form of the Boy Scout movement. Most schools of renown had their own corps. Whilst the number of Tiger Cubs was just over 8,800 in 1917, by 1922 it had grown to almost 21,500 young participants,[73] and in 1924/25 the total number was reported as 38,735.[74] At the annual army maneuvers the king would invite delegations of Tiger Cubs to take part. Wachirawut also continued to promote competitive sports. In the 1920s Bangkok boasted golf courses, tennis courts, and almost monthly horse races alternately at the Sports Club and the Turf Club; there were football, hockey, rugby, and cricket matches, though the latter two sports did not attract much attention.[75]

The king's most important pursuit, however, was that of writing for the benefit and education of the Siamese people. Unlike some of his predecessors, he rarely chose the medium of

[71] For details, see Batson, 'End of the Absolute Monarchy', pp. 26-31.

[72] *Straits Times*, 9 October 1925.

[73] Cucherousset, *Quelques informations*, p. 48.

[74] *The Directory for Bangkok and Siam*, 1928, p. 128.

[75] Information on sports in Bangkok can be found in the *Straits Times*, 23 June 1923 and 22 October 1925; *Souvenir of the Siamese Kingdom Exhibition*, pp. 248-52; and Vella, *Chaiyo!*, pp. 144-51.

the formal royal decree, but communicated by means of short articles, generally written under a pseudonym, and plays, usually written under his own name. Wachirawut's literary output was phenomenal. For the theatre alone he wrote thirty-four original dramas and translated and adapted a further twenty-six plays. Many of his plays were intended to propagate his messages to his people. The hero on stage would exhort the audience to love and respect the king, nation and their religion. Some plays were written specifically to foster a cause: to be respectful to military virtues, give to the Navy League fund, rally behind Siam's involvement in the First World War, or sponsor a Wild Tiger fund. The king did not write solely for didactic purposes, however, and many of his writings for the stage appear to have no other aim but to thrill and entertain.[76] When the king was ill and doctors prescribed a long rest, he would spend most of his time writing. Thus during much of the time between July and October 1925 Wachirawut translated into English the play he had written during another illness two years earlier, but died before he could finish it.[77]

On 11 November 1925 the king left his sickbed to attend some of the celebrations for the fifteenth anniversary of his coronation, but by the evening he felt so unwell that he took to his bed again. As part of the celebrations he had devised an event on a massive scale: a Siamese Kingdom Exhibition to be held in January 1926. For this purpose the king had presented the nation with a large piece of land which he named Lumbini, after the Indian pleasure garden where the Lord Buddha had been born. The exhibition was to present Siam to the world as never before. During the first week it was planned to organize an international Boy Scout jamboree. Hotel accommodation was expanded by the king's lending a palace to the Railway Department. Meanwhile the proffered grounds became the scene of frantic building activity between September and mid-November 1925, when a violent storm broke over Bangkok, destroying eight newly erected buildings in the exhibition grounds. At the same time the king had become seriously ill and was operated on for an abdominal abscess. In the evening of 25 November he lost consciousness, dying early next morning. One of the first acts of the new government was to cancel the grand exhibition.[78]

The Succession

At the beginning of the reign it had been publicly announced that if the king should die without male issue, the succession to the throne would pass presumptively through the line of the queen mother's other sons according to their respective ages. Prince Chakraphong had therefore been automatically the heir

[76] Vella, 'Siamese Nationalism', pp. 7-8.

[77] H.H. Prince Dhani Nivat, 'King Rama VI's Last Work', *Collected Articles*, pp. 121-7.

[78] Vella, *Chaiyo!*, p. 258.

to the throne. Since his elder brother Wachirawut had often been ailing, notably in 1918, Prince Chakraphong had been widely regarded as the nation's hope. It had been expected that he would become a good and popular king, and therefore it came as a severe shock when on 13 June 1920 Chakraphong died at the age of thirty-eight. One author has repeated the gossip that he was poisoned by an unseen hand.[79] However, there seems no substance in this rumor. Prince Chakraphong had become ill with influenza while travelling with his family to Singapore; this had turned into the pneumonia from which he died in spite of the best medical care available, surrounded by family and friends.[80]

His brother's unexpected death, probably coupled with the realization that he himself would soon be forty years old, caused Wachirawut to consider the succession seriously. His three remaining younger brothers, the princes Atsadang, Chuthathut and Prachathipok, may have appeared unsuitable compared with the firm, strong, and able Chakraphong, and this could have been the reason why Wachirawut decided to create a family of his own. On 10 November 1920, on the eve of the festivities for the tenth anniversary of the king's reign, he announced his engagement to *phra'ongchao* Wanlaphathewi. However, owing to 'incompatibility of temperament', the betrothal was officially annulled some four months later.[81] In 1921 a new bride was found; she received the name of Laksamilawan and officially became the king's consort in August 1922. Meanwhile the king's desire for an heir caused him to set aside his earlier views regarding the benefits of monogamy and to take as concubines two sisters, *phra* Sucharit and *phra* Intharasak. The younger sister, *phra* Intharasak, reportedly became pregnant and was elevated to the rank of queen. However, this and other pregnancies ended in miscarriages. In July 1923 the king was still without children when his younger brother Chuthathut died. In February 1925 yet another of the late Queen Saowapha's sons died and only Prince Prachathipok remained in the first line of succession. During 1925 another consort, Suwathana, emerged. During the eighth month of her pregnancy she replaced Intharasak as queen in anticipation of the birth of an heir. On 24 November 1925 a daughter was born to the king, who was then dangerously ill, and the baby was shown to him on the following day. A short time afterwards the king sank into a coma from which he did not wake.[82] Wachirawut had left instructions that if the child was male, Prachathipok should be appointed as head of the council of regency.

[79] Phra Sarasas, *My Country Thailand*, p. 135.

[80] See the accounts in the *Straits Times*, 14, 15, and 16 June 1920; Chula Chakrabongse, *The Twain Have Met*, pp. 112-3; and Hunter and Narisa Chakrabongse, *Katya and the Prince of Siam*, pp. 158-9.

[81] Wachirawut's unsuccessful attempts to produce an heir are reported in Prayut Sitthiphan, Phramahathira-ratchao, pp. 219-20; and Vella, *Chaiyo!*, pp. 157-8.

[82] See the account in the *Straits Times*, 3 December 1925.

Assessment

The sixth reign had lasted fifteen years. Wachirawut had been a controversial figure when he came to the throne; by the end of his reign it was almost universally accepted that he had not made a good king. Prince Damrong summed up the situation as follows: 'The authority of the sovereign had fallen much in respect and confidence, the treasury was on the verge of bankruptcy, and the government was corrupted and the services more or less in confusion.'[83]

It was not that Wachirawut lacked intelligence or sensitivity. He undoubtedly was a very gifted man, an innovator in many respects. Nor could he be accused of unbridled selfishness; many of his projects were intended to educate and advance the Siamese people. He attempted, not without success, to instill in the masses a heightened awareness of Siam's great history and the strengths of its civilization. Wachirawut demonstrated for the first time that the Siamese people could become aroused and enthusiastic about nationalistic ideals.

Yet King Wachirawut lacked a dimension that would have enabled him to become a truly nationalistic leader: he had little personal charm and could not easily relate to other people. His social awkwardness was a constant embarrassment to himself and to many who came in contact with him. It caused him sometimes to be brusque and undiplomatic, and it made him retreat from much of the daily administrative routine through which an absolute monarch keeps in touch with reality. Increasingly the king slipped into a fantasy world, one of his own creation. With immense sums of money he bought the favor of all close to him, thus creating around his immediate presence an atmosphere of popularity and good cheer. The confrontation with the cabinet in July 1925, where strong advice was given to curb his spending, threatened to undermine the basis upon which his masquerade was built. Therefore, he was compelled to reject the cabinet's suggestions forcefully. He died a rather pathetic figure, a man whose impersonation of a popular ruler had long ago ceased to convince his associates.

[83] Prince Damrong's words are quoted in Batson, 'End of the Absolute Monarchy', p. 33.

Plate 17. Front page of a special issue of Siam Rat, *3 March 1925, on the coronation day of King Prajadhipok (Rama VII).*

10

RESTORATION, REVOLT, AND THE RISE OF THE MILITARY

(1925-1945)

S iam's history between 1925 and 1945 can be divided neatly into two periods. The first, lasting less than seven years, is marked by attempts to restore faith in the system of government that had prevailed towards the end of the fifth reign. The second, from 1932 to 1945, is characterized by the growth of the military, beginning with a *coup d'état* and an attempted counter-*coup*, leading up to the Japanese invasion and the convolutions caused by the Second World War. This is the time when a new elite comes into power and Siamese nationalism gains unprecedented support among the people.

Part 1. The Restoration

The New King and His Council

When Wachirawut died in November 1925, his youngest full brother Prachathipok was just thirty-two years old, the youngest of Chulalongkorn's seventy-seven children still alive. Although he was of *chaofa* rank and had always known he was in the line of succession, others had been closer to the throne, and during most of his youth he had neither expected nor aspired to succeed to the throne. It was only after Prince Atsadang died, in February 1925, that he came to be regarded as the official heir apparent, and only from that time dated his appointment to senior government committees. With less than a year's experience in statecraft and a deplorable inheritance from his elder brother, young King Prachathipok relied upon the respect, the knowledge, and the experience of senior members of the royal family, several of whom had already been called in to deal with the growing conflict between Wachirawut and his government.

Three days after Wachirawut's death, the new king announced the appointment of a Supreme Council of State, an advisory body consisting of five princes, all experienced men who had expressed concern at the way Siam was governed during the sixth reign. In order of age they were the new king's three uncles, the princes Phanurangsi, Damrong, and Narit, and his half-brothers Kitiyakon (better known as Prince Chanthaburi) and Boriphat. Although the role and the duties of members of the Supreme Council were never specified, it was clear from the outset that they would be a sort of 'super-cabinet', that all matters of importance would be discussed between the king and his five relatives, and that under normal circumstances he would follow their advice.

In February 1926 the new king was formally crowned, and a month later the remains of his predecessor were cremated. By this time the king and the Supreme Council had worked out the composition of the new cabinet and the government's priorities.[1] All those closely associated with the previous reign, from the mighty *chaophraya Yomarat* downward, were dropped from the executive. The new ministry consisted of seven princes and four nobles. Only three members of the previous cabinet were retained. The changes therefore represented a sudden shift in direction, the greatest about-face since the accession of Rama I. The king obviously wanted to demonstrate a clear break with the discredited sixth reign, and the choice of men to fill the top positions appeared to be guided largely by a wish to restore a Chulalongkorn-type government.

The preparation of the budget for 1926/27 also represented a dramatic break with the past. Royal expenditure was drastically curtailed, the number of ministries was reduced by two, and the number of administrative divisions (*monthons*) from eighteen to fourteen. Virtually every government department was forced to retrench and dismiss a number of officials.[2] Several of the king's advisers suggested that the largest cuts be made in the military budget. Siam's armed forces had grown sufficiently to deal with possible internal emergencies. The country would never be able to afford to develop and maintain an army that could stand up against its colonial neighbors, however, and with the passage of time and with Siam's good international record, it was most unlikely that a large-scale armed conflict would arise between Siam and France on the one hand or Siam and Britain on the other. The king was aware of these views and was inclined to agree with them; in a letter summing up Siam's problems, he admitted as much. Yet cutting defense costs, he felt, was a very serious matter that very few people would dare to advocate; it might encourage foreign incursions.[3] In addition, the king could have mentioned that Prince Boriphat, who was not only a member of the Supreme Council but also Minister of War, would not allow defense to be seriously undermined.

The letter in which Prachathipok gives first one argument and then its opposite may be seen as indicative of the style of government during the seven years that preceded the *coup d'état*. The king was painstaking and conscientious; he would elicit comments and suggestions from a range of experts and study them assiduously, noting the good points in each submission, but when various options were available he would seldom be able to select one and abandon others. He would often rely upon the Supreme Council to persuade him in a particular

---

[1] The 1925 cabinet is listed in Charnvit Kasetsiri, 'Each Generation of Elites in Thai History', *Journal of Social Science Review* 1, no. 1 (1976), pp. 219-20; and that of 1926 can be found in B. A. Batson, 'The End of the Absolute Monarchy in Siam', pp. 241-3.

[2] The need for reduction in numbers of administrators had been recognized for some time (see the *Straits Times*, 3 December 1925).

[3] The king's exact words can be found in B. A. Batson, ed., *Siam's Political Future: Documents from the End of the Absolute Monarchy*, p. 21. Much of the information on the events between 1925 and 1932 has been found in Batson's works; in 'Naisuchinda', *Phrapokklao Kasat Nakprachathipatai;* and in Sonthi Techanan, ed., *Phaenphathana Kanmu'ang pai Su Kanpokkhrong rabop Prachathipatai tam Naew Praratchadamri khong Phrabatsomdet Phrapokklaochaoyuhua* (Ph.S. 2469-2475).

direction. This meant that in practice for day-today decision-making Siam depended upon a royal oligarchy. Yet Prachathipok did not institutionalize this situation; he did not formally relinquish any of the powers of the absolute monarch.

Unlike his predecessor, the king diligently read virtually all state papers that came his way, from ministerial submissions to petitions by citizens. Late in 1926 or early in 1927 he received a petition from the father of Pridi Phanomyong (*luang Praditmanutham*) about Pridi's recall from France. Pridi was the principal force behind a petition from the organization of Siamese students in France to have their allowances increased. The Siamese minister in France had asked for his recall, mentioning among other things that Pridi was dangerous, so proud of his own cleverness that he would 'go his own way whether right or wrong', of a class the minister considered 'the danger of Siam in the future, namely, the half educated class'.[4] The king was swayed by Pridi's father's petition and countermanded his earlier telegram ordering recall, and Pridi was allowed to complete his studies. 'Once he enters the government in a responsible position', the king said, 'he will probably work well, and I don't much believe that he will become a 'serious danger to the government' as Prince Charoonsakdi has reported'.[5] Ironically, Pridi, after obtaining a very responsible position, did not abandon his critical stance. He became one of the leaders of the movement for drastic government reform and later played an important role in the *coup d'état* of 1932.

Considering Fundamental Change

Already before his accession, Prachathipok had been aware of weaknesses in Siam's system of government; indeed, he had already discussed the idea of a Supreme Council before Wachirawut died. This committee of senior princes was created as a safeguard against the potential mistakes and excesses of a 'bad king'. Prachathipok received many petitions for more fundamental changes, and as early as July 1926 he sought the opinion of one of the most honored and prestigious foreigners, Francis Sayre,[6] asking him *inter alia* whether Siam ought to have a constitution, how the succession ought to be regulated, what the role of the Supreme Council ought to be, whether a prime minister ought to be appointed immediately, and whether there should be a legislative council. The king indicated that he himself was firmly of the opinion that Siam was not ready for a representative form of government. Sayre, who believed that some such form of government would eventually come about, agreed with the king that the country was not yet ready for it, as did Prince Damrong, who joined the debate.[7]

[4] Batson, 'End of the Absolute Monarchy', p. 76.

[5] *Ibid.*, p. 74.

[6] Francis B. Sayre, an American, had been Siam's Adviser in Foreign Affairs in 1924 and 1925. He had been largely active in the negotiations for revision of treaties with European countries, negotiations he had successfully concluded and which had assisted greatly in boosting not only the self-esteem of senior Siamese administrators but also the state's income by allowing an increase in import duty.

[7] For details, see Batson, *Siam's Political Future*, pp. 13-41.

Early in 1927, however, spurred on by agitation for radical constitutional change, the king appointed a committee under Prince Boriphat to study the possibility of creating an advisory body which would be more representative than the Supreme Council and less unwieldy than the Privy Council. The Privy Council had survived since the early days of the fifth reign but had ceased to have any administrative function; membership of it had developed into one of the many types of honors a king could distribute, and in 1927 there were more than two hundred men who had earned that honor. The king ruled out a parliamentary form of government not only because the country had not reached the required stage of development but also because he could foresee that under it Siamese politics would be entirely dominated by the Chinese. Even if the Chinese were formally excluded from the political process, through their financial power they could still be expected to dominate the situation.[8] Fear of the increasing power of the Chinese seems also to have been the reason why in 1927 the Siamese government passed a law restricting immigration.

A parliament having been ruled out, the king favored the creation of a *Kammakan Ongmontri*, a committee selected from Privy Counselors who could practice the methods of parliamentary debate and whose views might reflect something of the general public opinion. This Privy Council Committee consisted of forty senior men, including some members of the royal family and former ministers of state. The committee had the right to select its own chairman, and at any time a group of members could request the king's permission to discuss a topic that had not yet been placed on its agenda. The committee was in due course given a number of minor laws to discuss, but there was little advance in the process of education in parliamentary debate. By 1932, when drastic changes were brought about through the *coup*, the Privy Council Committee had still not developed into a widely known forum, nor did it appear to reflect public opinion. The Privy Council Committee was not the only place where the Siamese people were given a chance to gain experience in self-government. From 1926 onward there were moves to develop the concept of *prachaphiban*, or 'municipality', which had emerged late during the fifth reign in a law regarding sanitation. Information was obtained regarding local self-government in surrounding countries, and proposals to allow certain municipalities to raise local taxes and manage their own budgets were drawn up. There were two main problems militating against the success of this administrative venture. Firstly, it was thought that in the provinces the public was not sufficiently educated to make the scheme work. Secondly, it was feared that in Bangkok a freely elected representative body would be dominated by the Chinese.[9] Nevertheless, the idea of teaching the Siamese the concept of

---

[8] Batson, *Siam's Political Future*, p. 48; Sonthi Techanan, *Phaenphathana Kanmu'ang*, p. 165.

[9] Sonthi Techanan, *Phaenphathana Kanmu'ang, passim.*

democracy through a measure of decentralization of power in municipalities had become, in the king's mind, fundamental to future policy-making.[10] Before practical steps could be taken, however, the days of the absolute monarchy were over.

Prachathipok's Travels

Early in his reign, during January and early February of 1927, King Prachathipok went with his wife, Queen Ramphai, on an official state visit to the north. The royal train took him via Phitsanulok, Phrae, and Lampang to Chiang Mai, and he went by car further north to Chiang Rai and Chiang Saen.[11] A royal voyage to Singapore and the Dutch East Indies was planned to follow, but, because of the death of Prince Phanurangsi in June 1928, it was postponed. Phanurangsi, as the eldest *chaofa* prince and a member of the Supreme Council, was the most senior member of the royal family, and his cremation entailed full state involvement. Eventually the tour to Singapore, Java, and Bali took place in mid-1929, lasting more than two months. While the king was abroad, Prince Boriphat acted as regent.

Boriphat had emerged as the strongest and most forceful member of the Supreme Council, the only one of that body also to hold a cabinet post. In a cabinet shuffle in March 1928 he had been moved from the War to the Interior portfolio, a promotion that had made him in all but name the country's prime minister. His post as minister of war had been given to Prince Boworadet, another forceful and able man whose career had been interrupted during the sixth reign and who was recalled from retirement to serve Prachathipok.[12]

The state visit by the Siamese king and queen was quite a diplomatic success. Various favorable reports on Siam and its good immediate prospects were published.[13] Indeed, the Siamese leaders had reason to regard the seventh reign as being generally successful. The economic problems of the early 1920s had been overcome, the country's balance of payments showed a healthy surplus, and by 1928 there was no longer any thought of retrenchments or cutbacks in government departments. Suddenly there was scope for initiative, and investment and the future could be faced with optimism, a situation that lasted until the serious economic crisis which began in 1930.

In April and May 1930 the king and queen made a state visit to French Indo-China, and Boriphat again became regent. Meanwhile, the king was worried by the state of his health, especially his failing eyesight and threatened blindness. Various proposals were considered, such as to invite an ophthalmologist to Siam or for the king to visit a clinic in France. Finally, however, the king decided that he would rather travel to the United States.[14] The king and queen spent most of 1931 overseas, trav-

[10] See the king's statements of April 1931, as reported in the *New York Times*, reprinted in Sonthi's book, pp. 103-8.

[11] For details, see Naisuchinda, *Phrapokklao*, pp. 136-219.

[12] Prince Boworadet was one of the grandsons of King Mongkut, a son of Prince Naret. In 1929 the king honored Boworadet by raising him from *momchao* to *phra'ongchao* status.

[13] See, for example, H. Ch. G. J. van der Mandere, 'Het tegenwoordige Siameesche Koninkrijk', *De Indische Gids* 51, pt 2 (1929): 919-36; and J.G. Loohuis and L.D. Petit, ed., *Siam: Muang-Thai*. Petit's contribution on architecture was reprinted as Siameesche Bouwkunst.

[14] In his typically unassuming manner, the king wrote to a close relative who had tried to dissuade him from going to the United States: 'I am very keen on America unless it is an impossibility' (see Batson, 'End of the Absolute Monarchy', p. 211).

elling to Japan, Canada, and the United States. Again Boriphat was regent, this time during a period when Siam's financial problems rapidly worsened and some difficult decisions had to be made. When the king returned in mid-October 1931, the economic crisis had reached a stage where firm and decisive measures were needed, measures apparently beyond the powers of a man of Prachathipok's character and constitution.

Between late 1925 and early 1932 King Prachathipok had traveled through most of Siam and also extensively abroad. Though some of the journeys were primarily undertaken for reasons of health and recuperation, most of them were official state visits. Prachathipok considered these formal visits to be an intrinsic part of his duties as king. As such, they may be seen as consistent with his general policy of restoration and emulation of his father's most popular actions. At the same time the frequency and long duration of some of the voyages may be seen as an indication of the king's willingness to drop the executive burdens of the absolute king. *En route*, Prachathipok did his duty towards his country, by listening to innumerable speeches and complying with the programs devised by local committees. Meanwhile, he relied heavily upon his uncles and brothers to handle affairs of state in Siam.

The Economic and Domestic Crisis

Whereas the economic difficulties at the beginning of the seventh reign had been largely the result of domestic imbalances and relatively easily remedied, the crisis that began in 1930 was essentially an international crisis that had suddenly emerged in October 1929 with the collapse of the American stock market.

A combination of a bad rice crop and falling prices for some other commodities and a slackening off in trade made it clear by the end of 1930 that the Siamese government could expect a drop in revenue. In order to balance the budget for 1931/32 it was decided to cut all official salaries.[15] The budget for defense was severely slashed by one-third, a remarkable feat considering that the responsible minister, Prince Boworadet, had during the preceding year bitterly fought to safeguard and even increase funds for military expenditure. Indeed, it soon was apparent that Boworadet did not intend to adhere to the spirit of economic restraint, because in May 1931 he told cabinet that he had promoted more than two hundred officers, who would thus receive an increase in their salaries, and that he had also decided to offer salary increases without promotion to another ninety-one officers. In the ensuing debate, cabinet decided to cancel the ninety-one raises and Boworadet offered his resignation. The Supreme Council decided to contact the king, who was recuperating from his eye operation in

[15] Apparently ministers of state had their salaries cut by ten per cent, senior civil servants by seven per cent, and all lower salary earners by five per cent (see *La Revue du Pacifique* 11 [1932]: 447).

New York, recommending that he accept the resignation, to which the king reluctantly agreed.[16]

In September 1931 Britain abandoned the gold standard and devalued the pound by 30 per cent. Despite the fact that Siam's foreign holdings were mainly in sterling, that the bulk of its imports originated in Britain, that much of its exports were to British-held regions, and that British firms dominated the teak and tin industries, the (British) Financial Adviser, E. L. Hall-Patch, advocated that Siam break its link with the pound sterling and retain its own gold standard. By October there was a run on the *baht*, and an increasing number of sources publicly doubted whether Siam could hold out. This was the situation when in mid-October the king returned to Siam. Hall-Patch advocated new taxes, especially taxation of the richer classes, in conjunction with further cuts in government expenditure, while the Supreme Council had come to favor devaluation. The debate continued until March 1932, over five months, in which the king desperately sought a solution that would satisfy all opposing parties. Repeatedly he publicly made what amounted to an apology for not making a decision:

> *The financial war is a very hard one indeed. Even experts contradict one another until they become hoarse. Each offers a different suggestion. I myself do not profess to know much about the matter and all I can do is listen to the opinions of others and choose the best. I have never experienced such a hardship; therefore if I have made a mistake I really deserve to be excused by the officials and people of Siam.*[17]

The falling price of rice meanwhile seriously affected the farmers, and during the first months of 1932 the government received a large number of petitions for relief from economic hardship. Finally, in March 1932, after the purchasing power of the *baht* had been artificially maintained long after public confidence had fallen, the decision to abandon the gold standard was made. The king's wavering attitude had undoubtedly contributed to the depletion of Siam's foreign reserves.

Soon afterwards some new taxes were announced. During the previous months the prospect of increased taxation had been widely debated, and taxes on the wealthy and on businesses had been suggested in the local press, measures that had found little favor in the Supreme Council. Of the new taxes announced in April 1932 the most important was a tax on salaries, effectively reducing even further the income of government officials who had borne the brunt of the cost-saving exercise of the previous year. Royalty and the higher nobility also were to be taxed on their salaries, but since they often derived much of their income from other sources, they again escaped relatively unscathed. Among middle-ranking officials

---

[16] See Batson, 'End of the Absolute Monarchy', pp. 224-9.

[17] *Ibid.*, p. 248.

and intellectuals this was felt to be unfair and iniquitous. The enactment of this tax law must have strengthened the resolution of the parties busily devising a scheme to overthrow the government.

The Sesquicentennial

Prachathipok knew that during the seventh year of his reign, in 1932, the city of Bangkok would be 150 years old, and during the years of economic prosperity between 1928 and 1930 he had instigated planning for the event. In one of his rare strong and decisive moves, he decided to neglect the advice of a special committee and ordered the construction of a new bridge to span the Chaophraya River. In 1927 he had already opened a railway bridge, a project that had been started during the sixth reign, and he decided that the 1932 memorial bridge would be the first for general traffic. He donated considerable funds towards the construction. The bridge was called Phraphuthayotfa Bridge, in honor of the founder of the Chakri dynasty, and it was duly opened on Chakri Day, 6 April 1932, with appropriate pomp and ceremony and a military parade.[18]

The celebrations for Bangkok's sesquicentennial were somewhat overshadowed by the worsening economic crisis. The official announcements made on the occasion may also have come as a disappointment to many. Ever since his return from the United States, the king had intended, as part of the sesquicentennial celebrations, to present the nation with its first constitution. His advisers had drawn up a first draft, which had in early March 1932 been submitted to the Supreme Council, and which provided for a prime minister and a legislative council.[19] Apparently the proposal met with opposition from the princes, and the king, true to his own assessment himself as a person who saw both sides of every question,[20] allowed the sesquicentennial to pass without alluding to a more democratic form of government.

The organizers must have breathed a sigh of relief when the celebrations passed without incident. The economic depression and the concomitant hardship had created a political climate in which there was among many educated Siamese a resurgence of the debate on alternative forms of government. In March 1932 a senior adviser mentioned to the king that there were rumors of an attempt to overthrow the government.[21] These rumors were partly based upon an old prophecy, reputedly stemming from King Rama I, saying that his dynasty would last but 150 years.[22] At this time of economic troubles such a prophecy could be regarded as a factor adding to the general instability.

---

[18] Photographs of the military parade have been published in Naisuchinda, *Phrapokklao*, opp. p. 276.

[19] The full text appears in Batson, *Siam's Political Future*, pp. 86-9.

[20] Chula Chakrabongse, *The Twain Have Met*, p. 156.

[21] Batson, *Siam's Political Future*, p. 92.

[22] Batson, 'End of the Absolute Monarchy', pp. 159 and 282.

Part 2. Revolt and the Rise of the Military

The Coup d'état

Just as Prince Charun, the Siamese minister in France, had predicted, Pridi, having completed his studies and having returned to Bangkok to teach law at the university, continued to criticize the Siamese system of government and to disseminate revolutionary ideas. Gradually he became the undisputed leader of a group of idealists who all agreed to co-operate to bring about a drastic change in the system of government. Pridi's friends from the time he was in France were among the core of this group. They included some young military officers such as Plaek Khittasangkha (*luang* Phibunsongkhram, usually known as Phibun), Thatsanai Mitphakdi (*luang* Thatsanainiyomsu'k), and Prayun Phamonmontri, with whom he could practice speaking French and share reminiscences of the exciting days when they were all studying abroad. Most members of this group hoped that democracy would put a stop to the abuses of a privileged class and lead to greater prosperity. They had sworn secrecy, knowing that their discussions often touched matters that, if publicized, would harm their careers. Yet, up to 1931 this group had not developed a practical plan of action, not conceiving how to accomplish violent change. If King Prachathipok had proceeded to announce his plan for a constitutional monarchy, it would have satisfied at least some of Pridi's fellow-conspirators.

The situation changed during the second half of 1931, when several senior army officers who had heard about the growing numbers of young officers and civil servants wishing to overthrow the government decided to join forces with them. The two most important of these were Phot Phahonyothin (*phraya* Phahonphonphayuhasena, usually known as *phraya* Phahon) and Thep Phanthumasen (*phraya* Songsuradet), both colonels who had studied in Germany. The former was deputy-inspector of the Bangkok artillery and the latter headed the educational section of the Military Academy. The senior army officers and their friends appeared to have been motivated both by personal grievances and by more general dissatisfaction with the way in which Siam was ruled. Some were influenced by the Supreme Council's lack of support for Boworadet, the Minister of War, who resigned over the case for salary increase. Others felt frustrated in their career prospects because preference was often given to members of the royal family. Again others disagreed with some of the measures taken by the country's executive in a time of a worsening economic climate.[23]

It was these senior officers and their friends who finally devised the plans for the overthrow of the government, *phraya* Songsuradet being the general coordinator. Details of the over-

[23] Opinions vary greatly regarding the forces that led to the *coup*. See, for example, V. Thompson, *Thailand, the New Siam*, pp. 64-5; B. A. Batson, in his review of Thawatt's book, *JSS* 61, pt 2 (1973), pp. 193-5; and the references from the *Bangkok Times*, cited in Batson's 'End of the Absolute Monarchy', pp. 293-4. See also R. de Lapomarède, 'The Setting of the Siamese Revolution', *Pacific Affairs* 7 (September 1934): 251-9, and other contemporary documents, such as those published in Prida Wacharangkun, *Phrapokklao kap Rabop Prachathipatai*, pp. 96-9. A most fanciful account, in which he assigns a major role to himself, is given by Phra Sarasas in *My Country Thailand*, pp. 223-31.

all plan were kept from most of the *coup* sympathizers, and so efficient was the preparation that the *coup* took everybody by surprise. On the night of 23 June 1932 the telephones of senior government ministers were quietly disconnected and naval units, acting on false orders to suppress Chinese riots, were mobilized, armed, and transported to the vicinity of the throne hall. A gunboat took up position opposite Prince Boriphat's residence. Boriphat was the acting head of government, because earlier during that month the king had gone to his seaside resort at Huahin. In the early hours of the morning all key government members were arrested and brought to the throne hall. The *coup* was officially announced to the unsuspecting public by means of proclamations from the *Khana Ratsadon*, or People's Party.[24] The first public announcement drawn up by Pridi contained a strongly worded denunciation of the Chakri dynasty and the Prachathipok government. It was probably intended to arouse the population and elicit spontaneous support. The people, however, not knowing the character of the new party, generally reacted with restraint, awaiting the reaction of the forces that were being ousted.

Prachathipok had meanwhile received a message from the *coup* leaders informing him of the fall of his government, and that hostages were being held, and asking him to return to Bangkok as a constitutional monarch. Some of the king's advisers urged him to march up to the capital and fight, but Prachathipok decided, after some hesitation,[25] that the best course of action was to accept the offer. On 26 June the leaders of the People's Party met the king, who appeared genuinely happy with the idea of relinquishing much of his power, a move he had come close to implementing himself. Pridi, the author of the anti-monarchial statement, formally apologized, and the king forgave all *coup* members for having acted contrary to the existing laws. Prachathipok accepted a draft constitution by which executive authority was given to an Assembly, and the Supreme Council and Privy Council were dissolved. In return, the hostages were released, Prince Boriphat agreeing to go abroad.

The leaders of the People's Party rapidly proceeded to nominate an Assembly, consisting of seventy members, which in its turn chose a leader, *phraya* Manopakon, a lawyer who had come to the fore because he had recently proposed in the Privy Council Committee that there be a cut in the annual princely allowances.[26] *Phraya* Manopakon then chose fourteen members of an Executive Committee, consisting of the most influential members of the *coup* party, and on 29 June a small cabinet of seven ministers was announced.[27] The Executive Committee and Cabinet formed an interim government to implement the first measures in accordance with the policies of the People's Party; a special committee set about creating a 'final' draft of the constitution.

[24] A detailed account can be found in Thawatt Mokarapong, *History of the Thai Revolution: A Study in Political Behaviour*. Various personal reminiscences can be found in Thak Chaloemtiarana, ed., *Thai Politics: Extracts and Documents 1932-1957*, pp. 4-93.

[25] Chula Chakrabongse, *The Twain Have Met*, p. 161.

[26] Prida Wacharangkun, *Phrapokklao*, p. 130.

[27] *Phraya* Prasoetsongkhram (acting. Defense), *chaophraya* Wongsanupraphan (Agriculture and Commerce), *phraya* Chasaenbodi (Interior), *phraya* Pramuanwichaphun (acting, Public Instruction), *phraya* Siwisanwacha (Foreign Affairs), *phraya* Manopakon (Finance), and *phraya* Thepwithun (Justice).

The first priority was given to the nation's economic situation. In July 1932 it was decided that the depressed state of the economy was mainly the result of international forces which the government could not control. It was also clear that the situation in Siam was far from bad. Rice and teak, the main export items, were still finding buyers.[28] The previous government's controversial salaries tax was changed into a more general tax on incomes and businesses. Various other taxes that were particularly burdensome to the poorer people were reduced and some even repealed. The most sweeping reform took place in the military, where practically all high-ranking officers were retired, making way for *coup* members and their sympathizers. Although there were voices urging the confiscation of all princely fortunes, *phraya* Manopakon opposed such a drastic move, and various members of the royal family were even allowed to continue holding government positions.

By the end of November 1932 the constitutional committee had managed to produce a text that was agreeable to Prachathipok and to the Assembly, and on 10 December it was formally approved. It provided for a new National Assembly, with half its members to be appointed and half to be elected, in a two-tiered election process; eventual development of a fully elected Assembly was foreseen. According to this constitution, princes were deemed to be 'above politics', a measure that was understood to mean they were not to engage in political activities and were barred from holding ministerial positions. By the end of 1932 it seemed that the *coup* had been eminently successful. With little violence, an outmoded oligarchical system had been overthrown and Siam had, at least from a political point of view, joined the countries where power would be exercised by people responsible to the elected representatives of the people.

Early in 1933, however, a serious rift developed between the more radical idealists and the more conservative members of the Assembly over the issue of Pridi's far-reaching national economic policy plan. He suggested that the government pay monthly wages to all citizens; that farmers should no longer work individually, but as members of government-supervised co-operative societies; and that the government should control all productive land and machinery and work towards abolishing private enterprise.[29] The plan, which in Pridi's words followed 'the socialist pattern with an admixture of liberalism',[30] passed the committee stage with a dissenting minority opinion. Among the dissenters were *phraya* Manopakon and *phraya* Songsuradet. When the controversial plan reached the Assembly, heated debate took place and fundamental differences of opinion became clear. Late in March 1933 *phraya* Manopakon prorogued the Assembly; not long after, it was dissolved. A new State Council, without Pridi, who had been

[28] *La Revue du Pacifique* 11, no. 8/9 (August-September 1932), p. 576.

[29] The text, translated from the Siamese, appears in K. P. Landon, *Siam in Transition*, pp. 260-302. For an analysis and background see P. Fistie, *Sous-développement et utopie au Siam, le programme de réformes présenté en 1933 par Pridi Phanom-yong.*

[30] Landon, *Siam in Transition*, p. 307. The text of the minutes of a meeting in which the plan is discussed appears on pp. 303-18. The Siamese original is reprinted in Naisuchinda, *Phrapokklao*, pp. 321-37.

sent to Europe into what amounted to exile, ruled the country. At the same time an 'anti-communistic' law was proclaimed, making it illegal to advocate doctrines implying nationalization or impinging upon the right to private property. To counter possible criticism that the government had no firm economic policy at all, an economic council was appointed, including some foreign advisers.[31]

Even without Pridi and some of his radical friends, and with a no longer unruly Assembly, the governing body soon split up. On 10 June 1933 the four senior military officers in the State Council submitted their resignations. One of these disgruntled men, *phraya* Phahon, was persuaded by a group of younger army officers under the leadership of Phibun, to stage another *coup*. On 20 June this took place, and *phraya* Manopakon's government collapsed in the face of a military threat. Ironically, again King Prachathipok was at his seaside palace at Huahin when he received the request from the *coup* leaders to recall the (provisional) Assembly. *Phraya* Phahon formed a new cabinet, and Pridi was invited to return to Siam. It was made clear, however, that his economic plan would not be considered. Nevertheless, Pridi remained the symbol of revolution, and his return in late September contributed to the unsettled atmosphere which preceded yet another attempt to change the government by force.

The Rebellion

On 11 October 1933 a full-scale rebellion broke out in the provinces. Under the leadership of the former Minister of War, Prince Boworadet, the garrisons of Nakhon Ratchasima, Ubon Ratchathani, Prachinburi, Saraburi, Ayutthaya, Nakhon Sawan, and Phetburi declared themselves in favor of a rebellion against the Bangkok government. Troops from the north-east of the country marched on Bangkok, seized the airport, and entered the northern suburbs. The commander-in-chief of the navy declared himself neutral and withdrew his battleships from the capital. The rebels sent an ultimatum, threatening to seize Bangkok by force if the government did not resign.

At this stage, Boworadet, who reputedly espoused a democratic-royalist cause, probably hoped that at least some Bangkok army units would join him and that the king would show his preference by remaining strictly neutral and non-committal. In actuality, however, none of the Bangkok garrisons revolted. The government declared martial law, and *phraya* Phahon revealed that the king had declared himself against the action of the rebels, who meanwhile had let their ultimatum drop and had sent a much milder set of suggestions. *Luang* Phibun became field commander, and during the evening of 13

[31] The names of four foreign advisers – two American, one French, and one English – are mentioned in *La Revue du Pacifique* 12 (1933), p. 507.

October he opened a heavy artillery attack on the rebels' positions. For three days the two opposing parties shelled each other, causing many casualties and great damage. The government force, better supplied and aided by fresh reinforcements from the city, then recaptured the airport and forced the rebels to retreat. An attempt by Phetburi troops to come to Boworadet's aid failed, and by the end of October, after several skirmishes in the provinces, the central government was again firmly in control. Most of the rebel forces surrendered. Of the leading figures, some had been killed in action and seventeen were captured. These latter were sentenced to death, but later all the sentences were commuted, and no executions took place. Twenty-two officers, including Boworadet himself, managed to flee the country and find asylum in French Indo-China.[32]

The October rebellion had been an ambitious and daring attempt by Boworadet and various senior officers to seize power. At one moment the fate of the uprising seemed to hang in the balance. The government had not panicked, however; it was given time to organize resistance, and, through Phibun's military action, it had gained a resounding victory. The result of the Boworadet uprising was a severe setback to many princes, together with their known supporters among the prestigious noble families. Some were arrested, some exiled, and some were retrenched.[33] In addition, some senior officers, such as *phraya* Songsuradet and his friends, who had kept aloof from the military conflict, obviously hoping that *phraya* Phahon and *luang* Phibun would be toppled, found their hopes of power and influence dashed. Phibun had now emerged as a real force. While in 1932 he had been simply one of the junior *coup* members, he had now risen to prominence and was put forward as the savior of the country.

As if to demonstrate its post-uprising confidence, in late 1933 the government held the nation's first elections. Under the provisions of the first constitution of 1932, one half of the members of the House of Representatives had to be appointed by the king, who chose from a list, supplied by the ruling People's Party. The other half had to be chosen by all members of the general public who were at least twenty-one years of age (excluding members of the royal family and Buddhist monks). In order to ensure that also those who were illiterate would be able to identify candidates and vote for them, boards displaying photographs were set up, each candidate having a number, both displayed as a numeral and with the corresponding number of black dots. The voter was given a strip of paper with a series of numbers and only had to detach the number that corresponded with their choice.

Once the large number of *tambon* representatives had been elected, as representatives of the general populace, they pro-

---

[32] Documents regarding the Boworadet uprising can be found in Nai-suchinda, *Phrapokklao*, pp. 506-28. A short account is given in Landon, *Siam in Transition*, pp. 36-9. See also B.A. Batson's review of Chai-Anan Samudvanija, '*14 Tula*', in *JSS* 63, pt 2 (1975), pp. 386-91.

[33] The most prominent member of the royal family and critic of the government to leave the country not long after the Boworadet rebellion was Prince Damrong.

ceeded with to choose seventy-eight Assembly members. Among the chosen were many retired government officials (eight of them of high rank), three journalists, two professors, and three men who had played a key role during Siam's first abortive *coup* just over twenty years earlier. Another seventy-eight members were appointed by the king, among them forty-five army officers and five from the navy.[34]

King Prachathipok's Position after the failed rebellion

One effect of the repression of the insurrection was the diminishing of the king's prestige. When the revolt had broken out, Prachathipok, at his Huahin palace, had been warned by *phraya* Phahon that the rebels had reached the aerodrome, the government had proclaimed martial law and the army intended to stand firm. At the same time Phahon had reiterated his loyalty to the king.[35] The king had answered by telegram that he regretted the strife and civil disturbances. This message had played an important role in the first propaganda battles between the Bangkok regime and the rebels. During the days following the telegram the king realized that the rebellion had much more support than Phahon had made him believe. Apart from the Ayutthayan and Nakhon Ratchasima troops mentioned by Phahon, many other provincial garrisons were involved in the uprising, including the one at Phetburi, not far from Huahin.

It is not clear whether the king was motivated by fear of being captured by rebels, or by the wish to avoid having to make further choices between Phahon and Boworadet, the fact remains that at the height of the fighting the king and queen fled, taking refuge in Songkhla, near the Malay border. The king's withdrawal from the scene when there was a crucial battle going on near Bangkok, was interpreted by the victorious party as a sign that he had failed to do his duty. By refusing to throw his full support behind the government forces he had undermined his credibility.[36]

One of the first items to be discussed in Siam's first half-elected Assembly was the king's plan for another lengthy visit overseas for further medical treatment. It was widely felt that the king's proposed travel was ill timed, it would strengthen the impression that a rift had developed between the crown and the cabinet. The government offered to invite the world's best ophthalmologists to come to Siam rather than let the king make the strenuous journey. Prachathipok insisted, however, and in January 1934 he left for Europe. On the way he stopped at Belawan, Sumatra, where he was met by a large gathering of exiled Siamese, including his uncles Damrong and Sawat, his half-brothers Boriphat and Burachat and the former prime minister *phraya* Manopakon.[37] Early in 1934 the king and his

---

[34] *La Revue du Pacifique* 13, no. 2 (February 1934), pp. 122-4.

[35] The text of the telegram is given in Landon, *Siam in Transition*, p. 38.

[36] Batson, 'End of the Absolute Monarchy', pp. 307-10.

[37] Landon, *Siam in Transition*, p. 253, where an article from the *Bangkok Times*, 27 January 1934, on the reunion is reprinted.

party arrived at Marseilles and went for a while to Paris, and later to London. From Europe he kept up a regular correspondence with the Bangkok government, increasingly demonstrating his dissatisfaction with the manner in which Siam was governed by a *clique* of strong men. He protested against measures that whittled away the few remaining royal prerogatives that had been safeguarded in the constitution, and suggested some practical changes that would make his role as constitutional monarch more significant. When his suggestions were not heeded, he threatened to abdicate. In November 1934 a special government mission was sent to England to negotiate Prachathipok's return. The rift between king and government could not be bridged, however, and on 2 March 1935 the king formally abdicated.[38]

As Prachathipok had no children, the committee considering the succession decided to turn to another branch of Chulalongkorn's offspring. They proposed Prachathipok's nephew, Ananda Mahidon, the eldest son of *chaofa* Mahidon, as the new king. Ananda Mahidon was still a young boy at school in Lausanne. A council of regents was therefore appointed to act for him.

The seventh reign had lasted less than a decade, a time during which the king had presided over the dismantling of the system that had placed him on the throne. Prachathipok had been a kind, sincere, and diligent king. In his own mild way he had stimulated debate and encouraged a fundamental reassessment of the state system. He had done this at a time when there were serious economic fluctuations in the nation causing widespread hardship. While the king was aware of the new forces in Siamese society and was more open-minded than his predecessor regarding different approaches to sharing responsibility, it was his personal tragedy that he was easily swayed by any well-argued opinion and that he lacked the measure of decisiveness needed to lead the nation in a new direction.

The Creation of a Stable Government

In Prachathipok's abdication speech he accused *phraya* Phahon and his party of having no regard for democratic principles, employing methods of administration incompatible with individual freedom and the principles of justice, ruling in an autocratic manner and not letting the people have a real voice in Siam's affairs. As an idealistic democrat, the former king had good grounds for complaint. The Executive Committee and Cabinet did not seem eager to develop an atmosphere of debate or to be guided by resolutions of the Assembly. In 1934 a Press Act came into effect forbidding the publication of material detrimental to public order or undermining morals and this law

[38] The abdication statement is reprinted in Batson, *Siam's Political Future*, pp. 101-2; and the government's official reaction in Thak Chaloemtiarana, *Thai Politics*, pp. 238-40.

was strictly applied. All publications had to be submitted for censorship, and the government Press Bureau dictated what items of news were allowed to appear. Similarly, all speeches over the radio were subject to censorship.[39]

Military officers having toppled Manopakon's government, thereby gained considerable influence in the nation's decision-making processes. This is apparent in the generous budget allocations for military spending. By 1935 some 27 per cent of the total ordinary expenditure went on defense and this was to increase in the years to follow.[40] The drive to democratize from below, by setting up local government councils with independent funds derived from local taxes – a key project in Prachathipok's plan to educate the Siamese in the handling of political power – was actually slowed down by the form of the legislation implementing it in 1934. Although the law provided for the creation of municipal councils and election of local counselors, the central authorities reserved the right to appoint all office-bearers and thus retained effective control.[41]

Yet *phraya* Phahon probably did not regard himself as an autocratic ruler. He presided over a cabinet that could be considered representative of various different groups and opinions. It contained not only those who were firmly linked with the army and the navy but also men who were sponsored by different sections of society. The most notable non-military face in the cabinet was Pridi, who in February 1934 was formally declared to be free of the 'stigma of communism' which had been imputed to him at the time of his controversial economic plan,[42] and who soon afterwards was appointed as Minister of the Interior. Another representative of the 'intellectuals', *phra* Sarasat, became Minister of Economic Affairs, but his opinions were so much at variance with those of the military that he was dropped in September 1934 during the first cabinet reorganization.[43]

In the years to follow, the influence of the military remained such that its hand can be seen in many of the decisions made at cabinet level. In the five years between 1933 and 1938 Siam's army, navy, and air force were equipped as never before. The navy, which had in 1932 a small number of rather outdated vessels, was augmented by twenty-four modern warships, built in Italy and Japan. The army was expanded to thirty-three battalions and boasted an armored division and three sections of artillery. The air force had two hundred warplanes of the most modern American type. This investment in offensive weaponry caused some concern in the region, especially in French Indo-China.[44]

Japan's Growing Image

Siamese leaders had long had an image of Japan as a major

[39] For details, see Landon, *Siam in Transition*, pp. 49-50.

[40] J. C. Ingram, *Economic Change in Thailand 1850-1970*, pp. 192-93; and Landon, *Siam in Transition*, pp. 54-5.

[41] Thompson, *Thailand, the New Siam*, p. 254.

[42] Landon, *Siam in Transition*, pp. 319-23; provides the text of the investigating committee.

[43] *La Revue du Pacifique* 13 (1934), pp. 565-7.

[44] *De Indische Gids* 61, pt 1 (1939), pp. 467-8.

Asian country which was managing its own affairs and thus countering the myth, current in the colonies, that Asian peoples were incapable of ruling themselves. It was not until after 1932, however, that this general feeling was translated into measures that rapidly brought about fraternization between the two countries. The pro-Japanese attitudes of Siam's rulers were dramatically demonstrated in 1933. When the League of Nations passed a censure motion against Japan's invasion of Manchuria, Siam was the sole nation abstaining. At the same time, Siam was receiving a share of the rapidly expanding Japanese exports to Southeast Asia. During 1934 there were official trade negotiations between Siam and Japan, giving rise to rumors that a secret military alliance between the two countries was being drafted and that the Japanese were proposing to build a canal through the Isthmus of Kra.[45] During 1935 the first groups of young Siamese officers arrived in Japan to complete their training in the Japanese army.

One of the strongest supporters of closer relations with Japan was Siam's Defense Minister. Phibun's personal views were frequently expressed in articles published by the Defense Ministry. He noted Siam's need for a strong leader in these days of 'nation building' and world crisis, much as 'an animal herd needs its leader'.[46] Phibun was attracted by the effective and quite popular movements in Japan, Turkey, and Italy, where large numbers of people, inspired by national goals, managed to perform seemingly impossible tasks. Clearly influenced by these foreign examples, Phibun encouraged the development of a system of military training for Siamese youth. In 1935 he set up the *Yuwachon* movement, to complement the less-militant Scouts. Dressed in smart, attractive uniforms, the *Yuwachon* boys trained voluntarily for two or three hours a week.[47] In September 1938 the movement comprised some six thousand boys, and it was decided to set up a section for schoolgirls.[48]

The Civilian and Military Factions

Phraya Phahon was Prime Minister from 1933 to 1938. He remained the only one of the senior officers who had led the 1932 *coup* to maintain an executive position. *Phraya* Songsuradet, who had in 1933 been outwitted by *luang* Phibun, refused to return to active politics, though reputedly he was once offered a cabinet post and later sounded out for the post of prime minister.[49] Phahon presided over a cabinet in which two rather different groups were represented. One was the 'young military clique', led by Phibun; the other was the 'civilian faction', with Pridi as its leader. The military faction's strength was reflected in many of the cabinet decisions, but at the same time Pridi was given the opportunity to implement some of his

[45] See, for example D. F. van Wijk's article in *Onze Stem* of October 1934, reprinted in *De Indische Gids* 57, pt 1 (1935): 76-7; and Thompson, *Thailand, the New Siam*, pp. 129-33.

[46] Charnvit Kasetsiri, 'The First Phibun Government and Its Involvement in World War II', *JSS* 62, pt 2 (1974), p. 35.

[47] Phibunsongkhram's love for attractive uniforms is well documented in 'Withetkaram', *Sarakhadi Prawatisat Thangkanmu'ang Thai, Hetkan Thangkanmu'ang 43 Pi Haengprakop Prachathipatai*, pp. 53-7.

[48] Thompson, *Thailand, the New Siam*, pp. 308-9.

[49] The offer of a cabinet post is mentioned in *La Revue du Pacifique* 13 (1934), p. 567, and the 1938 request to consider the ministership is m̲ Manzooruddin Ah *Land der Freien*, p. ʼ

ideas. Thus, in 1934, as a result of Pridi's planning and preparations, the Law School was detached from Chulalongkon
University to become the nucleus of a new tertiary institute,
Thammasat University, where the emphasis was to fall on political and social science. It was in this institution that Pridi hoped
to be able to train large numbers of young Siamese in critical
analysis of various aspects of society. Before Thammasat
University even opened its doors, more than seven thousand
applications for enrolment were received.[50]

Although the two faction leaders pursued quite different
goals, one attempting to raise the defense budget quite attracted by fascism, the other wanting to spend more on the people's general education and attracted by socialism, they were
at that time quite friendly with each other. As far as possible,
each allowed the other scope to develop the nation. They had
co-operated since their student days in France and while they
both held senior cabinet posts they could afford a measure of
generosity. Siam had weathered the international economic
crisis rather well, so between 1933 and 1938 budget expenditure rose dramatically.[51]

Phraya Phahon maintained a fairly neutral stance with
respect to any move towards fascism or socialism. Not all citizens remained as uncommitted and aloof. Phibun came to be
regarded as the most likely candidate for leadership of a fas-
cist Siam and in February 1935 he was the victim of an assassination attempt. Though shot in the neck and shoulder,
Phibun escaped mortal injury. In August of that year the police
discovered an army plot for another *coup*. Fifteen officers
were arrested and their leader condemned to death.[52] In mid-
1937 Phibun was seriously embarrassed by members of the
Assembly asking questions regarding the sale of the land that
had been in the king's possession. A list of people who had
bought these lands at a very low price was published; among
them was the Defense Minister. Eventually the lands were
returned. In 1938 the tension between Assembly and cabinet
grew much worse. *Luang* Wichit Wathakan (usually abbreviated to Wichit), the Director-General of the Department of
Fine Arts, had publicly made anti-Chinese statements. Members of
the Assembly demanded an inquiry, and eventually the offensive remarks were publicly retracted. When the budget came
up for discussion, a sizable number of Assembly members
insisted that they ought to exert full control over it. Cabinet
and Assembly could not solve the ensuing conflict. Eventually
it was decided to dissolve the Assembly, which had proved too
hostile to the executive, and call for new elections.

Phraya Phahon, who had often indicated his distaste for
the political arena, announced that he would no longer be
willing to serve as Prime Minister. Therefore, the first major
task of the new half-elected half-appointed Assembly was the

[50] Thompson, *Thailand, the New Siam*,
p. 785.

[51] Ingram, *Economic Change*, p. 329.
For a contemporary account of Siam's
economic situation, see 'L'activité
economique du Siam', *La Revue du
Pacifique* 15 (1936), pp. 69-73.

[52] Ahmad, *Thailand, Land der Freien*,
p. 231.

choosing of Phahon's successor. Phibun was the candidate sponsored by most of the military. In late 1938 his enemies organized two further attempts on his life. Both the shooting and the poisoning failed to remove him from the scene and in December 1938 he was elected Prime Minister.

The Military Regime

Phahon's resignation and Phibun's rise to power marked a distinct change in Siam's government. The new Prime Minister emulated Phahon in that he maintained Pridi and various other liberals in the cabinet. However, the chief ministries were given to his personal army friends, whilst at first he retained his old Defense portfolio. Within a month of coming to power there were rumors of widespread discontent with the new government and Phibun ordered a large number of arrests. Some members of the royal family, Assembly members, and Phibun's army rivals were charged with treason. After a rushed court-martial, eighteen were found guilty and executed, another twenty-six were condemned to life-imprisonment and others, including *phraya* Songsuradet, were exiled.[53]

The young King Ananda Mahidon had meanwhile come of age, and late in 1938 returned to Siam. However, in January 1939 he went back to Europe, probably because there was no significant role for him at that particular time. The new government had dismissed many royalist officials with the Ministry of the Royal Household being downgraded to a simple Bureau.

An outspoken critic of the autocratic regime was ex-King Prachathipok. It retaliated in 1939 by accusing him of having misappropriated some six million *baht*. The subsequent court procedures were not yet concluded when Prachathipok died in May 1941. Eventually a court declared him guilty, and his Siamese possessions were confiscated. The government decided to prohibit any display of Prachathipok's image.[54]

Phibun's ideas about leading the nation became visible in a series of measures which were intended to stimulate pride in the nation, its military might and its leader. In 1939 the name Siam was dropped in favor of Thailand.[55] This name change was formally part of a campaign to foster values that would be recognized as 'cultured' in the international world: 'We must be as cultured as other nations otherwise no country will come to contact us. Or if they come, they come as superiors. Thailand would be helpless and soon become colonized. But if we were highly cultured, we would be able to uphold our integrity, independence, and keep everything to ourselves.'[56] In reality, the name change also reflected the idea of the country being the land of all Thais, also those living beyond the borders.

[53] Charnvit Kasetsiri, 'The First Phibun Government', p. 36.

[54] These measures were rescinded after World War II.

[55] In the local vernacular, the name of the country was changed from Sayam to Mu'ang Thai. The change became effective on 24 June 1939, the seventh anniversary of the 1932 *coup*.

[56] From the minutes of the cabinet meeting, 30 August 1939, as cited in Thamsook Numnonda, 'Pibulsongkram's Thai Nation-Building Programme during the Japanese Military Presence, 1941-1945', *Journal of Southeast Asian Studies* 9, no. 2 (September 1978), p. 234.

A government-sponsored program to create a new, civilized Thailand began. During the latter half of 1939 six 'cultural mandates' were announced by the Prime Minister's office. They dealt with the name of the country, warned the people against endangering the nation's security, abolished the names for regional groups of Thais, stipulated paying respect to the national flag and the anthem, advocated the use of locally made consumer goods and proclaimed the new words of the national anthem.[57] Almost every night government policies were discussed over the radio by two fictitious characters, Man and Khong, whose dialogues were designed and often directed by the Prime Minister himself.[58]

Another six cultural mandates followed between March 1940 and January 1942. They stressed the need to work hard, announced a minor change in the national anthem, emphasized the unity underlying all Thai dialects, told the populace that they should be decently dressed in public, presented a healthy daily routine of work and relaxation and asked all Thais to be quick to assist aged people or invalids. Naturally, the unprecedented interference with regard to private habits met with some resistance. The proclamation that loose shirt-tails, or lack of a shirt, was not proper and not in accordance with cultured Thai behavior must have been greeted in some circles with disbelief. However, in October 1940 the National Cultural Development Act was promulgated, in which it became the duty of all Thai people to comply with the aspirations of the national culture (as determined by the government) and to foster and promote national progress.[59] Orderliness in dress, good etiquette, efficient use of time and an appreciation of Thai culture could now be enforced, and people convicted of disobeying the law could be fined. In 1941 it became unlawful, among other things, to make unnecessary noise, to use improper language, or to ridicule those who attempted to promote national customs.[60] In the same year a campaign was launched to persuade people to wear hats in public.[61] The nationalistic program also encompassed the fine arts. Fiercely nationalistic plays and films were sponsored by the government. Often these depicted a glorious past when Thai warriors fearlessly gained freedom for the country, defended their honor, or sacrificed themselves.[62] Patriotism was taught in schools and was a recurrent theme in song and dance.

The Confrontation with France

In August 1939, when political tension in Europe was high, the French government proposed to Phibun that France and Thailand should conclude a mutual non-aggression pact.[63] In reply to this overture, the Thais suggested that the two countries

[57] For the text in translation, see Thinaphan Nakhata, 'National Consolidation and Nation-Building, 1939-1947', in Thak Chaloemtiarana, *Thai Politics*, pp. 245-50.

[58] Charnvit Kasetsiri, "The First Phibun Government", p. 39. Several of the dialogues have been published in Thak Chaloemtiarana, *Thai Politics*, pp. 260-316.

[59] Prince Wan Waithayakon, 'Thai Culture', *JSS* 35, pt 2 (1944), p. 140.

[60] Thak Chaloemtiarana, *Thai Politics*, p. 258.

[61] Prem Chaya and Alethea, *The Passing Hours: A Record of Five Amazing Years*, taken from the weekly features in the Bangkok Chronicle between 1941 and 1945. The entry for 23 July 1941 refers to the hat campaign.

[62] Some extracts of plays are given in Thak Chaloemtiarana, *Thai Politics*, pp. 317-22.

[63] The details of the treaty negotiations and Phibunsongkhram's secret alliance with Japan can be found in E. T. Flood, 'The 1940 Franco-Thai Border Dispute and Phibun Songkhram's Commitment to Japan', *Journal of Southeast Asian History* 10, no. 2 (1969), pp. 304-25.

negotiate a border revision by which the position of various islands in the Mekong River would be reconsidered. The French minister at Bangkok and his superiors in Paris were sympathetic to the Thai requests. When the pact was signed in June 1940 the Thais expected a high-level committee to look into the border question. The Thais had some hopes that the French enclaves on the west bank of the Mekong opposite Luang Prabang and Pakse, which had been ceded to France in 1904, would be returned. Before the end of that month, however, Paris was seized by German forces and the burden of the negotiations thus fell upon the French rulers of Indo-China, men committed to the idea of maintaining the French presence and resisting Thai encroachment.

In August 1940 Phibun sounded out what German, Italian, British, American, and Japanese reactions would be to Thailand recovering territories formerly lost to Indo-China. The British and American governments were not encouraging, the German and Italian views were firmly in favor of the idea, while the Japanese saw the overtures as a good opportunity to draw Thailand into a much closer relationship. When all attempts to gain territorial concessions from the French seemed to fail, Phibun proceeded to respond favorably to the Japanese offers of friendship. In late September he let the Japanese diplomats know that he wished to join the Japanese camp. On 1 October 1940 he expanded on this and told the Japanese naval attaché that Japanese troops would be permitted to cross Thai territory if necessary and he would consider supplying such troops. In return he expected Japan to assist Thailand in regaining lost territories. This agreement was a carefully guarded secret which Phibun did not discuss in the cabinet.

While these secret negotiations were taking place, great publicity was being given to alleged French border violations. Throughout October and November there were reports of French airplanes entering Thai airspace and of reputedly unprovoked acts of aggression against Thai citizens. On 28 November two bombs were dropped on the north-eastern town of Nakhon Phanom. Thai planes retaliated by bombing Thakhek and Savannakhet, towns on the French side of the Mekong River. From then on acts of military aggression became commonplace.[64] Early in January 1941 the French were reported to have attacked Aranyaprathet, near the Cambodian border. This gave Phibun the excuse to launch a large-scale invasion of French Indo-Chinese territory. After three weeks the Thai armies had taken not only the disputed enclaves on the western side of the Mekong River but also a large stretch of Cambodian territory. As early as November 1940 Japan had offered to arbitrate in the dispute,[65] and on 21 January 1941 great pressure was brought upon the French to accept Japan's intervention. Eventually protracted negotiations took place both

[64] Some partisan accounts are given in M. Sivaram, *Mekong Clash and Far East Crisis: A Survey of the Thailand-Indochina Conflict and the Japanese Mediation;* and *luang* Vichitr Vadakarn, *Thailand's Case.* A detailed account is also given in phon'ek Net Khemayothin, *Ngan Tai Din khong Phon'ek Yothi* 3, pp. 65-120.

[65] See the editorial comment by J. G. Keyes in Direk Jayanama, *Siam and World War II*, p. 40.

on a Japanese cruiser off Saigon and in Tokyo and in March 1941 an agreement was reached. Thailand was permitted to keep almost all occupied land. The results were widely celebrated in Thailand, but insiders were quite aware of the fact that Phibun was deeply disappointed by the relatively meager gains and the apparent duplicity of the Japanese, who had traded off Thai interests against gaining access to military installations on Indochinese territory. As a result Phibun no longer felt bound to his secret agreement with the Japanese.

Nevertheless, the conflict between the French and the Thais and its outcome eminently suited the nationalistic propaganda machinery. Thai troops had valiantly crossed the border and put a colonial power to flight. Regions inhabited by members of the great Thai race had been liberated from a colonial regime and become part of Thailand. The Prime Minister, a dapper and handsome military figure, was photographed at the battlefront, courageously facing in the direction of the enemy. For the first time in living memory, Thai troops had been able to shoot and capture European troops with impunity. There was widespread popular support for Phibun's decision to press for border readjustments, and during much of 1941 he basked in a feeling of being truly the nation's leader. As if to celebrate the occasion, he promoted himself to field marshal, skipping the ranks of lieutenant-general and general.

Between May and December 1941, while Phibun and his cabinet remained publicly committed to strict neutrality, gradually the Japanese managed to strengthen the links between the two countries. Japan was permitted to borrow at first ten million *baht*, and later another twenty-five million to purchase Thai produce such as rubber. During the last months of 1941 a Japanese invasion of Mainland Southeast Asia was widely expected, and the Thai government, while reiterating its neutral stance, sought to strengthen its military position by requesting planes, arms, and ammunition from Britain and the United States. The British sent some field guns and aviation fuel, but the Americans were still considering a loan to Thailand when war broke out.[66] On 7 December 1941 the Japanese ambassador requested permission for Japanese troops to pass through Thailand into Burma and Malay. Just at this crucial time Phibun had chosen not to be in Bangkok and the cabinet was unable to come to a decision when the Japanese ultimatum ran out and invasion began. Thai troops resisted some of the invaders, but at noon on 8 December the Prime Minister, who had belatedly returned to discuss the matter in cabinet, announced an immediate cease-fire.

[66] J. V. Martin, 'Thai-American Relations in World War II', *Journal of Asian Studies* 21 (1963), p. 459.

The War Years

Phibun had already indicated in November 1940 that he had great sympathy for Japan's expansionist plans in Eastern Asia. It had been noted how the Japanese had rapidly extended their realm to include surrounding regions. In December 1941 the Japanese had destroyed many American military resources at Pearl Harbor and were demonstrating their ability to wage a very complex war on various fronts most effectively. It appeared that all of Asia was rapidly having its international borders redrawn. Phibun wanted to make sure that the Thais were going to be among the expanding nations. At this time the Thais had not completely given up hope of regaining more Cambodian and Lao territory. In addition they could envisage establishing themselves once again as overlords of some of the Malay States. Their main ambitions with regard to territorial expansion, however, lay to the north. Since the 1920s they had become aware of the existence of many closely related Tai-speaking minorities in Burmese, Indian and in particular Chinese-ruled regions, and had begun dreaming of a much larger pan-Thai realm.

In an unusually rapid succession of moves the Thais joined the axis powers and on 25 January 1942 they went as far as formally declaring war on Britain and the United States, even after the Japanese had advised against such a decision.[67] During the first months of 1942 events seemed to prove the Thai Prime Minister right. The Japanese quickly took the Philippines and the Dutch East Indies and the conquest of Singapore in particular seemed to herald a new era.

From the Japanese perspective the Thai attempts to play a major role in the region caused mixed feelings. On the one hand, the alliance with Thailand provided them with much-needed resources, greatly facilitated their attacks on Burma and the Malay Peninsula, and gave them the opportunity to organize garrisons where battle-weary Japanese troops could recuperate. On the other hand, they did not consider the Thais to be a firm, committed and dependable ally. As for the Thai wishes to regain lost territories, fulfilling them would be at the cost of neighboring areas, which had fallen largely under Japanese control.

In 1942 and 1943 the relationship between the two nations was depicted, at least to the Thai general public, as an extremely cordial one, the Thais hearing much propaganda, on radio and in cinema concerning the benefits of the alliance. Thus it was reported that at least some of the lost territories were regained. Thai troops had quickly invaded two Shan States, the Japanese reluctantly agreeing to accept these becoming Thai. After much pressure they also allowed the incorporation of four Malay states, so the country indeed expanded its borders both

[67] This fact has escaped the attention of most historians. Note, however, that Josef Goebbels wrote in his diary for January 21, 1942: 'Japan has notified us that it has requested Siam not to declare war on England for the present...'. See Louis P. Lochner, transl. and ed., *The Goebbels Diaries*, London: Hamish Hamilton, 1948, p. 1. See also Benjamin A. Batson, 'Siam and Japan: The Perils of Independence', in Alfred W. McCoy, ed, *Southeast Asia under Japanese Occupation*, Yale University Southeast Asia Studies, Monograph No. 22, New Haven: Yale University, 1980, p. 276.

north- and southwards. The height of pro-Japanese propaganda came in July 1943, when Premier Tojo visited the Thai capital.

The Prime Minister and a group of his closest associates, now comprising Wichit Wathakan, Wanit Phananon, Prayun Phamonmontri and Prince Wan Waithayakon Worawan stepped up the various programs to 'civilize' the Thais, mentioned above. Now the habit of betel-nut chewing was banned by law and in order to make sure that the people would comply, all provincial governors were ordered to instigate a cutting down of all areca palm trees. Various committees were set up who devised a proper dress code for various formal occasions.[68] Also a new national dance (the *ramwong*) was created and propagated. Phibun's admiration for Japan extended to considering emulating them, redefining the civilization process with a view of becoming closer to the Japanese concepts of the ideal Asians. Thus serious plans were devised to replace the traditional Thai way of greeting with the hands pressed together with the Japanese bow.

Nevertheless, it did not escape the attention of the general populace that the international situation was causing great concern. No amount of propaganda could hide the worrying effects of a galloping inflation, and everybody noticed the sudden scarcity of some basic household goods. Among the better informed and educated members of the public the view spread at first that the Japanese expansion had come to a halt, and later, that they were forced to retreat. Information differing from that distributed by the government was obtained by listening to foreign radio broadcasts, gradually undermining the credibility of the Thai government.

Therefore, before the pro-Japanese measures had time to affect the general public profoundly, the state-led reorientation lost its drive. Many leading politicians, including Phibun himself, began to plan for the eventuality that Japan might even lose the war. There were very few signs of an active resistance against the Japanese before 1943. The most prominent politician who had openly stated his opposition against an alliance with Japan was Pridi, who had been removed from the cabinet and appointed as one of the three regents acting on behalf of King Ananda who still lived in Switzerland. During 1942 Pridi had attempted in vain to contact the allied forces, but it was not until the latter half of 1943 that the beginnings of a resistance movement can be recognized.

In late July 1944 Phibun resigned over a relatively minor conflict with the House of Representatives. After a period of hesitation the regents found somebody willing to be nominated as prime minister, no simple matter, for Phibun had resigned once before and later rescinded this decision.[69] The new candidate was Khuang Aphaiwong, who was duly elected as Thailand's new premier. Khuang very ably pretended to contin-

[68] See the proclamation of 15 January 1941 (Rathaniyom No. 10) published in Thinaphan Nakhata, 'National Consolidation and Nation-Building', pp. 252-3. On Wednesday 3 September the formal dress rules as approved by the Cabinet were published in the *Bangkok Times*. The committe that prepared these rules was made up of seven ladies, all wives of leading politicians, chaired by Wichit Wathakan.

[69] B. A. Batson, 'The Fall of the Phibun Government, 1944', *JSS* 62, Part 2 (1974), pp. 89-120.

ue to foster the alliance with the Japanese, at the same time not jeopardizing the rapidly growing anti-Japanese resistance groups. The Thais began receiving large supplies of modern weapons by air and began preparing for a bitter campaign to subdue the Japanese forces who were in the country under the conditions of the formal alliance. The Japanese on their side were well aware of the changing conditions in the host country and began preparing for a sudden showdown with the Thais. They planned to disarm the Thais in September 1945, thus creating a safe base stretching from Burma to Indo-china. Before either side could move, however, the dropping of atom bombs on Hiroshima and Nagasaki caused the sudden end of the war in August 1945.

Plate 18. Front page of the Thai newspaper, Siam Rat, *25 June 1932 publishing an announcement about the coup d'état.*

11

THAILAND AFTER 1945

The Post-War Period

The Japanese surrender in mid-August 1945 placed the Thai government for an awkward situation. Although the recently formed and armed resistance forces had repeatedly offered to attack Japanese garrisons, they had been told by the allied forces to hold back until a joint concerted effort could be organized. Now the war was suddenly over without the Thais having had an opportunity to demonstrate their opposition to Japan. Rapidly the war declarations that they had sent three-and-a-half years earlier to Britain and the United States were rescinded. Also those Malay and Burmese territories that had been incorporated in 1943 were returned (but for the time being they held on to the territories taken from French Indochina in 1941). In order to disassociate themselves with the recent hyper-nationalistic fervor even the name Thailand was abandoned in favor of the old name Siam (a measure soon to be reverted).

With the Japanese surrender on the 15th of August 1945 the military responsibility for Thailand fell to the British. As soon as practicable British troops were flown in and these rapidly secured the safety of surviving prisoners of war. The British were surprised to find that the disarmament of the Japanese soldiers had already been largely completed by the Thais. They regarded the Thais as having been co-responsible for the rapid advances of Japanese troops in Burma and Malay and thus having caused immeasurable damage to the allied cause. They also noted that, in contrast to Indo-china and parts of the Dutch Indies where the Japanese interventions in the economy had contributed to severe food-shortages and famine, the Thai countryside was relatively intact and still produced rice. Therefore, in September 1945 it was proposed to the Thais that one of the conditions for formally ending the state of war was the delivery, free of cost, of a massive one-and-a-half million tons of milled rice.

The British, knowing that their American allies had a quite different view of the status of the Thais, pressed for an almost immediate agreement. The Americans had decided to regard the Thai declaration of war as a document issued under duress, not representing the will of the people. By the end of the war they had decided to count the Thais among the countries that had been oppressed and occupied, now liberated from the common enemy.[1]

Plate 19. Five cartoons taken from Phathanukrom Kanmu'ang, 1949 drawn by the cartoonist with the pen name of Thoetkiet. The upper cartoon shows Phahon in front of his troops at the Royal Plaza announcing the coup of 1932. The left one of the middle row shows Phibun holding his Field Marshal's staff, being carried by troops holding banners with slogans, such as: 'Thais are not slaves' and 'We fight for the honor of the Thai nation'. The right one, middle row, shows the difference between the former minister, standing left and the new breed of minister, to the right. Bottom left shows a candidate for the first election, stating: 'If you elect me, I shall help you and the public shouting: 'Hurrah'. The final cartoon shows Phibun (with Field Marshal's staff) and his wife La'iad in their home at Chidlom Road, surrounded by people asking for favors.

[1] Isorn Pocmontri, *Negotiations between Britain and Siam on the Agreement for the Termination of their State of War, 1945: An Instance of Intervention by the United States in British Foreign Policy*, Bangkok: Chulalongkorn University Social Research Institute, 1982.

The choice of a Thai interim Prime Minister was no doubt inspired by the wish to associate closely with the United States, for Seni Pramoj had been the Thai Minister in Washington during the war years. Seni found a troubled country and a plethora of complex decisions to make. Bangkok's infrastructure had been seriously damaged and the British occupation was causing many problems. Especially the disarmament of massive number of Freedom Fighters (who had been armed in 1944 and 1945 to help defeat the Japanese) proved difficult. The negotiations with the British about war reparations became more and more acrimonious and it was only America's intervention that helped Thailand eventually to conclude a relatively innocuous agreement. Seni's role was made all the more difficult because of the fact that he had little experience as a politician and almost no support in the assembly.

The post-war elections took place on 6 January 1946 and were won by the liberal forces, led by Pridi. At first he chose to remain in the background and persuaded Khuang Aphaiwong again to become Prime Minister. After two months, however, Khuang resigned and Pridi took over as Prime Minister. Pridi was the chief force behind a new, much more democratic, constitution which came into effect in May. During the first months of the Pridi government the war crimes trial against Phibun was dismissed on a legal technicality. Modern analysts have depicted the differences between Pridi and Phibun as being typical of an ideological chasm, Pridi standing on the socialist 'left' side and Phibun as right-wing ideologue. Such analysts have found it difficult to explain why Pridi did not use his influence to ensure that Phibun was punished for his role during the Second World War. In actuality, in this period, and also much later, Thai politics were usually not decided on ideological terms; instead they were governed by principles of patronage and clique-building. Up till 1946 there had been much to connect these two chief personalities. For example, Pridi and Phibun both belonged to the instigators of the 1932 *coup*, they also shared the experience of having studied in France. Up to the Japanese invasion they had effectively cooperated, Pridi occupying a ministerial position in Phibun's government. It may even be argued that the conciliatory gesture of dropping the charges against Phibun actually strengthened Pridi's network. In addition it is often overlooked that at the latest in 1943 Phibun had realized that Japan might lose the war and had begun hedging his bets, so that the case against him was by no means so clear-cut as the British believed it to be.

A major disaster arrived, however, from a completely unexpected angle. In the early morning of the 9th of June 1946 a pistol was fired in the bedroom of the King Ananda, a shot that killed the young monarch who had returned from Switzerland only six months before. Probably it was an accidental death, it may have been caused when a royal servant had tried to wrench the weapon from the young king's hands. However, the authorities, who had been taken by surprise, immediately announced that the king had accidentally killed himself, a version that not long afterwards was rejected by a commission appointed to examine the case. As a result of this inconsistency various rumors of conspiracy sprung up, which were to haunt Thai politics for years to come. Three of the king's attendants were put into jail and eventually executed in 1954. Pridi himself became a target of gossip and the rather absurd theory that the Prime Minister had masterminded an assassination was hotly discussed. In face of these accusations Pridi felt his authority undermined and in August he resigned in favor of Thamrong Nawasawat.[2]

In the months that followed, many high-ranking members of the military forces noted with dismay and growing irritation how inefficiently the cabinet and assembly seemed to be in dealing with the ills that beset Thailand. A continuing presence of British forces, commitments to deliver free rice to the British that caused shortages at home and a continuing inflation, made the government appear ineffectual. In addition, Pridi and his friends actively supported anti-colonialist forces in the region, a policy that was frowned upon by the more conservative factions. Some generals, led by Phin Chunhawan, began plotting a *coup d'état* and early November 1947 they sent tanks rolling in Bangkok and forcefully took power.

In order to forestall foreign criticism Phin persuaded the civilian Khuang Aphaiwong once again to accept the post of Prime Minister, his third time in office in just over three years. After a few months the generals decided that the new government had been too weak, they forced Khuang to step down in favor of no other person than Phibun, the same Phibun who had recently been cleared on technical grounds of the charge of war crimes.

The Thais and the Cold War

It was thus not without embarrassment that the new government presented itself to the world. For the British in particular there could hardly be a less appropriate person in charge of the Thais. Also internally there was strong opposition against Phibun, some of it in the army, but much more within the navy. Early in 1949 the navy staged an unsuccessful *coup d'état* and for several days battles took place in Bangkok. The Phibun government clamped down on all dissent, taking a harsh stand particularly towards Islamic dissidents in the South. A uniform Thai nationalism – a movement that had lingered on in the immediate post-war period – re-emerged in a different guise as

[2] Not Narasawat as Joseph Wright in *The Balancing Act*, p. 169 *et passim* insists on calling him.

a state-sponsored ideology, its chief war-time architects, such as Wichit Wathakan and Prince Wan Waithayakon, again taking up duties.

It must be seen as a sign of the political acumen of Phibun that he built up a new image on the platform of anti-communism. He did so at the very beginning of what later became known as the Cold War, the chief first signs of it in Asia being the communist gain of Mainland China in late 1949 and the outbreak of the Korean War in 1950. Stimulated by the idea that the Thais would receive American aid, Phibun ignored local critics who preferred a neutralist role and declared his country to be eager to do its share in defending the 'free world'.[3]

In September 1950 the first of a series of formal agreements with the United States was concluded, the beginning of a period of increased economic and technical exchange. Already before the war the United States had been attracting Thai students, but now a regular stream of young Thais left for tertiary education in America to profit from an intensive period of education there. Apart from the Ministry of Education also the Army (from 1954 under General Sarit Thanarat) and the Police Department (since 1951 under General Phao Sriyanon) were among the chief beneficiaries of the new international arrangements. After surviving a revolt in the Thai navy in June 1951, Phibun made some erratic moves in order to regain authority. In November he returned to the conservative 1932 Constitution, which gave the government the right to appoint half the seats in the National Assembly. The political scene, however, became increasingly dominated by a rivalry for political and economic power between two factions, one of them dominated by General Sarit, the other by Police General Phao.

The Indo-chinese anti-colonialist movements, primarily in Vietnam, but later also in Laos and Cambodia, had drawn the French authorities gradually into a costly war, culminating in a major military confrontation at Dien Bien Phu, the French being defeated decisively. The 1954 Geneva Agreements, which among other things regulated a temporary division of Vietnam, and also gave the communists in Laos a measure of legitimacy, caused alarm in prominent Thai circles. In face of the danger at the eastern borders Phibun pressed forward with his pro-American stance and Thailand joined the Southeast Asia Treaty Organization (SEATO).

As a result various forms of US aid continued to fill state coffers, indirectly enabling certain private individuals to accumulate immense wealth. Between mid-1952 to mid-1954 the flow of financial assistance grew from 6 million US dollars to 11 million, rising in the twelve months after signing the SEATO Pact to 38 million, dropping the following year to 24 million. It was a period when huge investments in Thailand's infrastructure were made, partly with assistance from the World Bank.

[3] With the commencement of the Korean War Phibun immediately offered assistance in the form of 20,000 tons of rice and thousands of troops. See Donald E. Nuechterlein, *Thailand and the Struggle for Southeast Asia*, Ithaca: Cornell University Press, 1965, p. 108.

Gradually a network of highways began to link the capital to ~~Modernisation~~ the outer provinces and to draw the flow of goods away from rivers and canals onto the roads. Electricity was brought to many remote villages, resulting at first in the dissemination of new consumer goods such as refrigerators and television sets, later setting the scene for a rapidly expanding manufacturing industry in the countryside.

The increased flow of money from abroad also fuelled corruption. The most important military leaders began controlling not only state enterprises, but several members of the top echelon also used their influence to set up their own business firms and acquire blocks of shares, in order to gain influence in private businesses and banks.[4]

In September 1957 General Sarit staged a successful *coup d'état*, causing Phibun to flee the country. Because Sarit soon had to be medically treated abroad, he chose his deputy Thanom Kittikachorn to be Prime Minister during most of 1958. Upon his return in October 1958 Sarit virtually ruled as dictator, with Thanom as his deputy and Praphat Charusathian heading the powerful Interior Ministry. Although Sarit and his team exercised dictatorial powers, the Prime Minister could count on a rather broad following. Not only did Sarit appear effective, but some of the support among the masses relates to the fact that he was the first Thai leader since the beginning of the twentieth century to have been educated in Thailand. Sarit did not try to convert the Thais to become civilized according to an alien recipe. The Prime Minister posed quite successfully as a man of the people. He overtly supported various Buddhist projects and also re-discovered the latent reverence for the office and person of the king. King Bhumibol turned out to be not only a worthy pinnacle of the Thai hierarchy but also a great success on state visits abroad while the beauty of his wife, Queen Sirikit, was widely celebrated in the foreign press and at home.

In December 1963 Sarit died and Thanom took over as Prime Minister. Thanom, and Praphat were to dominate Thai politics for the next ten years. Among the top echelon of the military the control over the political decision-making process led to an unprecedented intertwining of politics and industry, cabinet ministers beginning to vie for places on the board of industrial complexes and the accumulation of immense personal wealth.[5]

Interlude: the Democracy Period (1973-1976)

The confrontations that occurred between dissenters and the government authorities in 1973 had a long gestation period. In intellectual circles, notably in Thammasat University, the dis-

---

[4] For a list of companies controlled by the military at that time, see Chai-Anan Samudavanija, *The Thai Young Turks*, Singapore: Institute of Southeast Asian Studies, 1982, pp, 16-7.

[5] See Fred W. Riggs, *Thailand; The Modernization of a Bureaucratic Polity*, Appendix A, especially the entries for Field Marshals Phin and Sarit, Police General Phao and Generals Thanom and Praphat (by Riggs rendered Praphas), who held respectively 9, 22, 26, 17 and 19 seats on various boards (see pp.414-16).

advantages of being ruled by a small clique of military men had been a cause of strong dissatisfaction. Many intellectuals wanted fundamental improvements to the new constitution that had been promulgated in 1968. Others were angered by stories of corruption and graft at the highest level. There were those who disagreed principally with the Thai involvement in the Vietnam War and the presence of ever growing numbers of Americans using Thai army facilities. Others agitated against the perceived power of Japanese financial interests. Inspired by student protests in other countries in the late 1960s, the student organizers from fifteen universities and colleges began using the method of public protest to express their dissatisfaction.

By far the most effective student protests came from Thammasat University. It was here that in 1970 a referendum was conducted that helped coerce the government to accept a popular choice of a new rector. Late in 1971 the military government aggravated the situation by abrogating the constitution and dissolving parliament, thus stifling for the time being all public criticism. On 6 October 1973 some student activists and teachers distributed leaflets expressing the urgent need for a new constitution. As could be expected, all of them were arrested. The authorities announced not long afterwards that evidence of a communist-inspired plot to overthrow the government had been found in their homes and the culprits would have to face trial. During the days that followed this announcement the plight of those arrested triggered off demonstrations that grew to an unprecedented proportion. Several hundred thousand protesters gathered in the Thammasat campus and took to the streets. By the time the government offered to free the arrested ones, the protest had become a general spontaneous declaration of dissatisfaction. The king granted an audience to the spokesmen of the protest movement and was reported to be sympathetic to their wishes for immediate reform. It has been estimated that on October 13 up to half a million demonstrators took to the streets. It was then that the situation ran out of control, buses were turned over, government buildings set on fire, some army units began shooting and in a short time more than one hundred demonstrators were killed.

Unbeknown to the protestors, General Krit Sivara, the army-commander-in-chief, refused to declare martial law, thus challenging the power of the central government. As a result, Prime Minister Thanom and his deputy Praphat resigned and fled the country. To everyone's surprise, the protestors on the street appeared to have achieved a complete revolution.[6] A sense of euphoria broke out among the students, who had received support from all over the country and perceived themselves to be the saviors of the nation. Many felt that a new era had begun, one in which students, workers and peasants would reform Thailand.

[6] A discussion of the role of General Krit can be found in David Morell and Chai-anan Samudavanija, *Political Conflict in Thailand; Reform, Reaction Revolution*, Cambridge, Mass.: Oelgeschlager, Gunn &. Hain, 1981, pp. 147-50.

The king appointed Sanya Thammasak to head a new government, pending new elections. One of Sanya's innovative ideas was a plan to educate the general public speedily not to rely on powerful military men but to accept responsibility for their own future by practicing their democratic rights. At first hundreds, later thousands of students were chosen as a kind of Thai version of the US Peace Corps to propagate democracy in rural areas with films, slide shows and motivating group work.[7] A section of the students interpreted the plan as a platform from which to propagate a Marxist or Maoist future revolution. Notable at this time was the lifting of censorship. Many works that had hitherto been passed around secretly, such as Mao's Red Book and the collected works of Karl Marx and Ho Chi Minh, were now sold openly.

At the same time there already existed quite a different nation-wide organization to educate the general public. This was the *Luksu'achaoban* or Village Scout Movement, that had been sponsored since 1972 by the royal family. Its stated chief purpose was to foster a love and respect for the nation, the king and the Buddhist way of life. Unofficially the movement was intended to propagate and foster anticommunist attitudes.[8] The two organizations, the student movement on the one hand and the Village Scouts on the other, were in direct competition to win over the general populace. The students made great efforts to help develop trade unions, make farmers aware of their rights and duties, and carry conflict to the streets in frequent demonstrations, thus propagating a thorough re-make of Thai society. At the same time right-wing organizations, such as the *Nawaphon* (New Force) and the *Krathing Daeng* (Red Gaurs) were dedicated to combat any serious threat to the nation, with force when necessary. The two approaches are indicative of a general trend to polarization during the period between 1973 and 1976.

In 1975 the dramatic withdrawal of the United States from Vietnam, the Northern Vietnamese conquest of Saigon, and the defeat of non-communist forces in Cambodia and Laos, fuelled the debate. The left-wing movements saw these events as the predictable and inevitable steps towards a new world order, which soon would also apply to the Thais, while the conservative forces felt deeply threatened and perceived an urgent need to shield Thailand, Buddhism and royalty from the evils that would ensue when a communist revolution took place.

The elections of 1975 resulted in a rather chaotic coalition of no less than seventeen parties put together by Kukrit Pramoj. After a non-confidence vote new elections had to be held in April 1976, which brought about a right-wing coalition under Kukrit's brother Seni, who had already been Prime Minister in 1945. His government also proved to be rather ineffectual and unable to dispel the widespread unrest in the country. For the

[7] *Ibid.*, pp. 151-2.

[8] Good accounts of the Village Scouts and their five-day training programs can be found in Marjorie A. Muecke, 'The Village Scouts of Thailand', *Asian Survey*, Vol. 20, No. 4, April 1980, pp. 407-27 and Katherine A. Bowie, *Rituals of National Royalty*, New York: Columbia University Press, 1997.

first time in Thai history there were reports of obviously politically motivated violent crimes in the countryside.

Matters came to a head when former Prime Minister Thanom returned from exile (ironically the new liberal constitution, which he had prevented from being proclaimed, gave him the right to do so). The return of the former military ruler, who took refuge in the *Sangha* by becoming a Buddhist monk, was hotly discussed, notably when the king decided to pay his respects to this former Prime Minister. On October 5, 1976 several Thai newspapers published a report, accompanied by a photograph showing that Thammasat students had staged a mock hanging of a figure that bore the likeness of the crown-prince. Much later it has been revealed that this report was untrue and the photograph had been manipulated. It had been deliberately sent into the world in order to provoke a violent reaction among the groups opposing the students. The following day large numbers of Village Scouts and Red Gaurs were rushed to the campus of Thammasat, where they, assisted by police and army units, went on the rampage, killing and wounding a large number of unarmed protesters.

These excesses in turn triggered another *coup* and the National Administrative Reform Council was established. The three years of democracy had ended, as it had begun, with a bloodbath. The Democracy Period had been marked by unrest, political ferment, open conflict and instability. In face of the perceived communist threat from their neighbors many Thais were willing to condone the return of a more stable, military-dominated government. However, the debates had also greatly strengthened public awareness and may have played a role in combating political lethargy particularly in Bangkok. At some crucial moments fifteen years later the events of the mid-1970s assisted many Thais to overcome serious threats to democracy.

Confrontation and Reconciliation

Late in 1976 the military group announced their choice of Prime Minister. It was Thanin Kraivichien, a former high court judge. He presided over a government that displayed an unprecedented repressive style. The government quickly clamped down on dissent. Those who during the preceding years had openly voiced leftist opinion were suddenly hounded and punished. Some went into hiding, those who could afford it went abroad, but many others joined insurgents in the northern relatively inaccessible border regions. Thanin's authoritarian rule displeased the most important military men and in 1977 they intervened and replaced him with a compromise candidate from their own ranks, Kriangsak Chomanand. Kriangsak followed a policy of appeasement, offering an amnesty to most

286

of those who had fled and taken up arms. Many of the communist insurgents took up his offer, having become disillusioned
by internal strife and the difficulties of living in the jungle.
After the amnesty period had expired a few last pockets of
dissent were overrun by army troops.

The results of the elections of 1979 were indecisive and
forced Kriangsak into difficult negotiations before he obtained
a narrow majority. After a relatively short period he had to step
aside and make way for General Prem Tinsanulanonda. Prem
had more friends in key positions and managed to survive
various political crises, thereby growing both in experience and
stature. In 1981 a critical army faction staged a *coup d'état*,
managing to take key areas of Bangkok, a situation that in previous *coups* had usually led to a change of government.
However, Prem fled to an army base in the province and when
the king ostentatiously threw his full support behind the Prime
Minister by leaving Bangkok and traveling to meet Prem, the
coup attempt failed.[9] It was a clear demonstration of how the
prestige of the royal family had increased since the 1950s. The
elections of 1983 confirmed Prem as Prime Minister.
Altogether he stayed in power from March 1980 through five
cabinets until after the elections of 1988, when he handed over
power to Chatichai Choonhavan.

The Tiger that failed to Jump

In the mid-1980s the Thai gross national product that had
steadily grown since the early 1960s continued to rise. There
were several interacting reasons why the country remained
attractive for investors, particularly for those interested in the
manufacturing industry. One of these factors was that the infrastructure was fairly modern and reasonably well maintained.
The political system was stable and the cost of labor was relatively cheap. In order to keep labor costs down the government
discouraged the labor movement, refrained from heavy investments in the social services, avoided costly pension schemes
and shied away from an encompassing health insurance. In
addition the country remained relatively lenient to investors by
not strictly enforcing safety standards and by – at least until the
mid-90s – allowing environmental degradation.

At the end of the 1980s Prime Minister Chatichai moved
to diminish the power of the military in favor of business interests, which triggered a new *coup d'état* in February 1991 bringing the National Peace Keeping Council to the fore, whose self-
appointed chief task was to combat rampant corruption. For one
year a prominent businessman, Anand Panyarachun was placed
in the position of Prime Minister. Anand very capably managed
to check the power of the military clique. During this period the

[9] Background to the 1981 *coup* attempt
can be found in Chai-Anan Samudavanija, *The Thai Young Turks* and
Suchit Bunbongkarn, 'Political
Institutions and Processes' in
Somsakdi Xuto (ed.), *Government
and Politics* of Thailand, Singapore:
Oxford University Press, 1987, pp.
41-74.

military Council interfered with the drafting of yet another constitution, insisting on a clause giving the National Peace Keeping Council special rights. After the election of 1992 one of the *coup* leaders, General Suchinda Kraprayun, was installed as the new premier. All protests against the blatant manipulation of the political system to consolidate military power were at first rigorously suppressed. This caused a banding together of all forces in opposition, including some prominent politicians, academics, labor leaders, students and members of the educated middle class. An effort by military forces to break up a massive protest on the streets of Bangkok in May 1992 caused many casualties.[10] For the fourth time in twenty-five years the king successfully intervened to prevent the situation from worsening.

The elections of September 1992 brought Chuan Leekpai to the fore, an unusual politician with almost no backing from military or bureaucracy. In the mid-1990s business interests dominated Thai politics. For short periods Prime Ministers Banharn Silpa'archa and Chavalit Yongchaiyudh led the country, with little popular support. During the 1980s and much of the 1990s Bangkok was transformed by an immense building program; in the countryside innumerable factories were constructed. The country appeared to be rushing towards becoming one of the new industrialized, prosperous 'Asian Tigers'. This unusual growth was only possible through high-interest foreign loans, Thailand's foreign debt rising dramatically from around 31 billion *baht* in 1992 to over 90 billion four years later. In order to attract foreign investment the baht was kept firmly pegged to the American dollar. When the dollar appreciated in 1995 the Thai currency became overvalued, consequently the government, had difficulties maintaining interest payments.

In June 1997, after having spent almost all its currency reserves to prop up the *baht* – a situation reminiscent of the money crisis of 1920-1922 – the government was forced to sever the Thai currency from the US dollar, allowing the *baht* to float freely. The resulting devaluation and loss of confidence caused a shock wave that exposed various weaknesses in the financial sector. The property market fell dramatically and many banks suddenly realized that they had lent immense sums with too little collateral. During the second half of 1997 many banks found themselves in embarrassing circumstances, a large number of firms went bankrupt and large projects had to be abandoned. The economic crisis that befell Thailand spread to countries such as Japan, Indonesia and Malaysia began in Bangkok.

[10] Officially 50 deaths and more than 150 missing. Gerhard Reinecke and Ingvar Sander, 'Thailands Demokratisierung: Ein Schauspiel in vielen Akten', in Ingvar Sander and Gerhard Reinecke (eds) *Thailand: Aktuelle Wandlungsprozesse in Politik, Wirtschaft, Umwelt und Gesellschaft*, Mitteilungen des Instituts für Asienkunde Hamburg Nr. 328, Hamburg: Institut für Asienkunde, 2000, p.47.

A Constitution with a Difference

The constitution that was promulgated in 1997 differs considerably from the many Thai constitutions that preceded it. One difference was the breadth of the committee that drafted it, consisting of more than a hundred individuals representing a wide range of expertise and opinions. Another was the thoroughness with which the new constitution was prepared: countless regional local hearings were organized to discuss the scope of the enterprise and many fundamental issues were pondered, debated, drafted, re-drafted and finally decided upon.

The resulting long text, with more than 300 clauses, differed from previous constitutions in the depth of the reforms that were instigated. Thus the very basis of democracy was once more defined, and it was decided to ensure that under the new constitution the Senate would also consist of elected members. Access to the House of Assembly was made possible in two ways. On the one hand registered party members could be elected when their party gained sufficient support, but single-seat constituencies were also allowed. All elected members would have to have at least an academic qualification.

The most notable changes, however, were the creation of a series of measures and institutions that were designed to function as control mechanisms of the state's executive. A supervisory body would be empowered to control the electoral process, specifically designed to prevent and to combat various types of manipulation. Another commission was given the task to scrutinize the sources of wealth of politicians and in the case of coming across someone having hidden sources of income, or having obtained riches illegally, it could instigate a procedure that might lead to such a politician being removed from office. Another commission was created to investigate and report on state officials and their exercise of duties and the existing commission to combat corruption was given the power to prosecute.

These and similar clauses were clearly designed to combat graft and corruption on all levels of government. When the text of the draft constitution became known, many observers were skeptical and considered the document too ambitious. They predicted that it would most likely be rejected or rigorously amended in the House of Assembly and particularly in the Senate. It has been suggested that it was the dramatic situation created by the economic crisis of 1997 that made it possible for this rather revolutionary constitution to be accepted by both Houses of Representatives.[11] In October of that year it was promulgated and it was for the first time applied to an election in 2001, won by a rich businessman Thaksin Shinawatra, whose strong leadership gained him the favor of the voting public so that in 2005 his party won the absolute majority.

[11] This is suggested in the article by Michael Kelly Connors, 'Framing the 'People's Constitution'', in Duncan McCargo (ed.), *Reforming Thai Politics*, Copenhagen: NIAS Publishing, 2002, p. 53.

12

CONCLUDING REMARKS

Accelerated Change and Its Problems

During the period of time examined in the previous chapters the Thai landscape changed dramatically. This was chiefly the result of human activities. A main factor helping explain this change is the increase in population. In the eighteenth century that part of the surface of the earth now called Thailand may have contained – it has been argued above – between two and three million people. At the time of writing this book some sixty-five million humans dwell in that space. In other words, in little more than two centuries the human population increased by twenty to thirty times.

In the eighteenth century much of the land that is at present taken up by farms, industries, houses and roads was not even regarded as suitable for human occupation. There were large tracts, such as marshy grounds that had to be avoided because humans were pestered by mosquitoes or crocodiles were likely to attack.[1] Large tracts were covered by impenetrable grasslands where tigers hunted and there were areas with jungle only accessible to peoples with special knowledge of how to survive in that environment. Notwithstanding these restrictions there was ample land that could be occupied and transformed into rice-land or orchards. Traditionally any person could take possession of free land and raise a crop, paying one-fourth of the gross produce by way of tax.[2]

It has been shown that particularly in the first half of the nineteenth century the state was concerned with filling up such unused space with potential taxpayers. In various raids and during protracted periods of warfare it captured many peoples from surrounding regions, notably from Laos. The state also welcomed refugees, such as many Catholic families from Vietnam fleeing from religious persecution and many thousands of Mons from Tenasserim escaping from Burmese oppression.[3] All these newcomers were resettled in a wide belt surrounding Bangkok up to a distance of some 150 kilometers; to the south-west reaching the Phetburi and Ratburi region, to the west the land around Kanchanaburi was populated, in a northwestern direction new villages were established along the Suphanburi River, to the northeast the region around Saraburi and eastwards the valley of the Prachin River received many new settlers.

The same attitude of wanting to convert unused land and increase human-made produce underlies the measures taken to

---

[1] In 1778 the lower Chaophraya delta was the scene of many bounty hunters, for King Taksin had offered a reward for every crocodile killed. See Koenig, 'Journal of a Voyage from India to Siam and Malacca', p. 135.

[2] See Bowring, *The Kingdom and People of Siam*, Vol. 1, p. 187; Dilock, *Die Landwirtschaft in Siam*, p. 73.

[3] Details on the migrations of the Mons from Tenasserim in "Between Moulmein and Bangkok: The Mass Migration of Mons in the first half of the Nineteenth Century", in Leonard Blussé and Felipe Fernandez-Armesto (eds.) *Shifting Communities and Identity Formation in Early Modern Asia*, Leiden: Research School of Asian, African, and Amerindian Studies (CNWS), 2003, pp. 107-116.

stimulate Chinese immigration. Chinese entrepreneurs and Chinese labor responded in large numbers. They played a crucial role in transforming large tracts of land to plantations. Particularly the Chinese minority in Siam has been shown to play a very important role in the transformation of the country. It developed from a community of traders, tax farmers and entrepreneurs, to provide a laboring class, form a network of trading outlets and use the opportunities to invest in industrial enterprises.

Between the eighteenth and twenty-first century not only the landscape was transformed, the societal organization of the Thais also changed dramatically. The almost unlimited power of the king, the taxation system of the state, the hierarchy embedded in the *saktina* system of ranking, the names of the social classes and the system of slavery that once determined one's role, all these gave way to new organizational structures.

While the features which I have called elsewhere the 'formal structure' of the late seventeenth and eighteenth centuries can no longer be found, some remarkably persistent features may also be recognized, notably in eating habits, body language and attitudes towards authority.[4] Some circumstances mentioned in this book appear to recur. The measures taken by the Siamese king to combat drug abuse in the first half of the nineteenth century, which proved rather futile may be compared with equally unsuccessful efforts in modern times. Similarly, early in the nineteenth century, China was Siam's most important trading partner, in the early 21st century after the interlude of colonial oppression and protracted warfare China has rebounded and again is the dominating economic force in eastern Asia.

The transformation of Siam took place throughout the period of study, but this may not be thought of as a gradual process: notably in the most recent fifty years a dramatic acceleration took place in many aspects of society. Thus, at the end of the Second World War, Thailand's population numbered some 16.6 million people and more than ninety per cent of these still depended for their livelihood on agriculture and fishery. Most of these farmers and fishermen used simple, time-honored techniques that ensured an economic return without unduly jeopardizing the precarious ecosystem. Half a century later the position of agriculture in the national economy as well as the way plants were grown had been transformed. The percentage of people engaged in agriculture and fishery had dropped to about half of that of 1945 and most of those who remained as primary producers found their circumstances drastically changed. Most farmers now had to adjust to a complex situation whereby they depended on large-scale irrigation systems. Unlike their ancestors, now they were connected with a nation-wide electricity network. The new farmers used

[4] For details see B. J. Terwiel, 'Formal Structure and Informal Rules: An Historical Perspective on Hierarchy, Bondage and the Patron-Client Relationship', *in* H. ten Brummelhuis and J. H. Kemp (eds.), *Strategies and Structures in Thai Society*. University of Amsterdam: Department of South and Southeast Asian Studies, 1984, pp. 19-38.

mechanical tools, produced a greater variety of products and were concerned with methods of marketing these products.

It was not until the latter half of the 20th century that the population explosion, combined with mechanization and industrialization drastically affected the countryside and environment. Every year the surface devoted to agriculture, industry, and roads expanded by more than six per cent, human activity first spreading over various lowlands, then deep into the hills. The diversification of agricultural products also required new techniques. Since the Second World War agriculture grew on an average some three per cent annually. In order to boost production new types of rice were sown, needing increased chemical fertilizers and a liberal application of pesticides. The results were dramatic. While in 1913 some 75 per cent of Thailand's surface had been covered with forest, and in 1955 this cover had diminished to around 63 per cent, in 1992 it had been reduced to a mere 18 per cent.[5] Many of the regions recently occupied by farmers using modern production methods face erosion problems. During the fifteen years between 1976 and 1991 the amount of pesticides used quadrupled, the amount of fungicide grew by a factor of six and ten times the amount of herbicide was sprayed. Because of their incompatibility with sustainable production, many of these products had already been banned in Europe.

The fishing industry also faces severe problems. Thailand's rivers, once a never failing source of wealth, no longer produce a healthy staple source of protein. Even the Gulf of Thailand has been turned into a gigantic sewer. The massive amounts of waste products poured into the Gulf have damaged the sea fishing industry. Up till recently few Thais had a clear picture of what has been happening to their environment.[6]

The main responsibility for the massive ecological emergency lies with a rapid industrialization. Many of those who invested in Thailand have been interested in quick returns, not in long-term development. Although the Thai public authority has become aware of many problematic aspects of industrialization and has passed many sensible pieces of legislature to maintain public health, only too often such laws are circumvented. Public servants can often be bribed and the intimate links between political and financial interests often prevent an effective action against those who harm the environment.

The symptoms of an unbridled industrialization have become so aggravating that in Thailand a reaction appears to have set in. Central authorities now apply strict controls to food products, a measure primarily designed to protect the export market. A few pioneers have begun rethinking the basic production methods. In particular the Buddhist monasteries, with their tradition of gentle behavior towards all creatures, may well prove to perform a key role in raising public awareness

[5] David Feeny, 'The Coevolution of Property Rights Regimes for Land, Man, and Forests in Thailand, 1790-1990', in John F. Richards (ed.), *Land, Property, and the Environment*, Oakland, Cal.: ICS Press, 2002, pp. 196-197.

[6] A pioneer study dealing with these basic questions was Wolf Donner, *Thailand ohne Tempel; Lebensfragen eines Tropenlandes*, Frankfurt (Main): R. G. Fischer, 1984.

towards environmental issues. Some Buddhist monks have become heroes of the environmentalist movement. With the invention of 'tree ordination' a growing number of Thais have discovered a new way of shaking up the nation's conscience,[7] making people realize that mankind has been using natural resources, forgetting for a while that they themselves are part of nature.

The subtle craft of history writing in Thailand

Those who are unfamiliar with other books on Thai history should note that quite frequently the analytical and concluding segments in this book differ from the standard representations of Thai history. For example, King Taksin is usually depicted as someone who, during the final years of his reign, became mentally ill, a dangerous megalomaniac who had to be deposed for the well-being of the state. We have argued that this representation of a dangerously sick man may well have been an invention by his successor, or part of a political ploy to legitimate the new king.

Similarly, the nature of the economic developments in the first half of the 19th century described in Chapter 5 differs fundamentally from that described by others, as does the extent to which money was used prior to the Bowring Treaty and the impact of the huge experiment to attract Chinese labor under Rama III. Also this book mentions succession struggles, whereas it has become standard to describe a smooth change of rule. This book describes King Mongkut's attitude towards Britain in the 1860s, extrapolated from his own writing, as one whereby an eventual submission to its might was deemed to be almost inevitable. It has been suggested here that this was a quite understandable reaction to the results of the Opium War and the subsequent second war with Burma. In both instances the British demonstrated an unprecedented military might. The prevailing story, that during Mongkut's reign the chief diplomatic aim was to avoid colonization is in my view, ahistorical, an undifferentiated projection of a later concern to the past.

Further, both background and consequences of the domestic political crisis in late 1874 and early 1875 – in Chapter 7 it is called the Palace Incident – differ from its description in most textbooks. The same goes for the causes of the Paknam crisis in 1893. The reason why Siam escaped being colonized in the 1890s is commonly ascribed to the clever manipulations of Kings Mongkut and Chulalongkorn. In Chapter 8 a quite different scenario is depicted, whereby these Siamese kings were not in the situation of playing such glamorous roles.

In Chapters 8 and 9 it was noted that between 1890 and 1932 the cabinet was stacked with princes. Unlike the standard

---

[7] For details on the 'tree ordination' see John Taylor, 'Social Activism and Resistance on the Thai Frontier: The Case of Phra Prajak Khuttajitto', *Bulletin of Concerned Asian Scholars*, Vol. 25, No.2, 1993, pp. 3-17.

account, in this book it has been argued that this dominating role of the princely class must be regarded as a major deviation from the traditional political system, where executive posts were usually reserved for persons outside the royal family (the chief exception being the office of *Maha Uparat*). Thus I do not adhere to the idea that Chulalongkorn's placing his relatives in the cabinet was in accord with the traditional Thai system of government.

Some of the conflicts and controversies of the 1920s discussed in Chapter 9 have been avoided or trivialized in other history books. Another example in Chapter 10 is the anti-Japanese resistance movement during World War II, depicted as having gained momentum at a somewhat later date than commonly assumed. In all these and other instances this book differs, sometimes subtly, sometimes to a more radical degree, from what is usually written.

Such a wide range of differences with the standard account needs some explanation. They are the direct result of a fundamental methodological decision. During the many years that I have taught Thai history I have had the privilege of gaining access to many documents written during the nineteenth and twentieth century. It soon became apparent that many contemporary documents were in direct conflict with the standard depiction of Thai history. In other words, I have good cause to believe that the way the Thai past is presented in most accounts is distorted or wrong. It is also my opinion that this distortion has been part of a complex deliberate process.[8]

The re-writing of the Thai past, whereby changes are made to the historical record, can be demonstrated to have begun around the middle of the nineteenth century with the writing of the so-called Royal Autograph version of the State Annals. In this official account the manner of King Taksin's execution on April 7, 1782 was changed from an ignominious beheading to a clubbing, a death reserved for members of royalty. In this matter, as in numerous other instances the Royal Autograph edition may be regarded as the first deliberately embellished account of the Thai past.[9]

Thai history writing is burdened by this long practiced process of rewriting the past – with the aim of avoiding disagreeable events – in favor of an account that renders a more positive impression. The history of the state has been remade to serve the purpose of fostering admiration in the reader. Particularly works having the state's imprimatur tend to provide the reader with an account that in some cases is little more than a litany of great deeds and praiseworthy decisions.

While it is natural for the rulers of a country to look favorably upon attempts to portray the past from a positive angle, there are several reasons why in Thailand the state-sponsored rosy picture is overwhelmingly present. One reason is the indigenous traditional attitude towards knowledge and teachers. Ideally speaking, all traditional knowledge rests with the great teachers of the past. Each profession had its great anonymous 'teachers' who would be honored and respected by every

---

[8] See Barend Jan Terwiel, 'Van Denkmodellen en Vooroordelen: Thaise Geschiedschrijving over de Periode van de Eerste Helft van de Negentiende Eeuw', Inaugural lecture on the occasion of accepting the extraordinary chair for Mainland Southeast Asia at Leiden University, Leiden: IIAS, February 2000.

[9] The manipulation of the Thai record of the past is usually placed much later. Thongchai Winichakul, for example, opts for the late nineteenth and early twentieth century. See his *Siam Mapped: A History of the Geo-Body of a Nation*, Chiangmai: Silkworm, 1994, p. 161 f.

new generation of pupils. Those who became dancers, theatre performers, tattooers, boxers, all who learnt a traditional art, had to pay homage to the masters of the past. The revered position of all teachers derived from that teacher's link with an ancient fund of knowledge. Ideally speaking it is the task of a teacher simply to transmit that precious good, not to examine it critically.

The great classic works of literature, *Ramakien, Phra Aphaimani, Sam Kok, Inao, Khun Chang Khun Phen* and many others are available in Thailand in one authorized edition, usually proudly displaying the seal of the Department of Fine Arts. The same goes for basic historical texts. The more than fifty volumes of Collected Chronicles *(Prachum Phongsawadan)*, once assembled by the state's best minds, are reprinted exactly as in the original. The same goes for other primary sources, such as the Three Seals Law *(Kotmai Tra Sam Duang)*, the Collected Proclamations of the Fourth Reign *(Prachum Prakat Ratchakan thi Si)* and the official edition of the Thai inscriptions. There is a fascinating book, entitled *Chindamani*, already used in the seventeenth century as a teaching text for future scribes and courtiers. There are numerous quite distinct manuscript versions of this Chindamani, but only one edited version is in print. The Annals by *chaophraya* Thiphakorawong (Kham Bunnak) are available only in the standard edition, which has been subtly changed from the manuscript version. All of these prepared editions are authoritative; the persons who prepared them have made their decisions without leaving room for alternative readings or expressing doubt.

Related to the tradition of authoritative state-supervised primary sources is the phenomenon that in Thailand a strong interest in archival research never developed. The very gaining of access to the material that had been used to create standard versions may be felt to be presumptuous. To redo the work of great people who once have given their best, such as the statesman Damrong Rajanuphab, amounts to showing a disrespectful attitude towards this pioneer of Thai history writing. Even worse would be a direct challenge to the constructs he created.

Another circumstance hampering a critical examination of the historical record is the development, during the last seventy years, of an indigenous strain of nationalism. The presentation of history has been deeply embedded into the cult of Thai nationalism. History is to foster a pride of being part of the Thai Nation. Therefore, there are elaborate episodes depicting Thais behaving heroically during battles with Burma, while the case of the Burmese is systematically presented in less flattering terms. A related trend is to choose personalities and events as motifs to instill a love for the nation. This has caused the creation of a series of paradigmatic figures; Rama Khamhaeng has become the epitome of a wise ruler; Naresuan is the hero leading the Thais towards freedom, he has become the symbol of resistance against oppression; Queen Suriyothai is a paragon who offered her life for king and nation; the citizens at the Bang Rachan stockade stand for the principle of battling against those threatening the country. Historians who come across documents or interpretations that are not in agreement with these and many other nationalistic portraits are placed in a very awkward position. By publishing such thought-provoking material they risk being attacked as pursuing dangerous goals, they may be accused of wanting to undermine national morale.

A third reason why Thai historiography differs from that in many other countries is the unusual attitude towards the royal family, and in particular, the manner in which one may or may not write about members of the Chakri dynasty. In Thailand there is a very strong tradition of protecting royalty. In the early Bangkok Period this was usually limited to the person of the king himself. In modern times this protection is extended to members of the royal family and firmly embedded in the law of 'lèse majesty', which forbids any crime or offense against the sovereign or the dignity of his person. Any perceived attack or criticism is quickly punished. While there are comparable laws in other countries that have a constitutional monarchy, in Thailand this is interpreted relatively strictly. No adverse written or broadcast comment in relation to royalty is allowed. The strict interpretation of the law already causes minor problems to historians who write about the person of King Bhumibol Adulyadet, the ninth monarch of the Chakri Dynasty. As far as can be determined from the accounts available, this king has generally acted honorably and, with growing experience, increasingly statesmanlike. Even in his case, all historians are aware of the fact that an incautious remark would have severe repercussions, for there exists a veritable cult surrounding His Majesty.[10]

The chief problem for historians is, however, that in Thailand 'lèse majesty' is perceived to apply not only to the present extended royal family, but is felt to apply to many members already deceased. Thus, in 1999 there were negotiations with the Thai authorities for a re-take of the film 'The King and I' (a film that among others shows much of the private life of King Mongkut). These negotiations could not be concluded. The chief obstacle was that the filmmakers, like their predecessors who made earlier versions of the film, were perceived by the Thais to be disrespectful towards the memory of that beloved monarch by depicting him as willful and short-tempered.

Similar problems would befall those wanting to make a film of the life of King Mongkut's son and successor Chulalongkorn. Around this Thai king over time a dense web of legends has developed supporting the rather simplistic concept that the king was above making a wrong judgment. All his actions are widely perceived to have been pervaded by a single-minded love for the Thai nation. Innumerable amulets and photographs are the outward signs of a regular cult surrounding the fifth reign.[11]

For each of the Chakri kings a modern standard depiction exists in the form of school textbooks and short films made for general consumption. In these books and films every king

[10] A good summary of the cult surrounding King Bhumibol can be found in Irene Stengs, 'A Kingly Cult; Thailand's Guiding Lights in a Dark Era', *Etnofoor*, vol. 12, pt.2, 1999, pp. 41-75.

represents one or more particular virtues. King Rama I is the somewhat severe but just king who created peace. His son, Phraphutthaloetla, or Rama II is the gifted poet. The third reign of Phra Nangklao is usually described as a period with a caretaker king, preparing the way for the fourth reign of king Mongkut, the far-sighted scholar, devout Buddhist and clever diplomat. This is followed by the glorious and heroic King Chulalongkorn, guiding the state through turbulent times towards modernity. His son Vajiravudh is lauded for his nationalism as well as his writing. His brother Prachathipok was the king who wanted to present his people with a true democracy, but was forestalled by the *coup d'état* of 1932. The young King Ananda had just begun a glorious reign when his life suddenly tragically came to an end. His successor Bhumibol Adulyadet has succeeded to lead the nation, occasionally to point in the right direction, sometimes taking direct action in order to quell political turmoil.

In the face of these various circumstances historians covering the Bangkok Period from 1782 to the present face severe problems. Not the least among these is that the 'plot' of most Thai history books is clearly chauvinistic, a great number of historical documents can be shown to be at variance with the standard story. As soon as a historian begins to argue for a more balanced judgement, allowing past rulers their qualities but pointing out apparent weaknesses, the debates that follow quickly tend to degenerate into accusations of ill-will towards the nation. A common reaction has been to point out that the skepticism of the critical historian merely demonstrates that he is against authority, or to use a term that many Thais of the 1960s, 1970s and 1980s used for such impertinent persons: the offending academic obviously belonged to *'phuak khommunit'* (the Communists), which meant all people who were intent to undermine law and order.

The contents of this book are primarily based on contemporary documents, or those resting upon their perusal. Consequently much attention has been given to identify all these sources listed in the footnotes as well as in the bibliography. Where a period is dealt with here, particularly early ones, for which relatively few sources are available, primary sources largely determine the subjects so dealt with. Hence the works of *chaophraya* Thiphakorawong, who was the chief chronicler of the first half of the nineteenth century, necessarily play a large part. His accounts are complemented, however, with documents from the National Library in Bangkok, correspondence such as the Burney Papers, as well as the scant and incomplete accounts by European and American visitors. Moving towards more modern times, increasingly more information is available and often it is possible to rely with some confidence on the detailed analyses of previous scholars.

Given the relatively undeveloped state of Thai historiography, a history book such as this cannot claim to be definitive or authoritative. I hope that it will contribute to a more critical examination of what hitherto has been widely accepted as the story of Thai history.

[11] See Irene Stengs, 'Worshipping the Great Moderniser; The Cult of King Chulalongkorn, Patron Saint of the Thai Middle Class', Ph.D. Dissertation, Amsterdam University, 2002.

Glossary

abhiseka (Sanskrit). Anointing, consecrating, with particular reference to the inauguration of a king.

at Old copper coin, one sixty-fourth of a *baht* in value.

baht Siamese monetary unit. The name is derived from the *baht* unit of weight, 15 grams, which was its original weight in silver.

biawat Sum of money the Siamese king used to give to his ranking officers.

Chakri Traditional honorific name given to the head of the Mahatthai. Since the founder of the present dynasty once occupied that position, that dynasty is often referred to as Chakri dynasty.

chamu'n Military title indicating officer rank in the Mahatlek, also known as *chaomu'n*.

chang Unit of money and weight, corresponding to 80 *baht* or 1.2 kilograms.

changpu'n Armed soldier.

changwang Senior palace official; title of an officer in the Mahatlek.

chao Ruler, chief.

chao Prince, the class of noblemen.

chaochommanda Title indicating the king's concubine who has given birth to a child fathered by the king.

chaofa Title of a prince of the highest rank.

chaokrom Head of a department.

chaomu Leader of a small band of soldiers, comparable to corporal.

chaomu'ang Ruler of a city or country.

chaomu'n See *chamu'n*.

chaophaya Highest rank of conferred nobility; during the Bangkok period usually spelled *chaophraya*.

chedi Sacred mound; memorial edifice.

fu'ang Unit of money and weight, corresponding to one-eighth of a *baht*, at present obsolete.

hap Unit of weight, equivalent to 60 kilograms.

Jatakas Collection of stories of previous births of the Buddha; in the Buddhist canon there are 547 Jataka stories.

Kalahom Ministry of Defence.

kathin Annual religious ceremony, following the rainy season, during which robes are presented to some of the Buddhist monks.

khun Title of respect; during the Bangkok period it was one of the lower ranks of the conferred nobility.

khunnang Term denoting the general class of the conferred nobility.

khotchasi Mythical animal representing a lion with an elephant's trunk, found on the seal of the Kalahom.

krom Department, bureau; an element in conferred titles for royalty.

kromakhun Conferred title for royalty, higher than *kromamu'n*.

kromaluang Conferred title for royalty, higher than *kromakhun*.

kromamu'n Conferred title for royalty.

kromphra Conferred title for royalty, higher than *kromaluang*.

kromsomdetphra The highest conferred title for royalty.

kup Large hood, providing shade, found on ceremonial boats; a howdah.

liang To raise, bring up; to look after (someone else's) child.

luang Title of conferred nobility, higher than *khun*.

luksu'a chaoban Village Scout Movement, founded 1972.

Maha Uparat Literally 'Great Viceroy', the official rank of the occupant of the Front Palace, traditionally the highest office in Siam, second only to that of the king. Often referred to as *Uparat*.

Mahatlek Corps of Royal Pages.

Mahatthai Department of Civil Affairs; since the fifth reign the name of the Ministry of the Interior.

momchao Title of a member of royalty who is in the grandchild generation of royal descent, or treated as such.

mu'ang City; country.

mu'n One of the lower ranks of the conferred nobility, during most of the Bangkok period obsolete.

nai Master, owner, boss.

naimuat Chief or leader of a section.

niphan (Sanskrit: *nirvana*) State of salvation when an individual is released from the cycle of rebirth.

parien High grade of Buddhist religious instruction.

phaya High rank of conferred nobility, during most of the Bangkok period also known as *phraya*.

phonlaru'an Civilians, as opposed to *thahan*.

phra Rank of conferred nobility, higher than *luang*, but lower than *phaya (phraya)*.

phraratchaphithi boromaphisek Elaborate ceremonies of anointment and elevation to the status of absolute king.

Phra Thammasat (Sanskrit: *dharmasastra*) Body of laws, jurisprudence.

phrai Commoner, freeman.

phrai luang Commoner, for *corvée* duties assigned to one of the king's departments.

phrai rap Commoner.

phrai som Commoner, for *corvée* duties assigned to a private individual other than the king.

Phrakhlang The Treasury, traditionally also in change of Foreign Affairs.

phraya See *phaya*.

prang Tall religious monument with rounded top.

rai Square surface measure equal to 1,600 square metres.

ratchakhana Highest honorific title a Buddhist monk may receive.

saktina Elaborate system of degrees of rank expressed by numbers of *rai* in land.

salu'ng Unit of money and weight, corresponding to one-fourth of a *baht*.

samanokhrua Census of the Siamese populace, occasionally held during the Ayutthaya period.

samian Scribe.

Sangha The brotherhood of Buddhist monks and novices.

sarawat Assistant supervisor.

Satsadi Department of Registration, also known as Suratsawadi.

Sena Officer responsible for the collection of tax on rice lands.

Senabodi Ministerial committee, corresponding to a cabinet.

sodaban Person who has entered the stream of wisdom. It is believed that a true *sodaban* will not have more than seven rebirths before reaching the blissful state of *niphan*.

somdet An adjective meaning 'high, excellent', part of some exalted titles.

Suratsawadi See Satsadi.

tambon District.

thahan Military men, soldier, as opposed to *phonlaru'an*.

tham khwan Ceremony to restore or reinforce the 'vital power' of a person, animal, or venerated object.

thanai Legal counselor.

thang Capacity measure equal to 20 litres.

thawai tua (literally) 'To present one's body', to be presented to the king.

Tai Name designating the broad linguistic category of Tai-speaking peoples, of which the Thai are the branch situated in central Thailand.

Thai Word with which the people inhabiting central Thailand traditionally have indicated themselves; during the days of heightened nationalism it became equated with a homophonous word meaning 'free'.

tha (literally) 'Landing place; ships' berth', name of a subdivision of the traditional Siamese Treasury.

that Class of slaves.

Traiphumikhatha Sacred work on the 'Three Worlds', versions of which were known in Siam as early as the fourteenth century. It has provided the Siamese with a framework with which to view the universe and the role humans play in it.

Uparat See *Maha Uparat*.

Wang Na The 'Front Palace', traditionally the residence of the *Maha Uparat*.

wanphra Buddhist regular 'sacred' day held four times each lunar month.

ya Rank of conferred nobility used in Ayutthaya times, obsolete during the Bangkok period.

Yokrabat Legal officer appointed by the king and attached to a provincial centre.

Reference Bibliography

Only sources mentioned in the notes are listed. The bibliography incorporates the abbreviations used; immediately after the abbreviation the full reference is given. Only in a few instances, when they are repeatedly cited for primary source material, are periodicals listed here, together with the dates of the issues consulted. Thai names are listed under the 'first name'.

Unpublished source:

P. H. I. G. M. Kempermann, German Minister Resident, Bangkok, Report No. 82, dated 27 August 1893, Politisches Archiv des auswärtigen Amts, R 19230.

Published sources:

Abha Bhamorabutr. *A Short History of Thailand.* Bangkok: Department of Corrections Press, 1979.

Adey Moore, R. 'An Early British Merchant in Bangkok'. *JSS* 11, pt 2 (1914-15), pp. 21-39. Kraus. Reprint, 1969.

Ahmad, H. Manzooruddin. *Thailand, Land der Freien.* Leipzig: W. Goldmann, 1943.

Akin Rabibhadana. *The Organization of Thai Society in the Early Bangkok Period, 1782-1873.* Data paper no. 74, Southeast Asian Program. Ithaca, N. Y.: Cornell University, 1969.

Alabaster, Henry. *The Wheel of the Law. Buddhism Illustrated from Modern Siamese Sources by The Modern Buddhist, A Life of Buddha and An Account of the Phrabat.* London: Trübner, 1871. Republished by Gregg International, 1971.

Amat, R. d', and R. Limuzin Lamothe, (eds.). *Dictionnaire de biographic française*, vol. 10. Paris: Libraire Letouzey, 1967.

Amon Darunarak. *Dusit Thani.* Bangkok: National Library, 1970.

Ampha Otrakul. *König Chulalongkorns Reisetagebuch, 'Glai Baan' (Fern von Zuhause).* Bonn: Deutsch-Thailandische Gesellschaft, 2001.

An Englishman's Siamese Journals 1890-1893, Bangkok: Siam Media International Books, n. d.

Bangkok Calendar. Annual, edited by D. B. Bradley. Bangkok, 1859-1872.

Batson, Benjamin A. Review of Thawatt Mokarapong, *History of the Thai Revolution: A Study in Political Behaviour. JSS* 61, pt 2 (1973), pp. 186-196.

_____. (ed.). *Siam's Political Future: Documents from the End of the Absolute Monarchy.* Data Paper no. 96, Southeast Asia Program. Ithaca, N. Y.: Cornell University, 1974.

_____. 'The Fall of the Phibun Government, 1944', *JSS* 62, Part 2 (1974), pp. 89-120.

_____. Review of Chai-Anan Samudvanija, *14 Tula: Khana Ratsadan kap Kabot Bowaradet. JSS* 63, pt 2 (1975), pp. 386-391.

_____. 'The End of the Absolute Monarchy in Siam'. Ph.D. dissertation, Cornell University, 1977.

_____.'Siam and Japan: The Perils of Independence', in Alfred W. McCoy, (ed.), *Southeast Asia under Japanese Occupation*, Yale University Southeast Asia Studies, Monograph No. 22, New Haven: Yale University, 1980.

Battye, Noel A. 'The Military, Government and Society in Siam, 1868-1910: Politics and Military Reform during the Reign of King Chulalongkorn'. Ph.D. dissertation, Cornell University, 1974.

Blankwaardt, W. 'Notes upon the Relations between Holland and Siam'. *JSS* 20, pt 3 (1927), pp. 241-258.

Blofeld, John. *King Maha Mongkut of Siam.* Singapore: Asia Pacific Press, 1972.

Bock, Carl. *Temples and Elephants: The Narrative of a Journey of Exploration Through Upper Siam and Lao.* London: Sampson Low, Marston, Searle and Rivington, 1884.

Bowie, Kathrine A. *Rituals of National Royalty*, New York: Columbia University Press, 1997.

Bowring, Sir John. *The Kingdom and People of Siam.* 2 vols. Oxford in Asia Historical Reprints. Kuala Lumpur: Oxford University Press, 1977.

Bradley, W. L. 'Prince Mongkut and Jesse Caswell'. *JSS* 54, pt 1, (1966), pp. 29-41.

_____. 'The Accession of King Mongkut'. *JSS* 57, pt 1 (1969), pp. 149-162.

Brailey, Nigel. *Two Views of Siam on the Eve of the Chakri Reformation*, Whiting Bay: Kiscadale Publications, 1989,

Bristowe, W. S. *Louis and the King of Siam.* London: Chatto and Windus, 1976.

Brown, Ian. 'British Financial Advisers in Siam in the Reign of King Chulalongkorn'. *Modern Asian Studies* 12, no. 2, (1978), pp. 193-215.

_____. 'Siam and the Gold Standard, 1902-1908'. *Journal of Southeast Asian Studies* 10, no. 2 (1979), pp. 381-399.

Bruijn Kops, G. F. de. *Statistiek van den Handel en de Scheepvaart op Java en Madura.* 2 vol. Batavia: Lange & Co., 1857-1858.

Brummelhuis, H. C. F. ten, 'De Waterkoning; J. Homan van der Heide, staatsvorming en de oorsprong van moderne irrigatie in Siam, 1902-1909', Ph.D. Dissertation, Amsterdam University, 1995.

Burney Papers, Bangkok 1910-1914, The. 5 vols. Reprinted by Gregg International, 1971.

Caron, F., and J. Schouten. *A True Description of the Mighty Kingdoms of Japan and Siam*, with introduction, notes and appendixes by C. R. Boxer. London: Argonaut Press, 1935.

Cartwright, B. O. 'The Huey Lottery'. *JSS* 18, pt 3 (1924), pp. 221-239.

Chaen Patdiusanon and Sawat Chantham, (eds.). *Koraniphiphat rawang Thai kap Farangset lae Kanrop thi Paknam Chaophraya samai r. s. 112*. Bangkok: Kromyutha-su'ksathahanru'a, 1967.

Chai-Anan Samudavanija. *The Thai Young Turks*. Singapore: Institute of Southeast Asian Studies, 1982.

Chaloem Yongbunkoet. *Thonabat Thai*. Bangkok: Thaikasem, 1961.

Chaloem Yuwiengchai. 'Prawatisat Nakhon Si Thammarat samai Krung Thonburi'.Raingankan-samanaprawatisat Nakhon Si Thammarat, Nakhon Si Thammarat Withayalaikhru, *Prawatisat Nakhon Si Thammarat*, Krung Sayamkanphim, 1978, pp. 218-268.

Chandler, David P. 'Cambodia's Relations with Siam in the Early Bangkok Period: The Politics of a Tributary State'. *JSS* 60, pt 1 (1972), pp. 153-169.

Chandran, Jeshurun. *The Contest for Siam 1889-1902: A Study in Diplomatic Rivalry*. Kuala Lumpur: Penerbit Universiti Kebang-saan Malaysia, 1977.

Chaofa Thammathibet, Phraprawat lae Phraniphon bot Roykrong: Bangkok: Bannakhan, 1973.

Charnvit Kasetsiri. *The Rise of Ayudhya: A History of Siam in the Fourteenth and Fifteenth Centuries*, Kuala Lumpur: Oxford University Press, 1976.

_____. 'The First Phibun Government and Its Involvement in World War II'. *JSS* 62, pt 2 (1974), pp. 25-88.

_____. 'Each Generation of Elites in Thai History'. Translated by Chantima Ongsuruksa. *Journal of Social Science Review* 1, No. 1 (1976), pp. 189-226.

Chatthip Nartsupha and Suthy Prasartset, (eds.). *Socioeconomic Institutions and Cultural Change in Siam, 1851-1910, a Documentary Survey*. Southeast Asian Perspectives No. 4. Singapore: Institute of Southeast Asian Studies, n.d.

_____. *The Political Economy of Siam, 1851-1910*. Bangkok: The Social Science Association of Thailand, n.d.

_____. Suthy Prasartset, and Montri Chenvidyakarn, (eds.). *The Political Economy of Siam, 1910-1932*. Bangkok: The Social Science Association of Thailand, 1978.

Chen, Chingho A. 'Mac Thien Tu and Phraya Taksin: A Survey of their Political Stands, Conflicts and Background'. *Proceedings, Seventh IAHA Conference, 22-26 August 1977, Bangkok* vol. 2, pp. 1534-75. Bangkok: Chulalongkorn University Press, 1979.

Cho, Hung-Guk. 'Die thailandische Denkschrift des Jahres 1885 und ihre historische Bedeutung (Mit einer vollständigen Ubersetzung des Original textes)', unpublished M. A. thesis, Hamburg University, 1987.

Chotmaihethon, chabap Phraya Munlathonrak. Bangkok: Sophonaphiphathanakon, 1921.

Chotmaihet Phraratchakitraiwan nai Phrabatsomdet Phrachunlachomklao Chaoyuhua Pi Tho Chunlasakarat 1241. Bangkok: Cremation volume for Phra Patiwetwisit (Sai Lekhayanon), 1970.

Chotmaihet Ratchakan thi Song, C. S. 1173. Bangkok: Munlanithi-phraboromarachanuson Phrabatsomdetphraphuthaloetlanaphalainai Phraboromarachupakam, 1961.

Chotmaihet ru'ang Ballestier Thut Amerikan khaoma nai Ratchakan thi Sam mu'a pi cho Ph.S. 2393. PP. vol. 35 (1969), pp. 3-71.

Christian, J. L. 'The Kra Canal Fable'. *Amerasia* 1 (February 1938), pp. 559-563.

Chula Chakrabongse, Prince. *Lords of Life: A History of the Kings of Thailand*. London: Alvin Redman, 1967.

_____. *The Twain Have Met, or An Eastern Prince Came West*. London: Foulis, 1956.

Chulachomklao Chaoyuhua, *phrabatsomdetphra. Phraratchahatlekha mu'a Sadetphrarat-chadamnoen Praphat Yurop Ph.S. 2440.* 2 vols. Bangkok: Khurusapha, 1962.

Coedès, George. *The Making of South East Asia.* Translated by H. M. Wright. London: Routledge & Kegan Paul, 1967.

_____. (ed.). 'The English Correspondence of King Mongkut'. *JSS* 21 (1927), pt 1, pp. 1-35, pt 2, pp. 127-77; 22 (1928), pt 1, pp. 1-18.

_____. and Charles Archaimbault. *Les trois mondes (Traibhumi Brah Rvan).* Publications de 1'École Française d'Extrême-Orient, vol. 89. Paris: École Française d'Extrême-Orient, 1973.

Collet, O. J. A. *Étude politique et économique sur le Siam moderne.* Brussels: Hayez, 1911.

Collis, Maurice. *Wayfoong, the Hongkong and Shanghai Banking Corporation.* London: Faber and Faber, 1965.

Connors, Michael Kelly. 'Framing the 'People's Constitution', in Duncan McCargo (ed.), *Reforming Thai Politics*, Copenhagen: NIAS Publishing, 2002, pp. 37-55.

Cosenza, M. E., (ed.). *The Complete Journal of Townsend Harris.* New York: Japan Society, 1930.

Cowan, W. L. 'The Role of Prince Chuthamani in the Modernizing of Siam and His Court Position During the Reigns of Rama III and Rama IV'. *JSS* 55, pt 1 (1967), pp. 41-59.

Crawfurd, John. *Journal of an Embassy to the Courts of Siam and Cochin China*. Oxford in Asia Historical Reprints. Kuala Lumpur: Oxford University Press, 1967.

Crawfurd Papers, The Bangkok: Vajiranana National Library, 1915. Reprinted by Gregg International, 1971.

Crosby, Sir Josiah. *Siam: the Crossroads*. London: Hollis and Carter, 1945.

Cucherousset, H. *Quelques informations sur le Siam*. Hanoi: Éditions de 1'Éveil Économique, 1925.

Curtis, L. J. *The Laos of North Siam*. London: Fleming H. Revell, 1903.

Cushman, Richard D. (transl.), *The Royal Chronicles of Ayutthaya, A Synoptic Translation*. Edited by David K. Wyatt, Bangkok: The Siam Society, 2000.

Damrong Ratchanuphap, *kromphra. Phraratchaphongsawadan Krungratanakosin Ratchakan thi Song*. 2 vols. Bangkok: Khurusapha, 1952.

_____. *Phongsawadan Ru'ang Thai Rop Phama*. PP, pt 6, vols. 5 and 6. Bangkok: Khurusapha, 1963.

_____. *Tamnanwangna*, PP, pt 13, vol. 11, pp. 1-176. Bangkok: Khurusapha, 1964.

_____. *Phraratchaphongsawadan Krungratanakosin Ratchakan thi Ha*. Bangkok: Cremation Volume for Chayan Phlachiwa, 1964.

DC First R – Chaophraya Thiphakorawong. *The Dynastic Chronicles Bangkok Era, the First Reign*. Edited by Thadeus and Chadin Flood. Vol. 1. Tokyo: The Centre for East Asian Cultural Studies, 1978.

DC Fourth R – Chaophraya Thiphakorawong, *The Dynastic Chronicles Bangkok Era, the Fourth Reign*. Translated by Chadin Flood. 5 vols. Tokyo: The Centre for East Asian Cultural Studies, 1965-1974.

Dhani Nivat, *kromamu'n*. 'The Reconstruction of Rama I of the Chakri Dynasty'. *JSS* 43, pt 1 (1955), pp. 21-48.

_____. 'The Age of King Rama I of the Chakri Dynasty'. *JSS* 46, pt 1 (1958): 51.

_____. 'The Inscriptions of Wat Phra Jetubon', *in Collected Articles by H. H. Prince Dhani Nivat Kromamu'n Bidayalabh Brdihyakorn*, pp. 5-28. Bangkok: The Siam Society, 1969.

_____. 'King Rama VI's Last Work', *in Collected Articles by H. H. Prince Dhani Nivat Kromamu'n Bidayalabh Brdihyakorn*, pp. 121-27. Bangkok: The Siam Society, 1969.

Dilock, Prinz von Siam. *Die Landwirtschaft in Siam: Ein Beitrag zur Wirtschaftsgeschichte des Königreichs Siam*. Tübingen: Laupp'schen Buchhandlung, 1907.

Direk Jayanama. *Siam and World War II*. Translated and edited by J.G. Keyes. Bangkok: The Social Science Association of Thailand, 1978.

Donner, Wolf. *Thailand ohne Tempel; Lebensfragen eines Tropenlandes*. Frankfurt (Main): R. G. Fischer, 1984.

Engel, David M. *Law and Kingship in Thailand During the Reign of King Chulalongkorn*. Michigan Papers on South and Southeast Asia, no. 9. Ann Arbor: The University of Michigan, Center for South and Southeast Asian Studies, 1975.

Englehart, Neil A. *Culture and Power in Traditional Siamese Government*, Ithaca: Cornell University Southeast Asia Program Publications, 2001.

Eulenberg-Hertfeld, P. zu. *Ost-Asien 1860-1862 in Briefen des Grafen Fritz zu Eulenberg*. Berlin: Mittler, 1900.

Farrington, Anthony (ed.). *Early Missionaries in Bangkok; The Journals of Tomlin, Gutzlaff and Abeel 1828-1832*, Bangkok: White Lotus, 2001.

Feeny, David. 'The Coevolution of Property Rights Regimes for Land, Man, and Forests in Thailand, 1790-1990', in John F. Richards (ed.), *Land, Property, and the Environment*, Oakland, Cal.: ICS Press, 2002, pp. 179-221.

Finlayson, George. *The Mission to Siam and Hue, the Capital of Cochin China, in the Years 1821-2*. London: John Murray, 1826.

Fistie, Pierre. *Sous-développement et utopie au Siam, le programme de réformes présenté en 1933 par Pridi Phanomyong*. The Hague: Mouton, 1969.

Flood, E. Thadeus. 'The 1940 Franco-Thai Border Dispute and Phibun Songkhram's Commitment to Japan'. *Journal of Southeast Asian History* 10, no. 2 (1969), pp. 304-325.

Fouser, Beth. *The Lord of the Golden Tower, King Prasat Thong and the Building of Wat Chaiwatthanaram*. Studies in Southeast Asian History, No. 3, Bangkok: White Lotus, 1996.

Frankfurter, O. 'The Mission of Sir James Brooke to Siam'. *JSS* 8, pt 3 (1911), pp. 19-33.

_____. 'Events in Ayuddhya from Chulasakaraj 686-966'. *The Siam Society Fiftieth Anniversary Commemorative Publication. Selected Articles from the Siam Society Journal*. Vol. 1, 1904-29. Bangkok: The Siam Society, 1954, pp. 38-64.

_____. 'The Unofficial Mission of John Morgan, Merchant, to Siam in 1821'. *JSS* 11 (1914-15), pp. 1-8.

Gerini, G. E. 'Trial by Ordeal in Siam and the Siamese Law of Ordeals'. *Asiatic Quarterly Review*, April 1895, pp. 415-24, and July 1895, pp. 156-175.

_____. 'Shan and Siam'. *Imperial and Asiatic Quarterly Review*, 1898, pp. 145-163.

_____. 'Historical Retrospect of Junkceylon Island'. *JSS* 2, pt 2, (1905), pp. 1-141.

_____. *A Retrospective View and Account of the Origin of the Thet Mahā Ch'at Ceremony*. Bangkok:Sathirakoses-Nagapradipa Foundation, 1976. Reprint of the 1892 edition.

Gervaise, Nicolas. *Histoire naturelle et politique du royaume de Siam*, Paris: Claude Barbin, 1688.

_____. *The Natural and Political History of the Kingdom of Siam*. Translated by H. S. O'Neill. Bangkok: Siam Observer Press, 1928.

Gesick, L. M. 'Kingship and Political Integration in Traditional Siam, 1767-1824'. Ph.D.dissertation, Cornell University, 1976.

Giles, F. H. 'A Critical Analysis of Van Vliet's Historical Account of Siam in the 17th Century'. *JSS* 30 (1938), pt 2, pp. 155-240, pt 3, pp. 271-380.

Goldman, M. F. 'Franco-British Rivalry over Siam, 1896-1904'. *Journal of Southeast Asian Studies* 3, no. 2 (1972): 210-228.

Graham, W. A. *Siam: A Handbook of Practical, Commerical, and Political Information*. 2 vols. 3ʳᵈ ed. London: Moring, 1924. Originally published in 1912.

Greene, Stephen L. W. 'King Wachirawut's Policy of Nationalism', *in In Memoriam Phya Anuman Rajadhon, Contributions in Memory of the Late President of the Siam Society*, Tej Bunnag and M. Smithies, (eds.), pp. 251-9. Bangkok: The Siam Society, 1970.

_____. *Absolute Dreams; Thai Government Under Rama VI, 1910-1925*. Bangkok: White Lotus, 1999.

Griswold, A. B. 'King Mongkut in Perspective'. *JSS* 45, pt 1 (1957), pp. 1-41.

_____. 'The Rishis of Wat Pho'. *Felicitation Volumes of Southeast-Asian Studies Presented to His Highness Prince Dhanivat Kromamun Bidyalabh Bridhyakorn*, vol. 2. Bangkok: The Siam Society, 1965, pp. 319-328.

Guehler, U. 'A Letter by Sir Robert H. Schomburgk H.B.M.'s Consul in Bangkok in 1860'. *JSS* 37, pt 2 (1949), pp. 149-154.

Gutzlaff, Karl. *Verslag van een Driejarig Verblijf in Siam, en van eene Reize langs de Kust van China naar Mantchou-Tartarije*. Rotterdam: Wijt & Zonen, 1833. The English version was published under the title 'Journal of a Residence in Siam and of a Voyage along the Coast of China to Mantchou Tartary' in the *Chinese Repository* 1 (1832), pp. 16-25, 45-64, 81-99, 122-40, and 180-196.

Hell, Stefan. 'The Role of European Technology, Expertise and Early Development Aid in the Modernization of Thailand Before the Second World War'. *Journal of the Asia Pacific Economy*, 6 pt 2 (2001), pp. 158-178.

Hirshfield, C. 'The Struggle for the Mekong Banks, 1892-1896'. *Journal of Southeast Asian History* 9, no. 1, 1968, pp. 25-52.

Homan van der Heide, J. 'The Economical Development of Siam During the Last Half Century'. *JSS* 3, pt 2 (1906), pp. 74-101.

Hong, Lysa. *Thailand in the Nineteenth Century: Evolution of the Economy and Society*, Singapore: ISEAS, 1984.

Htin Aung, Maung. 'Three Unpublished Papers by Harvey, Introduced, Explained and Commented Upon'. *Journal of the Burma Research Society* 58, pt 1 (1975), pp. 1-52.

Hunter, Eileen and Narisa Chakrabongse, *Katya & The Prince of Siam*. Bangkok: River Books, 1994.

Ingram, J. C. *Economic Change in Thailand 1850-1970*. Stanford, Cal.: Stanford University Press, 1971.

Ishii, Yoneo. 'A Note on Buddhist Millenarian Revolts in Northeastern Siam'. *Journal of Southeast Asian Studies* 6, no. 2 (1975), pp. 121-126.

_____. Osamu Akagi, and Shigeharu Tanabe. *An Index of Officials in Traditional Thai Governments, vol. 1, pt 1*, discussion paper no. 7. Kyoto: The Center for Southeast Asian Studies, 1974.

Isorn Pocmontri. *Negotiations between Britain and Siam on the Agreement for the Termination of their State of War, 1945: An Instance of Intervention by the United States in British Foreign Policy*, Bangkok: Chulalongkorn University Social Research Institute, 1982

Johnston, D. B. 'Opening a Frontier: the Expansion of Rice Cultivation in Central Thailand in the 1890's'. *Contributions to Asian Studies* 9 (1976), pp. 27-44.

Jones, R. B. *Thai Titles and Ranks, Including a Translation of Traditions of Royal Lineage by King Chulalongkorn*. Data Paper no. 81, Southeast Asia Program. Ithaca: Cornell University, 1971.

JSS – The Journal of the Siam Society, 1904 to the present. (Between 1942 and 1944 the journal appeared under the title *Journal of the Thailand Research Society*).

Kanlaya Chunnuan, (comp.). *Chaophraya Aphairat-chasayamanukunkit (Khutsatap Rolin Yakhmin)*. Bangkok: Krom Sinlapakon, 1972.

Kantaengtangkhunnangthai nai samai Ratchakan thi Ha. Bangkok: Konghochotmaihethaengchat Krom Sinlapakon, 1978.

Kemp, Jeremy. *Aspects of Siamese Kingship in the Seventeenth Century*. Bangkok: Social Science Association Press of Thailand, 1969.

Khana Kammakan Fu'nfu Burana Khai Bang Rachan. *Wirachon Khai Bang Rachan*. Bangkok: Rongphim Kansasana, 1966.

Ki Thanit. *Prawat Khana Song Thai kap Thammayut prakan*. Bangkok: Thamrat, 1975.

Kiernan, V. G. 'Britain, Siam and Malaya: 1875-1885'. *Journal of Modern History* 27, no. 1 (March 1956), pp. 1-20.

Koenig, J. G. 'Journal of a Voyage from India to Siam and Malacca in 1779'. *Journal of the Straits Branch of the Royal Asiatic Society*, no. 26 (January 1894), pp. 58-201; and no. 27 (October 1894), pp. 57-133.

KTSD – Kotmai Tra Sam Duang. 5 vols. Bangkok: Khurusapha edition, 1963.

L'Asie Française – Bulletin Mensuel du Comité de l'Asie Française. Paris: Comité de l'Asie Française, 1910-1917.

La Loubère, Simon de. *The Kingdom of Siam*. Oxford in Asia Historical Reprints. Kuala Lumpur:

Oxford University Press, 1969. Reprint of the 1693 edition.

La Revue du Pacifique – monthly, May 1922-March 1937.

Landon, Kenneth P. *Siam in Transition*. New York: Greenwood Press, 1939.

_____. *The Chinese in Thailand*. New York: Institute of Pacific Relations, 1941.

Lapomarède, R. de. 'The Setting of the Siamese Revolution'. *Pacific Affairs* 7 (September 1934), pp. 251-259.

Le May, Reginald, H. A. Ramsden, Ulrich Guehler and W. Harding Kneedler, *Siamese Coins and Tokens*, London: Andrew Publishing, 1977.

Leonowens, A. H. *The English Governess at the Siamese Court: Being Recollections of Six Years in the Royal Palace at Bangkok*. London: Trubner, 1870.

_____. *The Romance of the Harem*. Philadelphia: Porter and Coates, 1872. Lindenberg, P. P. 'The Early Postal History of Thailand'. *Journal of the Thailand Research Society* 35, pt 1 (1944), pp. 77-94.

Lingat, R. *L'esclavage privé dans le vieux droit siamois*. Paris: Éditions Domat-Montchrestien, 1931.

_____. 'La vie réligieuse du roi Mongkut'. *The Siam Society Fiftieth Anniversary Commemorative Publication*, 1, pp. 18-37. Bangkok: The Siam Society, 1954.

_____. 'Les suicides réligieux au Siam'. *Felicitation Volumes of Southeast-Asian Studies Presented to His Highness Prince Dhaninivat Kromamun Bidyalabh Bridhyakorn*, vol. 1, pp. 71-75. Bangkok: The Siam Society, 1965.

Lochner, Louis P. (transl. and ed.) *The Goebbels Diaries*, London: Hamish Hamilton, 1948.

Loohuis, J. G., and L. D. Petit, (eds). *Siam; Muang-Thai*. The Hague: Het Genootschap 'Nederland-Siam', 1931.

Low, James. 'On the Government of Siam'. *Asiatic Researches* 20, pt 2 (1836), pp. 245-284.

_____. 'On the laws of Mu'ung Thai or Siam'. *The Journal of the Indian Archipelago and Eastern Asia* 1 (1847): 327-429.

McFarland, George Bradley. *Thai-English Dictionary*. Stanford: Stanford University Press, 1954. First printed in 1944.

McGilvary, D. *A Half Century Among the Siamese and the Lao*. New York: Fleming H. Revell, 1912.

MacGregor, J. *Through the Buffer State: A Record of Recent Travels through Borneo, Siam, and Cambodia*. London: White, 1896.

Mandere, H. Ch. G. J. van der. 'Het tegenwoordige Siameesche Koninkrijk'. *De Indische Gids* 51, pt 2 (1929), pp. 919-936.

Manich Jumsai, *mom luang. King Mongkut and Sir John Bowring*. Bangkok: Chalermnit, 1970.

_____. *Popular History of Thailand*. Bangkok: Chalermnit, 1972.

_____. *Prince Prisdang's Files on His Diplomatic Activities in Europe, 1880-1886*. Bangkok: Chalermnit, 1977.

Maps of Bangkok AD. 1888 - 1931. Bangkok: Royal Thai Survey Department, 1984.

Martin, J. V. 'Thai-American Relations in World War II'. *Journal of Asian Studies* 21 (1963), pp. 451-467.

Minney, R. J. *Fanny and the Regent of Siam*, London: Collins, 1962.

Moffat, A. L. *Mongkut, the King of Siam*. Ithaca, N.Y.: Cornell University Press, 1961.

Mongkut, King of Siam. 'Brief Sketches of Siamese History, Facts from H.S.M. the late King Phra Chaum Klau in 1850'. *Siamese Repository*, 1869, pp. 254-67. This also appeared in the *Chinese Repository*, 1851 as well as in Bowring, *The Kingdom and People*, vol. 2.

_____. 'The English Correspondence of King Mongkut'. See under G. Coedès, ed.

Montri Umavijani. *A Poetic Journey Through Thai History*. Bangkok: privately published, n.d.

Morell, David and Chai-anan Samudavanija. *Political Conflict in Thailand; Reform, Reaction Revolution*. Cambridge, Mass.: Oelgeschlager, Gunn &. Hain, 1981.

Muecke, Marjorie A. 'The Village Scouts of Thailand'. *Asian Survey*, 20, No. 4, April 1980, pp. 407-27.

Murdoch, J. B. 'The 1901-1902 'Holy Man's' Rebellion'. *JSS* 62, pt 1 (1974), pp. 47-66.

Nanamoli, The Venerable Thera, transl. *The Patimokkha, 227 Fundamental Rules of a Bikkhu*. Bangkok: Maha Maku Academy, 1966.

'Naisuchinda'. *Phrapokklao Kasat Nakprachat-hipatai*. Bangkok: Samnakphim Sayam, 1976.

Neale, F. A. *Narrative of a Residence in Siam*. London: Office of the National Illustrated Library, 1852.

Neon Snidvongs. 'Siam's Relations with Britain and France in the Reign of King Mongkut, 1851-1868'. Ph.D. dissertation, University of London, 1961.

Net Khemayothin, *phon'ek. Ngan Tai Din khong Phan'ek Yothi*. 3 vols. Bangkok: Kasoem-bannakit, 1967.

Notton, C., (transl.). *The Chronicle of the Emerald Buddha*. Bangkok: Bangkok Times Press, 1933.

_____, (transl.). *La vie du poète Sounthone-Bhou*. Limoges: Rougerie, 1959.

Nuechterlein, Donald E. *Thailand and the Struggle for Southeast Asia*. Ithaca: Cornell University Press, 1965.

O'Kane, J., (transl.). *The Ship of Sulaiman*. Persian Heritage series no. 11. New York: Columbia University Press, 1972.

Owen, Norman G. 'The Rice Industry of Mainland Southeast Asia, 1850-1914'. *JSS* 59, pt 2 (1971), pp. 75-143.

Pallegoix, J. B. *Description du royaume Thai ou Siam*. 2 vols. Farnborough: Gregg International, 1969. Reprinted from the 1854 edition.

Pavie, A. *Eine friedliche Eroberung, Indochina 1888*.Vienna: Buchgemeinschaft, n.d. Translated from the French edition of 1947 by S. Pruvost-Seguin.

Pensri (Suvanij) Duke. *Les relations entre la France et la Thailande (Siam) au XIXe siècle d' après les archives étrangères*. Bangkok: Chalermnit, 1962.

Periodicals and Newspapers Printed in Thailand between 1844-1934, a Bibliography. Bangkok: Department of Fine Arts, 1970.

Petit, L. D. *Siameesche Bouwkunst*. Mouseion-reeks, no. 3. Amsterdam: Van Munster, n.d.

Photchananukrom Chabap Ratchabanthitsathan. Bangkok: Ratchabanthitsathan, 1950.

Phraison Salarak, *luang* (transl.). 'Intercourse between Burma and Siam as Recorded in Hmannan Yazawindawgyi'. *JSS*, 11, Pt.3, pp. 1-67,

Phraratchaniyom nai Phrabatsomdet Phramongkutklao Chaoyuhua. Bangkok: Cremation volume for Nang Charatsi Sucharitkun, 1971.

Piyachat Pitawan. *Kanyokloekrabopphrai nai Ratchasamai Phrabatsomdetphra Chulachomklao rawang Ph.S. 2411-2453*. Bangkok: Munlanithikhrongkantamra Sangkhomsat lae Manutsayasat, 1980.

PKRt Sam – chaophraya Thiphakorawong. *Phraratcha-phongsawadan Krungratanakosin, Ratchakan thi Song*. Bangkok: Khurusapha, 1961.

PKRt Song – chaophraya Thiphakorawong. *Phraratchaphongsawadan Krungratanakosin, Ratchakan thi Song*. Bangkok: Khurusapha, 1961.

PP – Prachum Phongsawadan. The collected chronicles of Siam, a multi-volume series published between 1961 and 1970. Where I have consulted other versions than this recent Khurusapha edition, these are mentioned separately.

Prachoom Chomchai, (ed. and transl.).*Chulalongkorn the Great*. East Asian Cultural Studies Series, no. 8. Tokyo: The Centre for East Asian Cultural Studies, 1965.

Pradit Kraiwong. *Taksin Maharat*. Bangkok: Pramuanson, 1965. *Prap Ngiew Ton Thi 1, PP*, pt75. Bangkok: Cremation volume for *mom* Yu'an Thongyai na Ayutthaya, 1974.

Prawatkitchakanthahan samai Krungratanakosin. Bangkok: Cremation volume for *phan' ek phraya* Damkoengronaphop (That Pathamanon) and *nangsaw* Phian Pathamanon, 1967.

Prayut Sitthiphan. *Phramahathiraratchao*. Bangkok: Sayam, 1972.

Prem Chaya and Alethea. *The Passing Hours: A Record of Five Amazing Years*. Bangkok: Chatra Books, 1945.

Prida Wacharangkun. *Phrapokklao kap Rabop Prachathipatai*. Bangkok: Phranakhon Printers, 1977.

Programme of the Coronation of His Majesty Vajiravudh, King of Siam. Bangkok, 1911.

Prungsi Wanliphodom. 'Phraprang Wat Arunratchawaram', in *Chaloem Phrakiet Phrabatsomdet Phraphuthaloetla*, pp. 41-51. Bangkok, 1978.

Ratchaburidirekru't, *kromaluang*. *Kotmai Lem* 1. Bangkok: Cremation volume for *phanahua phontho* Amphon Sichaiyan, 1970.

Ratchasakunwong. Bangkok: Cremation volume for *nai* Sanan Bunsiriphan, 1969.

Rajaretnam, M. *Thailand's Kra Canal: Some Issues*. Research Notes and Discussions Paper no. 8. Singapore: Institute of Southeast Asian Studies, 1978.

Ramsay, J. A. 'The Development of a Bureaucratic Policy: the Case of Northern Siam'. Ph.D. dissertation, Cornell University, 1971.

Reynolds, C. J. 'The Buddhist Monkhood in Nineteenth Century Thailand'. Ph.D. dissertation, Cornell University, 1973.

_____. (ed. and transl.). *Autobiography: The Life of Prince-Patriarch Vajirañana of Siam, 1860-1921*. Athens, Ohio: Ohio University Press, 1979.

Reynolds, E. E. *Baden-Powell: A Biography of Lord Baden-Powell of Gilwell*. 2nd ed. London: Oxford University Press, 1957.

Rian Sichan and Net Phunwiwat. *Kabot R.S. 130 (Kanpatiwat khrang raek khong Thai)*. 5th printing. Bangkok: Khamphi, 1976.

Riggs, Fred W. *Thailand, The Modernization of a Bureaucratic Polity*. Honolulu: East-West Center Press, 1966.

Roberts, Edmund. *Embassy to the Eastern Courts of Cochin-China, Siam and Muscat; in the U. S. Sloop-of-War Peacock, David Geisinger, Commander, During the Years 1832-3-4*. New York: Harper & Brothers, 1837.

Rong Syamananda. *A History of Thailand*. 2nd edition. Bangkok: Thai Watana Panich, 1973.

Rosenberg, Klaus. *Nation und Fortschritt: Der Publizist Thien Wan und die Modernisierung Thailands unter König Culalongkon (r. 1868-1910)*. Hamburg: Mitteilungen der Gesellschaft für Natur-und Völkerunde Ostasiens (OAG), vol. 78, 1980.

Saengsom Kasemsri, *momratchawong*, and Wimon Phongphiphan, comp. *Prawatisat Thai Samai Ratanakosin Ratchakan thi Nu'ng thu'ng Ratchakan thi Song*. Bangkok: Khanakammakan Chamra Prawatisat Thai Samnak Nayokrathamontri, 1980.

Saint-Hubert, C. de. 'Rolin-Jaequemyns (Chao Phya Aphay Raja) and the Belgian Legal Advisers in Siam at the Turn of the Century'. *JSS* 53, pt 2 (1965), pp. 181-190.

Sander, Ingvar and Gerhard Reinecke (eds.). *Thailand: Aktuelle Wandlungsprozesse in Politik, Wirtschaft, Umwelt und Gesellschaft*, Mitteilungen des Instituts für Asienkunde Hamburg Nr. 328. Hamburg: Institut für Asienkunde, 2000.

Sarasas, Phra. *My Country Thailand (Its History, Geography and Civilisation)*. Tokyo: Maruzen, 1943.

Sarasin Viraphol. *Tribute and Profit: Sino-Siamese Trade 1652-1853*. Cambridge, Mass.: Harvard University Press, 1977.

SarDesai, D. R. *British Trade and Expansion in Southeast Asia, 1830-1914*. New Delhi: Allied Publishers, 1977.

Schaek, I. de, *S. A. I. le grand-duc Boris de Russe aux fêtes du Siam pour le couronnement du roi*. Paris: Plon, 1914.

Seni Pramoj, M. R. and M. R. Kukrit Pramoj. *A King of Siam Speaks*. Bangkok: The Siam Society, 1987.

Senn van Basel, W. H. *Schetsen uit Siam*. Amsterdam: J. H. de Bussy, 1880.

Shunyu, Xie. *Siam and the British, 1874-75: Sir Andrew Clarke and the Front Palace Crisis*, Bangkok: Thammasat University Press, 1988.

Siam Repository – Bangkok: quarterly, 1869-1874.

Sithi-Amnuai, P. *Finance and Banking in Thailand: A Study of the Commercial System, 1888-1963*. Bangkok: Thai Watana Panich, 1964.

Sivaram, M. *Mekong Clash and Far East Crisis: A Survey of the Thailand-Indochina Conflict and the Japanese Mediation*. Bangkok: Thai Commercial Press, 1941.

Siworawat, *luang*. Phongsawadan *Mu'ang* Phathalung. *PP*, vol. 12, pt 15. Bangkok: Khurusapha, 1964.

Skinner, Cyril. *The Civil War in Kelantan in 1839*, Monographs of the Malaysian Branch, Royal Asiatic Society, Singapore: Malaysia Printers, 1965.

Skinner, G. William. *Chinese Society in Thailand: An Analytical History*, Ithaca: Cornell University Press, 1957.

Skrobanek, Walter. *Buddhistische Politik in Thailand; mit besonderer Berücksichtigung des heterodoxen Messianismus*, Beiträge zur Südasien-Forschung, Südasien-Institut, Universität Heidelberg, Band 23, Wiesbaden: Franz Steiner verlag, 1976.

Small, L. E. 'Historical Development of the Greater Chao Phya Water Control Project: An Economic Perspective'. *JSS* 61, pt 1 (1973), pp. 1-24.

Smith, B. A. 'The King of Siam'. *The Contemporary Review* 71 (January-June 1897), pp. 884-891.

Smith, H. B. 'Historic Proposals for a Kra Canal: Their Impact on International Relations in Southeast Asia with Emphasis on British Perspectives'. *Asian Profile* 3, no. 1 (February 1975), pp. 43-58.

Smith, M. 'The Families of the Kings of Siam of the House of Chakri'. *Annals of Eugenics* 12 (1943-45), pp. 151-157.

_____. *A Physician at the Court of Siam*. London: Country Life, 1947.

Smith, M. J. 'Taksin the Savior of Siam'. *Sawaddi*, March-April 1968, pp. 18-20 and 29-31.

Smith, R. B. *Siam or the History of the Thais, from 1569 A.D. to 1824 A.D.* Bethesda, Maryland: Decatur Press, 1967.

Somathat Thewet. *Chaofa Chuthamani*. Bangkok: Phrae Phithaya, 1970.

Somdetphraboromorotsathirat Sayammakutratchakuman. Commemoration volume at the Installation of Crown Prince Mahawachiralongkon, 18 December 1972. Bangkok: *krom* Sinlapakon, 1972.

Sonthi Techanan, ed. *Phaenphathana Kanmu'angpai Su Kanpokkhrong rabop Prachathipatai tam Naew Phraratchadamri khong Phrabatsomdet Phrapokklaochaoyuhua (Ph.S. 2469-2475)*. Bangkok: Kasetsat University, 1976.

Souvenir of the Siamese Kingdom Exhibition at Lumbini Park B. E. 2468, The. Bangkok: Siam Free Press, 1927.

Stengs, Irene. 'A Kingly Cult; Thailand's Guiding Lights in a Dark Era'. *Etnofoor*, vol. 12, pt 2, 1999, pp. 41-75.

_____. 'Worshipping the Great Moderniser; The Cult of King Chulalongkorn, Patron Saint of the Thai Middle Class'. Ph.D. Dissertation, Amsterdam University, 2002.

Sternstein, L. 'From Ayutthaya to Bangkok'. *Hemisphere* 17. no. 11 (November 1973): 14-21.

Stockmann, H. *Muay-Thai: The Art of Siamese Unarmed Combat*. Bangkok: Duang Kamol, 1979.

Stoughton, E. W. 'The Opium Trade – England and China'. *Hunt's Merchants' Magazine* 2 (1840), pp. 394-413.

Straits Times. I have consulted issues between 1854, when it appeared as a weekly, *The Straits Times and Singapore Journal of Commerce*, and 1926 when it was a daily, the *Straits Times*.

Stransky, J. *Die Wiedervereinigung Thailands unter Taksin, 1767-1782*. Hamburg: Gesellschaft für Natur- und Völkerkunde Ostasiens, 1973.

Stuart-Fox, Martin. *The Lao Kingdom of Lan Xang: Rise and Decline*, Bangkok: White Lotus, 1998.

Suchit Bunbongkarn. 'Political Institutions and Processes' in Somsakdi Xuto (ed.), *Government and Politics of Thailand*. Singapore: Oxford University Press, 1987, pp. 41-74.

Tanabe, Shigeharu. 'Historical Geography of the Canal System in the Chao Phraya River Delta'. *JSS* 65, pt 2 (1977), pp. 23-72.

Tarling, N. 'Siam and Sir James Brooke'. *JSS* 48, pt 2 (1960), pp. 43-72.

_____. 'The Mission of Sir John Bowring to Siam'. *JSS* 50, pt 2 (1962), pp. 91-118.

_____. 'Harry Parkes' Negotiations in Bangkok in 1856'. *JSS* 53, pt 2 (1965), pp. 153-180.

_____. 'The Bowring Mission: The Mellersh Narrative'. *JSS* 63, pt 1 (1975), pp. 105-126.

Taylor, John. 'Social Activism and Resistance on the Thai Frontier: The Case of Phra Prajak Khuttajitto'. *Bulletin of Concerned Asian Scholars*, Vol. 25, No.2, 1993, pp. 3-17.

Tej Bunnag. *The Provincial Administration of Siam, 1892-1915: The Ministry of the Interior under Prince Damrong Rajanubhab*. Kuala Lumpur: Oxford University Press, 1977.

Terwiel, Barend Jan. 'The Tais and Their Belief in Khwans'. *South East Asian Review* 3, no. 1 (1978), pp. 1-16.

_____. *Monks and Magic: An Analysis of Religious Ceremonies in Central Thailand*. Scandinavian Institute of Asian Studies Monograph Series no. 24. 2nd ed. London: Curzon Press, 1979.

_____. 'Tattooing in Thailand's History'. *Journal of the Royal Asiatic Society*, 1979, pt 2, pp. 156-166.

_____. *The Tai of Assam and Ancient Tai Ritual. Vol. 1, Life-cycle Ceremonies*. Gaya: Centre for South East Asian Studies, 1980.

_____. 'Towards a History of Chanthaburi, 1700-1860: The French Sources', International Conference on Thai Studies, August 22-24, 1984, Bangkok, Vol. 8, pp. 1-19.

_____. 'Formal Structure and Informal Rules: An Historical Perspective on Hierarchy, Bondage and the Patron-Client Relationship', in H. ten Brummelhuis and J. H. Kemp (eds.), *Strategies and Structures in Thai Society*. University of Amsterdam: Department of South and Southeast Asian Studies, 1984, pp. 19-38.

_____. 'Asiatic Cholera in Siam: Its First Occurrence and the 1820 Epidemic', in N. G. Owen (ed.) *Death and Disease in Southeast Asia*, Singapore:Oxford University Press, 1987, pp. 142-161.

_____. 'The Bowring Treaty: Imperialism and the Indigenous Perspective', the *JSS* 79, pt 2 (1992), pp. 40-47.

_____. 'Thailand', *in* Bernhard Dahm and Roderich Ptak (eds.), *Südostasien-Handbuch*. Munich: Beck, 1999, pp. 320-32.

_____. 'Van Denkmodellen en Vooroordelen: Thaise Geschiedschrijving over de Periode van de Eerste Helft van de Negentiende Eeuw'. Inaugural lecture on the occasion of accepting the extraordinary chair for Mainland Southeast Asia at Leiden University. Leiden: IIAS, February 2000.

_____. 'Between Moulmein and Bangkok: The Mass Migration of Mons in the first half of the Nineteenth Century', in Leonard Blussé and Felipe Fernandez-Armesto (eds.) *Shifting Communities and Identity Formation in Early Modern Asia*, Leiden: Research School of Asian, African, and Amerindian Studies (CNWS), 2003, pp. 107-116.

Thak Chaloemtiarana, (ed.). *Thai Politics: Extracts and Documents, 1932-1957*. Bangkok: The Social Science Association of Thailand, 1978.

Thamsook Numnonda. 'The Anglo-Siamese Secret Convention of 1897'. *JSS* 53, pt 1 (1965), pp. 45-60.

_____. 'Khabuankan R. S. 130'. *Warasan Thammasat* 8, pt 2 (October-November 1978), pp. 2-29.

_____. Pibulsongkram's Thai Nation-Building Programme during the Japanese Military Presence, 1941-1945. *Journal of Southeast Asian Studies* 9, no. 2 (September 1978), pp. 234-247.

Thawatt Mokarapong. *History of the Thai Revolution: A Study in Political Behaviour*. Bangkok: Chalermnit, 1972.

The Directory for Bangkok and Siam for 1894, Bangkok: Bangkok Times, reprinted as *The 1894 Directory for Bangkok and Siam*, Bangkok: White Lotus 1996.

Thinaphan Nakhata. 'National Consolidation and Nation-Building (1939-1947)', in Thak Chaloemtiarana, ed., *Thai Politics*, pp. 243-562.

Thiphakorawong, *chaophraya*. See *DC First R, DC Fourth R, PKRt Sam* and *PKRt Song*.

Thompson, V. *Thailand, the New Siam*. New York: Paragon Book Reprint, 1967.

Thongchai Winichakul. *Siam Mapped: A History of the Geo-Body of a Nation*. Chiangmai: Silkworm, 1994.

Turton, A. 'Thai Institutions of Slavery', in *Asian and African Systems of Slavery*, ed. J. L. Watson. Oxford: Blackwell, 1979.

Turpin, F. H. *Histoire civile et naturelle du royaume de Siam*. Paris: Costard, 1771.

_____. *History of the Kingdom of Siam*. Translated by B.O. Cartwright. Bangkok: American Presbyterian Mission Press, 1908.

Udom Poshakrishna. 'Geschichte der Chirurgie in Thailand, 1828-1922'. *JSS* 51, pt 1 (1963), pp. 59-73.

Vella, Walter F. *Siam Under Rama III*. Locust Valley, N. Y.: Augustin, 1957.

_____. 'Siamese Nationalism in the Plays of Rama VI'. Paper presented at the 28th International Congress of Orientalists, Canberra, 1971. Mimeographed.

_____. *Chaiyo!: King Vajiravadh and the Development of Thai Nationalism*. Honolulu: The University Press of Hawaii, 1978.

Vichitr Vadakarn, *luang. Thailand's Case*. Bangkok: Thai Commercial Press, 1941.

Vickery, Michael. Review of *Thai Titles and Ranks*, by R. B. Jones. *JSS* 62, pt 1 (1974), pp. 158-173.

_____. 'A Note on the Date of the Traibhumikatha'. *JSS* 62, pt 2 (1974), pp. 275-284.

_____. Review of Yoneo Ishii et al. An Index. *JSS* 63, pt 2 (1975), pp. 419-430.

Vincent, F. *The Land of the While Elephant.* London: Sampson Low, Marston, Low and Searle, 1873.

Wales, H. G. Q. *Siamese State Ceremonies: Their History and Function.* London: Bernard Quaritch, 1931.

_____. *Ancient Siamese Government and Administration.* New York: Paragon Book Reprint, 1965. A reprint of the 1934 edition.

_____. *Supplementary Notes on Siamese State Ceremonies.* London: Bernard Quaritch, 1971.

Waley, Arthur. *The Opium War through Chinese Eyes.* London: Alien and Unwin, 1958.

Wan Waithayakon, Prince. 'Thai Culture'. *JSS* 35, pt 2 (1944), pp. 135-145.

Warrington Smith, H. *Five Years in Siam, From 1891-1896, Volumes 1 and 2,* Bangkok: White Lotus, 1994 (reprint of the 1898 edition).

Weiler, L. *Anfang der Eisenbahn in Thailand.* Bangkok: Chalermnit, 1979.

Wells, Kenneth E. *History of Protestant Work in Thailand, 1828-1958.* Bangkok: Church of Christ in Thailand, 1958.

Wenk, Klaus. 'Ein Lehrgedicht für junge Frauen – Suphasit son ying – des Sunthon Phu'. *Oriens Extremus* 12, pt 1 (1965), pp. 65-106.

_____. *The Restoration of Thailand Under Rama I, 1782-1809.* The Association for Asian Studies Monographs and Papers, no. 24. Tucson: University of Arizona Press, 1968.

_____. *Phali Lehrt die Jungeren – Phali son nong.* Hamburg: Gesellschaft für Natur- und Völkerkunde Ostasiens, 1977.

Wilson, Constance M. 'State and Society in the Reign of Mongkut, 1851-1869: Thailand on the Eve of Modernization'. Ph.D. dissertation, Cornell University, 1970.

Wira Wimoniti. *Historical Patterns of Tax Administration in Thailand.* Bangkok: Institute of Public Administration, Thammasat University, 1961.

'Withetkarani'. *Sarakhadi Prawatisat Thangkonmu'ang Thai, Hetkan Thangkanmu'ang 43 Pi Haengprakop Prachathipatai.* Bangkok: Ruamkanphim, 1975.

Wood, W. A. R. A *History of Siam, from the Earliest Times to the Year A. D. 1781.* Bangkok: The Siam Barnakich Press, 1933.

Wook Moon, J. 'United States Relations with Thailand: The Mission of Townsend Harris'. *Asian Profile* 1, no. 2 (1973), pp. 355-363.

Wuthichai Munsin. *Kanpatirupkansu'ksa nai Ratchakan thi 5.* Bangkok: Samakhom Sangkhomsat haeng Prathet Thai, 1973.

Wright, Joseph J. *The Balancing Act: A History of Modern Thailand.* Bangkok: Asia Books, 1991.

Wyatt, David K. 'Siam and Laos, 1767-1827'. *Journal of Southeast Asian History* 4, no. 2 (September 1963), pp. 13-32.

_____. 'Samuel McFarland and Early Educational Modernization in Thailand, 1877-1895'. *Felicitation Volumes of Southeast-Asian Studies Presented to His Highness Prince Dhaninivat Kromamun Bidyalabh Bridhyakorn,* vol. 1, pp. 1-16. Bangkok: The Siam Society, 1965.

_____. 'Family Politics in Nineteenth Century Thailand'. *Journal of Southeast Asian History* 9, no. 2 (1968), pp. 208-228.

_____. *The Politics of Reform in Thailand: Education in the Reign of King Chulalongkorn.* New Haven, Conn.: Yale University Press, 1969.

_____. 'King Chulalongkorn the Great: Founder of Modern Thailand'. *Asia,* supplement no. 2, 1976.

Young, Edward M. *Aerial Nationalism: A History of Aviation in Thailand.* Washington: Smithsonian Institution Press, 1995.

Warasan lae nangsu'phim nai Prathet Thai su'ng tiphim rawang Ph. S. 2387-2477, Bannanukrom, Nuai Warasan, Hosamuthaengchat. Bangkok: Krom Sinlapakon, 1970.

Zoomers, Henk. 'De Siamese elite in de perceptie van Nederlandse bezoekers van Siam: 1857-1863', in Raymond Feddema (ed), *Wat beweegt de bamboe? Geschiedenissen in Zuidoost Azië.* Amsterdam: Het Spinhuis, 1992, pp. 41-69.

Index

Dilok, *kromamu'n* 243
Directions of the compass, ritual function of 14
Dit Bunnak *see* Phrakhlang of the Third Reign; Elder Somdet
Dusit Samit 245
Dusit Tham 244-246

Economic crisis 246-247, 258-260, 288
Economic development 161-164
Edict: on combatting cholera 94
    on gambling 49, 69
    on prisoners 85
    on selling slaves 69-70
    on tattooing 50-51, 85
Education reform 178, 185, 213, 216-217
Ekathat, King of Siam 34-36, 40, 43, 70
Elder *somdet* (Dit Bunnak) 138, 145, 179, 194, *see also* Phrakhlang of the Third Reign
Elephants 25
    in warfare 36, 37, 143
    white 103, 116, 145-146
Emerald Buddha, temple of the 70, 82, 236, *see also* Wat Phrakaew
Etiquette 140, 271-272
Exhibition, national 193, 248, 249

Fang, *Phra* 42, 44, 46-48
Finlayson, George 101-102, 115, 122
First Foot Guard 189-191, 200
Food shortage 45, 47, 71, 72, 74, 112, 246, *see also* Rice
Foreign advisers 210, 212, 219, 220-221, 224-225, 244, 248, 255-256, 259
France: and liquor licenses 191
    and the Kra Canal 192-193
    confronting Siam 206-212
    relations with Siam 154-156, 185, 200, 215
Front Palace, *see* Wang Na; *Uparat*

Gambling: abolition of 178, 204
    decree on 49, 67-68
    fn 40, 78, 221
    state lottery 110
    tax on 164
Gold mine 115
Guard, royal 13-14
Gulf of Thailand 11, 292
Gutzlaff, Karl 112, 115, 120

Harris, Townsend 147 fn 56
Ha Tien 50, 56-57, 116
Hillier, C. B. 147-148, 150
Ho gangs 186, 199-200, 207
Hsinbyushin, King of Burma 33, 36, 51, 53
Huahin 262, 264, 266
Hunter, Robert 112, 117-118, 124-126, 128, 132, 145

In, *mu'ang* 89
Inao 80
Income of princes: during Ayutthayan times 14
    during the first reign 79
    during the fourth reign 136, *see also bia-wat*
Insignia of rank 17, 20
Inthaphat 80
Intharaphitak, *kromakhun* 59, 60
Inthra Aphai, *phra* 92
Isthmus of Kra 11, 77, 192-193, 224
Itsaret, *kromakhun* 120, 126, 130, 136-137, *see also* Chuthamani; Phra Pinklao
Itsarasunthon, prince 85 fn 1, *see also* Rama II

Jatakas 118
Java 164
Johore 121

Kabinburi 11
Kalahom, *krom* 11, 17, 18 fn 29, 22, 66-7, 72, 87, 102-103, 115, 166, 205
Kamphaeng Phet 20, 40, fn 16, 87, 89-90
Kancha, use of 122
Kanchanaburi 72, 89, 119, 290
Kanlayanmit family 179, 205
Kaset, *krom see* Na
Kathin robe giving 82, 176
Kawila, *phraya* 73, 76, 80
Kawilorot 186
Kedah 73, 93, 121-22, 123, 224
Kelantan 73, 97, 121, 224
Kham Bunnak *see* Rawiwong; Thiphakorawong
Khamphran 89
Khmer language 11
Khotchasena family 179
Khotchasi 17
Khorat plateau 42, 212
Khridet family 179
Khuang Aphaiwong 276, 280, 281
Khunnang 22, 172
Kitchanukit 159
Kitiyakon *see* Chanthaburi
Knox, Fanny 187-188
Knox, Sir Thomas 182, 187-188
Koenig, J. G. 54-55
Kot, *krom see* Phrakhlang
Kotmai Lilit 81
Kotmai Tra Sam Duang 81, 295
Kriangsak Chomanand 286
Krit Sivara 284
Krom ranks 15, 21, 66, 67, 92, 108, 114, 136, 138
Kuiburi 11, 33
Kukrit Pramoj 285

La Loubère, Simon de 12, 37
Lamduan 80-81

and Sri Lanka 93, 94
and United States 93, 95-96, 129, 208, 279
Siam Land, Canals and Irrigation Company 205, 212, 220
Siam Observer 241
Singapore 118, 158, 161, 184
    and opium 121
    and royal travel 176, 177, 257
    and trade 96, 97, 130, 164
Singapore Free Press 136
Singapore Straits Times 136, 154
Singhasena family 173, 179, 195
Sing Singhasena *see* Bodindecha; Nikorabodin; Rachasuphawadi
Singu, King of Burma 53
Siphiphat, *phraya* (That Bunnak) 109, 129, 138. *See also* Younger *somdet*
Sirikit, Queen of Thailand 283
Sisorarak, *chamu'n* 139
Sisuren, *kromamu'n* 92
Sisuriyawong *chaophraya* (Chuang Bunnak) 131, 139, 152, 166, 171-173, 175, 177
    and modernization 140, 153, 161, 181
    and the Palace Incident 181-185
    general assessment of role 194-196
    relation with Rama IV 147, 156-157
    relation with Rama V 188-191, 195-196, 214
    role in making Bowring treaty 144-146, 161
    travel 142, 184
Sithammathirat, *phraya* 18, 73
Skinner, G. W. 74-75
Slavery 90-91
    abolition 178, 180, 194
    rules 69-70
Slaves 26, 86, 99, 174
    runaway 105
Smallpox: epidemic 72
    inoculation 121, 238
Sodaban 55, 57-58, 67
Songkhla 74, 123, 166, 266
Songsuradet, *phraya* (Thep Phanthumasen) 261, 263, 265, 269
Sorawichit, *luang* 64, 67, 79 *see also* Phiphatkosa
Sport 241, 248
    boat racing 79
    boxing 76-77
    football 241, 248
Sri Lanka 93, 94
Steam engines 146, 153, 162
Suan Kulap school 241
Succession: considerations on 131, 171-172
    rules of 13 fn 6, 231, 249-250
    struggle 27-28
Suchinda Kraprayun 288
Sugar 96-97, 124, 162-163, *see also* Taxation
Sukhothai 87, 89, 101
Sunthon Phu, *phra* 94 fn 26

Suphanburi 35, 34, 35, 38, 89, 290
Sura, *luang* 67
Surasak, *chaophraya* 205, 219, s*ee also* Choem Saengchuto; Waiworanat
Surasena, *phraya* 139
Surasi, *chaophraya* 59, s*ee also* Bunma
Suratsawadi, *krom see* Satsadi
Surawongwaiyawat, *chaophraya* (Won Bunnak) 173, 190, 192, 196, 202, 203
Suriya, *phraya* 225
Suriya Aphai, *phraya* 59, 64, 67 *see also* Anurakthewet
Suriyawongkosa, *phraya* 98

Tak, *mu'ang* 34, 40, 50, 71
Tak, *phraya see* Taksin
Taksin, King of Siam 39-41, 64-68, 74-75, 92, 293
    administration 53-63
    and Buddhist monks 45-49, 57-58
    and Catholic missionaries 51-53
    conqueror of Siam 41-49
    cremation 70
    execution 60, 294
    protector of the people 43, 45, 49
    relation with southern region 60 fn 76
Talapoin, origin of the word 54 fn 61
Tattooing 16 fn 22
    decree 50; drive 77, 86, 129, 150, 174, 190
Tavoy 35, 32, 34, 43, 74, 77-78, 108
Taxation 29-30, 87-90, 100-2, 105, 127, 164-168, 213-214, 259
    evasion 61
    on alcohol 22, 101, 115, 164
    on bamboo 113
    on fruit trees 23, 87, 164
    on gambling 164
    on rice land 22, 87, 90, 100, 166, 180, 213-214
    on salt 108
    on sugar 124, 125, 127, 167, 168
    on teak logs 113
Teak 113, 115, 124
Telegraphy 194, 218
Tenasserim 11, 20, 33, 35, 36, 38, 77
Tha, *krom* 18, 67, 87, 166
Tha Chin River 110
Thailand, name change from Siam to 271, 279, *see also* Siam
Thaksin Shinawatra 289
Tham *khwan ceremony* 90
Thammapurohit, *phraya* 80
Thammasat, *luang* 81
Thammasat, *phra*, legal code 12
Thammasat University 270, 283-284, 286
Thammathikon, *chaophraya* 139
Thammathibet, *chaofa* 34
Thammayutikanikaya 120
Thamrong Nawasawat 281
Thanai 23, 174

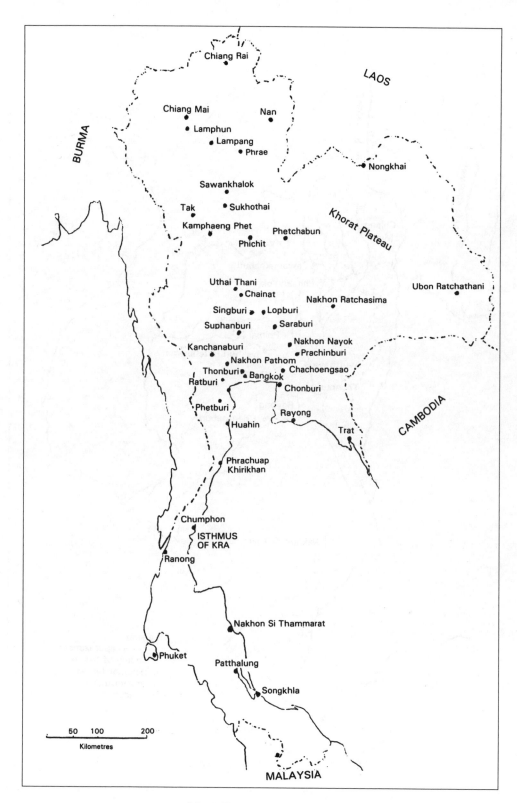

Map 1. Thailand (present borders).

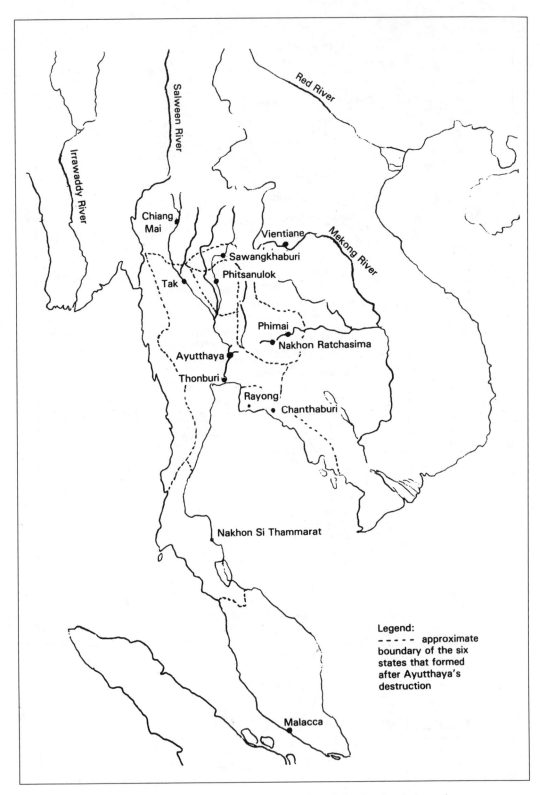

Map 2. Approximate boundary of the six states that formed after Ayutthaya's destruction.

Plate 20. Crown Prince Maha Vajirunahis, seated on a palanquin while King Chulalongkorn looks on in front of the Aphonphimok Prasat Throne Hall in the Grand Palace at the occasion of the tonsure ceremony.
From: *Voyage autour du monde par le Comte de Beauvoir*, Paris: 1868, p. 521.

Plate 21. The female armed guards at the women's compound.
From: *Voyage autour du monde par le Comte de Beauvoir*, Paris: 1868, p. 516.

Plate 22. Elephants captured near Ayutthaya.
From: G. B. Bacon, *Siam – the Land of the White Elephant as It Was and Is*. New York, 1893, p. 127.

Plate 23. Ayutthaya in ruins.
From: *Die Katholischen Missionen*, 1883, p. 52.

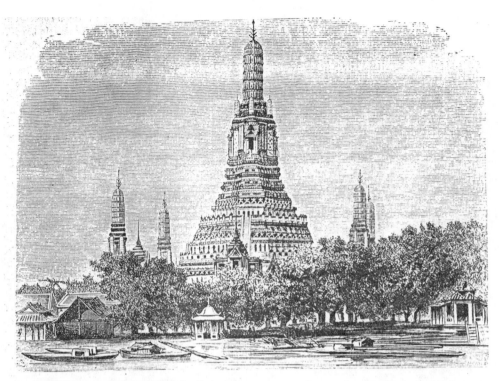

Plate 24. Wat Chaeng (now called Wat Arun).
From: *Die Katholischen Missionen*, 1883, p. 36.

Plate 25. The reclining Buddha, Bangkok.
From: *Die Katholischen Missionen*, 1883, p. 81.

Plate 26. King Mongkut on a palanquin during the royal *kathin* ceremony at Wat Pho.
From: *Voyage autour du monde par le Comte de Beauvoir*, Paris: 1868, p. 473.

Plate 27. Siamese Eating.
From: *Die Katholischen Missionen*, 1883, p. 37.

Plate 28. Letter by King Mongkut, writing
Thai in Roman characters.
From: *Voyage autour du monde par le
Comte de Beauvoir*, Paris: 1868, p. 536.

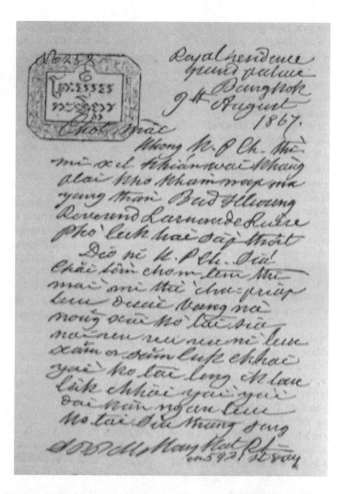

Plate 29. Paknam.
From: G. B. Bacon, *Siam – The Land of the White Elephant as it Was and Is*. New York, 1893, p. 129.

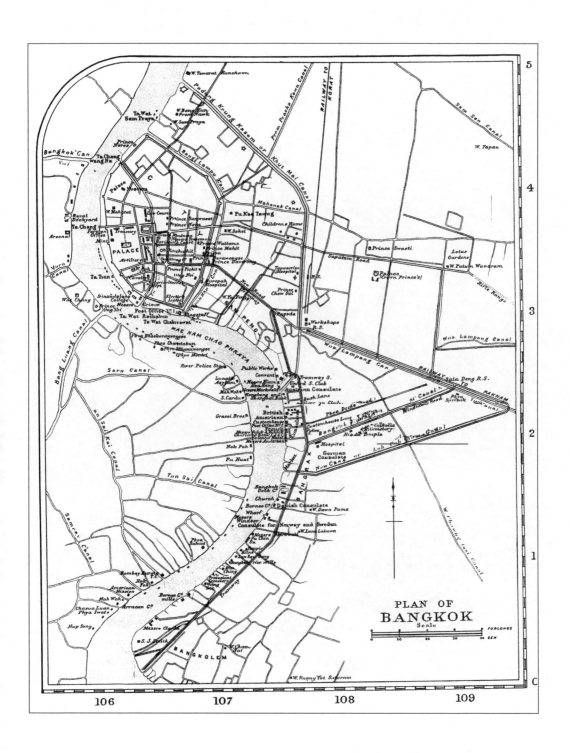

Map 3. Bangkok in 1888, from *Maps of Bangkok AD. 1888-1931*. Bangkok: Royal Thai Survey Department, 1984.

Plate 30. The King of Siam and his Children.
From: *L'Illustration*, 29 July 1893, title page.

Street in Bangkok.

Plate 31. Colored-in photograph of a street in Bangkok, circa 1910, probably New Road.

SIAM ELECTRIC CORPORATION, LIMITED.

BANGKOK, SIAM.

TELEGRAMS :—"GAELIC"

Bankers: HONGKONG and SHANGHAI BANKING CORPORATION.
BANQUE BELGE pour L'ETRANGER, LONDON.
DEN DANSKE LANDMANDSBANK, COPENHAGEN.

ELECTRIC LIGHT AND POWER SUPPLY.
CHEAP RATES TO LARGE CONSUMERS.

SUPPLIES OF ELECTRICAL MATERIALS
OF EVERY DESCRIPTION.

ELECTRIC INSTALLATION DEPARTMENT.

TELEPHONES:

Managing Director and General Manager	No. 1158
Secretary	No. 851
Electrician's Office (regarding electric installations)	No. 1455
do. (outside office hours)	No. 850
Store, Pratu Samyot	No. 1455
Account Dept. (with extension to Bills Dept.)	No. 286
Power Station	No. 85
Workshop and Garage	No. 873
Tramway Office, Samyek	No. 405
do. Sapan Dam	No. 705

SIAM ELECTRIC CORPORATION, LIMITED.

Plate 32. Advertisement from *The Directory for Bangkok and Siam*, 1930.

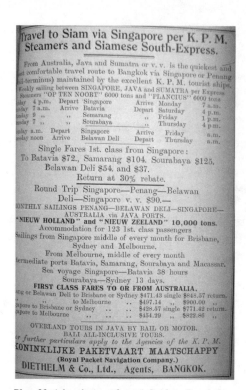
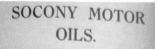

Plate 33. Advertisement from *A Guide to Bangkok* with notes on Siam, 1928, p. III.

Plate 34 Advertisement from *A Guide to Bangkok* with notes on Siam, 1928, p.VII.

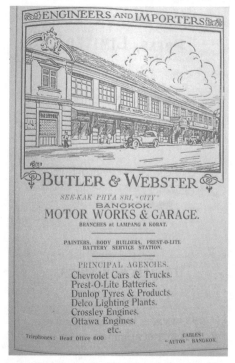

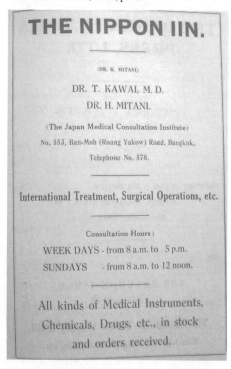

Plate 35. Advertisement from *The Directory for Bangkok and Siam*, 1930, opp. p. 356.

Plate 36. Advertisement from *The Directory for Bangkok and Siam*, 1930, opp. p. 378.